COMPUTER BOOK SERIES FROM IDG

Macs For Dummies

Cheat Sheet

Surviving the First Half Hour

You may only need this information at the very beginning of your Mac career — but you'll *really* need it.

Turning on the Mac

1. Press the On button. If you have a compact, one-piece Mac (called a Classic, Plus, or SE), the rocker switch is on the back of the machine, left edge, about halfway up. Otherwise, it's the big key on your keyboard, separate from the others, with a left-pointing triangle.

If nothing happens, go directly to Chapter 9, "When Bad Things Happen to Good Machines."

Turning off the Mac

1. If you've typed or drawn anything, make sure it's safely stored on your disk by choosing Save from the File menu.

2. If you've been working in a program (like a word processor), choose Finder from the Application menu at the right side of your screen.

   See Chapter 1 for instructions on choosing a command from a menu.

3. From the Special menu, choose Shut Down.

4. If your Mac is a one-piece model like a Classic, Plus, or SE, you now have to turn off the power, using the same switch you used to turn it on.

Working with Several Programs

One of the handiest features of the Mac's latest System software (that is, the stuff in your System Folder that the Mac requires to run itself) is that it lets you run more than one program at once. If you keep launching programs, eventually you'll be told you're out of memory. Until then, here are some pointers.

Launching a program

1. Find its icon.

   You may not have bought *any* programs with your Mac. If that's the case, peruse Chapter 3. Otherwise, the icon for a program is usually (not always) diamond-shaped. Here are some typical program icons:

   Microsoft Word   DiskDoubler   TeachText   Claris Works

2. Put the cursor on the icon, and double-click the mouse button quickly.

Determining what programs are running

1. Put the cursor on the icon in the far upper right of your screen, and hold down the mouse button.

   The *Application menu* drops down, listing (below the dotted line) all the programs you've launched. The frontmost one, the one you're working in, is indicated by a check mark.

Working with Windows

Opening or closing a window

A window is simply your view into something that's normally closed. When a window is closed, it's not a window at all — it's represented by an icon (of a disk, a folder, or a file).

1. Double-click any icon to open its window.

2. To close a window, click the *close box* in the upper-left corner.

Moving a window

Point to its striped *title bar* (where the name of the window appears). Hold the mouse button down, and drag the window into a new position.

Bringing concealed icons into view

Sometimes a window is too small to show you all the icons within it. If that's the case, you'll see gray *scroll bars* along the bottom and right side.

1. Point to one of the small arrows on the scroll bar, as shown, and press the mouse button continuously.

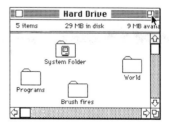

Your view of the window will slide in the direction of the arrow, showing you what's hidden beyond the edges.

2. To make the window as large as necessary to view all the icons (limited by screen size), click the *zoom box*, as shown.

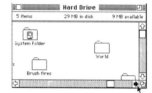

Making a dimmed window active

1. Click in it.

. . . For Dummies: #1 Computer Book Series for Beginners

Macs For Dummies

COMPUTER
BOOK SERIES
FROM IDG

Cheat Sheet

Working with Icons

Finding a file

Each file you create is represented by an icon and is usually stored inside an electronic folder, which looks like a file-folder on your screen. Beginners and pros alike occasionally lose files or forget where they filed a certain file.

1. Choose Find from the File menu.

2. Type a few letters of the missing file's name.

   You don't have to type the whole name . . . only enough to distinguish it; type *Wonk* to find the file called *Willy Wonka Quarterly Earnings*. Capitalization doesn't matter.

3. Press the Return key, or click the Find button.

   The Mac roots through your files and displays the first icon it finds (that matches your request) by opening its folder and *highlighting* (blackening) the icon.

4. If the Mac found the wrong file, choose Find Again from the File menu.

   Keep choosing Find Again until you find what you're looking for, or until the Mac beeps, telling you that it's done searching.

Renaming a file

1. Point to its icon, and click the mouse button.

   The icon is now highlighted (selected).

2. Press the Return key, and type a new name.

   A file's name can be up to 31 letters long. If you make a mistake, backspace over it by pressing the Delete key.

   If you're used to other kinds of computers, a Mac filename can have almost any kind of letters you want (uppercase, lowercase, symbols — anything but a colon) and doesn't have to have a period in it.

3. Press Return when you're done typing.

Copying a file onto a disk

1. Drag the icon (below left) onto the disk's icon (below right), and let go.

Alternatively, you can drag the file into the disk's *window*, instead of on top of the disk's icon.

Locking a disk

1. Eject the disk.

2. Slide the small square tab in the corner of the disk so that you can see through the hole.

A disk you've locked in this way can't be erased, and nothing on it can be thrown away.

To ruin a disk forever

1. Leave it near a phone, a printer, a stereo speaker, or any other magnetic source.

2. Store it near the right rear of your Mac (or, if you have a one-piece Mac like a Classic, near the left side).

3. Leave it in a hot car.

What to Do When You See Something Like This:

They call this box a *dialog box* because the Mac is asking you some questions it needs answered. Here are the elements of a typical dialog box and what they do.

Radio buttons

Paper: ● US Letter   ○ A4 Letter
       ○ US Legal   ○ B5 Letter

Named after the pushbuttons on a car radio, where only one can be pushed in at a time. If you push a different one, the first one pops up. Likewise, only one Mac radio button can be selected at a time.

Checkboxes

☒ Text Smoothing?
☒ Graphics Smoothing?

Used to indicate whether an option is on or off. Click once to place the X in the box; click again to remove the X (and turn off the option).

Text fields

Reduce or   [100] %
Enlarge:

You're supposed to type text or numbers into these blanks. To move from one blank to another (if there's more than one), you can either click in a blank with the mouse or press the Tab key to jump from one to the next.

Pop-up menus

Tabloid ▼
    ✓ Tabloid
      A3 Tabloid
      Envelope - Center Fed
      Envelope - Edge Fed
      LaserWriter II B5

When you see some text in a rectangle, marked by a down-pointing triangle, you're seeing a *pop-up menu*. Point to the text, hold down the mouse button, and make a selection from the mini-menu that drops down.

Buttons

Some buttons, like Options (in the dialog box above), make *another* dialog box appear, where you can make even more choices.

Every dialog box, though, has a clearly-marked button or two (usually OK and Cancel) that make the box go away — your escape route. (New Mac users often get frustrated when they try to get on with their work, only to find that the Mac keeps beeping and won't respond — because a dialog box is still on the screen, waiting for a click of the OK or Cancel buttons.)

Click OK (or Print, or Proceed, or whatever the main button says) to proceed with the command you originally chose from the menu. Click Cancel if you want to back out of it, as though you'd never issued the command.

And a power-user tip: See the thick black outline around the OK button picture above? That's your cue that you don't have to use the mouse to click that button; you can press either the Return or Enter key on your keyboard instead.

Ethiopian Reg. Eleel. -
Alem Gaitom
2711

Boston Af Stu Assoc.

Af Amer. Inst.

Friends of Eth / Eritea

P.O. BOX 65684

Wash DC. 20035

LaVerel Barry

Library Congress.
202 - 245 - 5222

...t to establish "changed circum-
...

...record below does not contain sub-
...evidence that changed conditions re-
...Dhine's well-founded fear of persecu-
...consequently, Dhine is statutorily eli-

The Discretionary Aspect

Dhine establishes that he is statutori-
...le for asylum, he must show that he
...be granted asylum in the exercise of
...on. The BIA found that even if
...were determined statutorily eligible,
...ld be denied asylum in the exercise of
...on. See BIA Decision II, at 4. That
...is reviewed for abuse of discretion.
...ch, 962 F.2d at 238.

...factor that figured most prominently
...BIA's analysis (as well as the decision
...immigration judge who determined
...ine should be denied asylum in the
...of discretion) was Dhine's drug con-
... Between 1982 and 1990, Dhine was
...d of four misdemeanors involving
...three involving possession, and one
...g attempted distribution (of marijua-
...hine's drug history was the only ad-
...ctor cited by the BIA in affirming the
...of asylum in the exercise of discre-

...pport of his application for asylum,
...mentioned a number of factors he
...should militate in favor of a positive
...of discretion. Dhine notes that he is
...al who speaks up to nine languages.
...r, he is a practicing Jew, who has
...ned his faith and his observance un-
...t trying conditions while in custody.

...religion focus on Protestant and Orthodox
...ns, rather than Judaism.

...a note that even if the INS had established
...d conditions in Ethiopia, Dhine would be
...rily eligible on the basis of past persecu-
...See Matter of Chen, BIA Interim Decision
...1989 WL 247532 (1989) ("If an alien es-
...es that he has been persecuted in the past
...of the five reasons listed in the statute, he
...ble for a grant of asylum.") The INS does
...spute that Dhine suffered persecution in
...a Accordingly, he is statutorily eligible
...lum.

He also notes that since being incarcerated,
he has held a number of jobs in the Varrick
Street facility, and has managed to save a
sum of money, some of which he has donated
to charity. He has volunteered his language
abilities at Varrick Street, translating in the
infirmary and in grievance procedures.
Most importantly, he has never tested positive for drugs since being in custody, and has
never received a disciplinary ticket for any
infraction.[6]

Dhine has also cooperated in an investiga-
tion directed by the United States Attorney's
Office for the Southern District of New York
into activities at a INS Processing Center.
Dhine not only provided information to inves-
tigators, but he also volunteered to, and indeed did, wear a "wire" in an attempt to
gather more information.

A psychologist submitted a letter on behalf
of Dhine suggesting that Dhine's drug use
might be attributable to the traumatic expe-
riences he suffered in Ethiopia. The psychologist explained that Dhine, entering a
strange country at the age of 16, where he
had no friends, family, or community, after
losing his parents and brother in a brutal
murder, and being tortured personally, un-
derstandably became depressed, and turned
to drugs to counter the difficult feelings he
was experiencing. Without excusing his
drug use, Dhine asks that it be viewed in the
context in which it developed.

Dhine also put in evidence that an array of
social services would be available to him if he
was granted asylum. A social worker from
the United Jewish Appeal Federation promised to assist Dhine in obtaining housing,
employment and counseling, and an immigra-

5. The BIA also mentioned the "small likelihood
of persecution" as a factor militating against a
favorable exercise of discretion. See BIA Decision II. Since this finding was inappropriate, it
shall not be considered in the discretionary analysis.

6. While one's behavior in custody is not the
greatest indicator of how one would behave
when released, I note that the petitioner's excep-
tionally clean record since being confined, under
what I am aware are less than ideal circumstances, indicate a strength of will which can be
drawn upon to assist him in future endeavors.

...tion attorne...
...based on h...

The imm...
Dhine was...
...tate himsel...
petitioner...
...story of...

The Cou...
...abuse of dis...
...these factor...
In Dhine's...
...at a young...
...ment. An...
...custody, h...
...tale his w...
...that furthe...
...ing, housi...
...available...
Adversely,...
...convictions...
...immigratio...
...belief that...
...whelming...
...positive fa...
...conclusion...

Taking...
...cumstance...
Decision...
...believe D...
...granted a...
...discretion...
...convictions...
...tors.

Moreov...
...has overc...
...that arise...
...persecutio...
...must pre...
...likelihood...
...militating...
...discretion)...
...alien does...
...cation lik...
...ger of per...

2. "I onc...
...record w...
...of this c...
...certainly...
...rice cust...
...no doubt...
...is makin...
...integrate...
...migratio...

Macs For Dummies Testimonials

"It's a lot easier to deal with than the *"Mac Bible."*
— Mrs. Maryellen Kitchen
Scottsdale, Arizona

"Easy to understand and hard to put down; told me things I never knew I could do!"
— Rick Bettencourt
Brampton, Ontario Canada

"It takes a lot of thinking, editing, and re-editing to comprise a 'context' book that is readable, not just 'referenceable.' Congratulations on accomplishing such a feat!"
— Anthony Pendino & Debra McKeown
Tampa, Florida

"Refreshing, down to earth, understandable, and enjoyable method of becoming comfortable with the world of Macs."
— R.I. Trudel
Danbury, Connecticut

"It makes computer use easy to incorporate without feeling like a total fool."
— Ginger Bechtold
Atlantic, Iowa

"This is a GREAT book! Extremely intelligent, witty, sophisticated . . . and I couldn't believe how up-to-date it was!"
— Charles McCraw
New York, New York

"If my house were on fire, and I could save only one book, it would be *Macs For Dummies*. (The book saved me from flaming stupidity.)"
— Jay Frederick
Composer
Westport, Connecticut

TM

By David Pogue

Macworld Magazine's Desktop Critic

IDG BOOKS

IDG Books Worldwide, Inc.
An International Data Group Company
San Mateo, California 94402

Macs For Dummies
Published by
IDG Books Worldwide, Inc.
An International Data Group Company
155 Bovet Road, Suite 310
San Mateo, CA 94402
(415) 312-0650

Library of Congress Catalog Card No.: 92-72344

ISBN 1-878058-53-3

Printed in the United States of America

10 9 8

Distributed in the United States by IDG Books Worldwide, Inc.
Distributed in Canada by Macmillan of Canada, a Division of Canada Publishing Corporation; by Woodslane Pty. Ltd. in Australia; and by Computer Bookshops in the U.K.

For information on translations and availability in other countries, contact Marc Jeffrey Mikulich, Foreign Rights Manager, at IDG Books Worldwide. Fax: (415) 358-1260.

For sales inquiries and special prices for bulk quantities, write to the address above or call IDG Books Worldwide at (415) 312-0650.

is a trademark of IDG Books Worldwide, Inc.

COMPUTER
BOOK SERIES
FROM IDG

Acknowledgments

I can't tell you how much I've appreciated the patience of everyone whose projects got back-burnered for the sake of this book: Carol Person, Liza Weiman, and Adrian Mello of *Macworld;* Coda Music Software; Freddie Gershon and the gang at Music Theatre International; Joseph Schorr (and Max); and Poppa, for whose creative chromosomes I'll thank him personally at his 103rd birthday.

Thanks to John Kilcullen, David Solomon, Terrie Lynn Solomon, and Jeremy Judson, without whose support this book would have failed to not be impossible. Thanks, too, to Londa Holsinger for her borrowed wit, and to my students — the ranks of born-again Mac nuts whose first steps, questions, and impressive strides constitute my research.

(The publisher would like to give special thanks to Patrick J. McGovern, without whom this book would not have been possible.)

About IDG Books Worldwide

Welcome to the world of IDG Books Worldwide.

IDG Books Worldwide, Inc., is a division of International Data Group (IDG), the world's largest publisher of computer-related information and the leading global provider of information services on information technology. IDG publishes over 190 computer publications in 60 countries. Thirty million people read one or more IDG publications each month.

If you use personal computers, IDG Books is committed to publishing quality books that meet your needs. We rely on our extensive network of publications, including such leading periodicals as *Macworld, InfoWorld, PC World, Computerworld, Publish, Network World, and SunWorld,* to help us make informed and timely decisions in creating useful computer books that meet your needs.

Every IDG book strives to bring extra value and skill-building instruction to the reader. Our books are written by experts, with the backing of IDG periodicals, and with careful thought devoted to issues such as audience, interior design, use of icons, and illustrations. Our editorial staff is a careful mix of high-tech journalists and experienced book people. Our close contact with the makers of computer products helps ensure accuracy and thorough coverage. Our heavy use of personal computers at every step in production means we can deliver books in the most timely manner.

We are delivering books of high quality at competitive prices on topics customers want. At IDG, we believe in quality, and we have been delivering quality for over 25 years. You'll find no better book on a subject than an IDG book.

John Kilcullen
President and Publisher
IDG Books Worldwide, Inc.

IDG Books Worldwide, Inc. is a division of International Data Group. The officers are Patrick J. McGovern, Founder and Board Chairman; Walter Boyd, President; Robert A. Farmer, Vice Chairman. International Data Group's publications include: **ARGENTINA's** Computerworld Argentina, InfoWorld Argentina; **ASIA's** Computerworld Hong Kong, PC World Hong Kong, Computerworld Southeast Asia, PC World Singapore, Computerworld Malaysia, PC World Malaysia; **AUSTRALIA's** Computerworld Australia, Australian PC World, Australian Macworld, Reseller, IDG Sources; **AUSTRIA's** Computerwelt Oesterreich, PC Test; **BRAZIL's** Computerworld, Mundo IBM, Mundo Unix, PC World, Publish; **BULGARIA's** Computerworld Bulgaria, Ediworld, PC World Bulgaria; **CANADA's** Direct Access, Graduate Computerworld, InfoCanada, Network World Canada; **CHILE's** Computerworld, Informatica; **COLUMBIA's** Computerworld Columbia; **CZECH REPUBLIC's** Computerworld Elektronika, PC World; **DENMARK's** CAD/CAM WORLD, Communications World, Computerworld Danmark, Computerworld Focus, Computerworld Uddannelse, Lotus World, Macintosh Produktkatalog, Macworld Danmark, PC World Danmark, PC World Produktguide, Windows World; **EQUADOR's** PC World; **EGYPT's** PC World Middle East; **FINLAND's** Mikro PC, Tietoviikko, Tietoverkko; **FRANCE's** Distributique, GOLDEN MAC, InfoPC, Languages & Systems, Le Guide du Monde Informatique, Le Monde Informatique, Telecoms & Reseaux; **GERMANY's** Computerwoche, Computerwoche Focus, Computerwoche Extra, Computerwoche Karriere, edv aspekte, Information Management, Macwelt, Netzwelt, PC Welt, PC Woche, Publish, Unit; **HUNGARY's** Computerworld SZT, PC World; **INDIA's** Computers & Communications; **ISRAEL's** Computerworld Israel, PC World Israel; **ITALY's** Computerworld Italia, Lotus Magazine, Macworld Italia, Networking Italia, PC World Italia; **JAPAN's** Computerworld Japan, Macworld Japan, SunWorld Japan; **KENYA's** East African Computer News; **KOREA's** Computerworld Korea, Macworld Korea, PC World Korea; **MEXICO's** Compu Edicion, Compu Manufactura, Computacion/Punto de Venta, Computerworld Mexico, MacWorld, Mundo Unix, PC World, Windows; **THE NETHERLANDS'** Computer! Totaal, LAN Magazine, MacWorld Magazine; **NEW ZEALAND's** Computer Listings, Computerworld New Zealand, New Zealand PC World; **NIGERIA's** PC World Africa; **NORWAY's** Computerworld Norge, C/World, Lotusworld Norge, Macworld Norge, Networld, PC World Ekspress, PC World Norge, PC World's Product Guide, Publish World, Student Data, Unix World, Windowsworld, IDG Direct Response; **PANAMA's** PC World; **PERU's** PC World; **PEOPLES REPUBLIC OF CHINA's** China Computerworld, PC World China, Electronics International; **IDG TECH BEIJING's** Electronics New Product World; **IDG SHENZHEN's** Computer News Digest; **PHILLIPPINES'** Computerworld, PC World; **POLAND's** Computerworld Poland, PC World/Komputer; **PORTUGAL's** MacIn; **ROMANIA's** InfoClub Magazine; **RUSSIA's** Computerworld-Moscow, Mir-PC, Sety; **SLOVENIA's** Monitor Magazine; **SOUTH AFRICA's** Computing S.A.; **SPAIN's** Amiga World, Autoedicion, Computerworld Espana, Macworld Espana, NeXTWORLD, PC World Espana, Publish, Sunworld; **SWEDEN's** Attack, ComputerSweden, Corporate Computing, Lokala Natverk/LAN, Lotus World, MAC&PC, Macworld, Mikrodatorn, PC World, Publishing & Design (CAP), Datalngenjoren, Maxi Data, Windows World; **SWITZERLAND's** Computerworld Schweiz, Macworld Schweiz, PC & Workstation; **TAIWAN's** Computerworld Taiwan, Global Computer Express, PC World Taiwan; **THAILAND's** Thai Computerworld; **TURKEY's** Computerworld Monitor, Macworld Turkiye, PC World Turkiye; **UNITED KINGDOM's** Lotus Magazine, Macworld, Sunworld; **UNITED STATES'** AmigaWorld, Cable in the Classroom, CD Review, CIO, Computerworld, Desktop Video World, DOS Resource Guide, Electronic News, Federal Computer Week, Federal Integrator, GamePro, inCider/A+, IDG Books, InfoWorld, InfoWorld Direct, Laser Event, Macworld, Multimedia World, Network World, NeXTWORLD, PC Games, PC World, PC Letter, Publish, SunWorld, SWATPro, Video Event, Video Toaster World; **VENEZUELA's** Computerworld Venezuela, MicroComputerworld Venezuela; **VIETNAM's** PC World Vietnam

 The text in this book is printed on recycled paper.

About the Author

Ohio-bred David Pogue never touched a computer — nor wanted to — until Apple Computer suckered him into it by selling Macs half-price at Yale, from which he graduated *summa cum laude* in 1985. Since then, Pogue has merged his two loves — the musical theatre and Macs — in every way he could dream up: by writing manuals for music programs like Finale; by being the computer-consultant guy for Broadway musicals like *Carrie* and Lincoln Center's *Anything Goes*; by teaching Mac music seminars around the country; and by becoming the Mac guru to every Broadway and Hollywood creative-type who wanted to take the Macintosh plunge — Mia Farrow, Mike Nichols, Gay Talese, Stephen Sondheim, John Kander, Cy Coleman, Susan Stroman, and others.

In his other life, Pogue is a straight-ahead theatre musician, having conducted 1½ Broadway shows (the second one flopped out of town), played piano for some Off-Broadway productions, and composed a number of small-time musicals. In his other other life, he's a magician, and teaches courses in magic in New York City.

And in his *other* other other life, Pogue is a Contributing Editor for *Macworld* magazine. His column, *The Desktop Critic*, appears in the magazine each month.

In between crises, Pogue wrote a novel called *Hard Drive* — a Macintosh techno-thriller, in fact — published in April 1993 by the Berkley Publishing Group.

Pogue's résumé also boasts some *real* accomplishments, like winning the Ohio spelling bee in seventh grade, being the only nonlawyer in three generations, and getting a Viewer Mail letter read on *David Letterman*.

President and CEO
John J. Kilcullen

Vice President and Publisher
David Solomon

Managing Editor
Mary Bednarek

Project Editor
Jeremy Judson

Acquisitions Editor
Terrie Lynn Solomon

Copy Editor
Mary Ann Cordova

Technical Reviewer
Dennis Cohen

Production Manager
Beth J. Baker

Editorial Assistant
Megg Bonar

Text Preparation and Proofreading
Cindy L. Phipps
Charles A. Hutchinson

Indexer
Matthew Spence

Book Design and Production
Peppy White
Francette Ytsma
Tracy Strub
(University Graphics, Palo Alto, California)

university graphics

Contents at a Glance

Introduction 1

Part I: For the Absolute Mac Virgin 9

Chapter 1: How to Turn On Your Mac
(and What to Do Next) 11

Chapter 2: High-Tech Made Easy 27

Chapter 3: Doing Windows, Getting Floppy 35

Chapter 4: Actually Getting Some Work Done 49

Chapter 5: A Quiet Talk About Printers, ...89

Part II: Increasing Your Coolness Quotient 119

Chapter 6: Faking Your Way
Through the Top Ten Programs 121

Chapter 7: More Stuff To Buy and Plug In 179

Chapter 8: Putting the Mouse to the Metal 195

Part III: Becoming Your Own Guru 223

Chapter 9: When Bad Things Happen
to Good Machines 225

Chapter 10: Beyond Point-and-Click:
Where to Go From Here 273

Appendix A: How To Buy (And Set Up) a Macintosh 277
Appendix B: The PowerBook Survival Guide 295
Appendix C: The Resource Resource 303
Appendix D: The Techno-Babble Translation Guide 307
Appendix E: Long-Distance Computing: AppleTalk Remote Access 323
Index 329
Reader Response Survey ....back of book

Table of Contents

• •

Acknowledgments vii

Introduction 1

A Formal Welcome to the 20th Century 1
Why a Book for Dummies? 2
How to Use This Book
(Other Than as a Mousepad) 3
Macintosh conventions 5
Conventions in this book 5
Why a Mac? 6
A free psychological confirmation of your
taste and intelligence 6
Apple and obsolescence 7

Part I: For the Absolute Mac Virgin 9

Chapter 1: How to Turn On Your Mac
(and What to Do Next) 11
I Took Off the Shrink-Wrap! Now What? 11
Switching the Mac on 11
What you hope to see 12
What you might see 13
What you hope not to see 13
Your First Moments Alone Together 15
The big turn-off 15
Moving the mouse 15
What's on the menu? 15
Shutting down 17
A one-on-one guided tour 18
Moving things around on the desktop 20
Understanding icons, windows, and Macintosh syntax 21
Using multiple windows 24
Using multiple views 24
Top Ten Similarities Between You and Your Mac 25
Summary 26

Chapter 2: High-Tech Made Easy 27
Understanding How a Mac Works 27
Storing things with floppy disks 27
Conceptualizing the hard disk 28

Understanding memory 29
Who's Meg? 30
Understanding RAM 31
Putting it all together 31
"I lost all my work!" 32
Top Ten Differences Between Memory and a Hard Disk 33
Ready for Action 34
Summary 34

Chapter 3: Doing Windows, Getting Floppy **35**
Becoming Manipulative 35
Foldermania 35
Keyboard shortcuts 36
Having Fun with Floppies 41
Top Ten Window and Disk Tips 45
All About At Ease 47
Summary 48

Chapter 4: Actually Getting Some Work Done **49**
Obsolescence Therapy II 49
Credit Card Workout #2: Buying Software 50
Where to get it 51
Your very first software 52
Desk Accessories 53
The Calculator 53
The Note Pad 54
Selecting text 55
The cornerstone of human endeavor: Copy and Paste 55
The Application menu 56
Control Panels 60
Word Processing 101 61
Top two rules of word processing 62
Form and format 67
The return of Return 68
Appealing characters 69
Formatting paragraphs 70
Someone Save Me! (Working with Documents) 72
Navigating the Save File (and Open File) box 74
Closing a file, with a sigh 77
How to find out what the heck you're doing 78
Those crazy relationships: parents and children 79
Fetch: How to retrieve a document 80
Save Me Again! 82
Learning to be a quitter 83
The other most important rule of computing 84
Top Ten Word Processing Tips 85
Summary 87

Chapter 5: A Quiet Talk About Printers, Printing, and Fonts **89**

Credit Card Workout #3: A Printer Primer 89

Low-cost, low-quality 90

Low-cost, high-quality, low-speed 91

PostScript printers 91

How History Messed Everything Up 92

The LaserWriter era 93

Special type, special fonts 95

System clutter land 95

Technology to the rescue 97

Ferment at the core of Apple 97

The TrueType spectacle 98

The current mess 99

The output upshot 103

How To Print 104

Plugging in a 'Writer 104

Plugging in a laser printer 104

Letting the Mac know it has company 105

The Chooser 106

Background printing 108

After all that: How you actually print 109

Using the Tab key in dialog boxes 110

Canceling printing 110

Just Your Type 110

How to install a font 111

How to remove a font 111

Top Ten Free Fun Font Factoids 112

Summary 117

Part II: Increasing Your Coolness Quotient **119**

Chapter 6: Faking Your Way Through the Top Ten Programs **121**

HyperCard . . . Not! 122

ClarisWorks 122

Launching ClarisWorks 122

Your first database 123

Data entry time 125

Forming the form letter 128

The graphics zone: designing a letterhead 131

The return of Copy and Paste 132

MacDraw Pro, Canvas 3.0, SuperPaint 3.0 134

Concepts 135

Selecting and grouping multiple objects 136

Text FX 137

MacPaint, SuperPaint, UltraPaint, Studio/1, and Others 138
    Marquee and Lasso 139
    Pencil 140
    Text Tool 140
    Spray can 141
    Eraser 141
    Line Tool 141
    Rectangle, Rounded rectangle, Ellipse, Polygon, Arc 142
    Hand grabber 142
    Magnifying glass 142
Microsoft Word 5.0 143
    Views 143
    To change the margins 144
    Using the Ribbon and Ruler for quick formatting 145
    Moving text by dragging it 147
    Page numbers, headers, date-stamping 148
    Raw power: Style sheets 148
    Checking your spelling 149
PageMaker 150
    Starting a new document 150
    The Master Pages 150
    Adding text 151
    Tweaking to perfection 153
QuarkXPress 154
    The basics 154
    Linking to page C4 156
    Master Pages; rearranging pages 156
    Measurement Palette 157
Excel 157
    Starting up 157
    Formatting numbers and text 157
    Spreading the sheet 159
    Creating automatically calculating cells 160
    Fill right, feel right 161
    From here to infinity 162
    Making a chart 162
FileMaker Pro 163
    Step 1: Starting a file 164
    Step 2: Data entry 166
    Step 3: Designing a layout 167
    Finding 169
    Sorting 169
    Other steps 170
QuicKeys 170
    Teaching by example 171
    Opening QuicKeys 173
Apple File Exchange 175
Top Ten Programs That Aren't in the Top Ten 177
Summary 178

Chapter 7: More Stuff To Buy and Plug In **179**
   Microphones 179
      Casper, the friendly technology 180
   Scanners 180
      O say can u OCR? 181
   Modems 182
      Coping with bauds 183
      Fax/modems 183
      On-line services 184
      Bulletin boards 185
   CD-ROM 185
   Music and MIDI 186
      A one-person orchestra 187
      What you need 187
      Other things MIDI can do 188
   A Camcorder 188
      The caveats of the proletariat 188
   SyQuests, Bernoullis, and Tapes, Oh My! 189
      Remove it 189
   Networks 190
   Plugging the Stuff In 191
   Top Ten Non-Costly Mac Add-Ons 192
   Summary 194

Chapter 8: Putting the Mouse to the Metal **195**
   The Efficiency Nut's Guide to the Option Key 195
      Closing all windows at once 196
      Windows and folders: developing tunnel vision 197
      Taking out the trash 198
      Multitasking methods 199
      Making an instant document copy 201
      Alphabetize them icons! 201
      Funny little hidden Option key stunts 202
   Buried Treasures 202
      How to find a lost file 202
      Make an alias of a file 203
      Creating the L.L. Mac catalog 206
      Have it your way — at "Icon King" 207
      Taking a picture of the screen 208
      Just saying no 208
   Colorizing, Editing the Menus, and Other Cool Acts of Vandalism 209
      Changing the background pattern 209
      Color-coding your icons 210
      Blue language 211
      Views 212
      ResEdit: Menu-editor of the gods 214
      Using that microphone 216

Utilities with No Monthly Bill 217
    Compression programs 217
    Screen savers 218
    Anti-virus software 219
    The Talking Moose, and other just goofy stuff 219
Top Ten Free or Almost-Free Utility Programs 220
Summary 221

Part III: Becoming Your Own Guru **223**

Chapter 9: When Bad Things Happen to Good Machines **225**
Introduction to Computer Hell 225
    The three most common causes of computer problems 226
    Shooting your own troubles 227
The Top Ten Beginner Troubles
(That Don't Actually Need Shooting) 228
Error Messages 233
    "Application is busy or missing," or
        "Application not found." 234
    "There is not enough memory to open Word." 236
    "The application *LightningDraw* has unexpectedly quit." 236
    "The disk is full." 236
    "The Print Monitor has reported an error." or "Can't open
        printer." 237
    "Can't empty trash." 237
    "An error occurred while writing to the disk." 238
    "Microsoft Word prefers 2048K of memory.
        2000K is available." 238
Out of Memory 238
    First resort: Quit programs 240
    Second resort: Make the Mac give back some memory 240
    Third resort: Defragment your RAM 242
    Fourth resort: Starve your software 243
    Fifth resort: Virtual memory 243
    Last resort: Buy more 245
Starting Up 246
    No ding, no picture 246
    Ding, no picture 246
    Picture, no ding 247
    Four separate musical notes 247
    A question mark blinks on the screen 248
    "Sorry, a System error has occurred." 249
    Some crazy program launches itself every time
        you start up 250

System Crashes and Freezes 250
   Escaping a System crash 251
   System freezes 253
   A note about the ID numbers or error messages in the
      bomb box 253
Scuzzy SCSI 254
   What's SCSI? 254
   System crashes, slow-as-molasses performance, no external
      drive icon, scanner won't work 254
Printing Problems 257
   "Printer could not be opened."
      or "Printer could not be found." 257
   A million copies keep pouring out 258
   You get jagged text in your laser printouts 258
   While printing, you get a message that a font is "not found,
      using Courier" 259
   Nothing comes out of the printer 259
   Print Monitor won't go away 260
   Streaks on Laser printouts 260
   Every time you turn on the laser printer, it cranks out a
      stupid start-up page 260
Finder Foulups 261
   The Find command doesn't find a file that you know is
      there somewhere 261
   You try to rename an icon, but the Mac highlights some
      other icon 261
   You can't rename a file 262
Floppy Disk Flukes 262
   When copying a file to or from a floppy disk,
      you get a message that a file "could not be
      copied and will be skipped" 262
   The Mac keeps asking for a disk that you've ejected 263
   You can't rename a disk 263
   You can't get a floppy disk out 264
   You insert a floppy, and the Mac says
      "This disk is unreadable. Do you want to initialize it?" 264
   Your floppy disks don't hold the amount they're
      supposed to 265
Software Snafus 266
   Disappearing text 266
   In FileMaker: Missing information 266
   In Excel: ##### in a cell 266
   In HyperCard: No menu bar 266
   A whole document window just disappears 267
   Miscellaneous crashes, freezes, beeps, and goofy or

Hard-Disk Horrors 269
    The hard-drive icon doesn't show up 269
    Sluggish behavior...269
    You threw something away by mistake 270
Cursor, Keyboard, and Mouse Nightmares....................270
    The mouse is sluggish, jerky, or sticky 270
    Double-clicking doesn't work 271
    The cursor freezes on the screen and won't move 271
    Something really weird starts suddenly: Beeps and
        menus get stuck down 271
    Nothing appears when you type 271
    Keyboard shortcuts aren't working 272
Summary 272

Chapter 10: Beyond Point-and-Click:
Where to Go from Here 273
Credit Card Workout #5:
Upgrades and Accelerators 273
Where to Turn in Times of Trouble 275
Save Changes Before Closing? 275
Top Ten Topics Not Covered in This Book 276

Appendix A: How To Buy (And Set Up) a Macintosh 277
Appendix B: The PowerBook Survival Guide 295
Appendix C: The Resource Resource 303
Appendix D: The Techno-Babble Translation Guide 307
Appendix E: Long-Distance Computing: AppleTalk Remote Access 323
Index 329
Reader Response Survey ....back of book

Foreword

It is certainly no surprise to me that I was asked to write the Foreword for this book. After all, I was David Pogue's first dummy. When we met five years ago, I was an aging composer, wearily putting quill pen to parchment, surrounded by mountains of erasers. The world of computers was as foreign to me as the craters of the moon.

Then along came Mr. Pogue, fresh from Yale, who guided me patiently and painlessly into the joyful world of Macintosh. He made it all seem so simple. And the Mac, my new friend, was helpful as well, with little admonitions like, "Are you sure you want to do this?" or apologies like, "I'm sorry I can't find this. If you find it for me, I promise I'll remember where it is next time." I was soon convinced that this machine really cared about me. In a short time, I became a mouse maniac.

Since then, I have written the scores for two musicals, two films, and countless letters of complaint to my Congressmen on this wonderful contraption, thanks to my two wise, kind friends, David and the Mac.

In this book, you'll find many reminders, explanations, and shortcuts. *Macs For Dummies* will stay by me at my desk. After all, once a dummy . . .

John Kander

John Kander, with lyricist Fred Ebb, has written the scores for Cabaret; Chicago; Zorba; New York, New York; *and the new musical* Kiss of the Spider Woman.

Introduction

A Formal Welcome to the 20th Century

Something has driven you to learning how to use a computer — your friends, your job, or fate. If you're just tuning into the computer world now, you've either lacked the need, the budget, or the courage to dive in before this. In any case, you couldn't have chosen a better time; technology and price wars have made computers affordable, comprehensible, and almost fun. The Macintosh, of course, is the primary example.

The 5th Wave   By Rich Tennant

In 1984, the ad people called the Macintosh "the computer for the rest of us." The implication of this catch phrase, now famous in computer circles, was that *other* computers were hard to learn. Previous computers required you to learn jargon, have technical skill, and memorize dumb keyboard codes. The Macintosh was as simple as a toaster — nothing to assemble, nothing to install, no manual to puzzle through.

And sure enough, the first Mac pretty much fit that description. Its factory-sealed case meant that you didn't have to install any parts (like you do on IBM-style computers). Unless you were a real soldering gunslinger, the first Macintosh wasn't expandable. It was a complete, self-contained unit. You unpacked it and plugged it in. Like a toaster.

But Apple Computer learned about a funny catch-22 in the computer business. The people who influence computer sales (like computer magazines, consultants, industry spokespeople) all were people who *liked* the jargon, the keyboard codes, the messy circuit board stuff! These were people who prided themselves on having *mastered* the convoluted, dim-witted design of pre-Mac computers . . . people who not only didn't appreciate the simplicity of the Macintosh but actually *resented* it. In reviews, editorials, and interviews, the Powers That Were said over and over again that the Macintosh would never survive unless Apple opened it up. Let people expand it, customize it, juice it up, just like IBM owners had done (and had been required to do) for years.

Alas, that movement pushed the Mac out of its "computer for the rest of us" mold. Suddenly there were more models. They became available in separate modular pieces, so you had more to shop for. The computer weenies who ruled the press started imposing all their terminology and tech-talk on this poor little machine that was supposed to be simple enough for the most ardent computer phobe. Macintosh user groups sprang up — they're everywhere now — where you'd hear talk like, "How can I accelerate my 25MHz SE/30 fast enough to get a decent frame rate out of QuickTime?" or "How much RAM do I need for virtual memory on my 80MB Quantum?"

The Mac wasn't a toaster anymore.

Why a Book for Dummies?

Today, you'd be justified in saying that the Mac sometimes seems almost as intimidating as the computers it was supposed to replace. The way the techno-nerds throw jargon around (and the way the pages of Mac magazines have slowly been filling up with stories about Ethernet Hubs and 9600 bps modems with MNP and v42.BIS error-correction protocol), you'd think the Mac was no longer for the rest of us — you'd think it's now the private property of the dweeby intelligentsia all over again.

It's not. You hold in your hands a primal scream: "It's *not* as complicated as they try to make it sound!" Really, truly, almost everything said by the computer salespeople and magazines and books and computer consultants of the world is more complicated than it has to be. (Ever study psychology? A person who uses jargon where simple English would do is trying to underscore the listener's ignorance.)

This book is designed to help you

  ✔ Translate the tech-talk into useful information

  ✔ Weed out the stuff you'll never need to know

  ✔ Navigate the hype when it comes to buying things

  ✔ Learn the Macintosh and get useful things done

By the way: Of *course* you're not a dummy. Two pieces of evidence tell me so: For one thing, you're learning the Mac, and for another, you're reading this book! But I've taught hundreds of people how to use their Macs, and an awful lot of them start out saying they *feel* like dummies when it comes to computers. Society surrounds us with fast-talking teenagers who grew up learning English from their Nintendo sets; no wonder the rest of us can sometimes feel left out.

But you're no more a dummy for not knowing the Mac than you were before you knew how to drive. Learning the Mac is like learning to drive: After a lesson or two, you can go anywhere your heart desires.

How to Use This Book (Other Than as a Mousepad)

If you're starting from the very, *very* beginning, you might want to start this book from the end — with **Appendix A,** where you can find out how to buy a Mac (and which one to get) without getting scammed. It also contains an idiot-proof guide to setting up your computer.

Chapter 1 assumes that you do, in fact, have a Mac, and that it's been plugged in. You'll find out how to turn it on and off, for starters. In ten minutes (or 20 if you're trying to watch TV simultaneously), you'll have mastered the raw basics of driving your Mac.

Chapter 2 explains the very basics of a computer. And you'll learn a computer-nerd term or two that I really can't avoid teaching you.

Chapter 3's a Mac lesson for the absolute beginner: how to use the mouse (and what a mouse *is*), how to use menus (not the restaurant kind) — that kind of thing. In **Chapter 4,** you'll do some actual work; it includes a word processing lesson that won't destroy your self-esteem.

Once you've got your ideas typed into the computer, you'll want to print your work; that's one of the Mac's strong suits. **Chapter 5** lays bare the mysteries of printing and using typefaces.

Chapter 6 has the all-important "Faking Your Way Through the Top Ten Programs," which is an indispensable guide for anybody who wants to look cool without actually expending any effort.

In **Chapter 7,** you get to read about all the expensive equipment you can plug *into* the Mac: modems, scanners, and all that good stuff. By the time you get to **Chapter 8,** you'll be ready to start sailing with a priceless potpourri of sizzling shortcuts. You'll find out about the creative vandalism the Mac lets you do: colorizing the screen, recording your own sounds, and using utility programs that help you get extra mileage out of your computer.

When anything goes wrong, turn to **Chapter 9,** "When Bad Things Happen to Good Machines," the mother of all troubleshooting sections. It identifies the snafus you're most likely to encounter, how to prevent them, and what to do about them. Finally, read **Chapter 10** when the stuff in this book is starting to seem old hat, and you're ready to push off into the wider world of computing.

If you have a PowerBook laptop, savor **Appendix B.** It shows you how to coax every last milliwatt of juice from your laptop's batteries. Finally, the book wraps up with **Appendix C,** the Resource Resource (that lists contact info for a number of important Mac companies and organizations), and **Appendix D,** the Techno-Babble Translation Guide (you'd probably call it a glossary).

Finally, if you're ready for some real magic, and are equipped with two Macs, **Appendix E** lays bare the mysteries of connecting the two computers over the phone lines, even if they're thousands of miles apart.

Macintosh conventions

Macintosh conventions? Sure. They're called Macworld Expos, and there's one in Boston and one in San Francisco each year.

Conventions in this book

Oh, *that* kind of convention. Well, there are three. First of all, I'm going to take the liberty of defining terms in the margin whenever I think it'd be helpful to a wide-eyed, terrorized novice. If you already know the term, great — just breeze on past it; that's why I put them in the margins.

Second, I'm going to satisfy those beginners who have a recessive geek gene in their DNA, those who actually *want* to learn more about what's going on under the hood, with occasional sidebars on technoid topics. They'll be clearly marked with titles like "Stuff you'll never need to know." Unless you're actually interested, rest assured that you can live a rich and rewarding life without ever reading a word.

Finally, so that we'll be eligible for some of the more prestigious book-design awards, I've marked some topics in the main text with these icons:

Nerdy stuff that's OK to skip but will fascinate the kind of people who read Tom Clancy novels.

You can never, *ever* damage your Mac by "doing something wrong" (other than by pouring Diet Coke into the air vents or something). Occasionally, though, I'll alert you that there's a potential risk to your work.

The former Speaker of the House. Also a shortcut so you can show off.

Denotes an actual You-Try-It Experience. Hold the book open with a nearby cinder block, put your hands on the computer, and do as I say.

Indicates a deep glimpse into the psychology of Mac users: why people who already *know* how to use the damn things, for example, love to intimidate people who *don't.*

Why a Mac?

If there's one single *atom* of computer phobia in your bloodstream, but you need a computer, get a Macintosh. Trust me. And trust the ten million former computer phobes who are now happily computing away.

A free psychological confirmation of your taste and intelligence

You've heard it a thousand times: The Macintosh is the most user-friendly computer. What does that *mean?* In concrete terms?

For one thing, there's a lot less to install and set up. When you buy an IBM computer, for example, you're likely to spend your first weekend hunched over an open computer case filled with wiring. You squint at the manual that's filled with techno-babble and get depressed that you, a well-educated, perfectly good English speaker, can't understand the first thing it's saying. With a Macintosh, of course, you basically just plug it in and press the On switch.

Keyboard shortcut: *A combination of keys that you press to issue a command, instead of selecting a command from the menus. Some people think that typing (to issue a command, like Print) is faster than using the mouse; it's completely up to you.*

And another thing: There's a lot less to memorize when you use a Macintosh. Because the commands are all listed on the screen (in *menus*), you don't have to remember that Control-Alt-Escape-semicolon is the Print command. In the IBM world, of course, every single program has different commands in different places with different *keyboard shortcuts.* Out of 10,000 Macintosh programs, there are probably five that don't have exactly the same major commands in exactly the same menus with exactly the same keyboard shortcuts.

There are a bunch of other reasons you've done the right thing to go for the Mac — the screen looks better, it's easy to expand, it's the easiest to learn, and it has all kinds of high-tech goodies like a microphone for recording your own sounds. Of course, the last reason that a Mac is superior *is* that it's superior; it entitles you to gloat about owning the world's most hip, technologically evolved, shrewd computer.

Apple and obsolescence

Apple is the gigantic Silicon Valley computer company that started out as a couple of grungy teenagers in a garage. It's the target of incredible love and hate from the Macintosh community. Each time Apple introduces a new Macintosh model, you can bet that it's faster, more powerful, and less expensive than the model *you* already bought. Thus, the mixed passions — people love Apple for coming up with such great products but feel cheated at having paid so much for a suddenly outdated machine.

Feel whatever you want, of course. But if you're going to buy a computer, accept the fact that your investment is going to devalue faster than real estate in Three Mile Island. Here's a promise: No matter how carefully you shop or how good a deal you get on a Macintosh today, it's going to be obsolete in four years. Yeah, I know — it's a cruel, irritating fact, but it's a fact nonetheless.

With that quick and inevitable computer death looming, how can people psych themselves into laying out $3,000 for a computer? Simple: They believe that in those four short years, the computer will speed them up enough, and enhance their productivity enough, to cover the costs easily.

That's the theory, anyway.

Part I
For the Absolute
Mac Virgin

The 5th Wave

THE COMMITTEE FOR THE PROLIFERATION OF MACINTOSH COMPUTERS FINALLY PAY A VISIT TO LARRY.

In this part...

There are three general ways to learn how to work your Mac. You can prevail upon the good graces of your local computer dealer, who, having pocketed your money already, would just as soon have you blow away. You can read the manuals, which have about as much personality as a walnut. Or you can read a book like this one. (Then again, *no* book is quite like this one.)

Tough choice, huh?

In this part, you'll learn, as kindly and gently as possible, what you need to know to get up and running on your Mac system — and nothing else.

Chapter 1
How to Turn On Your Mac
(and What to Do Next)

• •

In This Chapter

▶ How to turn your Mac on (and off)

▶ Confronting weird new words like *mouse* and *menu*

▶ Doing windows

▶ Mindlessly opening and closing folders

• •

*I*f you haven't bought a Mac yet, go *immediately* to Appendix A. Don't speak to any salesperson until you've soaked in the material in this appendix.

If you have bought a Mac, but it's sitting in big cardboard boxes on your living room floor, read the second half of Appendix A, where you'll be gently guided through the not-harrowing-at-all experience of plugging everything in.

At this moment, then, there should be a ready-to-roll Mac on your desk. (Of course, I think that there should be a Mac on *every* person's desk, but that's Apple's job.)

I Took Off the Shrink-Wrap! Now What?

Switching the Mac on

Find your Mac model named as follows. Then find the power button!

Classic (I or II), Plus, or SE: The On/Off switch is in the middle of the rear left edge. **LC (I, II, or III), Performa (200 or 400):** The switch is at the rear *right* corner. It's a rocker switch; the On position is marked by a straight line, and the Off position is marked by a circle. Nobody can ever remember which is which. You may want to think of it this way: the *O* stands for *Off*. (Of course, it also stand for *On* . . . and they wonder why people are intimidated by computers?)

Color Classic, Mac II-something, Quadra-something, Centris 650, or Performa 600: The On switch is on the keyboard. It's a key all by itself with a left-pointing triangle on it:

Centris 610: This odd bird has a round nub of an On/Off button on the front panel, on the right side. **Normal PowerBook:** You have to open the back panel to get at the round, concave power button. On a **Duo,** you press the rubber capsule-shaped button on the keyboard.

Turn the Mac on!

You should hear a ding or a chord, and after a few seconds, an image appears on the screen.

What you hope to see

After a few seconds, you should see the smiling Macintosh on the screen. It looks like the following figure.

The power-on button

Every keyboard has a strange-looking button with a left-pointing triangle on it. On the low-cost Macs, it doesn't do anything (except possibly evoke primal feelings of Picassoesque geometry).

A few seconds after that, you'll see a "Welcome to Macintosh" message. Then the gray (or colored) pattern, called the *desktop,* appears. Congratulations! You're there; skip ahead to "Your First Moments Alone Together."

What you might see

The very first time you turn on your Mac, there's a chance that you'll see a disk with a blinking question mark, as shown in the following figure.

The Mac, in its charming universal picture-based language of love, is trying to tell you that it can't find a disk to start up from. More specifically, it can't find an electronic *System Folder,* which is where the Mac's instructions to itself live.

If you see the blinking question mark icon, you've just met your first computer problem. Now is as good a time as any to dog-ear the pages of Chapter 9, "When Bad Things Happen to Good Machines." This problem, and many others, is explained — and solved — for you there.

In this case, you have to give the Mac a disk containing a System Folder, or it will sit there like an idiot and blink at you until the warranty expires. The easiest way to provide it with a System Folder is to locate those white-labeled System floppy disks that came with the Mac. (They don't, alas, come with Performa models.) The one that contains a System Folder is called Disk Tools. Insert the disk into the slot on the front of the computer — metal side first, label side up. And then read Chapter 9 for the full troubleshooting scoop.

What you hope not to see

You do not want to see the icon shown in the following figure.

If you do, it means something is horribly wrong with the computer. Turn it off and on a couple of times to see if the icon goes away. If not, you have to haul the Mac in to be repaired.

And if you see the icon in the following figure, either you've had too many Buds for one afternoon, or you should try moving your Mac away from open flame.

"IT'S NOT THAT IT DOESN'T WORK AS A COMPUTER, IT JUST WORKS BETTER AS A PAPERWEIGHT."

Your First Moments Alone Together

Now that you've turned on your Mac, it's time to take a few minutes to get acquainted with the Apple of your eye by learning how to communicate with it. Read on.

The big turn-off

If you don't have time to continue at the moment, you can turn the Mac off. You already know where the On/Off switch on a low-cost Mac is. On the fancier Macs, the power-on button on the keyboard won't work to turn it off. You have to find the tiny, round, pea-sized On/Off button at the rear of the machine — it's on the left as you look at the back of the machine.

But turning off the Mac by chopping off its power is a no-no, according to Apple (although I've never heard of it hurting anything). The preferred method is to use the Shut Down command; we'll get to that in a moment.

Moving the mouse

The mouse is the gray, soap-sized plastic box on the desk beside your keyboard. Having trouble visualizing it as a rodent? Think of the cord as its tail, and (if it helps you) draw little eyeballs on the sloping side facing you.

 Now then, roll the mouse across the desk (or mouse pad), keeping the cord pointed away from you. See how the arrow pointer moves across the screen? For the rest of your life, you'll hear that pointer called the *cursor*. And for the rest of your life, moving the mouse will be called *moving the mouse*.

Try lifting the mouse off the desk and waving it around in midair like a remote control. Nothing happens, right? The mouse only controls the cursor when it's on a flat surface. (A ball on the bottom of it detects movement and moves the cursor accordingly.) That's a useful feature because it means that you can pick the mouse up when you run out of desk space, but the cursor will stay in place on the screen. Only when you set the mouse down and begin to roll it again will the cursor continue moving.

What's on the menu?

Let's try some real computing here. Move the cursor up to the white strip at the top of the screen. It's called the *menu bar*, named after a delightful little pub near Cupertino. Touch the arrow on the word Special.

The 5th Wave   By Rich Tennant

"THERE! THERE! I TELL YOU IT JUST MOVED AGAIN!"

Pointing to something on the screen in this way has a technical term: *pointing*. (Think you're going to be able to handle this?)

Now put your index finger on the square button on the mouse, and press the button down. Hold it down. Don't let go.

If all went well, you should see a list of commands drop down from the word Special, as shown in the following figure. Keep holding down the button.

Special	
Clean Up Window	
Empty Trash	
Eject Disk	⌘E
Erase Disk...	
Restart	
Shut Down	

PowerBook mouse buttons

If your Mac is a laptop Mac, you're probably half way to the bookstore to return this book. Yes, it's true: Your computer doesn't have a mouse. Instead, it has a *trackball,* which is essentially an upside-down mouse. The principle is the same: Roll the ball away from you, and the cursor moves up the screen. Instead of a square mouse button, you have two crescent-shaped buttons around the trackball. Both of these buttons act like the mouse button; they're identical in function.

I won't mention this distinction again, because if you're smart enough to have bought a Power-Book, you're smart enough to translate future references to the mouse into trackball terms.

Congratulations — you've learned how to *click the mouse* (by pressing the button), and you've also learned to pull down a *menu* (the list of commands). Try letting go of the mouse button: the menu disappears.

Shutting down

Click the word Special (in the menu bar) again. This time, when the list of commands appears, *keep the button pressed* and roll the mouse downward so that each successive command turns black. In Mac jargon, you're *dragging* the mouse (moving with the button pressed). And when each menu command turns black, it's *highlighted*.

The only commands that don't get highlighted are the ones that are dimmed, or "grayed out." They're dimmed because they don't make any sense at the moment. For example, if there's no disk in the floppy-disk drive, choosing Eject Disk wouldn't make any sense, so the Mac makes it gray, which means it's unavailable to you.

Roll the mouse all the way down to the words Shut Down so that they're highlighted, as shown in the following figure.

For budget-Mac owners only

When you use the Shut Down command on a compact Mac (or an LC or Performa 400), the computer doesn't go all the way off. Instead, it just tells you (with a message on the screen) that it's *ready* to be turned off. Now you have to reach around to the back and physically push the switch off, to the ⎯ position. Or was it the ○ position?

If you've had enough for one session, release the mouse button — the Mac turns itself off.

If your thirst for knowledge is unquenched, and you want to slog ahead with this lesson, then don't let go of the button yet. Instead, slide the cursor off the menu in any direction, and *then* let go of the mouse button. The menu snaps back up like a window shade, and nothing else happens. (You only invoke a menu command when you release the mouse while the cursor is on a command.)

When you're ready to slog ahead, read on.

A one-on-one guided tour

Hey, you've only read the first few pages of this book, and already you can turn your Mac on and off! Told you it was no harder than a toaster.

If you're smart, you should now drop everything and find the Macintosh Basics disk that came with your computer (or the Mouse Practice program that came with your Performa or PowerBook). It may have come pre-installed on your Mac, in which case you'll see it in your main window.

Don't have it?

The Macintosh Basics disk comes with every Macintosh sold in the last few years. It's buried in the manuals. Or maybe it's in its own folder on your hard disk.

If you bought your Mac used, and no Macintosh Basics disk came with the machine, call up the sellers and see if they've got it lying around some-where. If you have no luck, take a blank disk to an Apple dealer and see if they'll give you a copy.

If you still don't have the guided tour disk, don't sweat. I'll try to hit most of the same points as we go along.

Point, click, drag

You've already done some *pointing.* That's where you touch the tip of the arrow cursor on something.

You've already *clicked,* too — that's where you point to something and then click the mouse button. If you're pointing to an icon, like the Trash can, it turns black to show that it's selected.

If you point to an icon and hold the mouse button down, you can move the cursor and the icon will move along with it. The act of moving the mouse while the button's down is called *dragging.*

Eventually, you'll also be asked to *double-click* something. That is, hold the mouse still and press the mouse button twice fast. Feels great.

It's a clever, animated introduction to the Mac, and it shows you America's favorite computer skills (the ones you just learned): pointing, clicking, and dragging. Ponder the sidebar above if you need a refresher.

Because the Macintosh Basics disk does such a good job of teaching you the basics of Macintosh, I won't bother rehashing them further. Here's how you use the Macintosh Basics disk:

1. Turn on your Mac, if you haven't already done so.

2. Insert the Macintosh Basics disk into the floppy disk drive: metal side first, label side up. (When the disk is about 90 percent of the way in, the Mac grabs it and slurps it inside.)

3. Open the Macintosh Basics (or Mouse Practice) folder, if necessary, by pointing to it and clicking the mouse button twice, fast. Point to the little Macintosh Basics man (or Mouse Practice Woman) and double-click *that.*

Techno-babbler's notebook

You may occasionally hear cocky teenagers tell you to "boot up." No, they're not taking you fly-fishing. That's computerese for turning on the Mac. You also hear people say *power up, start up,* and just *boot.*

Furthermore, once the computer is on, you're sometimes asked to turn it off and on again. This is called *rebooting,* or *restarting,* or sometimes *turning it off and on again.*

From there, just follow the instructions on the screen. Turn down the corner of this page, and pick up here when you're ready to go on.

Moving things around on the desktop

So now you've earned your MMA — Master of Mouse Activity. Terrif.

Take a look around the Mac screen. You've already encountered menus (those words File, Edit, View, and so on at the top of the screen). Near the upper-right corner of the screen, you should see an *icon* (a small symbolic picture).

Icons represent everything in the Mac world. They all look different: one represents a letter you wrote, another represents the Trash can, another represents a floppy disk you've inserted. Here are some examples:

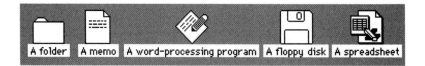

| A folder | A memo | A word-processing program | A floppy disk | A spreadsheet |

All systems are go

The only reason you might need to read this blurb is if you didn't see a Find command when you looked in your File menu as directed on page 21.

You know how General Motors comes out with a new model of each of its cars every year? Well, Apple does the same thing: It keeps making minor changes to its computers, trying to make them better (and provide more incentive to buy them).

Well, we've already encountered the System Folder, which holds software that the Mac needs for itself. Trouble is, in 1991 Apple came out with a newer version of this software, called System 7. (It replaces the older version, which, with great originality, was called System 6.)

System 7 has lots of terrific features, especially for the beginning Mac user. Every Mac sold since early 1991 is equipped with System 7.

If you bought your Mac used, or you bought it some time ago and you're only now starting to learn it, then you might have System 6. It's easy to tell which System you have: Look in the upper-right corner of the screen. Do you see this icon ? If so, you have System 7. If not, you have System 6.

In general, I'm going to assume that you're using System 7 (or 7.01 or 7.1 or 7-point-anything). I'll try not to leave System 6 users in the lurch, though. Watch the margins for special notes that refer to the differences between the two systems.

For now, if you don't see the Find command in the File menu, you should see its System 6 equivalent, Find File, under the *Apple* menu, which is marked by a at the left side of the menu bar. It serves the same purpose as System 7's Find command.

You can move an icon by dragging it. Try this:

1. Point to the Trash icon.

2. Drag it to a new position (move the mouse while the button's down).

Hey, this thing isn't so technical after all, right?

Other than the fact that there's a Trash can, nobody's really sure why they call this "home base" screen the *desktop*. It has another name, too: the *Finder*. Move the mouse to the File menu, and hold the button down. See the word Find? (If not, read "All systems are go" on the previous page.)

This command instantly roots through all your stuff and locates any file you ask for. Thus the name: the Finder.

Used in a sentence, you might hear it like this: "Well, no wonder you don't see the Trash can. You're not in the Finder!"

Understanding icons, windows, and Macintosh syntax

Point to the hard-disk icon (a rectangular box) in the upper-right corner of the screen. A hard disk is like a massive floppy disk. It's the filing cabinet that contains all your work, all your files, and all your software.

So how do you see what's in it? Where do you get to see its table of contents?

It turns out that any disk icon can be *opened* into a window, where you'll see every item inside listed individually. The window has the same name as the icon you opened. (It may already be open. If there's a window open on your screen, choose Close from the File menu. Choose Close again and again, until there are no windows open on your screen.)

Before we proceed, though, it's time for a lesson in Macintosh syntax. No, don't moan; it's nothing like English syntax. In fact, everything you do on the Macintosh has this format: Noun-Verb. Not much poetic nuance, but it's sure easy to remember.

Let's try a noun-verb command, shall we?

1. Click the hard-disk icon in the upper-right corner of the screen.

   It should turn black, indicating that it's *selected*. Good job — you've just identified the *noun*.

2. Move to the File menu, and choose Open.

File	
New Folder	⌘N
Open	⌘O
Print	⌘P
Close Window	⌘W
Get Info	⌘I
Sharing...	
Duplicate	⌘D
Make Alias	
Put Away	⌘Y
Find...	⌘F
Find Again	⌘G
Page Setup...	
Print Desktop...	

You guessed it — Open is the *verb*. And, sure enough, your hard-disk *opens* into a window, where you can see its contents.

Did any of that make sense? In the world of Macintosh, you always specify *what* you want to change (using the mouse), and then you use a menu command to specify *how* you want it changed. You'll see this pattern over and over again: *Select* something on the screen; then *apply* a menu command to it.

Look over the contents of your hard-drive window. See the following figure. (Everybody's got different stuff, so what you see on your screen won't exactly match these illustrations.) There are all kinds of neat things you can do to a window. They're worth learning because you're going to run into windows *everywhere* once you start working.

CLOSE BOX—Click here to close the window. It's the same as choosing Close from the File menu.

TITLE BAR—Drag anywhere in this striped area to move the entire window.

ZOOM BOX—Click here to make the window large enough to show all its contents.

VERTICAL SCROLL BAR— It's white, indicating that you're seeing everything in the window (top to bottom).

SIZE BOX—Drag in any direction to make the window bigger or smaller.

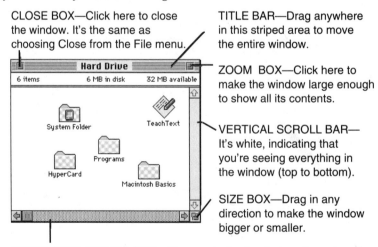

HORIZONTAL SCROLL BAR—It's gray, indicating that you're not seeing everything in the window (there's something off to the side). You can drag the little square to adjust your view of the window from side to side.

Go ahead and try out some of the little boxes and scroll bars. Click on them. Tug on them. Open the window and close it again. No matter what you do, *you can never hurt the machine by doing "the wrong thing."* That's the wonderful thing about the Macintosh: It's the Nerf appliance.

Now try this. Make sure your hard drive window is open. See the System Folder? Even if you don't, here's a quick way to find it: Quickly type SY on your keyboard.

Presto: The Mac finds the System Folder (which happens to be the first thing that begins with those letters) and highlights it, in effect dropping it in front of you, wagging its tail. (If not, absorb the wisdom in the sidebar below.)

Try pressing the arrow keys on your keyboard: right, left, up, down. The Mac highlights neighboring icons as you do so.

Take a look at what's in the System Folder. Of course, using your newfound noun-verb method, you could (1) click the System Folder to select it, and then (2) choose Open from the File menu.

But that's the sissy way. Try this power shortcut: Point to the System Folder icon so that the tip of the arrow cursor is squarely inside the picture of the folder. Keeping the mouse still, click twice in rapid succession.

If all went well, your *double-click* succeeded in opening a new window, showing you the contents of the System Folder. (If it didn't work, you probably need to keep the mouse still or double-click faster.)

Remember this juicy golden rule: *Double-clicking an icon is the same as opening it.* The precious moments and treasured calories you save by using this short-cut will add up rapidly.

Didn't work?

If typing letters of an icon name doesn't seem to do anything, it's because you're using System 6.

This is a System 7 feature. So is selecting icons using the arrow keys.

Using multiple windows

Now you should have *two* windows open on the screen: the hard drive window and the System Folder window. (The System Folder window may be covering the first one up; they're like overlapping pieces of paper on a desk.)

Try this: Click the title bar of the System Folder window, and drag it downward until you can see the hard drive window behind it. See the following figure.

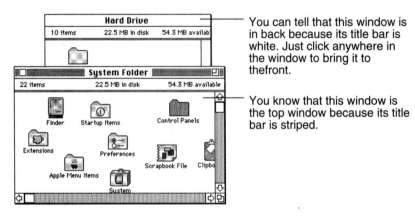

You can tell that this window is in back because its title bar is white. Just click anywhere in the window to bring it to the front.

You know that this window is the top window because its title bar is striped.

Take a stress-free moment to experiment with these two windows: Click the back one to bring it forward; then click the one that *was* in front to bring it to the front again.

If you need any more help fooling around with these windows, the Macintosh manual has a complete tutorial.

Using multiple views

There's one more aspect of windows that will probably make Type A personalities squirm with delight. Up 'till now, you've been viewing the contents of your disk as a bunch of icons. Nice, but wouldn't it be neat to see things alphabetically?

1. Make sure the System Folder is the active window (the one in front).

   We're going to use the System Folder because it's got a lot of stuff in it. Remember how to choose a command from the menu? Point to the menu's name and hold down the mouse button.

2. Locate the View menu at the top of the screen. From it, choose By Name.

   Suddenly, the big icons are replaced by a neat alphabetical list of the window's contents.

Top Ten Similarities Between You and Your Mac

Before you move boldly forward to the next chapter, ponder the significance of the following interesting — nay, frightening — similarities between yourself and your Mac.

1. Both weigh between five and 15 pounds when first displayed in public.

2. Both have feet on the bottom.

3. Both have slots to provide adequate ventilation of the innards.

For would-be weenies only (nonessential info)

When you view a window's contents in a list, each folder *within* the window is marked by a tiny triangle. The triangle points to the right.

You can open one of these folders-within-the-folder in the usual way, if you wish — by double-clicking. But it's much more satisfying for neat freaks to click the *triangle* instead. In the following figure, the before-and-after view of the Control Panels folder (inside the System Folder) shows how much more organized you can be.

System Folder			
17 items	22.5 MB in disk		54.3 MB available
Name		Size	Kind
▷ ☐ Apple Menu Items		105K	folder
☐ Clipboard		56K	file
▷ ☐ Control Panels		291K	folder
▷ ☐ Extensions		1,235K	folder
☐ Finder		356K	file
☐ Note Pad File		3K	file
▷ ☐ Preferences		20K	folder
▷ ☐ PrintMonitor Documents		zero K	folder

System Folder			
22 items	22.5 MB in disk		54.3 MB available
Name		Size	Kind
▷ ☐ Apple Menu Items		105K	folder
☐ Clipboard		56K	file
▽ ☐ Control Panels		78K	folder
☐ Color		12K	contr
☐ General Controls		17K	contr
☐ Monitors		41K	contr
☐ Mouse		9K	contr
▷ ☐ Extensions		1,235K	folder

When you click the triangle, in other words, your window becomes like an outline. The contents of that subfolder are indented. To "collapse," or close, the folder, click the downward-pointing triangle.

One more trick: See the words Size, Kind, and so on (at the top of the window)? Click any of these words. Instantly the Mac re-sorts everything in the window, based on the word you clicked. Example: Click Size, and you'll see the largest files listed first.

4. Both react to the movement of a nearby mouse.

5. Both sometimes crash when asked to do too much at once.

6. Both have a central button.

7. Both light up when turned on.

8. With considerable effort, both may be made to work with IBM computers.

9. Both may be connected to a phone line for days at a time.

10. Both have a built-in 1.4MB SuperDrive. (Well, OK, *you* probably don't, but you don't want to be *exactly* like your computer, do you?)

If you're panting from the mental exertion of learning so many new things at one sitting, go get something from the fridge. Believe it or not, you've already learned more than half of the skills required for operating a Mac.

Shut the Mac down now, if you want (by choosing the Shut Down command from the Special menu — but you knew that). Chapter 2 is something of a chalk-talk to help you explain what's really happening inside the computer's puny brain.

• •

Summary

▶ You turn your Mac on by pressing the On/Off switch (on the back of some Macs; on the keyboard of the expensive ones) to the On position.

▶ The *mouse* is the gray, plastic box you roll around on a flat surface to select commands and move objects on the screen.

▶ *Menus* are lists you access with the mouse that provide you with commands you can choose from to do something.

▶ An *icon* is a symbolic picture, such as the picture of the trash can, which represents the place you "throw away" files that you don't want.

▶ A *window* is a rectangular on-screen frame that displays documents, applications, and other data.

▶ You can have multiple windows open on the screen simultaneously, but only one can be active at any given time.

• •

Chapter 2
High-Tech Made Easy

In This Chapter

▶ How disks and memory work

▶ A look at the floppy disk

▶ Making the distinction between floppy and hard disks

▶ Why you'll never lose work to a computer glitch

▶ Understanding the differences between memory and a hard disk

Understanding How a Mac Works

I'm a little worried about sticking this chapter so close to the front of the book. Plenty of people firmly believe that the Mac has a personality — that when something goes wrong, the Mac is being cranky; and when a funny message appears on the screen, the Mac is being friendly. Don't let the following discussion of cold, metal, impersonal circuitry ruin that image for you; the Mac *does* have a personality, no matter what the wireheads say.

For the first time, you're going to have to roll up your brain's sleeves and chew on some real live computer jargon. Don't worry — you'll feel coolly professional and in control by the time it's over.

Storing things with floppy disks

Human beings, for the most part, store information in one of two places. Either we retain something in our memory — or, if it's too much to remember, we write it down on a legal pad.

Computers work pretty much the same way (except they're not quite as handy with legal pads). They can either store what they know in their relatively pea-brained *memory*, which we'll cover in a moment, or they can write it down. A computer writes stuff down on computer disks.

Floppy disk: *A hard 3½-inch square thing that data is stored on.*

The most common kind of disk is the floppy disk. Unfortunately for your efforts to understand the Mac, its floppy disks aren't floppy, and they're not disks. They're actually hard plastic squares, 3 ½ inches on a side.

Inside the protective hard shell, though, there's a circle of the same shiny brown stuff that tapes are made of. (I suppose that means there really is a floppy disk in there.) Anyway, instead of recording a James Taylor song or a Bruce Willis movie — as audio or videotapes would do — the computer records your documents: a letter to Aunt Millie, your latest financial figures, or notes for your first novel.

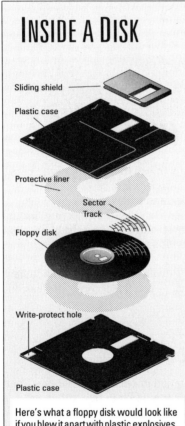

INSIDE A DISK

Sliding shield

Plastic case

Protective liner

Sector
Track

Floppy disk

Write-protect hole

Plastic case

Here's what a floppy disk would look like if you blew it apart with plastic explosives. In the middle, sandwiched between the two protective Stridex pads, there lies a shiny plastic disk to which you entrust your sacred data.

Floppy disks come in several capacities, but even the largest one only holds about 1,000 pages' worth of data. That may seem like a lot, but that's just text. Pictures, for instance, take up much more space; that same floppy disk can probably only hold one or two color pictures. You can see, then, that floppies aren't very handy for storing lots of information.

Conceptualizing the hard disk

Nearly every Mac has an even better storage device built inside it — a *hard disk*. The concept of a hard disk confuses people because it's hidden inside the Mac's case. Since you can't see it or touch it, it's sort of conceptual — like beta-carotene or God, I guess. But it's there, and a hefty chunk of your Mac's purchase price pays for it.

Hard disks differ from floppy disks in a few critical ways. A hard disk delivers information to the computer's brain about ten times faster than a floppy, holds about 50 times more than a floppy, and costs about 500 times as much as a floppy. (Floppies are dirt cheap.)

Why all this talk of disks? Because this is where your life's work is going to live when the computer is shut off.

Don't be confused if you hear (or see) the words hard disk and hard drive used interchangeably — they're the same beast.

Understanding memory

OK. Now we get to the good stuff: how a computer really works. I know you'd just as soon not know what's going on in there, but this is mental broccoli: It's good for you, and later in life, you'll be glad you were forced to digest it. If, at this point, your brain is beginning to hemorrhage and spill out of your ears, skip this section entirely and find serenity in Chapter 3.

There's actually a significant difference between a Mac's memory and your memory (besides the fact that yours is probably much more interesting). When the Mac is turned off at night, it forgets *everything*. It becomes a dumb, metal-and-plastic doorstop. That's because a computer's memory, just like yours, is kept alive by electrical impulses. When you turn off a Mac, the electricity stops. (Fortunately, few things can turn off a *person*, except possibly someone spitting tobacco juice, or something, which has little effect on our memories.)

Therefore, each time you turn on a Mac, it has to re-learn everything it ever knew, including the fact that it's a computer, what kind of computer it is, how to display text, and so on. Now we arrive at the purpose of those disks we've been droning on about; that's where the computer's knowledge lives when the juice is off. Without a disk, the Mac is like someone with a completely hollow skull (and we've all met *that* type). If you're ever unlucky enough to experience a broken hard drive, you'll see how exciting a Mac can be without any disks: It shows a completely gray screen with a small blinking question mark in the middle (I've met a few people like *that,* too).

When you turn on the Mac, there's whirring and blinking; the hard disk inside begins spinning. When it hits about 3,600 rpm, the Mac starts reading the hard disk (or, if the analogy helps you, it "plays" the disk like a record player). It finds out: "Hey, I'm a Mac! And this is how I display text!" and so on. It's reading the disk and copying everything it reads into *memory.*

Memory is really neat. Once something's in memory, it's instantaneously available to the computer; the Mac no longer has to read the disk to learn something. Memory is also expensive since it's really a bunch of complicated circuits etched onto a piece of silicon the size of a stick of gum.

Because it's expensive, most people's Macs have far less memory than disk space. For example, even if your hard disk holds every issue of National Geographic ever published, you're probably only going to *read* one article at a time. So the Mac reads "African Tribal Women: Pierced Noses in the Desert" from your hard disk, loads it into memory, and displays it on the screen. So it doesn't matter that your Mac's memory doesn't hold as much as your entire hard disk; the hard disk is used for *long-term, permanent* storage of *lots* of things, and memory is used for *temporary* storage while you work on *one thing at a time.*

The 5th Wave By Rich Tennant

©RICHTENNANT

"OH YEAH, AND TRY NOT TO ENTER THE WRONG PASSWORD."

Who's Meg?

You often hear computer jocks talk about megs. Trust me — they're almost certainly not discussing Meg Ryan and Meg Tilly. Meg is short for *megabyte*. (*Mega*=1,000,000 and *byte*=¹⁄₁,₀₀₀,₀₀₀ of a megabyte. That was fun, wasn't it?)

Megabyte: *A unit of memory or storage capacity, nicknamed* meg *or abbreviated* MB. *One meg equals 1,024 kilobytes, or K; a K is about one page of a romance novel.*

What's highly confusing to most beginners is that memory (fast, expensive, temporary) and hard-disk space (permanent, slower) are measured in the same units: megabytes. A typical

Mac has between two and eight megs of memory (silicon chips), but 40 or 80 megs of hard-disk space (spinning platters).

With this vital fact in mind, see if you can answer the following paradoxical dinner party question:

"How many megs does your Macintosh have?"

The novice's answer: "Um . . . say, have you tried those little cocktail weenies?"

The partly-initiated's reply: "I . . . I think 80?"

The truly enlightened response: "What do you mean, how many megs? Are you referring to memory or to *hard disk storage space?* . . . Here, have a cocktail weenie. . . ."

Understanding RAM

RAM: *When the Committee for Arbitrary Acronyms ratified this abbreviation, it probably stood for Random Abbreviation for Memory. Supposedly, it really stands for Random Access Memory, whatever that* means.

Let's add another term to your quickly-growing nerd vocabulary list. It pains me to teach you this word because it's one of those really meaningless terms that was invented purely to intimidate people. Trouble is, you're going to hear it a lot, so you may as well be prepared.

It's RAM. You pronounce it like the goat. RAM is memory. A typical Mac has four megs of RAM (in other words, four megs of memory).

Putting it all together

OK. Now that you know where a computer's information lives, let me take you on a tour of the computer's guts. If we were at Walt Disney World, you'd get on a little tram at this point, and I'd tell you to keep your hands and feet inside the car at all times.

When you turn on the Mac, as noted above, the hard disk spins, and the Mac copies certain critical information into its memory.

So far, the Mac only knows that it's a computer. It doesn't know anything else that's stored on your hard disk; it doesn't know about African Tribal Women, or your new screenplay, or how much you owe on your credit card — yet.

To get any practical work done, you now have to transfer the article (or screenplay or spreadsheet) into memory; in Macintosh terminology, you have to *open a file*. In Chapter 3, you'll find out how easy and idiot proof this is. Anyway, once you open a file, it appears on the screen. (It's in memory now.)

While your document is on the screen, you can make changes to it. This, of course, is why you bought a computer in the first place. You can delete a sentence from your novel or move a steamy scene into a different chapter (the term for this process is *word processing*). If you're designing a party invitation, you can make the border fatter, change your mind, and make it thinner again, without any eraser crumbs. And so on.

Perceptive readers (who haven't already gotten bored and gone off to watch TV) will recognize that you're making all of these changes to what's in *memory*. The more you change the screenplay that's up on the screen, the more it's different from that *permanent* copy that's still on your disk, safe and sound.

At this point, you're actually in a pretty precarious position. Remember that memory is sustained by electricity. In other words, if your four-year-old mistakes the Mac's power cord for a handy suckable plaything and jerks it out of the wall, then the electricity will stop, the screen will go blank, and all the changes you've made disappear forever. You're left with the original copy on the disk, of course, but any work you've done on it vanishes, along with anything else in the Mac's memory.

However, every Mac program has a simple command, called Save, that saves your work back onto the hard disk. That is, the computer updates the original copy that's still on the hard disk, and you're safe. Even if a sun storm wipes out all power plants in the Northern Hemisphere, your novel or letter or spreadsheet is safe on the disk, even though the Mac's memory gets wiped out. Most people use the Save command every five or ten minutes so that their work is always up-to-date and preserved on the disk. (You'll learn how to use the Save command in Chapter 3.)

"I lost all my work!"

So that you'll quit worrying about it, the precariousness of memory accounts for the horror stories you sometimes hear from people who claim that they lost their work to a computer. "I was on volume Y of the encyclopedia I've been writing," they'll say, "and I lost all of it because of a computer glitch!"

Now you can cry crocodile tears and then skip back to your office with a smirk because *you* know what happened. They probably worked for hours with some document on the screen but forgot to use the Save command. Then, when the unthinkable happened — someone tripped on the power cord — sure enough, all the changes they'd made got wiped out (along with everything else in the Mac's oh-so-temporary memory). A simple Save command would have stored everything neatly on the hard disk.

Top Ten Differences Between Memory and a Hard Disk

Just so you'll never confuse memory with a hard disk again, I've provided you with the ten major differences between the two.

1. You usually buy memory two or four megs at a time. Hard disks usually come in 20-, 40-, 80-, and 160-meg sizes (and on up).

2. Memory comes on chips — little brown mini-circuit boards. A hard disk is a big box made of metal (and sometimes housed in plastic).

3. You can only install memory inside the computer (something you usually hire a local guru to do). A hard disk may be either inside the Mac (an *internal* drive) or a separate box you just plug into the back (an *external* drive).

4. Memory delivers information to the Mac's brain almost instantly. The hard disk sometimes seems to take forever.

5. Memory is sometimes referred to as RAM. A hard disk has no abbreviation.

6. Not every Mac has a hard disk (some people still use very old models with nothing but floppy disks). But every Mac has memory.

7. When the Mac is reading some information off a hard disk, a little light flickers on and off (usually on the front of your Mac or on the case of an external hard disk). You can't tell when the Mac is getting information from RAM.

8. As a very general rule, RAM costs about $35 per meg, and hard drive space averages about $10 per meg.

9. Memory's contents disappear when you turn off the computer. A disk's contents stay there until you deliberately throw them away.

10. You can trick the Mac into thinking that some of your *hard-disk* space is RAM (called *virtual memory*). You can also trick the Mac into thinking that some of your RAM is a disk (called a *RAM disk*). (Actually, I guess this is really a similarity, not a difference. Oh well. Both of these advanced techniques are described in your Mac manuals, more or less. Neither is important except to power-users; most people don't use either one. I'm already sorry I brought it up.)

Ready for Action

Enough chalk talk. Let's hit the playing field; in Chapter 3, all this fancy jargon will turn into *action, action, action* (or, I suppose, *word processing, word processing, word processing*). Remember to read Appendix A for information about how to buy a Mac — or, if you already have one, to find out how yours ranks in the power hierarchy and what it can do.

• •

Summary

▶ A computer stores information on disks when it's off.

▶ Floppy disks are cheap, portable, slow, and don't hold much information.

▶ Hard disks are expensive, big, heavy, and hold lots of information. There's a hard disk built inside almost every Mac.

▶ Disks are too slow and inefficient to satisfy the Mac's insatiable appetite for information, so the Mac also has electronic memory.

▶ While you work on something, it's in temporary memory. You have to save it onto a disk unless you want it to say bye-bye when the power goes off.

▶ Hard disks and memory, which aren't very much alike, are both measured in megabytes, or megs.

• •

Chapter 3
Doing Windows, Getting Floppy

● ●

In This Chapter
▶ All about windows, folders, and icons
▶ Learning keyboard shortcuts
▶ Working with floppy disks
▶ Tips on using windows and floppy disks to raise your social status

● ●

Becoming Manipulative

All of this clicking and dragging and window-shoving you learned in Chapter 1 is, in fact, leading up to something useful.

Foldermania

I've said that your hard disk is like the world's biggest filing cabinet. It's where you store all your stuff. But a filing cabinet without filing *folders* would be about as convenient to handle as an egg without a shell.

The folders on the Mac screen don't occupy any space on your hard drive. They're electronic fictions whose sole purpose is to help you organize your stuff.

Mr. Folder

The Mac provides an infinite supply of them. Want a folder? Do this:

From the File menu, choose New Folder.

Ooh, tricky, this machine, eh? A new folder appears. Note that the Mac gracefully proposes "untitled folder" as its name. (Gotta call it *something,* I suppose.)

Notice something else, though: the name is *highlighted* (black). Remember our earlier lesson? Highlighted = selected = ready for you to *do* something. When *text* is highlighted, the Mac is ready for you to *replace* it with anything you type. In other words, you don't even have to backspace over it. Just type away.

1. Type *USA Folder*. Press the Return key.

   The Return key tells the Mac that your naming spurt is over.

   Now, to see how folders work, create another one.

2. Choose New Folder from the File menu again.

   Another new folder appears, once more waiting for a title.

3. Type *Ohio*. Press Return.

You're going to create one more empty folder. But by this time, your wrist is probably weary from the forlorn trek back and forth to the File menu. Don't you wish there was a faster way to make a folder?

There is.

Keyboard shortcuts

Pull down the File menu, but don't select any of the commands in it yet. See that weird notation to the right of some of the commands?

File	
New Folder	⌘N
Open	⌘O
Print	⌘P
Close Window	⌘W
Get Info	⌘I
Sharing...	
Duplicate	⌘D
Make Alias	⌘M
Put Away	⌘Y
Find...	⌘F
Find Again	⌘G
Page Setup...	
Print Window...	

Get used to 'em. They're *keyboard shortcuts,* and they appear in almost every menu you'll ever see. You're by no means obligated to use them, but you should understand that they let you select certain menu items without using the mouse.

Unimportant info regarding other symbols in menus

Besides the little keyboard-shortcut symbols at the right side of a menu, you'll occasionally run into a little downward-pointing arrow, like this:

Font
Avant Garde
Bookman
Chicago
Courier
Futura
Garamond
Geneva
Hartel
Helvetica
Monaco
Palatino
Symbol
▼

What that arrow is telling you is that the menu is so long, it doesn't even fit on the screen. The arrow is implying that there are still more commands in the menu that you're not seeing. To get to them, carefully roll the pointer down the menu all the way to that down-pointing triangle. Don't let it scare you: The menu commands will jump upward, bringing the hidden ones into view.

When you type, you press the Shift key to make a capital letter, right? They call the Shift key a *modifier key* because it turns ordinary, well-behaved citizen keys like 3 and 4 into wild symbols like # and $. Welcome to the world of computers, where everything is three times more complicated. Instead of having only *one* modifier key, the Mac has *three* of them! Look down next to your spacebar. There they are: in addition to the Shift key, one says Option, and another either says Command or has a little ⌘ symbol on it.

For weenies only

OK, there's yet another modifier key you've never seen before: the Control key. But the Control key doesn't do *anything;* neither do a number of other keys on the Mac keyboard (like those F1, F2, F3 keys, if you have them, or the Escape key).

Yet. (We'll whip it into submission in Chapter 6.)

It's that little cloverleaf symbol that appears in the File menu. Next to the New Folder command, it's ⌘-N. That means:

1. While pressing the ⌘ key down, press the N key.

   Bam! You've got yourself another folder.

2. Type *Michigan*, and press Return.

   You've just named your third folder. So why have you been wasting a perfectly good afternoon (or whatever it is in your time zone) making empty folders? So that you can pretend you're getting organized.

3. Drag the Ohio folder on top of the USA Folder.

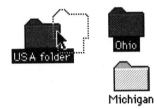

Make sure that the *tip* of the arrow actually hits the center of the USA Folder so that the folder becomes highlighted. When it turns black, let go of the Ohio folder — and watch it disappear into the USA Folder. (If your aim wasn't good, you'll now see the Ohio folder sitting *next* to the USA Folder; try the last step again.)

4. Put the Michigan folder into the USA Folder in the same way — by dragging it on top of the USA Folder.

   As far as you know, though, those state folders have *disappeared*. How can you trust me that they're now neatly filed away?

5. Double-click the USA Folder.

   Yep. Opens right up into a window, and there are your two darling states, nestled sweetly where they belong. If you were to double-click one of *them,* you'd open *another* window. (Having a million windows open at once is nothing to be afraid of. If you're a neatness freak, it might make you feel threatened, but it's easy enough to close them — remember the close box in the upper-left corner of each one.)

Double-click: *Without moving the mouse, click twice quickly on something, which will open it into a window. Doesn't matter if it's a disk icon, a folder icon, or a document icon.*

OK, so how do you get them *out* again? Do you have to drag them individually? That would certainly be a bummer if you had all 50 folders in the USA Folder.

Turns out there are several ways to select more than one icon at a time.

6. Click above and to the left of the Ohio folder (Example 1, below). Without releasing the mouse, drag down and to the right so that you enclose both folders with a dotted rectangle (Examples 2 and 3).

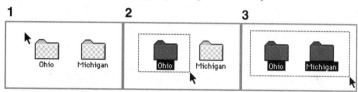

If you're using System 7, then each icon turns black as the dotted rectangle encloses it. (Otherwise, nothing turns black until you release the mouse.) In any case, release the mouse button when you've got both icons enclosed.

OK to skip this

The method of selecting several icons by dragging a rectangle around them is fine if all the icons are next to each other. But how would you select only the icons that begin with the letter A in this picture?

You can't very well enclose the A's by dragging the mouse because you'd also get all the *other* icons within the same rectangle.

The power-user's secret: Click each one *while pressing the Shift key.* As long as you're pressing Shift, you continually add additional, non-adjacent icons to the selection. (And if you Shift-click one by accident, you can *deselect* it by Shift-clicking *again.* Try it!)

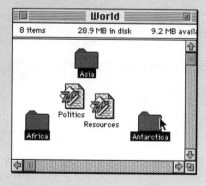

Now that you have several folders selected, you can move them en masse to another location.

Drag the Ohio folder outside of the USA Folder window. The Michigan folder goes along for the ride.

This was a somewhat unproductive exercise, of course, because we were only working with empty folders. It gets much more exciting when you start working with your own documents. All of these techniques work equally well with folders and with documents.

There's one more icon-manipulation trick you'll probably find valuable.

1. Close the USA Folder by clicking its close box.

2. Then drag the folder on top of the Trash can in the lower-left corner of the screen.

Don't let go until the Trash can actually turns black (when the tip of the arrow cursor is upon it). When you do let go, notice how the Trash can bulges, a subtle reinforcement of how important it thinks your stuff is. Anyway, that's how you throw things out on the Mac: Just drag them on top of the Trash can. (Technically, you've really only put that stuff in Oblivion Waiting Room because it doesn't disappear when it goes into the Trash. It'll sit there forever, in a bulging trash can.)

If you need to rescue something, just double-click the Trash to open its window; drag whatever-it-was right back onto the screen.

So if putting something into the Trash doesn't really delete it, how *do* you really delete it? Choose Empty Trash from the Special menu.

Trash and System 6

If you're using System 6 (that is, if no ⍰ icon appears in the upper-right corner of your screen), then the Trash can *doesn't* sit there, bulging, until you Empty Trash. It gets emptied automatically when you turn off the Mac, and sometimes sooner.

A trash tidbit for techies

Don't tell anybody, but *even after* you've Emptied the Trash, your file *still* isn't really gone forever. There are programs (like Norton Utilities and Complete Undelete) that can un-erase a file that's been trashed, as long as you haven't used your Mac much since. That's useful to remember in case (1) you ever trash something by mistake, or (2) you're a spy.

Having Fun with Floppies

For our next trick, you're going to need a floppy disk. If you didn't buy a box of blank disks with your Mac, you're going to need some eventually. Call up Mac Connection and order some. (Phone number in the Resource Resource at the back of the book.)

If you don't have a blank disk handy, you can use one of the white System disks that came with your Mac.

A floppy factoid barely worth reading

You know how an audio cassette has that small plastic tab, which you can pry out to prevent your little sister from accidentally recording over what's on the tape?

Well, a floppy has the same thing (a tab, that is, not a sister). In the corner of the disk, on the back, there's a little square sliding tab. On a disk, you don't actually have to pry out the tab (technology on the march, doncha know); you can just slide it back and forth. When you slide the tab so you can see through the hole, you've *locked* the disk, and you can't erase it or trash any of its contents.

When you slide the tab so that it *covers* the hole, the disk is unlocked, and you can erase it, trash it, or copy new stuff onto it.

Disk drive: The thin horizontal slot in the front of your Macintosh (or the side of your PowerBook or Duo Dock), where the floppy disk goes. Put the disk in metal-side first, label facing up.

1. Put the floppy disk into the disk drive slot.

   The Mac gulps it in with a satisfying *kachunk*. If it's a brand new disk, you see this message:

> **This disk is unreadable:**
> **Do you want to initialize it?**
>
> [Eject]   [Initialize]

   Go ahead. Click Initialize. (If you're asked whether you want to make it single-sided [the kind of disk that's way obsolete] or double-sided, select double-sided — unless you're going to be sending this disk to someone who bought a Mac in 1984 and immediately moved to Borneo.) You're then

TECHNICAL STUFF

More disk stuff you really don't need to know

The big floppy-disk makers, like Sony and Fuji, churn out disks by the trainload. They have a big market because both Macs and IBM-type computers use these 3½-inch disks.

The thing is, not all computers *format* the floppies in the same ways. Imagine that a little floppy-disk gnome runs around while the disk is being "initialized," making chalk-mark boundaries for the storage of your files. Well, Mac gnomes and IBM gnomes space their disk-surface boundary lines differently — the upshot is that an IBM disk will appear unreadable to a Mac, and vice-versa. So Sony and Fuji and the other disk companies don't bother pre-formatting these disks for you, since they don't know what kind of computer you have, and besides it's too much trouble.

As noted in Chapter 2, disks come in three capacities, although all the disks look almost alike:

the old 400K, or *single-sided* disks; 800K, or *double-sided* disks; and 1.4MB, or *high-density* disks. That is a *lot* of storage for such a little disk; 1.4 megabytes is around 1400K, or 3.5 times as much as the original single-sided disks. High-density disks are marked with the letters CH, for some reason:

Well, OK, it's really supposed to be an *HD,* for high-density, but the logo designer had a bad night. Anyway, all *recent* Macs can read high-density disks, but there are millions of Mac Plus and older SE models that can't. So when you exchange disks with somebody, give them 800K (double-sided) disks unless you've made sure they can handle the HD ones.

asked to name the disk; type a name and click OK and then wait about 45 seconds while the Mac prepares the disk for its new life as your data receptacle.

If it's *not* a new disk — for example, if you're using one of the disks that came with your Mac — the floppy-disk icon shows up on the right side, just beneath your hard-disk icon:

To see what's on the disk, double-click the icon. As you've no doubt tired of hearing repeated, a double-click on a disk icon opens its contents window.

This is important stuff: In your lifetime, you'll do a lot of copying from floppy disks *to* your hard drive (such as when you buy a program and want to put a copy of it on your hard drive). If you're smart, you'll also do a lot of copying onto floppies *from* your hard drive (such as when you make a backup copy of all your work, in preparation for the inevitable day when something will go wrong with your hard disk).

2. Double-click your hard-disk icon.

   If its window was closed, it now opens. If the window was open but hidden behind the floppy-disk window, the hard-disk window now pops to the front.

3. Drag the Ohio folder on top of the floppy-disk icon.

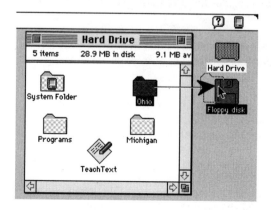

If you already trashed your Ohio folder, no big deal. Choose New Folder from the File menu (or press ⌘-N) to create a new folder. Drag that instead.

The point is that, on a Macintosh, making a copy of something is as easy as dragging it to the disk you want it copied onto. You can also drag something into the disk's *window* (instead of onto its *icon*).

Copying something from a floppy to your hard disk is equally easy. Open the floppy-disk window (by double-clicking the floppy-disk icon). Then drag whatever icons you want from the window onto the hard-disk icon (or into the hard-disk window).

For example, in the illustration below, two files are being copied from a floppy disk — not just into the hard-disk window, but into a *specific folder* on the hard disk:

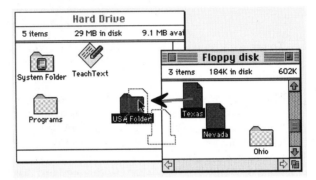

Rest assured that you can make as many copies of a file as you want without ever experiencing a loss of quality. You're digital now, kids. It's not like copying tapes, where each copy of a copy is a little bit worse than the previous generation. The ten-thousandth copy of your novel will be just as spicy as the first. (That makes software companies nervous because some unscrupulous people make a regular habit of making themselves free copies of their friends' expensive software.)

OK. So you've made a backup copy of your fourth-quarter report, or you've just copied a new program onto your hard disk. Now what? How do you get the disk out?

Well, you wouldn't be alone in guessing that you use the Eject Disk command in the Special menu. But you'd be sort of wrong. The Eject Disk command does spit out the disk — but it leaves the disk's *icon* on the screen so that the Mac thinks it's still available. The minute you try to go on with your work, the Mac will start displaying messages demanding that you give the disk back to it.

A much better way to get rid of the disk is to select it (noun) and choose *Put Away* (verb) from the File menu. That makes the disk pop out, *and* its image disappears from the screen.

Dweebs' Corner: Alternative disk tips

Another way to remove a floppy disk is to drag its icon to the Trash can! Yes, yes, I *know* it looks like you're erasing the entire disk. (It looks that way to *every* first-time Mac user.) But you're not — this action just pops out the disk.

Once every few months, you'll have a situation where a disk won't come out of the drive. If the Mac is still running, hold down the ⌘ and Shift keys together, and press 1. (This works even if

you're not at the desktop/Finder.) And even less often than that, you'll have a disk in the drive and the Mac is *off*. In that case, turn on the Mac while pressing the mouse button down continuously until the Trash can appears.

And if *that* doesn't work, straighten a paper clip. Push it slowly but firmly into the tiny pinhole to the right of the disk drive slot. That'll shove the disk out.

Top Ten Window and Disk Tips

"I don't do windows," you say? After reading the following tips, you'll find windows so easy to do that you might even consider cleaning the Venetian blinds or defrosting the fridge.

1. If you're looking at a windowful of file icons, you can select one by typing the first couple of letters of its name.

2. You're not condemned to spend the rest of your life viewing windows with mind-numbing numbers of icons, like this:

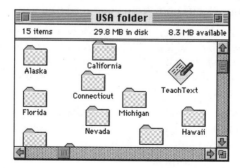

As a refreshing change of pace, use the oft-underestimated View menu (next page, left) to rearrange your icons into a *list view* (next page, right):

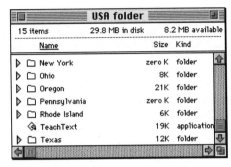

Once you're in a list view, you can press the up and down arrow keys to highlight neighboring files up and down the list.

3. Another list-view trick: When a folder name is highlighted, you can press ⌘-→ to expand it (as though you'd clicked the triangle to view its contents) and ⌘-← to collapse it again.

4. In System 7, every time you choose Empty Trash from the Special menu, the Mac asks you if you're absolutely sure. If you'd prefer it to simply vaporize the Trash contents without asking, select the Trash icon. Choose Get Info from the File menu, and click the "Warn before emptying" checkbox so that the X disappears.

5. If you're trying to make a copy of a floppy disk, and you only have one floppy-disk drive, you'll find that the Mac can only copy a little bit at a time. It winds up asking you to insert one disk, then the other; one disk, then the other . . . until your wrists are swollen and bleeding. A better, faster idea: Copy the entire disk to your *hard disk,* eject the floppy, insert the blank floppy and then copy the stuff from the hard disk to the new floppy. Using the hard disk as an intermediate holding tank in this way eliminates the disk swapping. (Just trash the superfluous copy from your hard disk when it's all over.)

6. If you have a very important document, you can prevent it from getting thrown away by accident. Click its icon. Choose Get Info from the File menu. Select the Locked checkbox. Now, even if you put it in the Trash and try to empty the Trash, the Mac will simply tell you that there's a locked item in the Trash, which it won't get rid of.

7. To rename an icon or disk, click carefully on its name. Wait for a second or so, until a rectangle appears around the name. That's your cue to type away, giving it a new name. Press Return when you're done.

   It works a little differently in System 6. Just click an icon and start typing. No rectangle, no waiting.

8. You already know how to copy a file from one disk to another. You can copy it on the *same* disk, too: Click the icon and choose Duplicate from the File menu. Or, while pressing the Option key, drag the icon onto a new folder.

9. See the question mark in the upper-right corner of the screen (?)? (It's the telltale signal that you're running System 7, remember?) It's really a menu, just like the other menus you've worked with. Point to the question mark, hold the button down, and choose Show Balloons.

   Now roll the cursor around the screen. Don't click; just point to things. As the cursor touches each one, a balloon pops up to identify it. Now move the cursor to a menu; press the button, and try pointing to different menu commands. When you're tired of seeing what things are and what they do, go back to the question mark menu. This time, choose Hide Balloons.

10. You don't have to eject disks and clean up your windows before you shut down the computer. The disks pop out automatically, and the windows will be right where you left them the next time you turn on the Mac.

All About At Ease

All this talk of folders, windows, and disks must make your head spin at first. Now imagine that you're a ten-year-old, and you'll understand why Apple invented At Ease (which you get free with a Performa model, or for around $59 from Apple or a mail-order place). It's a sweet little program that *covers up* all that stuff you've spent so much time and effort learning: folders, the Trash can, dragging icons around, and list views. In fact, the entire Finder (the desktop) gets hidden when At Ease is running.

In its place, you see something like this:

Click here to see the screenful of document icons.

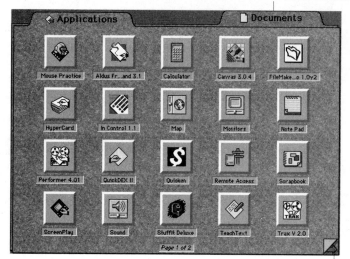

If there are more than 20 icons, click here to see the next screenful of them.

What's neat is that you can launch any program or document with a *single* mouse click, not a double-click. You hear a cool clicky sound when you click one of these icons. When you launch a program, the At Ease window itself disappears, only to reappear when you quit that program. (What's also neat, for those who care, is that At Ease takes up 200K less memory than the regular Finder desktop, and that means 200K more memory for your programs to use.)

At Ease is designed for teachers, parents, or trainers who want to hide the confusing world of folders and icons from beginning Mac fans. It's also good for *protecting* your regular Mac universe from unwitting (or witting) disrupters. Because At Ease denies a user access to Control Panels, the Trash, or moving or renaming files, your hard drive is safe.

You can switch back and forth from At Ease to the regular Finder by choosing the appropriate command from the File menu (Go to Finder, for example). If you want even *that* escape hatch closed, you can create a password so that only you, The Parent, can escape to the Finder.

Unfortunately, At Ease won't help *you* avoid learning the Mac because you still have to know the Mac just to install and set up At Ease. Still, At Ease is a nice idea if you have kids, students, or visitors of any kind; it provides a lot of simplicity and reassurance if you don't want your normal Mac environment messed with.

Summary

▶ Folders are electronic filing folders. You can have folders inside of folders. You put a file into a folder by dragging its icon on top of the folder.

▶ Open a folder by pointing to it with the mouse and double-clicking. The folder opens into a window that shows its contents.

▶ Power-user wannabes will tell you that, instead of choosing a command from a menu in the normal way, it's more efficient to use the keyboard shortcut, which usually involves pressing the ⌘ key.

▶ You can, thank God, easily throw away anything you create. Just drag its icon on top of the Trash can.

▶ You can copy files from one disk to another just by dragging their icons.

Chapter 4

Actually Getting Some Work Done

● ●

In This Chapter

▶ What software is, for those who care

▶ Copying and pasting

▶ Your very first word processing lesson

▶ Saving your work for posterity

▶ What desk accessories are and what fruit-shaped menu they're listed in

● ●

*B*uckle your mental seat belts: I'm about to stretch an analogy so far it might pop. Ready?

The Mac is like a VCR. The disks you slide into the Mac are like the tapes you slip into your VCR. Without tapes (disks), the VCR (Mac) is worthless. But with tapes (disks), your VCR (Mac) can take on any personality.

A VCR might let you watch a western one night, home movies another, and a "60 Minutes" exposé about a corrupt Good Humor man another night. In the same way, your Mac can be a typing instructor, a checkbook balancer, or a movie-editing machine, depending on the software you buy. Each piece of software — usually called a program, but sometimes known as an *application* — is like a different GameBoy cartridge: It makes the Mac look, feel, and behave differently. The average Mac user winds up using about six or seven different programs regularly.

Obsolescence Therapy II

Your relationship with a software company doesn't end when you buy the program. First of all, the company provides a technical help staff for you to call when things get rocky. Some firms are great about this — it's a toll-free number that's answered immediately by a smart, helpful, customer-oriented technician. More often, though, sending out an SOS is a long-distance call . . . and a long-distance five- or ten-minute wait before somebody can help you. And how can you find out how good a company's help line is? By asking around, and by reading the reviews in *Macworld* and *MacUser* magazines.

Like the computers themselves, software applications are continually being improved and enhanced by their manufacturers. Just as in owning a computer, owning a software program isn't merely a one-time cash outlay; each time the software company comes out with a new version of the program, you'll be offered the chance to get it for a small "upgrade fee" of $25 or $99, for example.

 You'd think people would get fed up with this endless treadmill of expenses and just stick with the version they've got, refusing to upgrade to successive versions. Some manage it. Most people, however, succumb to the fear that somehow they'll be left behind by the march of technology, and wind up forking over the upgrade fees once a year or so.

Credit Card Workout #2: Buying Software

(Credit Card Workout #1, by the way, was buying the computer.)

Unless you actually bought (or received) some software when you got your Mac, you won't be able to do much more than admire the Mac's contribution to the décor. So unless you bought a Performa model, which comes with a handsome bonus gift of software pre-installed on your hard disk, get ready for another buying spree.

Names and numbers

After you spend awhile with Macs, you start to notice some peculiar naming conventions in software. First of all, all programmers must have broken spacebars, because you never see spaces between words in the names of programs: Page-Maker, MacPaint, WriteNow, and even MyAdvancedLabelMaker (yuck). Today, having a space in your title is considered a social faux pas, like clipping your nails on the bus.

You learn to tell how recent a program is by the version number after its name. What begins as WordMeister version 1 becomes WordMeister 1.5 when its maker adds a spelling checker to the program, for example. Then they add built-in help messages and call it WordMeister 1.5.2. I don't know where the idea of multiple decimal points came from, but it's pretty dumb. It's ony a matter of time before we'll start seeing ads for things like MacFish 2.4.9.6 and Page Man 3.6.5.4.2.1.

Oh, and when a program gets upgraded too many times, the company adds the word Pro to its name.

Of course, every Mac comes with *some* software. For example, each Mac comes with the System software (those white floppy disks) that it needs for its own internal use. It comes with some mini-programs, like the Calculator and the Note Pad, called *desk accessories.* And it comes with HyperCard, which is a topic for a later, rainier day (Chapter 6). None of this free software will make you very productive on the day you set up your computer.

It's time to spend some more money; software, for the most part, is expensive. For example, the world's most popular Mac word processing program is Microsoft Word, and the lowest price I've seen for it is $300. If you plan to do number crunching, over 80 percent of Mac users use the spreadsheet Microsoft Excel (another $300). Want a database for handling order forms, tracking phone calls, and creating merged form letters? Check out the fantastic FileMaker Pro (around $200).

There are lower-priced alternatives, of course. If you really want to do some homework, read a few recent issues of *Macworld* and *MacUser* for some guidance. For example, WriteNow is a super, fast, easy-to-use word processing program, and it's only $150. It can even exchange files with Microsoft Word. Unfortunately, you may feel a little bit left out with one of the underdog programs, since almost all the talk, help, and articles will be about the big three (Word, Excel, and FileMaker).

If you're on a budget and don't much care about being in the vanguard, you can get a lot of power in the form of an *integrated* program like ClarisWorks (or any other program whose name ends with "Works") — which is the kind of program you get when you buy a Mac Performa. For the cost of a single program, you get several programs mashed into one: word processor, database, spreadsheet, drawing program, and so on. Of course, it doesn't do any *one* thing as well as a separate program would, but it does everything pretty well.

In any case, you definitely need a word processor. Most people could use an address book program like Super QuickDex and a calendar/reminder program like Now Up to Date. And then there's graphics: If you want to draw or paint, read Chapter 6 for some explanations and suggestions.

Where to get it

 There are two places to buy software: via mail order and at a store. Software stores give you a better dose of reality — something you, O Revered Beginner, could probably use: You get to pick up and heft the actual box, tap a live human being on the shoulder to ask questions, ask other customers what they've had luck with, and so on. In some stores you can even try out the software on a real live Mac, so you won't wind up buying something you don't need. As in the computer-hardware world, a good software dealer is an excellent resource.

Mail-order companies have different kinds of advantages: They give much bigger discounts; many of them take returns after you've opened the box; they don't charge sales tax; and so on. And, of course, you don't have to fire up the old Volvo; you get your order the next day (the overnight shipping charge is usually $3 per order).

At the risk of sounding like a broken CD, I'm going to direct you to the Mac magazines like *Macworld* and *MacUser* for more info on mail-order companies. They're called things like Mac Connection, Mac Zone, and Mac Warehouse. They all have toll-free phone numbers, and their catalogs and ads all appear in every single issue of those magazines. (Their numbers also appear in Appendix C, the Resource Resource.) Overnight mail-order companies like these are truly one of the bright spots in the Mac world. After being around them awhile, you'll start to wish there were overnight mail-order grocery stores, gas stations, and dentists.

In the next section, you're going to do some word processing. That's what 90 percent of Mac users do the most of (when they're not hang gliding, housing the homeless, and saving the environment, I mean). I have no way of knowing what software, if any, you bought with your computer. Maybe you already have a word processing program, maybe not. (Look over your pile of boxes. If there's one that says Microsoft Word, WriteNow, WordPerfect, Nisus, or anything that ends with the word *Works,* then you have a word processor.) If you don't have a word processor yet, call up Mac Connection or some other company and order one, right now, so you'll have it to work with tomorrow.

Until Federal Express delivers your new software, however, let me show you some of the basic principles of the computer. To make sure you've got the same thing on your screen I do, we'll start off by using the built-in programs that came with your Mac.

Your very first software

There are several menus across the top of the screen (remember these?). As you get to know the Mac, you'll discover that their wording changes from program to program. Right now, they say File, Edit, View, Label, and Special; in a word processor they might say File, Edit, Font, Size, and Format, and so on. The menu names (and the commands listed in those menus) are tailored to the function of the software.

There's one menu that's *always* on your screen, though: the Apple menu, which is the ⌘ at the left edge of the menu bar. Among other things, this menu provides immediate access to some useful miniprograms known as *desk accessories*. Desk accessories are sure-fire, nonthreatening, and fun — perfect for your first baby steps into the world of using software.

Desk Accessories

Let's start simple. Move your cursor up to the Apple menu and choose Calculator. The Calculator pops up in a tiny window of its own.

The Calculator

Using the mouse, you can click the little calculator buttons. The Mac will give you the correct mathematical answer, making you the owner of the world's heaviest and most expensive pocket calculator.

What's neat is that you can also type the keys on your *numeric keypad,* the block of number keys off to the right side of your keyboard. As you press these *real* keys, you can watch the *on-screen* keys in the Calculator window get punched accordingly.

Noncritical information about desk accessories

The Calculator, along with other miniprograms like the Note Pad, Alarm Clock, and so on (all in the Apple menu), is called a *desk accessory.* It's always available to you, no matter what Mac activity you're in.

In the olden days of System 6, the Apple menu *only* contained desk accessories. They were small, inexpensive, and cute. One of the new features in System 7, however, is that you can stick anything you want into that Apple menu: full-fledged software applications, a disk icon, a folder, a document you work on a lot, a sound, and so on. (Some people wind up with *very* long Apple menus.)

Want to know the secret of making your own Apple menu in System 7? Check it out: Point to your hard-drive icon in the upper-right corner of the screen, and double-click. Now double-click your System Folder icon. Inside that, you'll find a folder called Apple Menu Items. (Pretty cryptic, I know.) Go ahead and drag any icon into this folder: the Trash can, a letter, your word processing program, whatever; instantly it appears in the Apple menu for easy access.

Take a moment to reinforce your love of windows: By dragging the *title bar* (where it says "Calculator"), move the Calculator window into a new position. If you were good and tired of looking at it, you could also make the Calculator go away by clicking its close box (in the upper-left corner, like on all windows).

But don't close the Calculator just yet. Leave it open on the screen.

The Note Pad

Now go to the menu again, and this time choose Note Pad. Instantly, the world's most frill-free word processor appears on the screen.

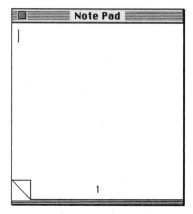

You'll learn more about word processing in the next section. For now, we're just going to do some informative goofing around. With the Note Pad open on your screen, type a math problem, like this:

    37+8+19*3-100

(In the computer world, the asterisk * means "times," or multiply.) If you make a mistake, press the big Delete key at the upper-right corner of your keyboard. This means "Backspace."

Now, by dragging the Note Pad's title bar, move it so that you can see the Calculator window too. You're going to use two programs at once, making them cooperate with each other — one of the most remarkable features of the Mac.

Selecting text

This is about to get interesting.

Using the mouse, carefully position the pointer at the left side of your equation (below, top). Press the button and drag to the right (middle). Release the mouse when you've highlighted the entire equation (bottom).

$]37+8+19*3-100$

$37+8+1]*3-100$

$37+8+19*3-100$ $]$

You've just *selected* some text. Remember in Chapter 1 when you *selected* an icon — and then used a menu command? Struggling, as always, to come up with a decent analogy, I likened this *select-then-operate* sequence to building a noun-verb sentence.

Well, it works just as well with text as it does with icons. You've now high-lighted, or selected, some text — so the Mac now knows what the noun is — what it's supposed to pay attention to. All you have to do is select a verb from one of the menus. And our verb du jour is *Copy*.

The cornerstone of human endeavor:
Copy and Paste

Choose Copy from the Edit menu.

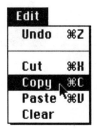

Menu refresher

"Choose Copy from the Edit menu." If that sentence stumps you, remember that you place the pointer on the *word* Edit at the top of the screen. Press the button to make the list of commands appear; don't let go. Move the pointer down the list until you reach the word Copy, which becomes highlighted. Release the mouse button. That's how you *choose* a command from a *menu*. And I won't say another word about it.

Thunder rolls, lightning flashes, the audience holds its breath . . . and absolutely nothing happens, as far as you can tell.

Behind the scenes, though, something awesomely useful occurred. The Mac looked at the selected equation and memorized it, socking it away into an invisible storage window called the *Clipboard*. The Clipboard is how you transfer stuff from one window into another, and from one program into another. (Some programs even have a Show Clipboard command, in which case I take back the statement about the Clipboard being invisible.)

Now then. You can't *see* the Clipboard at this point, but in a powerful act of faith, you put your trust in me and you believe that it contains the highlighted material (the equation).

The Application menu

Do you see the tiny Note Pad icon at the *right* end of your menu bar? It's next to that question mark thing.

Totally lost?

If you've gone bug-eyed from searching in vain for the menu I'm talking about, then you probably don't have System 7 installed in your Mac. (The Application menu, as well as the question mark icon, are both elements of System 7.)

This icon actually represents a menu — the Application menu. It lists all the programs you have running at once. And at this moment, you have *three* programs running at once: the Note Pad, the Calculator, and the famous Finder (or desktop).

You multitasking maniac, you.

Choose Calculator from the Application menu.

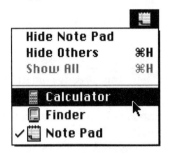

The Calculator window comes to the front, and the icon in the upper right changes to look like a Calculator.

Those of you still awake will, of course, object to using the Application menu to bring the Calculator forward. You remember all too plainly from Chapter 1 that simply *clicking* in a window brings it to the front, which would have required less muscular effort.

Right you are; watch for a bonus in your paycheck. However, learning to use the Application menu was a good exercise. There are going to be many times in your life where the program that's in front covers up the entire screen. So *then* how will you bring another program forward, big shot? That's right. You won't be able to *see* any other windows, so you won't be able to click one to make it active. You'll have to use the Application menu.

In any case, the Calculator is now the active application. (*Active* just means it's in front.) Now then: Remember that intricate equation that's still on the Mac Clipboard? Instead of having to type an equation into the Calculator by punching keys, let's just *paste* it in.

1. Press the Clear key on your Mac keyboard, or click the C button on the Calculator.

   You just cleared the display. We wouldn't want your previous diddlings to interfere with this tightly controlled experiment.

2. From the Edit menu, choose Paste. Watch the Calculator!

If you looked in time, you saw the number keys flashing like Las Vegas at midnight. And with a triumphant beep (sometimes), the Mac displays the answer to your math problem. (It should be 92.)

Did you get what just happened? You typed out a math problem in a word processor (the Note Pad), copied it to the Clipboard, and pasted it into a number-cruncher (the Calculator). Much of the miracle of the Mac stems from its capability to mix and match information among multiple programs in this way.

It's a two-way street, too. You can paste this number *back* into the word processor.

1. From the Edit menu, choose Copy.

   But wait! There was already something on the Clipboard. Where is the Mac to put this *new* copied info?

   On the Clipboard, of course. And whatever was there before (your equation) gets nuked. The Clipboard contains exactly one thing at a time — whatever you copied *most recently.*

2. From the Application menu, choose Note Pad (or just click the Note Pad window).

   The Note Pad is now the active application.

3. Type this:

   Dear son: You owe me $

   Stop after the $ sign. Move the mouse up to the Edit menu.

4. From the Edit menu, choose Paste.

Bingo! The Mac pastes in the result from the Calculator (which it had been keeping ready on the Clipboard).

Incidentally, whatever's on the Clipboard stays there until you copy something new or until you turn off the machine. It means you can paste it over and over again.

5. For a second time, choose Paste from the Edit menu.

Another 92 pops into the window.

Dear son: You owe me $9292

By now, you're probably cradling your wrist, which no doubt aches from all those trips to the menu. Although what you're about to learn is, technically speaking, a *power-user technique,* it will save you all kinds of time and chiropractor bills.

 You don't have to use the menu to issue a command like Copy or Paste. If you wish, you can use a keyboard shortcut to do the same thing. You may remember having used the ⌘ key in Chapter 3 to issue commands without using the mouse.

And how are you supposed to remember which letter key corresponds to which command? Well, usually it's mnemonic: ⌘+P for Print, ⌘+O for Open, and so on. But you can cheat; try it right now. Pull down the Edit menu, but don't let go of the mouse button.

There's your crib sheet, carefully listed down the right side of the menu. Note that the keyboard shortcuts for all four of these important commands (Undo, Cut, Copy, Paste) are adjacent on the keyboard: Z, X, C, V.

C is Copy. And V, right next to it, is Paste. Let go of the mouse button and let's try it.

1. While holding down the ⌘ key, type a V.

Bingo! Another copy of the Clipboard stuff (92) appears in your Note Pad. (In the future, I'll just refer to a keyboard shortcut like this as "⌘-V.")

2. Press ⌘-V again.

Yep, that kid's debt is really piling up. He now owes you $92,929,292.

But after all, it's your son. Why not just let him pay 10 percent down on the amount he owes you? In other words, why not *undo* that last 92 pasting?

3. From the Edit menu, choose Undo.

The most recent thing you did — in this case, pasting the fourth 92 — gets undone.

Rewriting history is addicting, ain't it?

Remember, though, that Undo only reverses your *most recent* action. Suppose you (1) copy something, (2) paste it somewhere else, and then (3) type some more. If you choose Undo, only the typing will be undone (step 3), *not* the pasting (step 2).

There are some other DAs, too. (No, not District Attorneys. Like everything in the Mac world, it's cooler to call something by its initials. DA = desk accessory.) Play around with (and look up in your Macintosh owner's guide) the Puzzle, the Alarm Clock, Key Caps, and all that stuff.

Control Panels

There's one item in your Apple menu that *isn't* a DA. It says Control Panels, and all it does is open up your Control Panels folder. And what exactly is your Control Panels folder? Well, it's a folder that lives inside your System Folder. It contains a bunch of icons, each of which controls some aspect of your Mac. Go ahead and choose it from the menu to make this window appear:

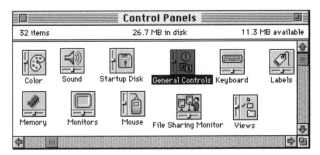

Everybody's got a slightly different set of Control Panels, so your screen may look different. In any case, I'll show you around one Control Panel, then you can take it from there.

1. Quickly type *GE* on your keyboard.

Remember this handy trick? You can select one icon in a folder just by typing the first couple of letters of its name. In this case, you get the General Controls window.

2. Double-click General Controls.

The General Controls window opens. It looks like . . . well, rather like a control panel. These controls govern the way your Mac works; you can customize your working environment, to a certain extent, or change the time, or whatever. (The Performa controls look slightly different.)

The Desktop Pattern is the shading that fills the background, behind the windows and stuff. You can change the design; see Chapter 8 for details.

When you type (as in the Note Pad), the Mac marks your place with a blinking *insertion point*. These buttons control how fast it blinks, in the event that the blinking rate has been triggering those inconvenient seizures.

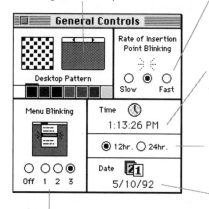

Click a number to change the time. Usually, when you buy a Mac, it is set to California time, so double-check this.

Click "24 hr." if you are a military-type person who wakes up at 0600 hours each morning.

Click a number to change the date.

When you choose a command from a menu (and release the mouse), the command blinks. This setting controls how many times. How did we *live* before we had this?

All right — close the General Controls window by clicking the close box in the upper-left corner; enough fooling around. Time to get some work done. (Fortunately, *working* on the Mac is almost as much fun as goofing off.)

Word Processing 101

If you have a word processing program, install it onto your hard disk now, if you haven't already done so. You'll find the instructions at the beginning of its manual.

Find the program's icon on your hard disk. It may be inside a folder, which you can open by double-clicking. In any case, once you find the word processing program icon, double-click it; you'll be presented, after a moment, with a blank white screen.

If you don't have a word processor yet, you can use your discount word processor, the Note Pad; choose its name from the Apple menu.

Top two rules of word processing

The first rules of typing on a computer are going to be tough to learn, especially if you've been typing for years. But they're super crucial. Here they be:

- ✔ **Don't press the Return key at the end of each line.** I'm dead serious here. When you type your way to the end of a line, the next word will *automatically* jump down to the next line. If you press Return in the middle of a sentence, you'll mess everything up.

- ✔ **Only put ONE space after a period.**

The point of no returns

Why aren't you supposed to hit Return at the end of each line?

First time in print! An actual example of the kind of mess you can get into by pressing Return after each line of text.

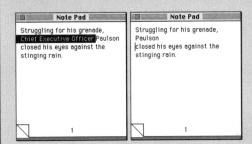

At left: the original passage. Suppose you decide to remove Paulson's title, "Chief Executive Officer," since everybody already knows what kind of

guy he is (left). But suppose you'd been foolish enough to press Return after each line of text; if you remove those three highlighted words, the word "Paulson" flops back to the left side of the line, but the rest of the sentence stays where it is, looking dumb (right). On the other hand, if you *hadn't* put Returns into your text, you'd get the figure below, where everything looks peachy.

See here?

There are two spaces after this sentence. It looks sort of wide.
There's only one space after this one. Looks pretty good.

If that statement gives you uncontrollable muscular facial spasms, I don't blame you. After all, I'm telling you to do something that you were explicitly taught *not* to do by your sharp-tongued high school typing teacher.

Nonetheless, don't put two spaces after a period. Typewriters print letters onto paper by slapping tiny metal blocks against a ribbon, and every block (every letter) is the same width. Including the space. But on a Mac, every letter has a different width; look how much wider this W is than this I, for example. On the Mac, a space is *already* extra-wide, thus saving you that precious calorie you would have exerted to press the spacebar a second time.

There are a few other rules, too, but breaking them isn't serious enough to get you fired. So let's dig in. Make sure you have a blank piece of electronic typing paper open in front of you — either a new, untitled word processing screen, or the Note Pad.

You should see a short, blinking, vertical line at the beginning of the typing area. They call this the *insertion point* because it shows you where the letters will appear when you start to type.

Type the passage below. If you make a typo, press the Delete key, just like Backspace on a typewriter. *Don't* press Return when you get to the edge of the window. Just keep typing, and the Mac will create a second line for you. Believe.

> *The screams of the lions burst Rod's earlobes as the motorboat, out of control, exploded through the froth.*

See how the words automatically wrapped around to the second line? They call this feature, with no small originality, *word wrap.*

But suppose, as your novel is going to press, you decide that this sleepy passage really needs some spicing up. You decide to insert the word *speeding* before the word *motorboat.*

Remember the blinking cursor — the insertion point? It's on the screen even now, blinking calmly away at the end of the sentence. If you want to insert text, you have to move the insertion point.

There are two ways to move the insertion point. First, try pressing the arrow keys on your keyboard. You can see that the up and down arrow keys move the insertion point from line to line, and the right and left arrow keys move the insertion point across the line. Practice moving the insertion point by pressing the arrow keys.

If the passage you want to edit is far away, though (on another page, for example), using the arrow keys to move the cursor is inefficient. Your fingers would be bloody stumps by the time you finished. Instead, use the mouse, like this:

1. Using the mouse, move the cursor (which, when it's near text, looks like this ⟨) just before the word *motorboat.* Click the mouse.

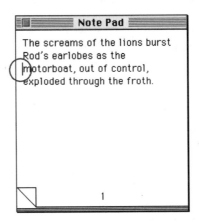

This is as confusing as word processing ever gets — there are *two* little cursors, right? There's the blinking insertion point, and this one ⟨, which is called an *I-beam* cursor. In fact, they're quite different. The blinking insertion point is only a *marker,* not a pointer. It always shows you where the next typing will appear. The I-beam, on the other hand, is how you *move* the insertion point to a different location; when you click with the I-beam, you set down the insertion point.

2. Type the word *speeding.*

The insertion point does its deed, and the Mac makes room on the line for the new word. A word or two probably got pushed onto the next line. Isn't word wrap wonderful?

So much for *inserting* text: You click the mouse (to show the Mac *where*) and then type away. But what if you need to delete a bunch of text? What if you decide to edit out the first half of our sample text?

Well, unless you typed the challenging excerpt above with no errors, you already know one way to erase text — by pressing the Delete key (which is called Backspace on some keyboards). Delete (or Backspace) takes out one letter at a time, just to the left of the insertion point.

That's not much help in this situation, though. Suppose you decide to take out the *first* part of the sentence. It wouldn't be horribly efficient to backspace over the entire passage, just so you could work on the beginning.

No, instead you need a way to edit any part of your work, at any time, without disturbing the stuff you want to leave. Once again, the Macintosh method, noun-then-verb, saves the day. Try this:

1. Using the mouse, position the I-beam cursor at the beginning of the sentence.

   This takes a steady hand; stay calm.

2. Click *just* to the left of the first word and keep the mouse button pressed down. Drag the I-beam cursor to the end of the word *as*.

   As you drag, the text gets highlighted, or *selected.* You've done this once before, in your copy-and-paste lesson.

```
                                                        I
The screams of the lions burst Rod's earlobes as the
speeding motorboat, out of control, exploded through
the froth.
```

If you're especially clever and forward-thinking, you'll have selected the blank space *after* the word *as,* as well. Take a look at the illustration above.

All right; in typical Mac syntax, you've just specified *what* you want to edit, by selecting it (and making it turn black to show it's selected). Now for the verb:

1. Press the Delete key.

   Bam! The selected text is gone. The sentence looks pretty odd, though, since it doesn't begin with a capital letter.

2. Using the mouse, position the cursor just before (or after) the letter *t* that begins the sentence. Drag it sideways across the letter so that it's highlighted.

```
    I
the speeding motorboat, out of control, exploded
through the froth.
```

Here comes another ground rule of word processing. See how you've just *selected,* or highlighted, the letter *t?* The idea here is to capitalize it. Of course, using the methods for wiping out (and inserting) text that you learned earlier, you could simply remove the *t* and type a T. But since you've selected the *t* by dragging through it, replacing it is much easier:

> 3. Type a capital T.

The selected text gets replaced by the new stuff you type. That, in fact, is the third ground rule: *Selected text gets replaced by the new stuff you type.* As your Macintosh life proceeds, keep that handy fact in mind; it can save you a lot of backspacing. In fact, you can select 40 pages of text so that it's all highlighted and then type one single letter to replace all of it. Or you could select only one letter but replace it with 40 pages of typing.

Take a moment now for some unsupervised free play. Try clicking anywhere in the text (to plant the insertion point). Try dragging through some text: If you drag perfectly horizontally, you select text just on one line (below left). If you drag diagonally, you get everything between your cursor and the original click (below right).

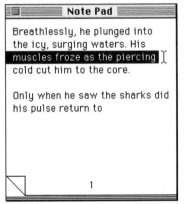 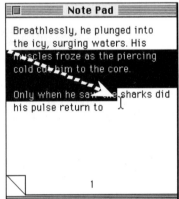

You de-select (or, equally poetically, un-highlight) text by clicking the mouse. Anywhere at all.

 Try pointing to a word and then double-clicking the mouse: You've easily selected exactly that word and without having to do any dragging.

As you experiment, do anything you want with any combination of drags, clicks, double-clicks, and menu selections. It's nice to know — and you might want to prepare a fine mahogany wall plaque along these lines — that *nothing you do*

with the mouse or keyboard can physically harm the computer. Oh, sure, it's possible to erase a disk or wreck one of your documents or something, but none of that requires a visit to a repair shop. You can't *break* the computer by playing around.

Form and format

For the rest of this lesson, you're going to need a real word processor. Sorry, kids, the Note Pad will only get you so far in life.

One of the most important differences between a typewriter and its replacement — the personal computer — is the sequence of events. When you use a typewriter, you set up all the formatting characteristics *before* you type: the margins, the tab stops, and (for typewriters with interchangeable type heads) the type style.

But the whole point of a word processor is that you can change anything at *any* time. Many people type the text of an entire letter or proposal or memo into the Mac and *then* format it. When you use a typewriter, you might discover, after typing the entire first page, that it's *slightly* too long to fit, and your signature will have to sit awkwardly on a page by itself. With a Mac, you'd see the problem, and nudge the text a little bit higher on the page to compensate.

Word processing has other great advantages: no crossouts; easy corrections that involve no white-out and no retyping; a permanent record of your correspondence that's electronic, not paper, and so it's always easy to find; a selection of striking typefaces — at any size; paste-in graphics, and so on. I think it's safe to say that once you try it, you'll never look back.

The return of Return

With all the subtlety of a Mack truck, I've taught you that you're forbidden to use the Return key *at the end of a line.* Still, that rectangular Return key on your keyboard *is* important. You press Return at the end of a *paragraph,* and only there.

To the computer, the Return key works just like a letter key — it inserts a *return character* into the text. It's just like rolling the paper in a typewriter forward by one notch. Hit Return twice, and you leave a blank line.

The point of Return, then, is to move text higher or lower on the page. Check this example, for instance.

¶ ¶ ¶ ¶ Dearest·Todd,·¶ ¶ I·have·never·loved·so·much·as·I·did·last· night.·Imagine·my·joy·as·I·watched·you· plunch·your·shining·scimitar·into·the· greasy·flesh·of·that—that—hideous·thing· from·the·deep.·¶ ¶ Unfortunately,·the·IRS·has·determined· that·you·failed·to·file·returns·for·the·years· 1982–1986.·They·have·asked·that·I·notify· you·of·¶

¶
Dearest·Todd,·¶
¶
I·have·never·loved·so·much·as·I·did·last·
night.·Imagine·my·joy·as·I·watched·you·
plunch·your·shining·scimitar·into·the·
greasy·flesh·of·that—that—hideous·thing·
from·the·deep.·¶
¶
Unfortunately,·the·IRS·has·determined·
that·you·failed·to·file·returns·for·the·years·
1982–1986.·They·have·asked·that·I·notify·
you·of·¶

Return characters move text down on the page. So, if you want to move text *up* on the page, drag through the blank space so that it's highlighted (above left); of course, what you've really done is to select the usually invisible Return characters. If you delete them, the text slides up the page (right).

Seeing the unseen

I said that Returns are *usually* invisible. However, every time you press the Return key, the Mac actually does plop down a symbol onto your screen. Same thing with the spacebar. Same with the Tab key.

You'll have to check your own word processor's manual to find out the exact command, but virtually every word processor lets you see these markings. The command may be called Show Invisibles; in Word, the command is called Show ¶. In any case, the result looks something like this:

> "Alison—my god, not that! Anything but that!"¶
>
> But it was too late. She had already disappeared.¶

Combine this knowledge with your advanced degree in Inserting Text (remember? you click to place the blinking insertion point and then type away), and you can see how you'd make more space between paragraphs or push all the text of a letter down on the page.

Appealing characters

Another big-time difference between word processing and typing is all the great *character formatting* you can do. You can make any piece of text **bold**, *italic*, underlined, all of the above, and more. You also get a selection of great-looking typefaces — only a few of which look like a typewriter.

Here's the scheme for changing some text to one of those character formats: noun-verb. Sound familiar? Go for it:

1. Select some text by dragging through it.

   Remember, you can select a single word by double-clicking it; to select a bunch of text, drag the cursor through it so that it turns black. You've just identified *what* you want to change.

   Each word processor keeps its Bold, Italic, and Underline commands in its own specially named menu, but they're definitely there. Drag your cursor through each menu name, reading the commands on each menu as it drops down, until you see the character formats like bold and italic.

2. From the Font menu (or Format menu, or wherever they are in your program), choose Bold.

Or Shadow or Outline or whatever. You've just specified *how* you want to affect the selected text.

You can apply several of these formats to the same text, too, although you won't win any awards for typographical excellence. Try changing the typeface, also; the various fonts are called things like Chicago, Geneva, Times, and so on. Changing fonts works the same way: Select text and then choose the font. And sizes — same deal: Select some text and then choose a type size from your word processor's menu. (Again, the name of the menu may vary. But for specifics on Microsoft Word, see Chapter 6.) The font sizes are measured in points, of which there are 72 per inch. Works out nicely, too — a Mac monitor has 72 *screen* dots per inch, meaning that 12-point type on the screen really is 12-point.

Before you know it, you can whip your document into mighty handsome shape.

Formatting paragraphs

Where type styles and sizes can be applied to any amount of text, even a single letter, *paragraph formatting* affects a whole paragraph at once. Usually these styles are easy to apply. To select a paragraph, you don't have to highlight all the text in it. Instead, you can just *click* anywhere within a paragraph to plant the insertion point. Then, as before, choose the menu command that you want to apply to that entire paragraph.

Guide to power typing

Because you *can* format text after you've typed it doesn't mean you *have* to. Most power users get used to the keyboard shortcuts for the common style changes, like bold and italic. They're pretty easy to remember: In every word processing program I know of, you get bold by pressing ⌘-B, and italic with ⌘-I.

What's handy is that you can hit this key combo just *before* you type the word. For example, without ever taking your hands off the keyboard, you could type the following:

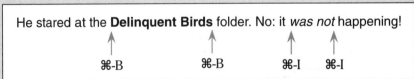

In other words, you hit ⌘-B once to turn bold *on* for the next burst of typing, and ⌘-B again to turn it off — all without ever having to use a menu.

This figure shows some of the different options every word processor provides for paragraph formatting — left-justified, right-justified, fully justified, centered, and double-spaced.

Her heart pounding, she looked toward the door. It swung open with a creak. The stench hit her first—an acrid, rotting swamp smell. She covered her mouth with the blood-soaked handkerchief and stepped backward, her naked back pressed hard against the fourposter.

Her heart pounding, she looked toward the door. It swung open with a creak. The stench hit her first—an acrid, rotting swamp smell. She covered her mouth with the blood-soaked handkerchief and stepped backward, her naked back pressed hard against the fourposter.

Her heart pounding, she looked toward the door. It swung open with a creak. The stench hit her first—an acrid, rotting swamp smell. She covered her mouth with the blood-soaked handkerchief and stepped backward, her naked back pressed hard against the fourposter.

Her heart pounding, she looked toward the door. It swung open with a creak. The stench hit her first—an acrid, rotting swamp smell. She covered her mouth with the blood-soaked handkerchief and stepped backward, her naked back pressed hard against the fourposter.

Her heart pounding, she looked toward the door. It swung open with a creak. The stench hit her first—an acrid, rotting swamp smell. She covered her mouth with the blood-soaked handkerchief and stepped backward, her naked back pressed hard against the fourposter.

There are other ways you can control paragraphs, too. Remember in high school when you were supposed to turn in a 20-page paper, and you'd try to pad your much-too-short assignment by making it two-and-a-half spaced? Well, if you'd had a Mac, you could have been much more sneaky about it. You can make your word processed document single-spaced, double-spaced, quadruple-spaced, or any itty bitty fraction thereof. You can even control how tightly together the letters are placed, making it easy to stretch or compress your writing into more or fewer pages.

Take this opportunity to toy with your word processor. Go ahead, really muck things up. Make it look like a ransom note with a million different type styles and sizes. Then, when you've got a real masterpiece on the screen, read on.

Someone Save Me!
(Working with Documents)

It might terrify you — and it should — to find out that you've been working on an imaginary document. It's only being preserved by a thin current of streaming electrical current. It doesn't exist yet, to be perfectly accurate, except in your Mac's *memory*.

You may recall from the notes you took on Chapter 2 that *memory is fleeting*. (Specifically, I mean computer memory, but if you find a more universal truth in my words, interpret away.) In fact, the memory is wiped away when you turn the Mac off — or when your coworker's trip over the power cord turns it off for you. At that moment, anything that exists on the screen is gone forever.

Therefore, almost every program has a Save command. It's always in the File menu, and its keyboard shortcut is always ⌘-S.

When you save your work, the Mac transfers it from transient, fleeting, electronic memory onto the good, solid, permanent disk. There your work will remain, safely saved. It will still be there tomorrow. It will still be there next week. It will still be there ten years from now, when your computer is so obsolete it's valuable again.

Therefore, let's try an experiment with your ransom note document on the screen.

From the File menu, choose Save.

Uh-oh. Something weird just happened: The Mac presented you with a box full of options. It's called a *dialog box,* because the computer needs to have a little chat with you before proceeding. (If you have a Performa, it says "Documents" at the top of this window.)

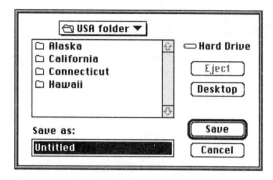

What the Mac mainly wants to know is: "Under what name would you like me to file this precious document, Masssssster?"

And how do you know this? Because in the blank where it says "Save as," there's a proposed title that's *highlighted* (selected already). And what do you know about highlighted text? *Anything you start typing will instantly replace it.*

The Mac, in its cute, limited dialog-y way, is trying to tell you that it needs you to type a title. Go ahead, do it: Type *Ransom Note.*

At this point, you could just click the Save button. The Mac would take every-thing in perilous, fleeting memory and transfer it to the staid, safe hard disk, where it would remain until you're ready to work on it some more.

However, there's a bunch of other stuff in this dialog box. Especially since this is the numero uno source of confusion to beginners, I think a tour of the Save File box is in order.

OK, OK, not all programs

The occasional program—Word, for example— doesn't propose a title (like "Untitled 1") in the text box of the Save as dialog box. Instead, you just see the little blinking insertion point in the empty blank. The message is the same, though: "Type your title *here.*"

Navigating the Save File (and Open File) box

You've already learned about the way your computer organizes files: with folders and with folders in folders. Remember this little exercise?

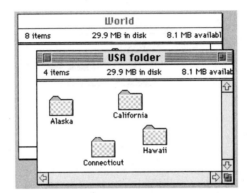

Well, the point of all the complicated-looking stuff in the Save File box is a miniature version of that same folder-filing system. Suppose you see this when you're trying to save your file:

Look at the open-folder "menu" above the list. It tells you that you're viewing the contents of the USA folder. (If you have a Performa, you always see the Documents folder at this point.) In other words, if you click the Save button, you'll file your new Ransom Note document in the USA folder, mixed in among the state folders.

But suppose you want to file the Ransom Note document *in* one of the state folders. You already know how you open a folder — by double-clicking it — so you'd point to Alaska, for example, and double-click.

Now the open folder "menu" above the list says Alaska, and you can see the stuff inside the Alaska folder. Most of their names are dimmed because they're all *documents;* the only things whose names are black in this dialog box are folders. (The Mac wants to know where you want to put your new document. Since you can't very well store one document inside *another* document, the document names are grayed out and unavailable, and only the folder names are black and available.)

OK. So now you're viewing the contents of the Alaska folder. What if you change your mind? What if you decide that the Ransom Note should really go in the World folder — the one that *contains* the USA folder?

You must retrace your steps. That's what the little open folder menu is all about (the open folder icon is in front of the word *Alaska*). They call this doohickey a *pop-up menu* because it's a menu but it's not at the top of the screen. The small black triangle beside the name Alaska tells you: "Click me!"

Sure enough, when you click the word Alaska (above left), you see the list of all the nested folders you had to travel through to get here (above right). This is where things get a little weird: The list is *upside-down* from the path you took!

In other words, if you were in the Finder instead of in this Save File dialog box, you started at the Desktop level (gray background). You'd have double-clicked the hard-disk icon to open its window. Then you'd have double-clicked the World folder to open that, and the USA folder inside of that, and finally the Alaska folder. If you look at the menu picture above, you'll see that, sure enough, your entire folder path is listed. You can view the entire hierarchy of folders — as long as you get used to the fact that the list is upside-down, and the outer levels (the hard disk and the Desktop) are listed at the bottom.

Therefore, if you wanted to file the Ransom Note in the World folder (below right), you'd simply slide down the pop-up menu list and choose World (below left).

Then, at long last, when you're viewing the contents of the folder you want to save the file in, you can click the Save button.

For the purposes of following along with this exercise, double-click a folder — any folder — to store your file in. And then click Save.

Your file gets snugly tucked away into the folder whose contents you're viewing.

Want proof, O Cynic? All you have to do is choose Finder from the Application menu. Remember, the Application menu is the icon at the upper-right side of the screen. (If you're not using System 7, never mind.) It lists all the programs that are running at once.

When you choose Finder, our friends the folders, windows, and Trash can pop up. If you wanted to make sure your file really exists, and it really got put where you wanted it, you could now double-click your way through folders until you found it. In our example, your Ransom Note would be in the World folder:

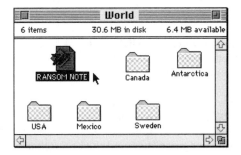

Why are we kicking this absolutely deceased horse? Because the same folder-navigation scheme (where you see an upside-down list of nested folders) is used for *retrieving* files you've already created. You need to know how to climb up and down your folder tree, as you'll see in a moment, to find your files again.

Closing a file, with a sigh

You've created a ransom note. It's got all kinds of text and formatting. You've saved it onto the disk so that it'll be there tomorrow. In a moment, you'll get a chance to prove it to yourself.

Click the close box in the upper-left corner of the window.

In the Mac's universal language of love, clicking the small white square up there means close the window, as you'll recall. If all went well, the window disappears.

The worrywart's balm

From the way I've described the terrifyingly delicate condition of a document that's on the screen (that you haven't Saved to disk yet) — that is, precariously close to oblivion, kept alive only by electric current — you might think that closing a window is a dangerous act. After all, what if you forgot to Save some work? Wouldn't closing the window mean losing that critical memo?

Not really — if you try to close a document, the Mac won't *let* you proceed until it asks you if you're *sure* you want to lose all the work you've done. It will say something like:

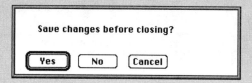

Click Yes if you do want to save your work. Click No if you were only goofing around or showing off your Mac to somebody and don't want to preserve your labors. Click Cancel if you change your mind completely about closing the document and want to keep working on it.

How to find out what the heck you're doing

This gets sort of metaphysical, so hold onto your brain.

Just because you closed your *document* doesn't mean you've left the *program*. In fact, if you pull down the Application menu at the right side of the screen, you'll see that the word processing program is, in fact, still running. (It's the one with a check mark beside it; your word processing program may be different.)

You could bring the Finder to the front by choosing its name from the Application menu — without exiting the word processor. They both can be running at the same time, but only one can be in front.

In fact, that's the amazing thing about the Mac (using System 7). You can have a bunch of programs all running at once. The more memory your Mac has, the more programs you can run simultaneously.

In this instance, I realize that it's hard for you to believe that you're using a word processor, when there are no words on the screen. But you have three clues as to what program you're using:

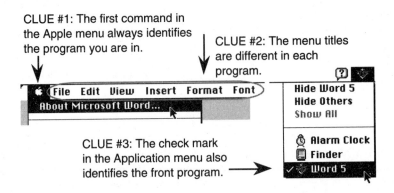

For the moment, I want you to stay in your word processing program.

Those crazy relationships: parents and children

OK. You've typed a ransom note. Using the Save command, you turned that typing on your screen into an icon on your hard disk. Now it's time for a concept break.

There are two kinds of files on your hard disk right now: *programs* (sometimes called *applications*) and *documents*. A program never changes; it's like a Cuisinart on your kitchen counter, sitting there day after day. Documents are what you *create* with a program — they're the cole slaw, crushed nuts, and guacamole dip that come out of the Cuisinart. You pay money to buy a program. Once you own it, you can create as many documents as you want, for free.

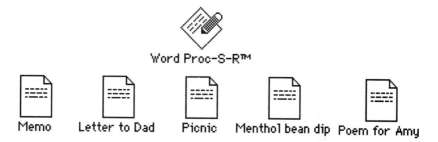

For example, you could use the Word Proc-S-R program (above top) to create all the different word processing documents below it and thousands more like them. If you love analogies as much as I do, you can think of the application as the mommy and the documents as the kiddies.

Here's what their family relationships are like:

1. Double-click the *program* icon when you want to open a brand new, untitled, clean-slate document.

2. Double-click a *document* icon to open that document. Unbeknownst to you, double-clicking a document simultaneously opens the program you used to create the document.

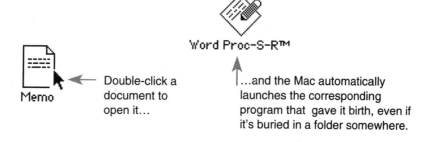

Double-click a document to open it...

...and the Mac automatically launches the corresponding program that gave it birth, even if it's buried in a folder somewhere.

Orphaned documents

The Mac's ability to launch the mommy program when you double-click a document may occasionally seem not to work. That is, you may double-click a perfectly innocent-looking icon but get a message like this:

 The document "Angela's Recipe" could not be opened, because the application program that created it could not be found.

OK

In its adorably inarticulate way, your computer is trying to tell you that it can't *find* the mommy program. You may have taken the application off your hard disk. You may have received the document from a friend, and you don't even own the program that created it. (If your friend gives you a music document, but all you own is a word processor, you're out of luck.) Then, too, some icons — mainly stuff in the System Folder — aren't *meant* to be opened. They're just helper files for programs or System features, and you're not supposed to mess with them.

This weirdness is described in greater detail in Chapter 9.

This may seem unimpressive to you. But in the dark days of DOS and other scary non-Macintosh computers, there was no such automatic program-launching. You'd have to know what program you used to create the document, launch it first, and *then* retrieve a document. And even then, you'd have to remember what you named it, exactly, and type that name precisely on the screen.

Fetch: How to retrieve a document

Let's return to our increasingly fruitful exercise with the Ransom Note, shall we?

Let's pretend it's tomorrow. Yawn, stretch, fluff your mustache, or take out your curlers. You find out that the person you've kidnapped actually comes from a wealthy Rhode Island family, and so you can demand much more ransom money. Yet because you created your ransom note on the Mac, you don't have to retype anything; you can just change the amount you're demanding and print it out again.

But if you've been following the steps in this chapter, then there's *no* document on the screen. You're still *in* your word processing program, though (or should be; look for the check mark in the Application menu). So how do you get your Ransom Note file back?

Like this:

1. Choose Open from the File menu.

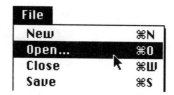

A dialog box appears.

You probably remember dialog boxes — in fact, you probably remember this one. It looks just like the Save dialog box, where you were asked to give your document a title. This one, navigationally speaking, works exactly the same way.

Double-click a folder to see what's in it.

Use this pop-up menu to see what folder *this* folder is inside of.

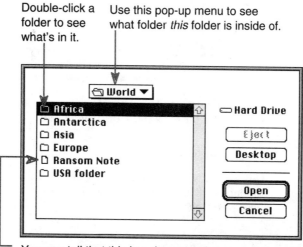

You can tell that this is a document because its icon isn't a folder. You can open it by double-clicking its name.

Unfortunately for my efforts to make this as instructional as possible, if you've been following these steps, your Ransom Note is staring you in the face right now. It's in whatever folder you saved it into. The Mac is nice that way — it remembers the most recent folder you stashed something in and shows you that location the next time you try to save or open something. (Unless you have a Performa, which shows you the Documents folder no matter what.)

If you want to emerge from this experience a better person, pretend you
can't find your Ransom Note. Pull down the pop-up menu and jump to
your hard-disk level:

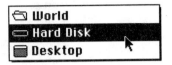

Now the display changes to show you the contents of your hard disk:

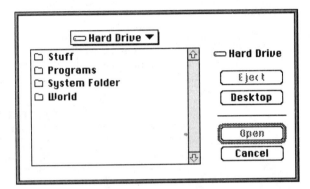

And from here, you know how to get back into the World folder, don't you?
Right — double-click the World folder, and you're right back where you
started.

2. Double-click the Ransom Note.

This is what you've been working up to all this time. The Ransom Note
appears on your screen in its entirety. Now, at last, you can edit it to your
heart's content.

Save Me Again!

To continue this experiment, make some changes to your document. Once
again, you have to worry about the fact that your precious work only exists in a
fragile world of bouncing electrons. Once again, turning the Mac off right now
means you'll lose the *new* work you've done. (The *original* Ransom Note,
without changes, is still safe on your disk.)

Therefore, you have to use that trusty Save command each time you make
changes that are worth keeping. (For you desk potatoes out there, remember

that ⌘-S is the keyboard shortcut, which saves you an exhausting trip to the menu.) The Save dialog box will *not* appear on the screen each time you use the Save command (like it did the first time). Only the very first time you save a document does the Mac ask for a title (and a folder location).

As mentioned in Chapter 2, you've probably heard horror stories about people who've lost hours of work when some glitch made their computers crash. Well, usually it's their own darned fault for ignoring the two most important rules of computing:

> **Rule 1. Save your work often.**
>
> **Rule 2. Never forget Rule 1.**

"Often" may mean every five minutes. It may mean after every paragraph. The point is to do it *a lot*. Get to know that ⌘-S shortcut, and type it reflexively after every tiny burst of inspiration.

Ever notice how you can control the weather? If you haul around an umbrella all day, it won't rain. If you forget the umbrella, it's Noah's flood.

It's precisely the same with computers. If you save your work often, you'll wonder why you bother because nothing will ever go wrong. The day — no, the *minute* you forget to save something you've typed, you'll get something called a system crash and lose your entire document into the electronic ether.

Learning to be a quitter

Now you know how to start a new document, edit it, save it onto the disk, reopen it later, and save your additional changes.

You know how to launch (open, or run) a program — by double-clicking its icon or by choosing its name from the Apple menu. You've discovered the fact that you can have more than one program open at once, which can be handy when you need to copy numbers from the Note Pad and paste them into the Calculator (for example).

But now you have to learn to get *out* of a program when you're finished for the day. It's not terribly difficult: Choose Quit from the File menu.

If the word processor was the only program you were running, then you return to the Finder. If you were running some other programs, then you just drop down into the next program. It's as though the programs are stacked on top of each other; take away the top one, and you drop into the next one down.

The other most important rule of computing

Duty compels me to keep this chapter going just long enough to preach one other famous word of advice to you: *Back up.*

To *back up,* or to *make a backup,* means to make a copy of your work.

When you're in the Finder, the documents you've worked on appear as icons on the hard disk. Your hard disk is like a giant-sized floppy disk. Like any mortal, these disks occasionally get sick and don't show up for work. On days like those, you'll wish you had made a *copy* of the stuff on the hard disk, so your life won't grind to a halt while the hard disk is being repaired.

Remember the cruel gods that make the computer crash when you don't save your work frequently? Those same deities have equal powers over your hard disk, and an equal taste for irony. That is, if you don't back up, your hard disk will *certainly* die. On the other hand, if you back up your work at the end of every day or every week, nothing will ever go wrong with your hard disk, and you'll mumble to yourself that you're wasting your time.

Life's just like that.

The idiot-proof guide to backing up

Put a blank floppy disk in the disk drive. (If it's a brand new disk, you'll be asked to *initialize* it [prepare it for use by a Mac]; do it.)

Now select the icons of the documents you want to back up. Drag them, together or one by one, onto the floppy disk icon. If the floppy fills up, insert another one and continue. Label the floppy disks *Backup* (and note the date). Keep them away from magnets and telephones.

If you're a business person, you might even want to invest in a backup *program,* which essentially does the above automatically. DiskFit, Redux, and Retrospect are some popular backup programs. If you have a Performa, you already own a backup program, you lucky dog, called Apple Backup.

Top Ten Word Processing Tips

1. Select a word by double-clicking — and then, if you keep the mouse down on the second click and drag sideways, you select more text in complete one-word increments.

2. Never, never, never line up text using the spacebar. It may have worked in the typewriter days, but not anymore. For example, you may get things lined up like this on the screen:

1963	**1992**	**2001**
Born	Elected President	Graduated college

   Yet, sure as the rain, you'll get this when you print:

1963	**1992**	**2001**
Born	Elected President	Graduated college

   So instead of using spaces to line up columns, use *tab stops* instead. Learn how your word processor does tabs, and use 'em!

3. You can select all the text in your document at once by using the Select All command (to change the font for the whole thing, for example). Its keyboard equivalent is almost always ⌘-A.

4. Aesthetics Rule of Thumb: Don't use more than two fonts within a document. (Bold, italic, and normal versions of a font only count as one.) Talk about ransom notes!

5. Don't use underlining for emphasis. You're a typesetter now, babe. You've got *italics!* Underlining is a cop-out for typewriter people.

6. The white box in the scroll bar at the right side of the window tells you, at a glance, where you are in your document:

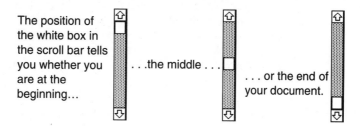

The position of the white box in the scroll bar tells you whether you are at the beginning... . . .the middle . . . . . . or the end of your document.

By dragging that white box, you can jump anywhere in the document.

There are two other ways to move around:

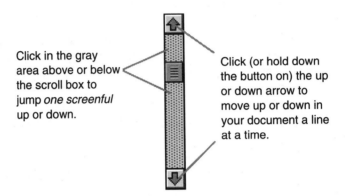

Click in the gray area above or below the scroll box to jump *one screenful* up or down.

Click (or hold down the button on) the up or down arrow to move up or down in your document a line at a time.

7. You've already learned how to *copy* some text to the Clipboard, ready to paste into another place. Another useful technique is to *cut* text to the Clipboard. Cut works just like Copy, except it snips the selected text out of the original document. (Cut-and-paste is how you *move* text from one place to another.)

8. It's considered uncouth to use "straight quotes" and 'straight apostrophes.' They hearken back to the days of yore (the days of your typewriter, that is). Instead, use "curly double quotes" and 'curly single quotes' like these. (See the difference?)

   You can produce curly double quotes by pressing Option-[(left bracket) and Shift-Option-[(right bracket) for the left and right ones, respectively. The single quotes (or apostrophes) are Option-] and Shift-Option-], for the left and right single quotes, respectively. Of course, any word processor I've ever heard of (like Word) has an automatic curly quote feature, which is a much better solution.

9. If there's an element you want to appear at the top of every page, like the page number or the date or *The Mister Rogers Story, Part VII: The Early Years,* don't try to type it onto each page. Not only is that a waste of effort, but the minute you add or delete text from somewhere else, this top-of-the-page information will become middle-of-the-page information.

   Instead, use your word processor's *running header* feature — it's a little window, into which you can type whatever you want. The program automatically displays this info at the top of each page, no matter how much text you add or take away. (There's also such a thing as a *running footer,* which appears at the *bottom* of the page, as well as a *running politician,* which you want to avoid at all costs.)

10. Be painfully aware that what you see on the screen isn't always what prints out. The number one source of rude surprises happens when you write with a Mac connected to *one* printer (like a StyleWriter) but print on a different one (like a laser printer). Since the typefaces are handled differently for these different printers, you'll discover that sentences, lines, and pages end in different places in the printout than they did on the screen.

The solution is simple. Before you print, trick the Mac into thinking it's got that laser printer already attached, so you can see what it's about to do to you. From the Apple menu, select Chooser. (You'll read more about this fascinating relic from the Stone Age in Chapter 5.) You should see the name of several printers there, like StyleWriter or LaserWriter (which is used for *all* brands of laser printer). Click the one you *plan* to print on, even if it's not currently connected.

If you don't see more than one printer icon in the Chooser, you have to reinstall it from your System or printer disks. (In the System 7 disk set, these little icons are on the disk called Printing.)

● ●

Summary

▶ What the Mac can accomplish depends on what software programs you buy.

▶ The Mac has a few built-in programs, called desk accessories (DAs), like the Note Pad and the Calculator. You can copy and paste information between them. You switch from one program to another using the Application menu at the upper-right corner of the screen.

▶ Word processing isn't quite like using a typewriter. For one thing, there's less need for white-out. For another, you don't press Return at the end of the line.

▶ You can change the format of type (like bold or italic) or of paragraphs (like single-spaced or double-spaced or centered) either before or *after* doing the typing.

▶ You can save a document into any folder you want. It'll still be there when you try to open it again.

▶ When you're done for the day, quit your programs using the Quit command — and make a backup copy of your work. Unless you thrive on tragedy, of course.

● ●

The Performa Page

Your Mac is a Performa if: (a) it says Performa on the front; (b) you bought it from an office or appliance store, not a computer store (see page 290); (c) when you say your Mac's name, you sound like a British guy trying to say "performer."

340 pages of this book apply equally well to Performas and non-Performas. This page, however, covers a few items exclusive to this, the Family Mac.

The Launcher

What the Launcher *is:* a control panel, just like the ones described on page 60. What it *does* is display a winderful wondow — I mean a wonderful window — containing jumbo icons for your programs.

As you know, you normally *double-click* an icon to launch a program. But anything in this window opens when clicked *once.* (This is progress, folks.)

You can move, resize, or close the Launcher window just as you would any window (page 22). Once closed, it will reappear if you double-click the little Launcher icon on the desktop.

So who decides what icons appear in the Launcher? You do. Inside your System Folder is a folder called Launcher Items. Any file or folder icon (or, more typically, any *alias* of an icon — see page 203) you put in Launcher Items shows up in the Launcher window.

And who decides whether or not the Launcher window appears when you first turn on the Mac? You again. Open the System Folder; open the Startup Items folder; and drag the Launcher alias outta there. From now on, the Launcher window won't appear until you double-click the Launcher icon on your desktop.

The Documents folder

See the Documents folder in the following figure? As you work with your Mac and create different documents, the Performa housekeeps for you by storing them all in this folder. Every time you use a program's Open or Save command, you're automatically shown the Documents folder's contents.

If this document magnet bothers you, just rename the Documents folder. Then you'll have to file your documents in your own folders, just like everybody else.

Turning It All Off

The Launcher is responsible for more Performa characteristics than just the Launcher window. It also creates the Documents folder. It's even responsible for *hiding* one program when you launch another (unlike other Macs, where all windows remain simultaneously on the screen).

To kill off these behaviors, thus de-Performatizing your Mac, choose Control Panels from your Apple menu. Drag the Launcher control panel clear out of the System Folder, and restart the Mac. From now on: no Documents folder, no program hiding. You *can* still use the Launcher window; double-click that Launcher control panel, wherever it is now (not in the System Folder), and the Launcher window will appear like always.

Apple Backup

Apple saved itself a precious $7 by failing to give you System disks with your Performa. Instead, the System comes preinstalled on your hard drive, and you're supposed to back it up onto your *own* floppy disks using the Apple Backup program.

Two extremely important points: (1) Do it! Back up your System Folder the day you get the Mac. (2) If your System Folder gets trashed before you've made a backup, call the toll-free Apple help line number that came with your Performa. Give the bad news. Apple will Fed Ex you a free set of System disks. (Methinks they should just include these disks to begin with.)

Chapter 5
A Quiet Talk About Printers, Printing, and Fonts

In This Chapter

▶ What the different kinds of printers are and how much they cost

▶ What the different kinds of typefaces are and why they can be annoying

▶ More than you ever wanted to know about PostScript and TrueType (and other words with no spaces in the middle)

▶ How to print

I hope you're seated for this chapter. In fact, I hope you're leaning way back with your feet up and a daiquiri in your hand.

Because there's no greater source of confusion and irritation for the beginning Mac user than understanding printers and fonts, and how to get the best of the latter from the former. After dropping $1,500 on a laser printer, some people still get jaggedy, irregular type in their printouts. Others aren't able to print at all — they get error messages. And still others have been printing their correspondence for years, in happy ignorance, using that ugly Chicago font — the heavy black type style that's used in the Mac menus.

It's time to make some sense of it. If possible.

Credit Card Workout #3: A Printer Primer

Printers come in all kinds of configurations and prices. You can spend next to nothing and get a dot-matrix printer whose printouts are so jagged that they look like Dante's *Inferno* written in Braille. Or you can spend a thousand clams or so and get a printer whose printouts look like they were typeset.

Dot matrix: *A printer named for the way it produces type on the paper — as a pattern of dots. (Matrix is computerese for pattern.) As the little printing head glides back and forth across the page, tiny metal pins shoot out against the ribbon, pressing it against the paper at specific moments. All of this happens really fast, and with very precise pin choreography. But dot-matrix printouts look like dot matrices — you can actually see the little dots that constitute each character.*

Low-cost, low-quality

I'm talking about the Apple ImageWriter II. It's called a *dot-matrix* printer because it prints by firing little pins against a ribbon that strikes the paper. The resulting collection of dots form the letters.

The ImageWriter is slowish and so noisy people regularly buy *mufflers* for them. The print quality isn't anything to write home about (but ironically, it's good enough for letters home. See the print samples below). Unless you regularly need to print onto multiple-page forms (like Fed Ex labels), read on.

ImageWriter
StyleWriter
LaserWriter

Low-cost, high-quality, low-speed

Yes, Virginia, there *is* a high-quality printer that won't bleed you dry: the Apple StyleWriter. Its quality almost matches a laser printer's. It's very small, very lightweight, and almost silent. You can feed all kinds of nonliving things through it: labels, envelopes, tagboard, whatever. And it costs less than $400.

So what's the catch? Well, for people who are used to laser printers, the StyleWriter II's speed — two pages per minute — seems pretty slow. (They shouldn't complain; the original StyleWriter only printed half a page per minute!) Still, the StyleWriter II is so compact, quiet, and inexpensive — and it prints grays (such as photographs) so beautifully — that it's hard to resist.

Both the StyleWriter II and its popular $400 rival, the Hewlett-Packard DeskWriter, are *inkjet* printers. They create a printed image by spraying a mist of ink. Note, therefore, that inkjet-printed pages smear if they ever get the least bit damp, and the printing isn't laser-crisp if your stationery is even slightly absorbent.

PostScript printers

If you can afford to pay something like $1,200 for a printer, though, some real magic awaits you: *PostScript laser printers.* Don't worry about the word Post-Script for now. Just look for the word PostScript in the printer's description, as though it's some kind of seal of approval.

A PostScript printer, like most of Apple's LaserWriter models, can print any text, in any style, at any size, and at any angle, and everything looks terrific. PostScript laser printers can also print phenomenal-looking graphics, like all the diagrams in Macintosh magazines. They're quick, quiet, and hassle-free; most can print envelopes, mailing labels, and paper up to legal-size (but not tagboard).

Remember the old saying, "The power of the press is limited to those who have one"? Well, the combination of a Mac and a laser printer put the Mac on the map, because it turns anybody into a self-publisher. If you can afford a PostScript printer, get it. If you're a small-time operation — a home business, for example — I'd say get the cheapest PostScript laser printer you can find. Almost all laser printers between $1,000 and $2,000 have exactly the same quality printouts. If you're going to print mainly normal-looking text without fancy graphics, you can save some bucks by getting one of the LaserWriter printers that *isn't* PostScript, such as the LaserWriter Select 300.

Anyway, that's the hardware part of printing. The software is the hard part.

As a matter of fact, this chapter gets pretty dense. Depending on your stomach for detail, you might want to skip down to the part called "The output upshot," where everything is nicely oversimplified.

How History Messed Everything Up

When the Mac first appeared, everything was incredibly simple. There were ten typefaces (which Apple calls *fonts*) to choose from. They were called *bitmap* fonts because each letter on the screen was composed of dots in a particular arrangement (a "map" of bits). (So why don't they call it a *dotmap?* You kidding? That'd be too easy to understand.) These fonts were named after cities: New York, Geneva, Athens, and so on.

The ten great city fonts

All of the original Mac bitmapped fonts are still around. If you're a System 7 user, you probably only see a few of them in your font menus because the Installer doesn't automatically give you all of them. (The remaining fonts are tucked away on your Fonts disk; drag them onto your System Folder to install them.)

Here, for the sake of history, are the city-named, non-PostScript fonts. Note the little jaggies at the edges, even though they've been printed by the most expensive printer in the world. (The picture font is Cairo.)

New York   San Francisco   Athens

London   Venice   [Cairo picture glyphs]

Monaco   Chicago

Geneva   Los Angeles

The Mac screen, then and now, has 72 tiny square dots per inch. (To make sure as many people as possible are left in the dark, everybody abbreviates "dots per inch" as *dpi.*) This screen resolution worked out incredibly well because the only Mac printer — the ImageWriter — *also* printed 72 dots per inch. In other words, each dot you saw on the screen produced a corresponding dot on the page. For the first time in the history of computers, you got a printout that looked *exactly* like what you saw on the screen.

In an inspired burst of cutesiness, the term *WYSIWYG* was born, which supposedly is pronounced wizzy-wig and stands for "what you see is what you get." (Too bad *people* aren't WYSIWYG, y'know?)

The LaserWriter era

Then the world changed. Apple created the LaserWriter printer. Its resolution was *300* dots per inch — over four times sharper than the ImageWriter.

The main thing about the LaserWriter, though, was a new technology called PostScript that was built into it. They call PostScript a "page description language." It was invented by a little California company called Adobe. Once Apple saw how cool PostScript was, they struck a deal with Adobe to build PostScript technology into each laser printer.

You can read all kinds of things about how PostScript works. But all *you* need to know is that:

> ✔ A laser printer can create extremely sharp, clear printouts that look published.

Explicitly mapped?

After reading page 94, you may wonder how you can tell for sure which bitmapped fonts have been included in a set. Just consult the Font Size menu in one of your programs, as shown at right.

If a point size number is hollow, you've got it. If it's black, you don't, and the type will look pretty lame on the screen.

Size
6 Point
9 Point
✓🄸🄾 🄿🄾🄸🄽🅃
🄸🄸 🄿🄾🄸🄽🅃
🄸🄸 🄿🄾🄸🄽🅃
🄸🄸 🄿🄾🄸🄽🅃
20 Point
🄸🄸 🄿🄾🄸🄽🅃
36 Point

✔ To print sharp text on a PostScript laser printer, you need a special set of fonts, and you have to install them in your Mac.

✔ PostScript typefaces can be printed at any size or angle — no matter how big, small, or stretched — with equal clarity.

If you think about it, you'll realize that the third statement was definitely not true of the previous, bitmapped technology. A bitmapped font can only be printed clearly at a single point size — the size at which its designer arranged the dots to look good. (See the sidebar on page 93 for details.) True, each bitmapped font usually comes in a selection of different sizes, each painstakingly mapped to screen dots — usually 10-point, 12-point, 14-point, 18-point, and 24-point sizes. But if you try to select an in-between type size, you get pretty gross-looking results.

For example, 12- and 24-point below looks fine, but no 17-point New York font bitmap comes with your Mac, as evidenced by the chunky example in the middle:

New York at 12-point size
New York at 17-point size
New York at 24-point size

PostScript fonts, on the other hand, don't print text by specifying the placement of each dot on the page. Instead, each letter in a PostScript font is a hollow outline — or, technically, the mathematical equations that describe the *curves* of an outline — and then the printer fills in that outline with solid black. Since a PostScript printer thinks of fonts by their shapes, it's simple to tell the printer "Make this bigger"; it just multiplies the outline-shape by a point size number you specify. Printouts of 12-, 17-, 35.8-, and 128-point type all look equally sharp on a PostScript printer.

Why get fancy?

So if PostScript printers are *laser* printers, how come people don't just say *laser printer?*

Excellent question. Glad I asked it.

Answer: Some laser printers *aren't* PostScript printers. They rely on a glorified bitmap scheme to produce their type — that is, you have a fixed number of point size choices for each font. Even Apple sells a couple of printer models, in the LaserWriter product line, that don't have PostScript. Be sure you ask!

Furthermore, although they don't exist yet, there will probably be such a thing as a PostScript printer that *doesn't* use laser technology inside. Like a PostScript inkjet printer, or something. (Well, maybe not.)

Special type, special fonts

If you've been reading carefully, you noticed in the second check mark above that PostScript printers require a special set of fonts. You can tell a PostScript font immediately — it *doesn't* have a city name. Times, Helvetica, Futura, and Palatino are *PostScript* fonts, and they look great when printed by a (PostScript) laser printer.

Unfortunately, the PostScript technology breakthrough came after the Mac had been designed. The Mac still displayed type as a bitmap on the screen and had no clue what PostScript was.

As a result, the Adobe company had to provide *two parts* for each PostScript font it sold. There was a regular bitmapped font for use on the Mac screen — hence the term *screen font* — with all the attendant problems (like the goofy, scrunched-looking letters if you tried to use an odd-numbered point size). And there was a separate file, called a *printer font,* that you put in your System Folder.

The printer fonts had the same names as the screen fonts, with the last letters lopped off. In your word processor's Font menu you'd see Palatino Roman — but in your System Folder, there'd be a printer font file called PalatRom. (You're not supposed to interact with a printer font — if you double-click it, you'll just get an error message. It's there exclusively for the printer's use.)

OK. So now we have a font that lives in two different places, in two different files — an awkward arrangement with two unpleasant side effects. First, WYSI was no longer WYG; what you saw on the screen (a bitmapped font) didn't necessarily match the layout of the printouts (the printer font). On the screen, your term paper seemed to be ten pages long — but when you printed it, it might come out only to nine pages.

The other non-WYSIWYG aspect of having two files for each font was that lousy-looking text on the screen looked great when printed. People would select an odd type size, like 17 points. But since the printer font couldn't care less what size you used, that chunky text on the screen would look perfectly fine on the printed page. People just gritted their collective teeth and learned to have faith that the printout would be OK. (Of course, this was nothing new to people who had used IBM computers.)

System clutter land

Another little inconvenience of this two-file font system soon arose. In the WYSIWYG days of the ImageWriter, you'd have a wonderful choice of type styles in your word processor. There was (and is) **bold,** *italic,* underline, outline, shadow, and any combination thereof. A lot of people went out of control with these styles at first, but the general result was a lot more flexibility than your average 1975 typewriter.

Behind the scenes, the Mac created these style variations by messing with the bitmap itself. To create bold, the Mac just put a second dot beside each existing dot that made up a letter, giving the whole thing a plumper look. For italic, each successive row of dots was offset to the right, sort of slicing up the character into one-dot horizontal segments and shifting them to give the letter a slanted look.

But PostScript didn't know anything about individual dots. It dealt with *outlines*, man, *outlines*. To re-create the same styles on the printed page, then, a Post-Script font had to include a separate printer font file for *each* style variation: one for bold, one for italic, one for bold italic, and so on. To this day, some PostScript fonts come with as many as six or eight printer font files, all of which have to take up space in your System Folder.

Now imagine that you own 20 PostScript type families. Your System Folder would be one sprawling storage bin for printer font files. Professional graphics people grumbled about all that clutter.

The 5th Wave   By Rich Tennant

"WELL, MR. BOND, I GUESS THIS IS FAREWELL. LOWER...THE...LASER...PRINTER!"

Yet another drag: Every time you wanted to install a typeface, you had to install both parts — the printer file and the screen font. And to install the screen font, you had to use this incredibly hard-to-figure-out program called the Font/DA Mover. (DA stands for desk accessory.) No single aspect of the Mac was responsible for as much wailing and teeth-gnashing as this little mutant program.

Technology to the rescue

As the font situation grew unmanageable, a guy wrote a program called Suitcase that solved two of the problems. First, it let you install fonts in one quick step, without having to set foot near the dreaded Font/DA Mover. Second, it let you stuff those cluttery printer font files into a folder by themselves, which didn't have to be in the System Folder at all. Life became worth living again. A rival program, MasterJuggler, soon followed, serving the same purposes.

That didn't solve the problem of screen display, though. People still had to look at strange-looking, jagged text on the screen, even though they knew the laser printout would be fine.

So Adobe, the company that developed the PostScript technology, introduced a clever little gizmo called Adobe Type Manager, or ATM. (At last you know that Mac people don't actually go to cash machines a lot. Half the time they say "ATM" they're *not* talking about automated teller machines.)

ATM made type on the screen look sharp at any size, just the way a PostScript laser printer did. The secret: It consulted the printer font in your System Folder, decided what each letter should look like based on its *outline*, and drew it on the screen. The price: ATM took up a good chunk of memory, and it slowed down the screen display a bit. At $99 per copy, Adobe sold a gazillion copies of ATM, and then promptly bought the state of Nevada for its employee parking lot.

Ferment at the core of Apple

All may have been well with the graphic design firms of America, but Apple began to get irked.

The Mac/laser printer combination was a megahit in the late '80s. The Mac was becoming established as a serious, important machine. Macs and laser printers flew out the showroom door. But Adobe, the inventor of PostScript, had no intention of letting Apple ride to fame and fortune without paying the piper. The price Adobe charged for putting PostScript technology into Apple printers: $1,000 *per printer.*

This licensing fee had two profound effects. First, it made PostScript laser printers incredibly expensive — about six grand in the early years. Second,

Apple Computer felt as though it was being held hostage by Adobe. And that's a feeling no multimillion dollar corporation enjoys.

So Apple's best brains concocted a brilliant scheme. They'd come up with their *own* version of PostScript! They'd create a new font technology that was every bit as good, but Apple would own it, not Adobe. They could sell laser printers for $1,000 less — and sell a lot more of them.

While they were at it, they'd solve all the remaining problems associated with the PostScript scheme. Instead of having two separate files — one for the printer and one for the screen — these new fonts would be self-contained. Likewise, instead of cluttering up your life with a separate font for each style variation (bold, italic, and so on), all the styles would be built into that one font file. Instead of needing ATM for crisp on-screen type at any size — a $99 add-on — the new fonts would always look good on the screen automatically.

And on the eighth day, Apple introduced TrueType.

The TrueType spectacle

TrueType does everything it promised. These new fonts are easy to use, look great, can be viewed or printed at any size, and are self-contained in a single font file in your System. Since they're built into System 7, TrueType fonts don't even add clutter to your System Folder — they are tucked inside the System *file,* (or in System 7.1's Fonts folder), where you never have to wade through them.

And did TrueType change the world? Did PostScript die away as a technological dinosaur? Did laser printer prices plummet?

No, no, and yes.

For a very short time, everybody said "Ooh, font fight!" Everybody geared up for a big tragic rivalry between TrueType and PostScript. People also expected all kinds of system crashes and goofy-looking printouts if both font types were installed at once.

None of it happened. The two technologies co-exist just fine.

TrueType didn't blow the world away, for two reasons.

> ✔ *There weren't any fonts in this new format.* Apple provided a half dozen. But that was nothing compared with the hundreds of PostScript fonts available. People had invested thousands of dollars buying PostScript typefaces. Even when some font companies announced that they'd soon

be making TrueType fonts, most people muttered that they couldn't afford to build a type library from scratch again.

✔ *TrueType is only a font technology.* PostScript, on the other hand, is a *graphics* technology. It can do much more than manipulate text. It can also create lines, circles, patterns, wild shadings, and three-dimensional re-creations of Marilyn Monroe standing over an air shaft. Indeed, two of the most famous professional graphics programs of all time, Illustrator and FreeHand, are PostScript drawing programs. TrueType, which deals only with type, can't possibly replace all the flexibility of PostScript.

But TrueType did do something wonderful — it scared the bejeezus out of Adobe. The very secretive Adobe became a loving, open, helpful company the minute it thought it might suddenly be wiped off the earth. It freely gave away the secrets of PostScript to other companies so that they could develop PostScript fonts for the first time. I don't know for sure, but I'd bet that the licensing fee per printer dropped. Laser printer prices have been dropping ever since — instead of $6,000 apiece, street prices around $1,000 aren't uncommon. Tensions between Apple and Adobe cooled down, but attendance dropped for the annual Adobe/Apple softball game.

In fact, Apple persuaded Adobe (or vice versa) to *give away* ATM, the must-have PostScript font screen utility. Unfortunately for everybody who'd paid $99 for it, you can now get ATM for a mere $7.50 shipping charge. (Call 800-776-2333.) It's font glasnost.

The current mess

Today, then, there are *three* kinds of fonts: bitmapped, TrueType, and Post-Script. With TrueType, Apple hoped to simplify the whole font deal. I guess they both succeeded and failed — TrueType itself *is* a much simpler system, but it adds yet another font format to an already complicated scenario.

The following guide will help you figure out what you have and why it makes any difference.

Before we delve, though, rest assured that you'll always get *something* when you print, no matter what font and what printer you use. But if you don't have at least a vague idea of what you're doing, you might get ugly low-resolution type when you print, even if you blew serious bucks on a laser printer.

OK. Yellow pad ready? Brain cells open? Here we go.

If a font has a city name: It used to be simple. Back in the days when men were men and savings and loans were fiscally sound, a city-named font was a bit-mapped font, suitable only for the ImageWriter.

No See 'Em?

If you open your System file (or your Fonts folder) and you see a list (instead of a bunch of icons), choose By Icon from the View menu.

Unfortunately, some of the new TrueType fonts have the same names as the old bitmapped fonts: New York, Chicago, Monaco, and Geneva. The nice part is that no matter *what* kind of printer you own, these TrueType fonts will look great when printed, and you don't have to worry about point sizes, or printer font files, or any of that jazz.

But if you *don't* have the TrueType versions of New York, Chicago, and Geneva — and only have the original bitmapped versions — you'll get jagged-looking printouts on your laser printer or StyleWriter.

If you're using System 7, read no further (into this paragraph, anyway) — you have the TrueType versions of everything. You can prove this to yourself by opening your System Folder and double-clicking the System file itself (or your Fonts folder if you have one). You'll see TrueType fonts displayed with this special icon:

New York

If you're not using System 7, you probably have the old bitmapped New York, Chicago, Monaco, and Geneva. If you plan to print on a StyleWriter or laser printer, steer clear of them when formatting your documents.

If a font doesn't have a city name (for laser printer owners only): The font is a PostScript font. That means it'll look terrific when you print — *if* you also have the printer font file equivalent in your System Folder. And remember, you need a separate printer font for each style of the font — one for bold, one for italic, and so on.

Technoid disclaimer

OK, there's a *chance* that you could be using TrueType and *not* have System 7. If you're using System 6.0.7, you can put a TrueType INIT into your System Folder and receive all the benefits of TrueType without upgrading to System 7.

But for me to mention that fact would require that

I define the word *INIT* (a small plug-in program that you drop into your System Folder) and also tell you how to figure out which System your Mac has (by choosing About the Finder or About This Macintosh from the Apple menu). But I have no intention of doing that.

Technoid disclaimer II

OK, just to save you the postage required for the angry letter correcting my oversimplification: Underline, shadow, and outline styles don't each require a separate printer font file in your System Folder. Only bold, italic, bold italic, roman, heavy, medium, and any other peculiar variants of a particular PostScript font do.

It *still* makes a rat's nest out of your System Folder.

There are 35 exceptions to that generalization — the 35 type styles *built into* your laser printer. These fonts *don't* need printer files in your System Folder. (Although *Oblique* and *Demi* may sound like part of a sleazy trapeze act, they are in fact the trendy words for *Italic* and *Bold,* respectively.) Here's the list:

Times Roman	New Century Schoolbook	Helvetica Roman
Times Bold	Roman	**Helvetica Bold**
Times Italic	**New Century Schoolbook**	*Helvetica Oblique*
Times Bold Italic	**Bold**	***Helvetica Bold Oblique***
	New Century Schoolbook	
Avant Garde Roman	*Italic*	Helvetica Narrow Roman
Avant Garde Demi	***New Century Schoolbook***	**Helvetica Narrow Bold**
Avant Garde Italic	***Bold Italic***	*Helvetica Narrow Oblique*
Avant Garde Demi Italic		***Helvetica Narrow Bold Oblique***
	Palatino Roman	
Bookman Roman	**Palatino Bold**	*Zapf Chancery*
Bookman Demi	*Palatino Italic*	
Bookman Italic	***Palatino Bold Italic***	αβχδεφγηιφκ (Symbol)
Bookman Demi Italic		
	Courier Roman	✦❖✳✦✳✳✳ (Zapf Dingbats)
	Courier Bold	
	Courier Italic	
	Courier Bold Italic	

If there's a font in your font menu that doesn't appear in this list (other than city-named fonts), then it didn't come with the Mac. You're going to need the printer font file equivalent of it in your System Folder.

One more word of advice, ye lucky laser-printer user: Nobody's ever gone to hell for this, but it's a good idea not to let the TrueType and PostScript versions of the *same* font co-exist on your system. Times, Helvetica, Courier, and Symbol are the fonts in question here. Make a decision to go with the TrueType versions or the PostScript versions, and stand by it — and remove the duplicate.

If a font doesn't have a city name (for nonlaser printer owners): The font is a PostScript font.

But you have either (1) a laser printer that doesn't have PostScript, like the Apple LaserWriter Select 300, or (2) a nonlaser printer, like a StyleWriter, ImageWriter, DeskWriter, or some other 'Writer.

For would-be weenies only

If you really, really give a darn about how ATM gives you great-looking type on nonlaser and non-PostScript printers, I'll indulge you. But please remember that there's not a reason in the world for you to actually know this info.

Even in the early days of Mac (1984), printouts on the trusty ImageWriter weren't quite as jagged-looking as text on the screen. The ImageWriter has a little bit of smarts; it gives you a choice of three print qualities — Draft, Faster, and Best. If you choose Faster, then you indeed get a printout with precisely the quality you see on the screen — one printed dot for every black dot on your screen.

If you choose Best quality, though, a clever thing happens. The ImageWriter can actually print 144 dots per inch. (Those of you handy with a calculator may note that 144 is exactly double the 72-dpi resolution of the Mac screen.) When you print a document containing (for example) 12-point New York type, and you choose Best quality, the printer ransacks your System file, looking for *24-point* New York. If its search is successful, the ImageWriter actually prints your document in 24-point New York but packs the dots onto the page twice as densely.

The result of these shenanigans: You get type that's 12-point *size* but twice as crisp. It's the same effect as using a photocopier with a reduction feature — the resulting copy is finer and crisper than the original.

Subsequent generations of non-PostScript and nonlaser printers have taken this theme and run

with it. The ImageWriter LQ, for example, is capable of printing with a resolution of 270 dpi. So if you want a printout at 12-point size, you need a *triple*-sized font installed in your System to get the highest quality printout. The printer does the same trick as the original ImageWriter — it consults that 36-point font and prints it at one-third the size (and triple the crispness of the screen display).

The best-selling Hewlett-Packard DeskWriter came along next, with a super-crisp resolution of 300 dpi. Now you were supposed to have a *qua-druple*-sized bitmapped font installed in your System Folder to get that juicy resolution.

As you can imagine, these higher resolution printers started requiring whopping System Folders, creaking at the seams with these jumbo fonts. To have a selection of 10-, 12-, 18-, or 24-point sizes, you'd have to have the 40-, 48-, 72-, and 96-point sizes installed — each of which takes up a good chunk of your hard disk space — *per type style*.

When the 360-dpi Apple StyleWriter came along, which would have required *quintuple*-size fonts, no wonder people welcomed TrueType and ATM, which eliminate all that math and inconvenience. Since TrueType and ATM can scale any font of its type to any size, you simply need the TrueType font file (or the PostScript printer font file) in your System Folder — a single smallish file — instead of the zillions of jumbo bitmapped screen fonts.

Aren't you glad you asked?

You, too, can reap the benefits of PostScript (and TrueType) technology. If you want to use PostScript typefaces, though, you'll have to spring that big $7.50 for Adobe Type Manager (ATM). In a now long-forgotten paragraph, I mentioned that ATM is great for giving you high-quality screen display of PostScript fonts. What I didn't tell you is that ATM is also great for getting high-resolution print-outs on *non*-PostScript printers.

So if you use either TrueType fonts or PostScript fonts and ATM, you'll get the highest quality printouts that your printer, whatever it is, can possibly produce.

The output upshot

System 7: *The most recent version of the Macintosh operating-system software. Even if you have 7.0.1 , 7.1, 7.1p, or 7.0.1p, it's still generically called System 7. You can tell if you have System 7 by the presence of the 🅿 in the upper-right corner of your screen.*

If you just bought a Mac, and you're using the type faces that get installed with System 7, you have nothing to worry about. Whether you know it or not, *all* of your fonts are TrueType fonts, which do their elfin-magic behind the scenes. And no matter what printer you own, you can rest easy knowing that TrueType will give you the highest quality printouts it's capable of. You can use any font in your System 7 font menu, without worrying that it will print jaggedly on a laser printer. End of story.

Things only get more complicated if you (1) crave more variety, (2) find fonts in your font menu that *you* didn't put there, or (3) have a Mac that's not running System 7.

If any of those conditions are true for you, then use this table to help you figure life out.

Your Mac	Your printer	Use TrueType fonts?	Use PostScript fonts?	Use city-named fonts?
System 7	PostScript laser	Sure	Yes, with ATM and the printer font files in your System Folder	Yup (cause they're really TrueType)
System 7	StyleWriter, DeskWriter, non-PostScript laser	You betcha	Yes, with ATM and the printer font files in your System Folder	Go for it ('cause they're really TrueType)
System 6	PostScript laser	No*	Yes, with ATM and the printer font files in your System Folder	No way

Your Mac	Your printer	Use TrueType fonts?	Use PostScript fonts?	Use city-named fonts?
System 6	StyleWriter, DeskWriter, non-PostScript laser	No*	Yes, with ATM and the printer font files in your System Folder	Only if you have the appropriate point size installed (see the sidebar on page 102)

*Unless you have System 6.0.7 *and* the TrueType INIT, as described in the sidebar on page 100.

How To Print

Bet you haven't had a lesson with *that* title since about first grade.

Plugging in a 'Writer

If you bought an ImageWriter, StyleWriter, or other 'Writer, a cable (printer-to-Mac) probably came with the printer. It's a no-brainer to connect them; there's only one possible place to plug the cable into the printer. The other end goes into the back of the Mac; there's a little round jack with a printer icon. (It's next to the jack with a telephone icon.) Of course, you also need to plug your new appliance into the wall.

Plugging in a laser printer

If you bought a laser printer, believe it or not, you probably did *not* get a cable with it. Like anything precious in the computer jungle, it'll take some bush-wacking through the technical underbrush to get at the explanation.

When Apple invented the LaserWriter — the very first PostScript laser printer — they charitably recognized that not every company could afford a $6,000 printer to sit beside each desk. They had a great idea, though: Invent a system where several Macs could all plug into the *same* printer.

Ladies and gentlemen, I hereby introduce you to the word *network*.

The wires and connectors that attach these Macs to a single shared printer (and which, by the way, can also connect Macs to each *other*) are called Local-Talk. These connectors aren't cheap — last I looked, a pair of connectors (what you need for *one* Mac and *one* printer) was about $100.

Soon thereafter, competitors got into the act, with rival connectors called things like PhoneNet and ModuNet. There were two brilliant concepts behind these rival wiring systems. First, they were much less expensive than Apple's product; second, they used ordinary phone wire to connect the connectors. (Apple's LocalTalk requires special cables.) If you decided to move your printer into the next room, no big deal — just buy a longer piece of phone wire from Radio Shack.

This is all relevant only if you believe that you *must* have a network in order to plug a Mac into a laser printer. And, in fact, that's exactly what the salespeople would like you to believe.

But here's another money-saving *Macs For Dummies* secret: You only need all that fancy wiring *if* you plan to share your laser printer with other Macs.

If it's just you, your Mac, and a cup of coffee on the desk, get a plain old Image-Writer II cable for $15. After all, one Mac and one printer hardly qualify as a *network*. Put the other $85 into a skiing weekend or something.

Network: *Macs and printers wired together, so they can share each other (and send messages back and forth).*

Anyway, if you do get the more expensive connectors, plug one connector into the back of the printer and the other into the printer jack in the back of the Mac. Then connect the connectors using LocalTalk cable or phone wire, as appropriate. And if you're just going to use an ImageWriter cable, see above under "Plugging in a 'Writer."

Letting the Mac know it has company

The hardest part of printing on a Mac comes at the very beginning — an unfortunate fact for the novice who simply wants to get going.

When you first plug a printer into the Mac, it's not smart enough to notice that it's got a new friend. You have to tell it explicitly; we'll get to that in a moment.

Imagine that you work in a big office; you have three different kinds of printers and a dozen Macs, and they're all wired together into a giant network. You want to print something. You have to be able to tell the Mac (1) what *kind* of printer you want to use (laser, StyleWriter, whatever), and, if there's more than one of each connected to the network, (2) which *one.*

That long-winded explanation was supposed to help you understand why there's a desk accessory in your Apple menu called the Chooser. Using this gadget, you can specify what kind of printer, and which one, you want to use.

If you're a one-person operation, of course, this stuff is utterly superfluous. But you have to go through it anyway. What the heck — maybe it'll give you some healthy sympathy for people who work in offices.

The Chooser

Once the Mac is connected to the printer, turn both machines on. Now choose Chooser from the Apple menu. You should see something like this:

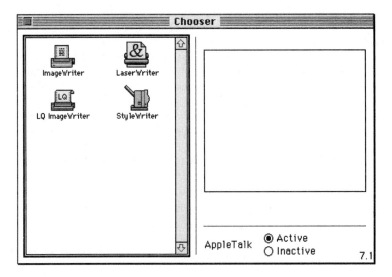

Your screen may look different, of course. The icons that appear in the left half of the window depend upon which *printer drivers* have been placed in your System Folder. A printer driver is a little piece of software that teaches the Mac how to communicate with a specific printer. Its name and its icon match the printer itself, as you can sort of tell from the figure above.

If you see a printer driver icon in the Chooser window that matches your printer, you're in luck! Click it. You should see your actual printer's name show up in the *right* side of the Chooser window (if it's turned on), as shown here:

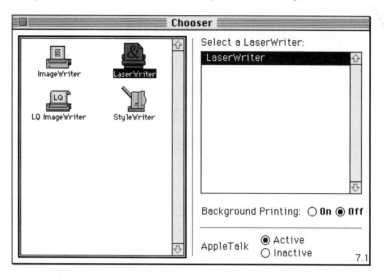

Good going! Everything's coming up roses. If the names of *several* printers show up on the right, then you're either part of an office network with several printers, or you're an unexpectedly wealthy individual. Congratulations. Click the one you want to print on.

If you don't see *any* icons in the left half of the Chooser window, then nobody bothered to install them. (Or, more likely, since the System 7 installer *automatically* places the printer drivers into your System Folder, somebody's probably taken them out.) No matter — you'll find all these icons on the original white Apple software disk called Printing. Find the one that matches your printer, and drag it on top of your System Folder icon. (If you have a laser printer and System 6, you need both the LaserWriter icon *and* the Laser Prep icon.) Don't worry if your laser printer isn't made by Apple — use the LaserWriter driver for any brand of laser printer. The Mac will install it automatically. Now you can repeat this Chooser business, and everything should go fine.

If you see *some* printer driver icons in the Chooser window, but none of them matches your printer, here again you need to copy the appropriate driver icon into your System Folder from the original Apple disk.

If things *still* aren't going well — for example, if you click the driver icon but your printer's name doesn't show up in the right side of the window — then see Chapter 9.

Anyway, once you click a printer driver icon, a couple of things happen. If you're selecting a laser printer, you'll be told to turn on AppleTalk. AppleTalk is related to LocalTalk, the networking system described above; remember that if you have a laser printer, you're supposedly part of a network even if just one Mac is attached to it. So make sure the little AppleTalk setting (in the lower-right corner of the dialog box) is Active if you have a laser printer.

When you close the Chooser, you'll get a soon-to-be-annoying alert message:

You have changed your current printer. Please choose "Page Setup..." in all of the open applications.

[OK]

It tells you (as if you didn't know) that you've just changed to a new printer. Its advice, though, is sound. After you select a printer driver, choose Page Setup from your File menu. A dialog box appears. Don't *do* anything in this box; just click OK.

You've just introduced the Mac to its new printer. All of this is a one-time operation, by the way; unless you have to switch printers or something, you'll never have to touch the Chooser again.

Background printing

In the Dark Ages of the 1980s, when you printed something, the printer's soul took over your Mac's body. You couldn't type, you couldn't work, you couldn't do anything but stare at the sign on the screen that said "Now printing." It was a dark and stormy era, a time of wild and rampant coffee breaks. Only when the paper came out of the printer were you allowed to use your computer again.

Since then, some clever engineer at Apple figured out how to allow *background printing*. When you use this handy feature, the Mac sends all the printing information at a million miles per hour into a *file* on your hard disk and immediately returns its attention to you and your personal needs. Then, quietly, behind the scenes, the Mac shoots a little bit of that file to your printer at a time. It all happens during the microseconds between your keystrokes and mouse clicks, making it seem as though the Mac is printing in the background. In time, the printer receives all the information it needs to print, the paper comes gliding out, and you've been able to keep working the whole time.

In practice, there are a few chilly background printing realities to consider. First of all, a document takes much longer to print in the background than it would if the Mac devoted all of its brainpower to printing. Similarly, making your Mac concentrate on two things at once also bogs down what *you're* doing; while something's being printed in the background, you can outtype your word processor, windows seem to take longer to open, and so on. Finally, background printing isn't available for ImageWriters (unless you buy a program, called a *spooler*, especially designed for the ImageWriter).

Turning the Background Printing feature on and off is easy. Select Chooser from the Apple menu. In the lower-right side of the box, you'll see the On/Off buttons. Go for it.

The reason I mention this tidbit is so that you'll remember it when the time comes: when it's 2 a.m. and your novel is due on the publisher's desk by 9 a.m.; or it's 1:55 p.m. and the meeting is at 2 p.m.; or you're leaving the house anyway and want to make sure your printout is ready when you get back. In all of these cases, it would be wise of you to turn *off* background printing to ensure that you get your printout as fast as possible.

After all that: How you actually print

OK. Suppose your printer is finally plugged in and, via the Chooser, has been introduced to the Mac. You've digested all that font information and have been careful to use only the appropriate fonts in your document. The moment has arrived: You actually would like to *print* the thing.

Choose Print from the File menu. This dialog box appears; it looks different depending on your printer, but the one pictured below is what you see if you have a laser printer:

```
LaserWriter  "Silentwriter 95"              7.1.1    [ Print  ]
Copies:[1▮]        Pages: ◉ All ○ From:[    ] To:[    ]  [ Cancel ]
Cover Page:    ◉ No ○ First Page ○ Last Page
Paper Source: ◉ Paper Cassette ○ Manual Feed
Print:        ◉ Black & White   ○ Color/Grayscale
Destination:  ◉ Printer         ○ PostScript® File
```

The main thing you do in this dialog box is tell the Mac which pages of your document you want it to print. If you just want page 1, type a 1 into *both* the

"From" and "To" boxes. If you want page 2 to the end, type 2 into the "From" box and leave the "To" box empty.

Specify how many copies you want by clicking and typing in the "Copies" box.

Using the Tab key in dialog boxes

Now would be a good time, I suppose, to mention what the Tab key does in dialog boxes. Suppose you want to print two copies of page 3. Instead of using the mouse to click in each number box on the screen, you can just press Tab to jump from box to box.

Therefore, you'd just type 2 (in the Copies box); press Tab, type 3 (in the From box); press Tab, type 3 again (in the To box). And the mouse just sits there gathering dust.

Anyway, once you're done filling out the options in this box, click OK. The Mac should whir for a moment, and pretty soon the printout will come slithering out of your printer.

If you can't get anything to work right, check Chapter 9 for trouble-sleuthing tips.

Canceling printing

If you want to interrupt the printing process, Command-period does the trick — that is, while pressing the ⌘ key, type a period. Several times, actually. Even then, your printer will take a moment (or page) or two to respond to you.

Just Your Type

You actually get more fonts with your Mac than you think — the Installer program, which you (or your dealer or your local computer whiz) used to set up your hard disk, only installs a handful of basic ones. As you go on through life, you may (and can) (and should) want to add new typefaces to your Mac or trash some of the ones you've already been given.

User group: *A Macintosh computer club in your area. Call Apple at 800-538-9696 to find out the nearest one. You can also get disks from most user groups by mail.*

So where do you get additional fonts? The universal response to that question is, of course: Buy them. Those on a budget, however, can still get tons of great fonts. On your white Fonts disk that came with your Mac, for example, there are about a dozen interesting ones. Or you can call up your local user group and pay about $5 for a disk full of new fonts. Or if you have a modem (as described in Chapter 7), you can dial up America Online or another online service and help yourself to as many fonts as your typographical taste buds can tolerate.

How to install a font

Quit all your programs (if you're running any) before trying this.

Drag the font file icon on top of the System Folder icon. That goes for both printer font files and screen font files, if it's a PostScript font you're installing. (Do *not* drag them into the open System Folder *window*. Do not drag them to the Trash can. Do not collect $200.)

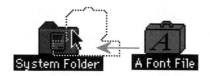

You'll see a message alerting you that the Mac is going to install the font for you. Just smile, wave, and click OK.

How to remove a font

First of all, choose About This Macintosh from the menu; read the little message that appears. If it says you've got System 7.1 or 7.1p, open your System Folder, then open the Fonts folder therein. If you've got System 7.0, 7.0.1, or 7.0.1p, open the System Folder and then double-click the System *file* icon itself. In any case, you'll now see a list of your fonts in a window:

Name	Size	Kind
System		
61 items 34 MB in disk 4 MB available		
Geneva 18	5K	font
Geneva 20	7K	font
Geneva 24	9K	font
Helvetica	60K	font
Helvetica 9	11K	font
Helvetica (bold)	58K	font
Helvetica 10	10K	font
Helvetica 12	11K	font
Helvetica 14	11K	font

System 6 corner

If you're using System 6, installing fonts is much uglier and more difficult. I'll make the effort, but you should feel free to consult your Mac manuals for more patient instructions.

Find the program called Font/DA Mover. It's either on your hard disk someplace or still on the white Apple disks that came with your Mac. Double-click the icon. You'll see two lists. One side lists all the fonts you *already* have in your System. The other side is probably empty.

Click the Open button on the empty side, and navigate your way to the font you want to install. Double-click its name; you return to the main Font/DA Mover window. Drag through the names of the fonts you want to install and then click the Copy button. (To remove fonts from your system, drag through their names on the System side of the list and click Remove.) And then think about getting System 7, where installing fonts isn't such a pain.

To see what a font looks like, double-click it; a little window opens, displaying a line from classical literature, displayed in the font you're investigating.

To remove a font, just drag it out of the window and into the Trash can.

Top Ten Free Fun Font Factoids

1. Every Mac comes installed with Times, Helvetica, Courier (which looks like an electric typewriter), Symbol (a bunch of Greek symbols), New York, Chicago (the font used for menu names), Geneva (the font used for icon names in the Finder), and Monaco (a really ugly *monospaced* font, where

For technology lovers only

When you look through your System file (or your Fonts folder), you may discover a bunch of icons that would seem to disprove what I just told you about fonts. That is, you'll see a TrueType font icon (like New York), all right, but you'll *also* see icons for a bunch of bitmapped fonts in specific sizes (New York 10, New York 12, and so on).

Don't freak — what I told you is still true. But remember when ATM came out and made everything slow on the screen? That's because it had to consult the printer font file to learn how to draw each letter. Apple didn't want TrueType

technology to give you the same problems, so along with each TrueType font, you also get a bunch of ready-made bitmapped screen fonts in common sizes. Any time you format a document in one of these fonts and sizes, the Mac doesn't have to consult the TrueType font file at all, since you've already got that point size installed as a bitmap. The result — faster screen display. You *could*, if you wanted to, throw away these specific point size files, leaving only the numberless TrueType font icon, and everything would still work OK...just a little bit slower.

every letter is exactly the same width). You can never remove the last three since the Mac uses them for various things on the screen.

2. Some of the bitmapped fonts that come with the Mac correspond to PostScript fonts. New York is pretty much like Times; Geneva is sort of like Helvetica; and Monaco is a lot like Courier (they're both monospaced).

   If you have a non-System 7 Mac, and you try to print a document prepared in New York, Geneva, or Monaco, the Mac will, at your request, *substitute* the PostScript equivalents (Times, Helvetica, Courier) automatically. ("At your request" means that, when you choose Print from the File menu and encounter a dialog box, you make sure that Font Substitution is selected.)

   However, you're much better off not using this feature. When the Mac does this font substitution for city-name fonts, it doesn't account for the fact that New York and Times (for example) have different *letter widths*. So you get really weird word spacing in the printout because the Mac tries to *position* every word in the same place (below right) as it's shown on the screen (below left).

"Agatha!" I screamed, my lungs bleeding and raw from the violent pounding of the vicious surf spray.	"Agatha!" I screamed, my lungs bleeding and raw from the violent pounding of the vicious surf spray.

   Much better idea: Format your documents with laser fonts to begin with! Unless you like the look of free-floating words in space, keep Font Substitution clicked off.

3. Ten font families are built into most PostScript laser printers. They are, as you'll recall, Times, Helvetica, Helvetica Narrow, Avant Garde, Palatino, Bookman, New Century Schoolbook, Symbol, Zapf Chancery, and Zapf Dingbats.

   Any PostScript font that doesn't appear on this list has to be *downloaded* (transferred) to the printer each time you turn on the printer and try to print. As such, they're called *downloadable* fonts. That's why their printer font files have to sit in your System Folder, where the Mac will know where to find them.

   Downloadable fonts impact your life in several ways. First, you have to buy them. Second, documents that use downloadable fonts take more time to print since the Mac has to teach the printer what each character looks like.

   Third, if you use several downloadable fonts in a document, it may not print at all. The printer's memory will get filled up with font information even before the Mac starts to send the document. The result: The printer keeps saying "Wait, wait, I'm not ready yet . . ." to the Mac, and the Mac keeps saying "Ready? Ready? Here it comes . . .", until you get disgusted and flip one of them off. (Marriage counseling for Macs and printers is not yet available outside California.)

The solution, of course, is to reformat your document using the built-in fonts (Times, Helvetica, and so on) instead of downloadable ones — or to install more memory into your printer. (You'll find more nitty-gritty on this topic in Chapter 9.)

4. Choose Page Setup from the File menu. The Page Setup dialog box has a handful of very useful options — what paper size you plan to use, for example, or how much you want your document enlarged or reduced.

In the upper-right corner, though, there's a nifty Options button (if you have a laser printer). Click it. Up comes a very useful dialog box:

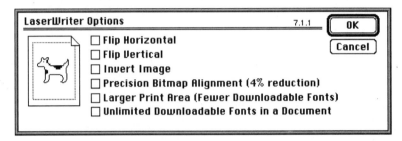

To get a little preview of each option, click the appropriate checkbox and watch the helpful Dogcow illustrate the effect on your printout.

Most noteworthy, though, is the item called Larger Print Area. The average laser printer can only print to within ¼ inch of the page edge. Select Larger Print Area, though, and you gain ⅛ inch all the way around — a very useful gain for graphics, music, page-layout, and other kinds of printing.

5. Suppose you select some text and make it bold. Then you try to print, but the text keeps coming out as *non*-bold on the printed page.

The problem is that you're using a PostScript typeface that *doesn't have* a Bold version — or maybe it does, but the corresponding printer font file isn't properly located in your System Folder. Remember how a PostScript font comes in two pieces — one for the screen and one for the printer? What happens here, then, is that the boldface style appears just fine on the

The Dogcow

No Mac book would be complete without at least a passing acknowledgment of the Dogcow.

His name, need I point out, stems from the fact that nobody can precisely figure out what kind of animal he is. In the inner sanctum of Apple Computer Corporation, it is said that, late at night, you can hear the sound made by the Dogcow: Moof!

screen; the Mac can make *anything* boldface, just by thickening the letters. When you try to print, though, the Mac can't find an appropriate printer font. In an attempt to be helpful, the Mac just uses the nonbold version for the printout.

Or, as I said, some fonts — notably Zapf Chancery — don't have a bold version at all. (Zapf Chancery doesn't even have an italic style since it's already sort of italic.)

6. Adobe's PostScript typefaces don't rely on the Mac's jury-rigged boldface-making feature, as described in Tip 5. Instead, you get a complete bitmapped screen font for each type style — bold, italic, and so on. Unfortunately, each style name appears in your Font menu prefaced by an initial: "I Times Italic, B Times Bold, BI Times Bold Italic," and so on.

Who came up with this dumb idea, I can't tell you. But I do know that your font menu lists fonts alphabetically. The result is that each typeface's style variations aren't listed together — they're scattered all over the darned menu, as shown below on the left. Your only chance of getting things into shape is to buy a utility program that combines them into family groups on your menu, with the style variations listed in a submenu (below right):

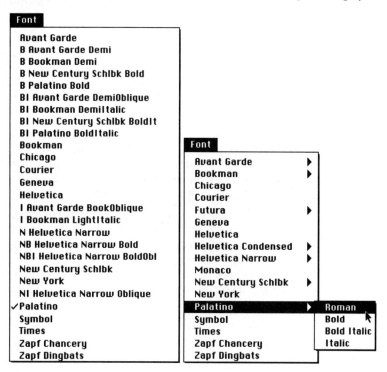

One such utility is sold by (guess who?) Adobe. Because they probably concocted the inconvenient font-naming scheme just so they could sell their utility program to correct it, I'm not going to play along by telling you what the thing is called. Instead, I'm going to recommend WYSIWYG Menus, an even better utility. It's part of the Now Utilities package (see Appendix C, the Resource Resource, in the back of the book).

7. In MacWrite II and some other word processing programs, you can actually see the names of the fonts in your font menu *in* those typefaces, like this:

There are a few other ways to get this feature, all of which involve spend-ing some money. Suitcase II, Now Utilities, and MenuFonts are a few programs that add this feature to any program you own.

8. When you first buy your laser printer, you may have noticed (and sworn at) the fact that it spits out a "startup page" every time you turn it on. This startup page contains a host of extremely unimportant information, like the number of pages you've printed in the printer's lifetime (including the useless startup page in your hand). Meanwhile, the Brazilian rain forests keep getting smaller.

You can tell the printer not to waste that paper and ink, if you want. Use the little program called LaserWriter Font Utility; it's on the Tidbits disk that comes with System 7. Double-click it, and choose Start Page Options from the Utilities menu. Click Off, and savor the fact that you made the world a better place for your grandchildren.

9. If you have something important to print, keep in mind that you don't actually have to *own* a laser printer to get that professional look. Even if you use an ImageWriter or other 'Writer at home, you can always take your disk in to an "output bureau" (a high-tech copy shop) and pay a certain amount per page for laser-printed (or even higher quality) print-outs. But if you do so, just remember the golden rules of which fonts to use, as described earlier in this section.

10. Want to look good the next time you're hanging out with a bunch of type geeks? Then learn to bandy about the terms *serif* (pronounced SAIR-iff) and *sans serif* (SANNZ sair-iff).

A serif is the little protruding line built onto the edges of the letters in certain typefaces. In the *serif font* pictured in the top example here, I've drawn little circles around some of the serifs:

Terrif serifs
Sans-serif

A *sans serif* font, on the other hand, has no little protuberances, as you can see by their absence in the little squares (in the lower example above). Times, Palatino, and the font you're reading are all serif fonts. Helvetica, Geneva, and the headlines in most newspapers are sans serif fonts.

And that information, plus 29¢, will buy you a first-class postage stamp in the United States.

• •

Summary

▶ A city-named, bitmapped font prints jaggedly on a laser printer and looks awful in any size except the ones it was explicitly designed for.

▶ If you have a laser printer, a PostScript font looks gorgeous at any size — provided you have both pieces of it (one part for the screen, one for the printer). If you throw ATM into the mix, you can get crisp letters at any size, both on the screen and on nonlaser printers.

▶ TrueType fonts are nifty: They always look great — any printer, any size.

▶ To print, you need the appropriate *printer driver* from your white Printing disk. And you have to select it in the Chooser desk accessory.

▶ *Sans serif* isn't the name of an expensive drink in a French café.

• •

Part II
Increasing Your Coolness Quotient

The 5th Wave By Rich Tennant

"WELL, RIGHT OFF, THE RESPONSE TIME SEEMS A BIT SLOW."

In this part...

Either you've faithfully plowed through the personally enriching material so far, nursing your inner child (the one that always wanted to use a computer), and are now ready for more . . .

. . . *or* you've just skipped over a lot of stuff to get here. Either way, you won't be disappointed: the mind-blowing *Faking Your Way Through the Top Ten Programs* will be your survival guide for maintaining status in the office, and *More Stuff to Buy and Plug In* will help you unleash you Mac's potential (and unload your wallet).

Chapter 6
Faking Your Way Through the Top Ten Programs

● ●

In This Chapter

▶ Faking your way through ClarisWorks

▶ Faking your way through graphics programs like MacPaint, MacDraw, and Canvas

▶ Faking your way through word/page processing programs like Word, PageMaker, and QuarkXPress

▶ Faking your way through famous number/data crunchers like Excel and FileMaker

▶ Plus excellent productivity-enhancers like QuicKeys and Apple File Exchange

● ●

*T*his chapter is a survival guide for stranded-on-a-desert-island, filling-in-for-Mr.-Big, my-son's-at-school-but-I-need-to-print-out-something, the-computer-just-arrived-but-the-board-meeting-is-in-two-hours, in-a-computer-store-to-try-something-but-don't-know-how-it-works situations.

I'm going to assume that you know the basics of saving files and retrieving them (from Chapter 4) and that you know how to use fonts and how to print (from Chapter 5). And if you want to do something fancier than what I'll be showing you, I'm assuming that you do have access to either (a) the manuals or (b) whoever got you into this mess to begin with.

Macintosh users are notorious for not reading their software manuals. They're actually belligerently *proud* of the fact that they never read manuals. Of course, two years down the line, one user will look at another user's techniques and intone, astounded, "I never knew it could do *that!*"

You're welcome to join this cult of instant gratification, with this chapter as your guide — but at least read the one for your word processor (or whatever program you spend the most time in).

The one thing this section *isn't* for is to help you use an illegal copy of one of these programs. Humor me on this; living in New York City is dangerous enough without worrying that some scary-looking goons in trench coats and dark glasses are gonna show up at my apartment accusing me of encouraging software piracy.

HyperCard...not!

In earlier copies of *Macs for Dummies,* this chapter started with HyperCard, because HyperCard used to come free with every Mac. HyperCard is often described as a "software Erector set," because you could create lots of neat things with it: an address book, a planning calendar, a recipe book, and so on.

At the time, you could also buy HyperCard from Claris Corporation — for $200. I guess not too many people were buying, though. Why would they, when they already had a free copy of the program?

So a funny thing happened near the end of 1992: without saying a word to anyone, Apple stopped giving away HyperCard with each Mac. Instead, you now get a stripped-down doodad they call HyperCard Player. You can't use it to design your own cool mini-programs. All the Player can do is open *other* people's HyperCard files.

Since HyperCard was yanked out of the Software Top Ten, I'm going to spend the following pages teaching you about a much more popular program: ClarisWorks. If you bought a Performa Mac, ClarisWorks probably came already installed on your hard disk. It's definitely one of the top ten programs and it's a durned fine program.

ClarisWorks

ClarisWorks is Swiss Army Knife software. Just look at all you get, even if you don't know what they are yet: a word processor, a database, and a spreadsheet. *Now* how much would you pay? But wait: you also get a graphics program that can even serve as a basic page-layout system. And if you order now, you even get a little communications program (to use if you own a *modem*—a phone hookup for your Mac).

All of these modules are neatly bundled into a single integrated program. You can write a letter and put a graphic in it; or design a flyer that has a little spreadsheet in it; and so on. This section will be worth reading even if you don't own this particular software because ClarisWorks works exactly like most other Mac programs.

Launching ClarisWorks

Double-click the ClarisWorks icon.

After the Claris logo disappears, you're asked to decide what it is you want to accomplish. Because you'll face this decision every time you use this program, a run-down may be in order here.

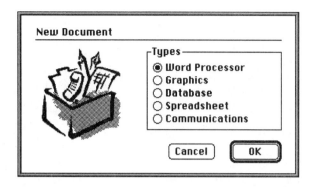

Word Processor: You know what a word-processing document is: something you type. A memo, a novel, a ransom note.

Graphics: This is ClarisWorks' version of MacDraw (see page 134). In this kind of document, you toy around with lines, shapes, and colors to produce logos, maps, Hangman game diagrams, and other important visuals.

Database: An electronic index-card file, very much like FileMaker (see page 163). You type in your lists—household expenditures; record collections; subscriber list to *Regis & Kathie Lee!* magazine—and the program sorts them, prints them, finds certain pieces of info instantly, and so on.

Spreadsheet: A computerized ledger sheet, almost exactly like Excel (see page 157). Crunches numbers: calculates your car's mileage per gallon, your bank account, how much of the phone bill your teenage daughter owes, that kind of thing.

Communications: You need this kind of program if you want to use your modem for dialing up (1) local "electronic bulletin boards," (2) a pay-by-the-hour information service like CompuServe, or (3) your local school's computer system.

To make ClarisWorks strut its stuff, I'll show you how to create a thank-you letter. But not just any thank-you letter — this is going to be the world's most beautiful and personalized *form letter.* You're going to merge a list of addresses into a piece of mail, creating what appear to be individually composed letters; thus, the technoid term for what you're about to do is *mail merge.*

Your first database

Suppose you just got married. You were showered with lovely gifts. And now it's your task to write charming thank-you notes to each of 100 people. You'll begin by typing a list of the gift-givers. The ideal software for organizing this kind of information is a *database.* Therefore, click the Database button, and click OK.

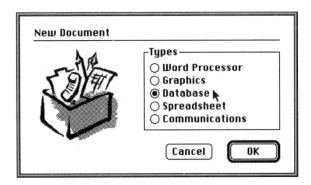

Don't be alarmed. The screen that now appears may look complicated, but it's actually not so bad — it simply wants to know what blanks you'll be wanting to fill in for each person in your list (name, address, gift type, and so on).

You're about to type names for these blanks (which the program calls *fields*). As always, if you make a typo, just press the Delete key to backspace over it. Here we go:

1. Type *First Name.* Press the Return key. (Pressing Return is the same as clicking the Create button.)

2. Type *Last Name.* Press Return.

3. Type *Address.* Press Return. (See how you're building a list?)

4. Type *Gift.* Press Return. Type *Adjective.* Press Return. (In this blank, you'll eventually type a word that describes the glorious present this person gave you.)

6. Finally, type *Part of House.* (You'll see why in a moment). Press Return.

Your masterpiece should look something like this:

7. Click the Done button in the lower-right corner. The dialog box goes away.

When you see what you've created, things should make a little bit more sense. You've just created the blanks (oh, all right, *fields*) to be filled in for each person in your list.

First Name	
Last Name	
Address	
Gift	
Adjective	
Part of	

Data entry time

To fill in the fields, you just type normally. To advance from one field to the next — from "First Name" to "Last Name," for example — press the Tab key. (You can also move to a new field by clicking in it, but the Tab key is quicker.) So here goes:

1. Make sure you can see a dotted-line rectangle for each field, like the ones in the figure above. If not, press the Tab key. The little blinking cursor should be in the "First name" blank. (If it's not, click there.) Type *Josephine*. Press the Tab key to jump to the "Last Name" field.

2. Type *Flombébé*. (See "Accent Heaven" on the next page.) Again, press Tab. Now you're in the Address blank.

3. Type *200 West 15th Street*. Now press *Return*. Note that you don't advance to the next blank; instead, the program thoughtfully makes *this* box bigger, so there's room for another line of address.

First Name	Josephine
Last Name	Flombébé
Address	200 West 15th Street
Gift	New York, NY 10010
Adjective	
Part of	

4. Go ahead and type *New York, NY 10010*. Then press Tab. (And don't worry that the second line of the address immediately gets hidden. The information you typed is still there.)

5. Type *acrylic sofa cover* (and press Tab); *practical* (and press Tab); *living room* (and stop).

You've just filled in the information for your first gift-sender. So that this won't take all day, let's pretend that it was a *very* small wedding, and you only received gifts from three people.

Accent heaven

Ah, mais oui, mon ami. C'est vrai, c'est la vie, c'est la résumé.

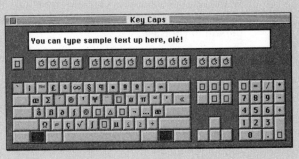

I know what you're thinking: What a smooth, sophisticated guy to be able to speak French like that! Thank you.

But you're also thinking: How did he get those cool accent marks? Very easily — and you, having been smart enough to choose a Mac over all its inferior competitors, can do it too.

The Mac has a ton of these special characters. Look at your keyboard — I bet you don't see ©, or ™, or •, or ¢, or any other useful symbols Mac people use all the time. That's because they're hidden. The secret that unlocks them is...the Option key.

It works like the Shift key: While pressing Option, you type a key. Here are some popular ones:

To get this . . .	Press Option and type this . . .
©	g
™	2
ç	c
¢	4
¡	1
£	3
•	8
®	r
†	t

Anyway, there are dozens of these things. What's nice to know is that you have a complete built-in cheat sheet that shows their locations on the keyboard. It's the Key Caps desk accessory, which is in your Apple menu.

Open it up and take a look. Now try pressing the Option key.

So *that's* where all those little critters live!

Anyway, there's one more wrinkle to all this. A few symbols, called *diacritical marks* (that's not a computer term, it's a proofreading one, I think) can be placed over *any* letter. They include the markings over this ü, this é, this è, and so forth. Since the Mac doesn't know ahead of time which vowel you're going to type, creating these is a two-step process:

1. While pressing Option, type the key as shown here:

To get this . . .	Press Option and type this . . .
é	e
ü	u
è	`
ñ	n
î	i

When you do this, *nothing will happen*. In other words, no marking appears on the screen — until you do step two.

2. Type the letter you want to appear under the diacritical marking.

Only now does the entire thing — letter and marking — appear on the screen. So if you think about it, typing the six-letter word *résumé* requires eight keystrokes. *C'est formidable, ça!*

But let's see: we need a new set of fields, don't we? Come to think of it, wouldn't life be sweeter if there were a computer term for "set of fields"? By gumbo, there is! A set of fields is called a *record*.

I wouldn't bother with that term if it didn't crop up in the next instruction.

1. From the Edit menu, choose New Record.

2. A new record appears, and you're ready to type the second person's information. Type anything you want or copy the example below, but remember to press Tab at the end of each piece of information. (Oh, and if you want a second line for the address, remember to press Return. Make up a town and state; you're a creative soul.)

First Name	Ginnie
Last Name	May
Address	42 Pocono La.
Gift	air conditioner w/ remote
Adjective	high-tech
Part of	bedroom

3. Once again, choose New Record from the Edit menu. Type a third set of information, perhaps along these lines:

First Name	Suzie
Last Name	Khiou
Address	1 Doormouse Ave.
Gift	Harley
Adjective	expensive
Part of	garage

4. Fabulous! You're really cooking now. As a final wise step, choose Save from the File menu. Type *Gift List* as the name of your database.

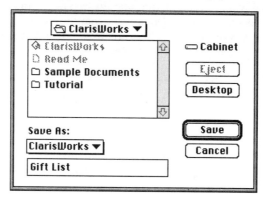

5. Click Save to preserve your database on the hard disk.

Forming the form letter

Next, you're going to write the actual text. At each place where you want to use somebody's name (or other gift-related information), you'll ask ClarisWorks to slap in the appropriate info.

1. Choose New from the File menu. (Once again, you're asked to choose the kind of document you want.)

2. Click Word Processor. Click OK.

   Now you get a sparkling new sheet of electronic typing paper.

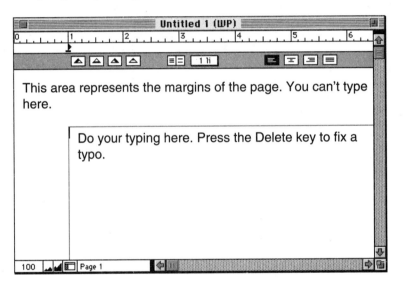

Incidentally, if you have a small-screen Mac like a Classic or a PowerBook, you probably don't want all that margin area eating up your screen. You can hide it easily enough: choose Document from the Edit menu. A dialog box appears; click the Show Margins checkbox to deselect it. And then click OK. Now your whole screen is filled with typeable area.

Now then — on with the form letter. You'll start the letter with the address, of course. Yet the address will be *different* on each letter! This is where mail-merging is handy:

3. From the File menu, choose Mail Merge. When the little window appears, you'll see your database name, "Gift List," prominently displayed. Just click OK (to tell ClarisWorks that Gift List is the database you want to work with).

Now a strange-looking window appears:

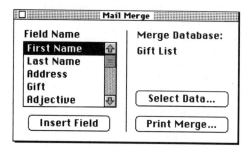

In the scrolling list you see the *field names* from your database. Here's how it works:

4. Point to *First Name* and double-click.

See what happened? The program popped a placeholder for the First Name right into your letter. When you print, instead of *<<First Name,>>* it will say *Josephine.*

5. Type a space. In the Mail Merge window, point to *Last Name* and double-click. Press Return; then point to the Mail Merge window again and double-click *Address.*

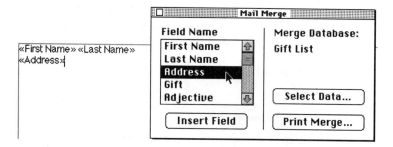

Before you continue typing, you may want to drag the little Mail Merge window off to the side of your screen as best you can. (To move the window, drag its title bar.) You're going to want to see both it and your typing simultaneously.

6. Press Return a couple of times. Type *Dear,* followed by a space.

7. Point to the words *First Name* in the Mail Merge window, as you did a moment ago. Double-click. Type a comma. Your letter should look something like this:

```
«First Name» «Last Name»
«Address»

Dear «First Name»,
```

8. This is where it gets good. Press Return a couple of returns. Type *I nearly cried when I unwrapped the incredible,* followed by a space.

9. Double-click the word *Gift* in the Mail Merge window.

10. Continue typing: *you gave me for my wedding. It is far and away the most* (and now double-click *Adjective* in the Mail Merge window) *gift I will ever receive.*

   Are you getting the hang of this? At each place where you want ClarisWorks to substitute a piece of information from your Gift List database, you insert a little <<placeholder>>. Check your work against the figure that follows.

   To see the last field name, *Part of House,* you have to use the Mail Merge window's scroll bar. Then finish the letter as follows:

11. Type: *It will look sensational in the* (double-click *Part of House* in the Mail Merge window) *of our new home.*

12. Press the Return key twice and finish up like this: *I had to write this personal note to you and you alone, so you'd know how much I treasure your gift above all the others. Love, Marge.*

```
«First Name» «Last Name»
«Address»


Dear «First Name»,

I nearly cried when I unwrapped the incredible «Gift» you gave me for my wedding. It
is far and away the most «Adjective» gift I will ever receive.

It will look sensational in the «Part of House» of our new home.

I had to write this personal note to you and you alone, so you'd know how much I
treasure your gift above all the others.

Love, Marge.
```

It may look impersonal now. But when these letters are printed, it'll be impossible to tell that each one wasn't typed separately.

Anyway, go ahead and choose Save from the File menu. Type *Thank-you letter,* and click Save.

The graphics zone: designing a letterhead

You'll read a lot more about graphics programs in the next couple of sections. But just to show you how you can tie everything together, let's whip up a quick letterhead in the Graphics module.

1. Choose New from the File menu. Our friend, the New Document dialog box, appears. As you've no doubt already figured out, this time you should select Graphics. Click OK.

   Claris Works shows you its drawing window. The grid of dotted lines is there to give things a nice architectural look; it won't appear in the finished printout.

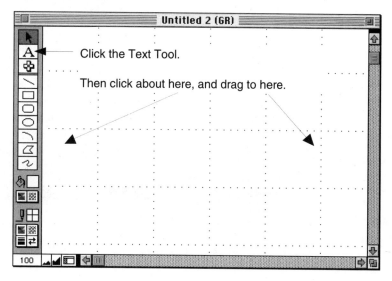

See the tool icons on the left side of your screen? They're pretty much covered on page 135. Now then:

1. Click the text tool (it looks like a letter A). Drag across the screen, as shown in the figure.

2. Use the Font menu; choose Times. Use the Size menu; choose 24 Point.

3. Type three spaces, then a long dash. (To make a long dash, hold down the Shift and Option keys, and type a hyphen.) Type *A Very Personal Note.* Type another long dash, then three more spaces.

4. Press the Enter key so that handles appear around your text. Using the Alignment submenu of the Format menu, choose Center.

5. Finally, you'll add that elegant white-lettering-against-black look that shows up on so many corporate annual reports. At the left side of your screen, there's a set of odd-looking icons. Find the one immediately below the tiny pouring paint can icon, as shown by the cursor below:

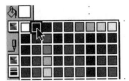

This icon is actually a pop-out palette. Keep the mouse button pressed, and drag carefully to the right, until the pointer is on the solid black square, as shown at right (above). (If you have a black-and-white Mac, choose the *word* "Black.") Release the mouse.

You've just used the Fill palette to color in the entire text block with black. Which is just great, except that now the text is a solid black rectangle! To fix the problem, you need to make the *text white*.

6. From the Text Color submenu of the Format menu, choose White. Ta-da!

The return of Copy and Paste

All that remains is for you to slap this letterhead into your mail-merge letter.

1. From the Edit menu, choose Copy.

2. Now you have to return to your word-processing document. Here's a quick way to pull it to the front: From the Window menu, choose Thank-You

Letter (WP). (WP stands for Word-Processing document, DB stands for Database, and GR stands for Graphics.) Your letter springs to the fore.

3. From the Format menu, choose Insert Header. (A *header* is an area at the top of every page, above whatever text you've typed. In this case, it looks like an empty text area.)

4. From the Edit menu, choose Paste.

Et voilà...your graphic pops neatly into the header.

You've actually done it: combined a database, a word processor, and a drawing program in a single project! For a real kick, choose Print from the File menu and watch how the program automatically replaces actual names for the <<placeholders>> on the screen.

—*A Very Personal Note*—

Suzie Khiou
1 Doormouse La.
San Francisco, CA 94108

Dear Suzie,

I nearly cried when I unwrapped the incredible Harley you gave me for my wedding. It is far and away the most expensive gift I will ever receive.

It will look sensational in the garage of our new home.

I had to write this personal note to you and you alone, so you'd know how much I treasure your gift above all the others.

Love, Marge.

The only parts of ClarisWorks we've left unexplored are the spreadsheet (which I couldn't figure out how to tie in to a thank-you letter) and the Communications module. Spreadsheets are covered on page 157. And if you have a modem and want to learn about the Communications program, then the little extra ClarisWorks manual does a nice job of explaining how to make your phone line a highway to the world of information.

MacDraw Pro, Canvas 3.0, SuperPaint 3.0

All of these programs, and a healthy helping of others, work essentially alike. They're called *drawing programs.* As much as that sounds like they'd be the same things as *painting programs,* they're not.

Painting programs create art called *bitmapped* graphics. When you lay down some "paint," it's stored as a bunch of dots. You can erase them, but you can't change the original shape you painted — a circle, say, or a letter of the alphabet — because the Mac no longer thinks of them as a circle or a letter. It just thinks of them as a bunch of painted little dots. The advantage: You have control over each individual dot, and you have dot-manipulation tools like the Spray Can. In the figure below, note (1) the speckled effect, and (2) the fact that you can drag a chunk of circle out of the original collection of dots:

Drawing programs, on the other hand, create *object-oriented* graphics. When you draw a circle, the Mac doesn't store it as a map of black dots. It remembers that you drew a *circle,* of a fixed shading and size. That means that you could never speckle it, and you could certainly never erase (or remove) a chunk of it.

But the advantage of drawing programs is that, later, you can return to that circle and move it by dragging it. Or you can overlap another object on top of it — and later change your mind. Or you can change a circle's shading long after you drew it. Or, as shown below, you can tug a circle's handles to stretch it.

Drawing programs tend to print out with much sharper quality than painting programs.

On beyond zebra

It's worth knowing that there's yet a *third* type of graphics program. Ever read *USA Today?* How about *Time* magazine? Well, then surely you've seen Sunday newspaper Stop-N-Shop ad inserts showing little line drawings of Clorox and Fig Newtons?

The drawings and diagrams in all of these fine publications are typically produced with either FreeHand or Illustrator, called *PostScript* graphics programs. Printouts from these programs are incredibly smooth and high quality. When used with a color printer, these illustration programs can be (and are) used for package designs, brochures, maps, you name it. These two professional programs may be in the top ten, but they sure ain't in the *beginner's* top ten, so I'm not even gonna touch them — but their operation has much in common with the drawing-type programs described here.

Concepts

The palette in all of these drawing programs contains the same basic tools. Here's the *Reader's Digest* condensed version:

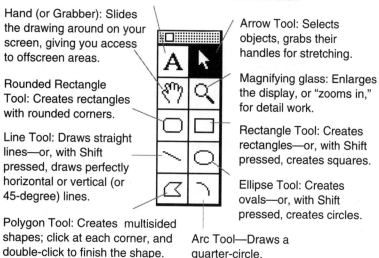

Text Tool: Lets you add type to your artwork. You can edit this text later.

Hand (or Grabber): Slides the drawing around on your screen, giving you access to offscreen areas.

Rounded Rectangle Tool: Creates rectangles with rounded corners.

Line Tool: Draws straight lines—or, with Shift pressed, draws perfectly horizontal or vertical (or 45-degree) lines.

Polygon Tool: Creates multisided shapes; click at each corner, and double-click to finish the shape.

Arrow Tool: Selects objects, grabs their handles for stretching.

Magnifying glass: Enlarges the display, or "zooms in," for detail work.

Rectangle Tool: Creates rectangles—or, with Shift pressed, creates squares.

Ellipse Tool: Creates ovals—or, with Shift pressed, creates circles.

Arc Tool—Draws a quarter-circle.

Each program has a few goodies of its own, too, but these basics are always included.

To draw something, click the tool (and release the button), move to a blank part of the screen where you want to place the object, hold down the mouse button, and drag. When you let go, you'll see the new line or shape enclosed by small black *handles*. Using the arrow tool, you can drag these handles to stretch or resize the object you just drew. Or click in the middle of it to drag the object to a new location.

Or just click an object to make its handles show. Once they appear — letting you know that the object is selected — you can use the menus to change the object's appearance. For example, suppose you draw a thin line (below left). While it's selected, you can choose a new line thickness (below middle) from the line thickness palette (every program has one). The result: The same line has a different thickness (below right).

Using the palette of colors (or of patterns), you can change the color (or pattern) that fills the inside of a shape the same way: Select, then apply.

When you press the Shift key while you draw something, the Mac constrains the movement of your mouse to flat or symmetrical movements. For instance, press Shift when you draw a line, and the line will be perfectly horizontal, vertical, or 45-degree diagonal. Press Shift while you draw a rectangle, and it will be a perfect square. And so on.

Selecting and grouping multiple objects

In the Finder, after you click one icon, you can select additional icons by Shift-clicking them (that is, clicking them while pressing the Shift key). In a word processor, if you have selected a word, you can extend the selection by Shift-clicking some place later in the paragraph.

Yes indeed, Mr. Watson, there is a pattern here. This Shift-click-to-extend-a-selection deal is a common Mac technique. Same thing in drawing programs: Click to select one object, Shift-click to select others.

Once you've got a bunch of objects selected, you can *group* them — combine them into a single new object — using (what else?) the Group command. You can even group groups. You may want to group objects in this way just to make sure their alignment to each other doesn't get disturbed.

Handiest yet, you can *un*group a group, or even ungroup a grouped group of groups. (I'll give you a moment to work on that.) Drawing programs ungroup objects in the same order in which they were grouped. So imagine that you group objects A and B together, and then group object C to the first group. The first time you use the Ungroup command, you'll wind up with the A/B group and the C object loose; apply Ungroup a second time to split up A and B.

Text FX

One of the nicest things about drawing programs is that text is text, and text it remains. Text in a bitmapped program (like MacPaint) turns into a text-shaped collection of painted *dots* instantly. You can't edit the text or change the font or correct a typo, once you're done typing. And the printout looks exactly as jagged as it does on the screen:

> A Green Onion

In a drawing program, though, each piece of text remains editable inside its little boundary rectangle. You can change the font or the size of the text or the dimensions of this rectangle at any time. And because the Mac still thinks of it as text (and not dots), it prints out at full text sharpness on a laser printer or StyleWriter:

> A Green Onion

Once you create a text block, you can paste it into a word processor and drag those little corner boxes. The word processor thinks it's just a plain old graphic and proceeds to squish it any way you like. The result is fantastic text effects you couldn't create in a word processor alone:

> A Green Onion
>
> A Green Onion

Beyond these concepts, a drawing program really doesn't require a degree in rocket science. I now release you to your creative juices.

MacPaint, SuperPaint, UltraPaint, Studio/1, and Others

There's about a dozen of these programs, all of which (except for Studio/1) end with the word *paint*. Most of them work alike — only the frills differ from program to program. Super-, Ultra-, and PixelPaint work in color (so do the expensive pro-level painting programs like Photoshop, ColorStudio, and Studio/32). The rest are black and white.

They're called *painting* programs because they produce *bitmapped* artwork. (For a discussion of what that means, see the introduction to the MacDraw section, above.) Printouts from bitmapped programs tend to be a little bit jagged since the Mac is reproducing the Mac screen when it prints out.

There's not much mystical hidden knowledge to be unearthed in paint programs. Once you've used a tool, you've pretty much mastered it for life. Here, then, is a typical Tool palette. You click a tool (and release), move the cursor to the page, and then drag across your white screen. With this guide — and the all-important Undo command in the Edit menu — you're well on your way to the world's toniest art galleries.

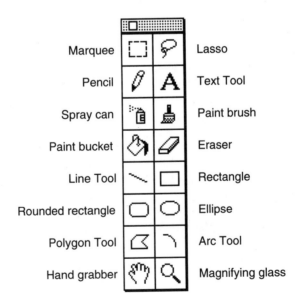

Marquee			Lasso
Pencil			Text Tool
Spray can			Paint brush
Paint bucket			Eraser
Line Tool			Rectangle
Rounded rectangle			Ellipse
Polygon Tool			Arc Tool
Hand grabber			Magnifying glass

Marquee and Lasso

These tools don't create any marks on the artwork. Instead, they're *selection* tools. They draw a dotted, shimmering line as you drag the mouse; you're creating an enclosure. Anything within the enclosure — the selected area — will be affected by your next move. For example, you can click within the selection to drag that chunk into a new position. Or press the Delete key to erase it. You can also apply special effects to the selected region, such as Invert (which swaps white areas for black, and vice versa) and Trace Edges (a bizarre one; try it).

There are two important differences between the Marquee and the Lasso. The Marquee always creates rectangular selected areas, *including whatever white space* is inside the rectangle. In the following illustration, you can see that when

Caveat lector for people who don't like generalizations

The Mac screen has 72 dots per inch. (In elite computing circles, this is abbreviated *72 dpi.*) A laser printer's printouts look much sharper because it crams in 300 dpi. Therefore, when you print a MacPaint document on a laser printer (or a StyleWriter), the results appear especially jagged.

There are two exceptions to this rule-o'-thumb. First of all, some programs — like SuperPaint, Studio/1, and ArtWorks — let you *edit* your painting at 300 dpi, the same as the laser. That way you have the best of both worlds: You get high-resolution printouts (typical of a drawing program), but you get the fine control over every dot (as in a painting program). The downside is that 300 dpi editing makes your Mac work harder. It takes

more memory, more disk space, and more time to process each editing move you make.

The other exception to the Jaggy-Printout Law is the Graphics Smoothing option. Before you print, choose Page Setup from the File menu (doesn't matter what program you're in — every program has this command). Make sure the Graphics Smoothing option is selected. When you print this way, the Mac's internal graphics gnomes run around with sandpaper and smooth out the rough edges of your graphics (see below for a before-and-after example). It's not quite as sharp-looking as the 300 dpi editing mode, but it's fine for flyers and stuff — and besides, the jagginess is actually a "look" that certain Greenwich Village artists I know think is kinda neat.

Jaggies

Smoothies

you drag a rectangular selection on top of a dark object (left), the white part of the selection remains opaque (right):

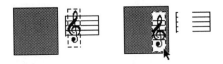

The Lasso, on the other hand, requires you to draw a circle all the way around the image you're trying to select. When you let go of the mouse, the dotted line snaps like a rubber band inward, enclosing only black regions of your artwork (below left). Therefore, when the selected part is dragged on top of a dark object, the latter shows through the former (below right):

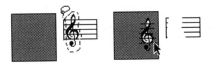

Pencil

The Pencil is pretty tame. Drag across the white area to draw a one-dot-thick line.

There's only one trick to it. If you begin your line by clicking in a *dark* spot, the line you draw will be white, even if you cross over into a white area.

Text Tool

Not much to this one: Click in a blank area, start typing. While you're typing, you can press Delete (or Backspace) to fix a typo; in some programs you can even use the mouse to drag through stretches of text for editing. But beware! The instant you click the mouse outside of the text box, your text freezes into a noneditable clump of dots (yes, a *bitmap*).

In most programs, you can double-click the Text Tool icon to set the font and size for your type (before you do the typing). Obviously, once you click the mouse outside the text box (and freeze the text into a bitmap), it's too late to change type characteristics. You have to delete the whole thing if you want to change it.

That's such a bummer that some programs, like Studio/1 and SuperPaint, have a separate transparent layer where you can type real, editable, word-processable text that never turns into a bitmap. Of course, bitmaps have some advantages; after selecting one with the Lasso or Marquee, you can apply any *transformation* commands to it (found in a menu): Stretch, Distort, Slant, whatever. See here:

Spray can

Painting at its finest. Drag it across the painting area to create a fine mist of dots, just like an airbrush or spray paint can. Dawdle over an area to make it darker; hurry across the screen for a lighter mist. The color (or pattern) of the spray is whatever color (or pattern) you've selected from the color (or pattern) pop-up menu. In some programs, you can double-click the Spray can icon to produce a dialog box, where you can adjust the rate and size of the spray. For post-pubescent thrills, try drawing a subway car and then spraypaint your name across it.

Eraser

Pretty basic. Drag across dark areas to erase them. Don't forget to zoom in (enlarge the screen image, using the Magnifying Glass) for detail work. For more mature thrills, draw your ex-spouse on the screen and then erase his/her head.

Line Tool

Choose a line thickness (there's usually a pop-up menu for this purpose) before you draw. Then drag to create a straight line. If you want a perfectly horizontal, vertical, or 45-degree line, press Shift while you drag. Some programs also let you specify the color or pattern of the line.

Rectangle, Rounded rectangle, Ellipse, Polygon, Arc

These shape tools pretty much work alike: Drag diagonally to produce the shape. (The Polygon Tool works differently — click once for each corner point of your multisided shape; then double-click to finish the shape.)

In any case, you can usually control both the color (or pattern) of the *interior* of the shape as well as that of the *outline* of the shape by using pop-up color (or pattern) menus. The Line Thickness pop-up menu governs the thickness of the outline. As before, the Shift key is the great constrainer: Press it to create a perfect square (with the Rectangle Tool), circle (with the Ellipse Tool), and so on.

Hand grabber

Unless you have a large monitor, you usually can't even see a full page of art at once. You can always use the scroll bars to slide your image up or down on your screen. But the Hand grabber is much more direct — just drag in the direction you want to shift the painting.

Each program has its own keyboard shortcut for this handy tool; usually it's the spacebar or the Option key. When this special key is pressed, your cursor turns into the Hand grabber; when you release the key, you return to whatever tool you had previously selected.

Magnifying glass

Click this tool then click the painting to zoom in and/or enlarge the display for detail work. Of course, you're not actually making anything bigger (in terms of its printout); you're really just magnifying the *screen* image to get more control over those pesky dots. Keep zooming in until you get an idea of how those little dots make up your painting. You can use the Pencil to click the dots either black or white.

To zoom out again or return to normal size, you usually press Option while clicking the painting.

Microsoft Word

Q: Where does an 800-pound gorilla sit?

A: Anywhere it wants.

Refer to this age-old discourse the next time somebody asks you why Microsoft Word, a program with numerous flaws and irritations, is the best-selling Macintosh program of all time. Microsoft is a gargantuan software company in Washington state. They sell so much software that the founder/owner (Bill Gates) is the youngest multibillionaire in history. Probably because of Microsoft's huge presence in the IBM-PC world, it's the 800-pound gorilla in the Mac world, too.

Of course, Microsoft Word isn't *bad*. In fact, it's got some truly wonderful features, one of which is that *everybody* uses Word. (Well, the vast majority of people do.) That means that when you hand your letter (on a disk) to a friend, you usually don't have to worry whether or not she's got the software needed to read it.

Anyway, you've already absorbed most of the basics of word processing (in Chapter 3). Word has a few fancy features worth learning, though (and does some basic features in interesting ways).

Views

To start a new document, double-click the Word icon. You arrive at a blank screen. Go ahead and start typing your Oscar-winning screenplay. Use the usual word processing techniques (Delete to backspace, drag through text to select it, use the Edit menu to copy and paste, and so on) to whip it into shape.

You'll discover, though, that your piece of paper appears to be endless, as though it's delivered on a never-ending roll of Bounty. That's because you're in Normal view, where you never see a page end. (The end of a page is symbolized by a thin dotted line, but you sort of have to watch for it.) In Normal view, you don't get to see page-related elements like page numbers, either. They're hidden until you go to another view.

If you want to see a more accurate display of what you'll get when you print, choose Page Layout from the View menu. Things start to bog down in Page Layout view — that is, it takes longer to scroll around and visit different corners of your document. But you clearly see where each page ends, and you get to see things like page numbers and multiple columns.

There's also an Outline view, which is pretty bizarre. I'll let you cuddle up to the manual for that one.

Finally, there's Print Preview, an absolutely vital and useful view. (Just to make sure the program isn't too easy to use, they've put the Print Preview command in the File menu, not the View menu with the others.) In Print Preview you get to see the entire page — in fact, two side-by-side pages — no matter what size monitor you have.

To change the margins

Print Preview also provides the easiest way to adjust the margins. Just drag the small black handles; remember that you're adjusting the margins for *all* the pages when you do this.

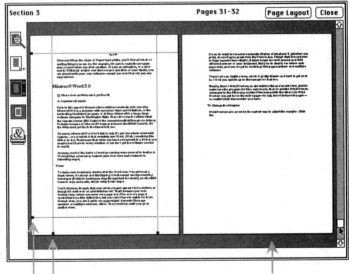

Drag these black handles (and the others like them) to adjust the margins . . .

. . . and then click the gray background to see the changes.

To return to Normal view from Print Preview, click Close.

Using the Ribbon and Ruler for quick formatting

When you're in Normal or Page Layout view editing text, there are two information strips across the top of the window. The Ribbon is the top one; the Ruler is below it. (If you don't see these strips, somebody must have hidden them. Choose their names from the View menu.)

For the most part, the Ribbon controls *character formatting:* the size of type, the style (bold or italic), and the font. To make them work, you *first* have to select some text you've already typed — by dragging through it. Of course, you can also make some of these settings just *before* you begin to type.

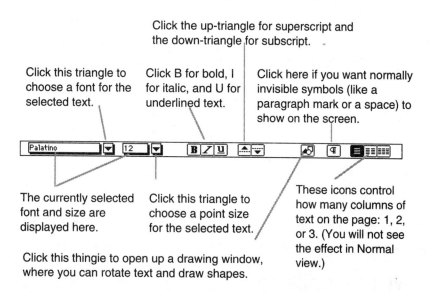

Click the up-triangle for superscript and the down-triangle for subscript.

Click this triangle to choose a font for the selected text.

Click B for bold, I for italic, and U for underlined text.

Click here if you want normally invisible symbols (like a paragraph mark or a space) to show on the screen.

The currently selected font and size are displayed here.

Click this triangle to choose a point size for the selected text.

These icons control how many columns of text on the page: 1, 2, or 3. (You will not see the effect in Normal view.)

Click this thingie to open up a drawing window, where you can rotate text and draw shapes.

Below the Ribbon is the Ruler. These icons apply to an entire *paragraph* at a time — and remember, a "paragraph" is anything you've typed that ends with a Return. To select a paragraph (which you have to do before using the Ruler), you don't have to highlight it. Just click inside so that the insertion point is

The lazy person's guide to selecting text

Word has a trillion shortcuts for selecting text, which greatly reduce the requirement for having a surgeon's hand with the mouse. Here are a few favorites.

Shortcut 1: Select one line of text by clicking in the *selection strip* to the left of the text.

> Linda choked back the sobs as the explosions shook the scarred earth around her. She fingered the ashy remnants of the glider.
> "Happy...happy Groundhog Day, Harry," she murmured noiselessly.

Shortcut 2: To select a paragraph, double-click in the selection strip. Or triple-click inside a paragraph.

> Linda choked back the sobs as the explosions shook the scarred earth around her. She fingered the ashy remnants of the glider.
> "Happy...happy Groundhog Day, Harry," she murmured noiselessly.

Shortcut 3: Select a longer stretch of text by clicking at the beginning of the part you want then *Shift* and clicking the end point, even if it is pages and pages away.

> Linda choked back the sobs as the explosions shook the scarred earth around her. She fingered the ashy remnants of the glider.
> "Happy...happy Groundhog Day, Harry," she murmured noiselessly.

Shortcut 4: Select one sentence by Command-clicking in it (in other words, click while pressing the ⌘ key).

> Linda choked back the sobs as the explosions shook the scarred earth around her. She fingered the ashy remnants of the glider.
> "Happy...happy Groundhog Day, Harry," she murmured noiselessly.

What's the difference?

What's the difference between Word 5.1 and previous versions? The primary addition is the Toolbar. You can rearrange these buttons, if you want, or create a different set, using the Toolbar menu. But here's what the factory-installed buttons do. (If you have a big screen, you'll see a few additional buttons.)

Open a document
Print   Cut   Paste
Turn paragraphs into a bulleted list
Print an envelope   Toolbar menu

Save your work   Copy   Undo   Un-indent   Indent   Change case
Start a new blank document
Check spelling

blinking within it. (If you want to select more than one paragraph, though, you do have to highlight the text by dragging.) Remember the Macintosh mantra: Select, then apply. Select, then apply...

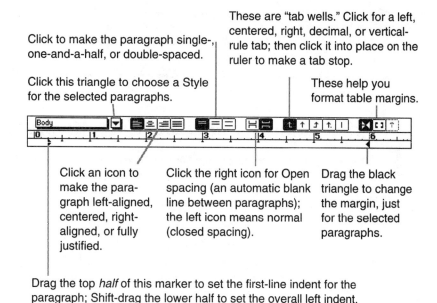

Click to make the paragraph single-, one-and-a-half, or double-spaced.

Click this triangle to choose a Style for the selected paragraphs.

These are "tab wells." Click for a left, centered, right, decimal, or vertical-rule tab; then click it into place on the ruler to make a tab stop.

These help you format table margins.

Click an icon to make the para-graph left-aligned, centered, right-aligned, or fully justified.

Click the right icon for Open spacing (an automatic blank line between paragraphs); the left icon means normal (closed spacing).

Drag the black triangle to change the margin, just for the selected paragraphs.

Drag the top *half* of this marker to set the first-line indent for the paragraph; Shift-drag the lower half to set the overall left indent.

Moving text by dragging it

One of the coolest features in Word 5 — a feature no other word processor has — is "drag-and-drop" text manipulation. You can highlight some text and simply drag it into a new position, without doing the tawdry cut-and-paste routine.

For example, in the sentence below, you select the word *miserable* by double-clicking it. Then point the cursor at the highlighted portion, and drag it carefully into a new position and let go. The result is shown in the lower example.

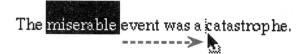

No go?

If you can't get drag-and-drop to work, somebody probably turned it off. Choose Preferences from the Tools menu, click General, and check the checkbox at the bottom of the list of options. (Of course, this trick, like this whole discussion, applies only to Word 5.0 or later.)

Page numbers, headers, date-stamping

Suppose there's something you want to appear at the top (or bottom) of every single page (like *TOP SECRET: Destroy this document after Xeroxing)*. Go to Normal view. From the View menu, choose Header (or Footer for the bottom of the page). A new window opens. Anything you type in here will conveniently appear at the top of every page.

If you click the little page number icon, Word will put a page number (at the insertion point) on every page. Click the middle icon, which is supposed to look like a calendar, to pop the date into this header. And click the clock to insert the time. Go ahead and use all the normal formatting controls — fonts, sizes, styles — to touch up the header text. If you want to see how it looks, choose Page Layout from the View menu.

Raw power: Style sheets

In this book, you see the same kinds of styles used over and over again. For example, this paragraph has specific margins and type characteristics, but the subhead ("Raw power: Style sheets") looks different. Yet I didn't have to reset all those margins and type styles for every appearance of a subhead. I just used styles.

You can read the manual for the full spiel on styles. But here's the easy way to do it.

Type some text. Format the heck out of it. Fiddle with the indents (see the Ruler diagram above). Change the type style. Make it double-spaced or whatever. Adjust the tab stops.

Finally, when it's good and ready, click the Style Name box and give this formatting a style name. Go ahead, just type it. Call it Subhead.

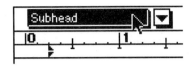

When you press Return, Word will ask you to confirm that you want to create a new Style called Subhead. Click OK.

Now the *next* time you need to format a paragraph this way, don't bother doing all that formatting. Just plop the insertion point anywhere in the paragraph; then, using the small black triangle to the right of the Style name box (on the ruler), choose Subhead. You've just changed all the formatting characteristics at once.

Now here's the beauty part. Let's say you've got 12,029 subheads in your document. (No *wonder* your editors say you're long-winded.) And now you decide that you want to change the font. For all 12,029 of them.

Fortunately, it's incredibly easy since you assigned them all to one style. Just triple-click *one* subhead to select it. (Triple-clicking highlights the entire para-graph.) Change the font (or make any other changes you want to make). Now, using the Style pop-up menu (that old black triangle again), choose the *same* Style name — Subhead.

Word will ask you what you're doing. Click "Redefine the style based on selection" and then click OK. In the blink of an eye, all 12,029 occurrences of this style change.

Checking your spelling

Click at the beginning of the document. Choose Spelling from the Tools menu. A dialog box appears, in which Word will display each spelling error it finds; click Suggest to see some guesses as to what word you intended. Double-click one to replace the misspelled word in the document.

If none of this happens, and you get some kind of message telling you that the Spelling command isn't installed, then, by gum, the Spelling command isn't installed. (When you first install Word, you're given the choice of which features to include. Thesaurus, Grammar, Hyphenation, and the drawing module are some of the others available. You can install them later, as long as you have the original Word floppy disks.)

PageMaker

The idea of *page layout* software is amazingly simple. You see a blank page. You dump different kinds of page elements onto it: text, graphics, straight lines, photos, whatever. Then you drag them around like tiles on the page, until they're in an attractive arrangement. This, kids, is page layout. Without a single union laborer being paid $180 per hour to paste waxed paper strips onto dummy pages (which is how they used to do page layout), you can publish and distribute your very own *Neighborhood Anarchist Weekly* — you can become a "desktop publisher." And since the Macintosh brought this fun new pasttime into people's homes and offices, every magazine, brochure, newsletter, flyer, and newspaper from *USA Today* to *Time* is designed this way.

Starting a new document

Double-click the PageMaker icon. You get a dialog box that asks what size paper you want to use: Letter (8 ½-inch × 11-inch), Legal (8 ½-inch × 14-inch), or Tabloid (11-inch × 17-inch), which is what the *National Enquirer* uses.

The Master Pages

Some elements of your publication are probably going to appear on every page: the logo, the page number, the issue date. Instead of making you retype *Bathroom Fixture Journal* at the top of every page, you can just type it once — on the Master Pages. To get to the Master Pages, you click the little dog-eared page icons in the far lower left of the window:

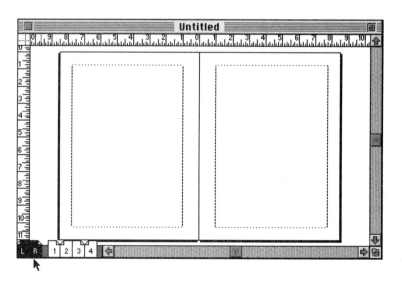

Now you see two blank pages — the Right and Left Master Pages (if your document has facing pages), whose image lurks behind every individual page of your publication. This is where the logo, the page number (which you create using the Text Tool by holding down ⌘-Option and typing a P), the chapter head, or whatever.

When you're done working with the Master Pages, click one of the individual page icons (each corresponds to a page of your document) to return to one-page-at-a-time editing.

Adding text

Ideally, you're supposed to write the articles for your newsletter (or whatever) in a word processor like Word. Then go to PageMaker and choose Place from the File menu. A list box appears; find your word-processed article, double-click it, and finally click the mouse (or drag to create a rectangle) on the appropriate starting page. The article spills onto the page, stretching from margin to margin (or filling the rectangle). Now, by grabbing the corner handles, you can resize or reshape the article's layout on the page:

You can also shorten the article's length by dragging the little window shade handle at the bottom:

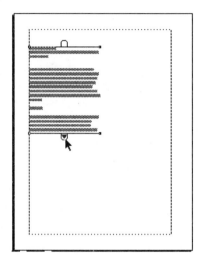

Of course, if you're thinking that an article needs shortening, window-shading it into a shorter box is only wishful thinking. All you've done is to place *less* of the article on the page — the rest of it is chopped off but needs to go someplace.

To specify where the rest of the article should go (as in, "continued on page C4"), ⌘-click the "windowshade handle" at the bottom of the text block. The cursor turns into a "loaded text" icon, telling you that the program is ready to pour the remainder of the article wherever your little heart desires. If you *click* someplace, PageMaker will dump the remainder of the article from margin to margin. If you *drag* to create a rectangle, the article will only fill that rectangle, as shown here.

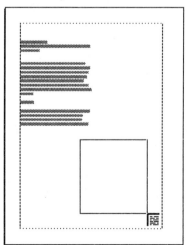

The neatest part of *flowing* text from box to box like this is that if you later have to cut some material from the beginning of the article, the text will flow, snake-like, through every text box it's been poured into. You'll never lose a single precious word.

If you could use some guidance in drawing text boxes, place your pointer in the ruler at the side (or top) of the screen and drag onto the page. A thin "guide" line comes with the pointer, which you can drag into position. (Hint: For consistent pages, place some guides on the *Master Pages,* so they'll be in the same place on every page.) These guides don't print; they're simply straight edges to help you align things, as you can see in the example below.

Tweaking to perfection

You can zoom in or out by using the Page menu commands and change the text style by selecting text (with the Text Tool, which looks like an A) and applying fonts, styles, and other attributes using the Type menu. For heavy-duty text editing, you'll want to use the built-in word processor, the Story Editor (choose Edit Story from the Edit menu).

Add straight lines, boxes, and other graphic accents using the appropriate tools on the PageMaker Tool palette; the Element menu controls line thickness and so on. You can either paste in graphics or import them using the Place command in the File menu.

Just remember that the Pointer Tool is what you need to draw, move, resize, delete, shorten, and lengthen text blocks. But you need the Text Tool to do everything that pertains to type, including changing fonts, sizes, styles, line spacing, and so on.

Once you become a power-user publishing mogul (God forbid), you may appreciate the Styles palette, which gives you a list of predefined paragraph and text formatting attributes. (See the description of Word, above, to get an idea of why these are useful and how to use them.)

QuarkXPress

QuarkXPress is PageMaker's rival. Both have ardent supporters. (In fact, if you're ever on a blind date with a Mac person, it's a sure conversation starter: "So which do you like — Quark or PageMaker?") The differences are getting smaller and smaller, as each company comes out with an update that duplicates the features of the other.

Anyway, this is not the book to solve the great debate. This *is* the book to help you muddle through a few basic tasks when they're thrown at you.

The basics

Quark (for some reason, everybody refers to this program by the name of its company) does pretty much the same thing as PageMaker, but the methods are different. The Tool palette looks like this:

⊕	Item Tool
🖑	Content Tool
↺	Rotation Tool
🔍	Zoom Tool
Ⓐ	Text Box Tool
⊠	Rectangular Picture Box Tool
⊠	Rounded-Corner Rectangular Picture Box Tool
⊗	Oval Picture Box Tool
⊘	Polygon Picture Box Tool
+	Orthogonal Line Tool
╲	Line Tool
⚭	Linking Tool
⚭	Unlinking Tool

The rules of thumb: Use the Item Tool to delete, move, and copy *boxes* (text and picture boxes), but use the Content Tool to resize or edit the *text and pictures themselves*. You can actually leave the Content Tool selected all the time since it's what you use for typing, editing, adjusting text box corner handles, cropping pictures, and so on — and whenever you need to move something, press the ⌘ key and drag. (The ⌘ key switches you temporarily to the Item Tool.)

To create a document, double-click the QuarkXPress icon and then choose New from the File menu. A dialog box appears, where you specify the page size and margins you want; then click OK.

To import some text, click the Text Box Tool and *draw a rectangle.* (You can't paste or import text or graphics in Quark without first drawing a box to contain it.) Quark switches back to the Content Tool automatically; from the File menu, choose Get Text and select the word processing document you want to import. It appears in the selected text box automatically. As in PageMaker, you can now edit the text, drag the text box's corners to adjust its dimensions, and so on.

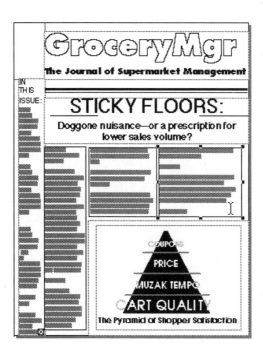

Linking to page C4

Quark's method of breaking a story up into separate text boxes requires the use of its Linking Tool. First, make sure you've actually drawn both text boxes on the screen, using the Text Block Tool. Now click the Linking Tool. Click the *first* text box and then the *second* text box — that's all there is to it. The text now flows freely from one to the other, even if you edit the text in either box.

What's especially useful about this method of linking is that you can *pre*-link text boxes that you've drawn on a Master Page. If you produce a newsletter, for example, that has roughly the same layout month after month, you could design an empty template containing ready-to-go, pre-linked, empty text boxes. When those lazy-slob writers are finally ready to turn in their stories, one Get Text command suffices to pour an article into your waiting Quark layout, and all flowing happens instantly.

Master Pages; rearranging pages

Quark's Document Layout palette shows a thumbnail view of all pages in your document, including any Master Pages. (You can have up to 127 *different* Master Pages, in case each section of your magazine has different common background elements.)

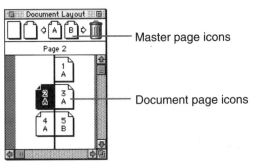

Master page icons

Document page icons

This Document Layout palette serves a number of useful functions:

✔ Double-click a page icon to make the document window jump to that page.

✔ Drag a page icon into a new position to rearrange your pages.

✔ Drag a Master page icon onto a Document page icon to change its background (master) elements.

✔ Double-click a Master page icon to edit that Master page.

✔ Drag a blank page (top left of the palette) or a Master page icon in between two existing Document page icons to insert a new page.

There's a bunch of other stuff the Document Layout window does, but this should get you started, and you can always use the QuarkXPress Help feature to read up on the other features.

Measurement Palette

Choose Measurement Palette from the View menu to see this useful little floating window full of precise numerical controls over the selected object. Click on any of these numbers to change them. Try changing the angle for a text box — it's fun!

Excel

Excel is the best-selling Macintosh *spreadsheet* program. If you're not familiar with a spreadsheet, get psyched — even if you only use 1 percent of its features, Excel can really be a godsend. It's for math, finances, balancing your checkbook, figuring out which of two mortgage plans is more favorable in the long run, charting the growth of your basement gambling operation, and other number-crunchy stuff.

Starting up

Double-click the Excel icon. A blank spreadsheet appears on your screen. It's a bunch of rows and columns, like a ledger book. The columns have letters and the rows are numbered. Each little rectangular cell is called, well, a *cell*. It's referred to by its letter and number: A1, for example.

To type a number into a cell, click the cell with the mouse and begin typing. Note that you don't do your typing (and editing) in the cell itself. Instead, all the action is in the editing strip at the top of the window. When you're done typing or editing, press Enter.

Formatting numbers and text

As you enter numbers, don't bother to format them with dollar signs, decimal points, and all that jazz. Formatting can be applied later. For instance, you could enter the following numbers, each of which has a different number of decimal places:

Now drag vertically through them with the pointer.

By now you can probably say it in your sleep: *In the world of Mac, you select something first and then act on it . . . Select, then apply . . .* Once the numbers are selected, you can format them all with dollar amounts in one fell swoop. See the little tiny pop-up menu at the upper-left corner of the screen? Choose Currency from this list.

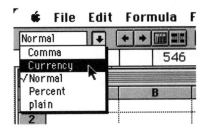

Instantly Excel formats all the selected numbers as dollar amounts. Note how it adds zeros (or rounds off excess decimal places) as necessary.

Spreading the sheet

Now it gets good. If you've been fooling around so far, erase everything you've done: Drag the cursor diagonally through it and then choose Clear from the Edit menu. We're gonna start you off fresh-like.

Click in cell B3 (that's column B, row 3; a spreadsheet is like a good game of Battleship). Type in *1963.*

To jump into the next cell to the right, press Tab. Or press the right arrow key. (You move to the *left* by pressing Shift-Tab — or the left arrow key.) In any case, enter *1973.* Repeat until you've filled in the years as shown below.

You move *down* a row by pressing Return or the down arrow key. Shift-Return moves you up a row, and so does the up arrow key. (There's a certain twisted logic to this, isn't there?)

You can also jump to any cell by clicking in it, of course. Now then: Go wild. With these navigational commands under your belt, type in the text and numbers as shown below. (Frankly, it doesn't make any difference *what* numbers you type. I made them all up anyway.)

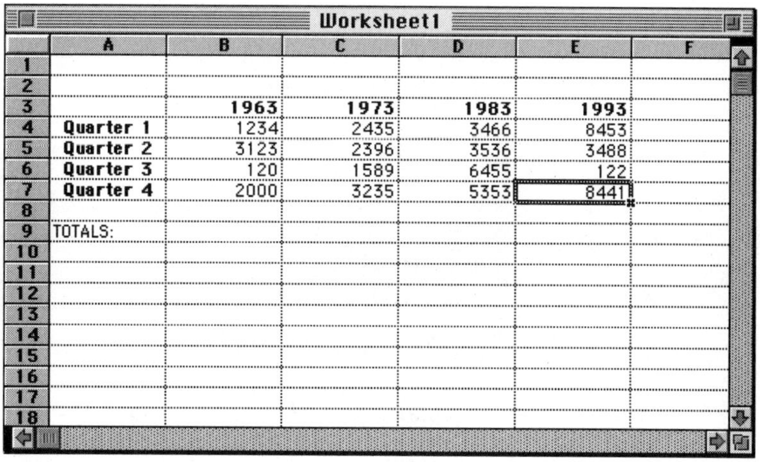

	A	B	C	D	E	F
1						
2						
3		1963	1973	1983	1993	
4	Quarter 1	1234	2435	3466	8453	
5	Quarter 2	3123	2396	3536	3488	
6	Quarter 3	120	1589	6455	122	
7	Quarter 4	2000	3235	5353	8441	
8						
9	TOTALS:					
10						
11						
12						
13						
14						
15						
16						
17						
18						

Worksheet1

Want to make the top row boldface, as shown above? Drag the cursor through the years. (Sounds like a high-tech country song, don't it?) Now click the B button in the ribbon at the top of the screen.

If you haven't guessed, **B** means Bold, and *I* means italic. (And I mean italic!)

Creating automatically calculating cells

Here comes the juicy part. Click in the Totals row, under the 1963 column of numbers. Click the funny Σ button on the ribbon. It's the Sum button, and it's some button.

In the formula bar at the top of the screen, you'll see that Excel has entered "=SUM(B3:B8)."

In English, the program is trying to say: "The number I'll enter into the cell you clicked (Total) is going to be the sum of . . . well, I suppose you mean the numbers directly *above* the cell you clicked — cells B3 down to B8." Isn't it smart to guess what you mean?

B3	X ✓	=SUM(B3:B8)	
			Fina
	A	**B**	**C**
1			
2			
3		1963	1973
4	Quarter 1	$1,234.00	$2,435.00
5	Quarter 2	$3,123.00	$2,396.00
6	Quarter 3	$120.00	$1,589.00
7	Quarter 4	$2,000.00	$3,235.00
8			
9	TOTALS:	=SUM(B3:B8)	
10			

Well, smart, but not quite smart enough. Because you *don't* want the number 1963 included in the total! So you can override Excel's guess by showing it which numbers you *do* want totaled . . . by dragging through them. Try it: While the dotted-line rectangle is still twinkling, drag vertically through the four cells *below* 1963. Then press Enter.

	B9		=SUM(B4:B7)
	A	**B**	**C**
1			
2			
3		1963	1'
4	Quarter 1	$1,234.00	$2,435
5	Quarter 2	$3,123.00	$2,396
6	Quarter 3	$120.00	$1,589
7	Quarter 4	$2,000.00	$3,235
8			
9	TOTALS:	6477	

Neat, huh? Excel automatically totals the four numbers you selected. But that's only the half of it. Now click one of the cells below the 1963 heading — and *change the number.* That's right, type a totally different number. (And press Enter when you're done typing. You always have to press Enter to tell Excel you're done working in a cell.) And voilà — the total *changed* automatically!

This is the origin of the phrase "What-if scenario." You can sit here all day, fiddling with the numbers in the 1963 column. As soon as you change a number and press Enter, the total will update itself. That's why it's so easy to compute a mortgage at 10 percent for five years, and see if it's better than one at 8 percent for seven years (or whatever).

Fill right, feel right

Now then. You have three other columns to contend with. Do you have to redo the Σ business each time? Nope. You've already explained to Excel how the Total row should work: It should add up the four numbers above it, *not* including the year at the top of the column.

So just take that magic total cell (B9 in the picture above) and *copy it* into the three cells to its right. Excel is smart enough to add up the right numbers in each column (no, it won't put the *1963* total into each cell).

Of course, you could use the regular Copy and Paste commands — but that's too tedious. Use the Fill Right command instead. Drag through the Totals row, starting with the 1963 total and extending through the three other years' total cells.

8				
9	TOTALS:	6477		
10				

Then, from the Edit menu, choose Fill Right (or press ⌘-R). Bingo! Excel intelligently copies the *formula* from the first cell and copies it into the other cells, totaling each column automatically. You may as well know that there's also a Fill Down command, used when you want to copy a formula to a series of cells *below* the one that contains it.

From here to infinity

Using the standard math symbols (+, –, / for division, and * for multiplication), you can build much more complicated auto-calculating cells than the simple SUM function described above. For example, you can use nested parentheses and the whole works. To make a cell calculate how many hours there are in ten years, for example, you'd click on it. Then, in the formula bar at the top of the screen, you'd type *=(24*365)*10* and press Enter. The formula always has to begin with the equal sign, but otherwise your equations can be as complicated as you want.

You can have formula cells that work with numbers from *other* formula cells, too — in the example above, you could create a Grand Total cell that would sum up the 1963, 1973, 1983, and 1993 totals automatically. There are even a few dozen more complex formula elements — financial, statistical, math, and time functions — listed in the Paste Function command (Edit menu), if you're into that kinky stuff.

Making a chart

There are a zillion options for charting, too, but here's the quick-and-dirty approach.

Drag through the table you created above — just the data part, not the totals in the bottom row. Once this section is highlighted, click the Chart Wizard button on the ribbon.

Now the cursor turns into a skinny little crosshair. Excel is waiting for you to show it where, and how big, to make the chart. Drag diagonally across the screen, either below the numbers (if your screen is big enough) or — what the heck — right on top of them. When you let go, a charming little chart pops up. (If a charming little *dialog box* appears instead, click the >> button.) Double-click the chart and then double-click an individual bar to adjust the colors and styles used in the chart.

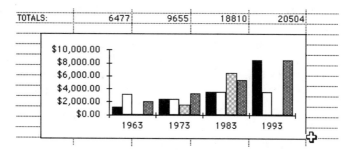

There are also outlining, drawing tools, macros, a database function, and probably a convenient toaster-oven . . . but this was supposed to be a crash course. If you want those frills, you'll have to actually put your nose in the manual.

FileMaker Pro

FileMaker is the king, queen, and princess of *database* programs. A database is just what it sounds like: a base of data — a pile of it, if you will — that you can view in a million different ways. Stop me if you've heard this one: Suppose you have a mailing list, and you want to know how many people in ZIP code 44122 have last names beginning with M. Or you have a list of 2,000 books and want to sort them by author's name or print a list only showing hardcover volumes or find out the publisher of a book of which you know only one word of the title. For all these tasks, a database is the way to go.

The really far-out feature of FileMaker is that you can set up several different *views* of the information. Suppose you have a mailing list for a party. You could set up your Data Entry view with great big 18-point bold type, which makes it easier for you to type in those names. You'd also want a Mailing Label layout, though, which neatly arranges the addresses side-by-side across the page, in a much smaller type size, so you can print and mail the invitations. Yet a third layout could be the Name-Tag view; it would place only the person's name (and not the address) in a cute font, preceded by the words "Hello! My name is:". Using these different layouts — of the same information — really lets you put the data to work, without having to do any retyping.

Weenie's world

At your favorite computer-nerd get-togethers, you'll occasionally hear the terms *relational database* and *flat-file database,* the latter with a sneer of technological superiority. These two types of databases have several distinguishing features.

A flat-file database is a simple list. You can sort it, print it, edit it, search it. It's fabulous for being a Rolodex, a recipe book, a mailing list, and a card catalog. It's easy to use.

A relational database is much more complex. Instead of being one list, it's *several* lists, inter-connected in clever ways. For example, you might have one list called Customers, and another called Phone Orders. When somebody calls up and orders one of your famous lemon meringue pies, you'd type his name into a Phone Order blank. With me so far?

Now then. If your Phone Order blank is a rela-tional database, when you type in the customer's name, the program *automatically* consults the Customers file and looks up the customer's ad-dress, phone number, and account number — and types all of this into the order blank. What's more, if the customer's address information (in

the Customer list) ever changes, the address on the order blank will change too. It's possible to construct huge complicated relational data-bases that link all aspects of a company's files to each other.

As you can imagine, flat-file database programs are better suited to you, Most Honorable Begin-ner. Relational databases are expensive, and even old-hand Mac users don't attempt to set them up (i.e., program them) personally — that's something you hire a full-time computer jock to do for you. Just so you'll be equipped when the names come up in conversation, the best-selling Mac relational databases are Omnis, Helix, 4th Dimension (known as 4D), and FoxBase.

So what's FileMaker? It's a *pseudo-relational* flat-file program. (I know, I know — just when you thought you'd gotten it straight.) That is, it *can* look up a bit of info from a different file, like fetching the customer's address in the example above. This address isn't *linked* to the Customer file, though; if you change the address in the Customer file, it doesn't get updated in the Phone Order blank automatically. Another great pseudo-relational program is Panorama II, by the way.

Step 1: Starting a file

Double-click the FileMaker icon. A dialog box appears, where you're either supposed to open an existing data file or create a new one; click New. In the next dialog box, type a name for your file and click New again.

Before you know it, a dialog box appears. Brace yourself for a couple more terms.

As you design your database, there are two units of information you'll be creating. First of all, there are the individual blanks: the name, the ZIP code, and the state. These are called *fields.* (The International Council of Nerds evidently

No Save command!?

Why the heck do you have to name your file *before* you type any information into it? Isn't that exactly opposite from the way most programs work, where you type some stuff and *then* choose Save (and give the file a name)?

Yup.

In FileMaker, though, you'll actually come to like this feature — the program saves your data *automatically*, without your having to remember. The result: Your data is always up-to-date, even when something goes wrong.

felt that calling them *blanks* wouldn't have made people feel confused and inferior enough.)

A set of fields constitutes one *record.* A record might be a complete name-street-city-state-ZIP set for a mailing list; if there are three people's addresses, there are three records in the database. Still with us?

OK then. In the dialog box now staring you in the face, you're being asked to create the *fields* (the blanks). First type the name of the field; it might be First Name or Last Name or Street or Account Number or Date or Eyebrow Thickness or whatever. Now tell FileMaker what *kind* of data is going to be in this blank, as shown here:

Table 6-1:	Data types and their consequences
If you select this data type . . .	*Then this will happen . . .*
Text	You can enter any kind of typed data.
Number	FileMaker won't let you type letters of the alphabet — only digits.
Date, Time	FileMaker will only accept dates or times in any format.
Picture	You can't type anything into this field, but you can paste a picture.
Calculation	You can't paste or type anything. FileMaker will fill in this field automatically by performing math on other fields, like adding up the Amount and Tax fields.
Summary	You can't paste or type anything. FileMaker will fill in this field automatically by performing global math on other fields, like adding them up, counting them, or giving you a running total.

A calculated maneuver

If you created a Calculation field, a dialog box will appear as soon as you click Create. In this box, you can build the equation you want FileMaker to use. It usually involves other fields — which are listed at the upper left — combined with the +, −, / (divided by), and * (times) symbols. For example, if you're crazy enough to live in New York City, you would define the Sales Tax field as *Purchase Amount * 1.0825* (8.25 percent is the sales tax rate).

For each field you'll want on the screen, then, type a name and select a data type, and click Create. Repeat for the other fields. (If you want FileMaker to automatically enter data, like today's date, then click Options just after creating a field.)

Anyway, once you're done defining every blank you'll want to use, click Done. You've just finished Step 1.

Step 2: Data entry

At this point, you can start typing away to input data. The rules are simple: It's just like a word processor, so you use the Delete key to backspace over a typo, cut, copy, and paste selected text, and so on. To advance to the next field, press Tab. To jump back to the previous field, press Shift-Tab. To create a new, blank record (for a new person's address, say), choose New Record from the Edit menu.

As you create more records, the little open book icon at the upper left will indicate that it has more and more "pages," each of which is a record. Click the upper page to see the previous record or the lower page to see the next one or use the slider to the right to jump to any record. Needless to say, if there are too many records to fit on one screen, use the vertical scroll bar to move through your records.

If your goal, in reading this section, is to perform the joyous task of entering data, this may be all the info you'll need. Put down this book and get busy.

If, on the other hand, you want to create a database of your own, or if you're supposed to modify an existing database, you may want to learn Step 3.

Step 3: Designing a layout

When you first create a new FileMaker file and define some fields, the program creates a simple default arrangement of the blanks so that you can type in some data. The default arrangement looks like this:

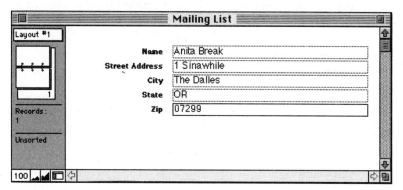

But suppose you want those same fields arranged in a more mailing-labelish layout, like this:

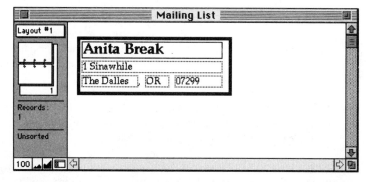

To accomplish this, you must enter the Layout Zone. Choose Layout from the Select menu. You enter a view that looks a lot like MacDraw (or any other drawing program). And, in fact, all the tools (line, rectangle, blah blah blah) work exactly as they do in a graphics program.

So: Click the Arrow Tool. Drag the fields around (make sure you can tell the difference between a field and its *label,* which you may or may not want to appear on the screen). Or click a field and then change its type style from the Format menu.

Since you can have as many different arrangements of your information as you want, use this pop-up menu to select the Layout you want to edit.

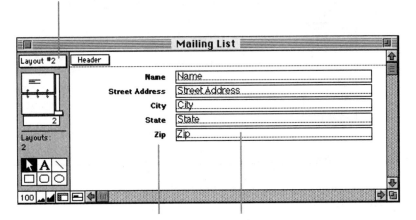

These are field labels. They do not have to appear in a layout if you do not want them to.

These are the fields themselves. To re-size one, click and then drag a corner handle. To move, drag from the center.

If you want to see more than one record at a time (when you're in data entry mode), drag the little Body tag upward until it's just below your fields, and choose View as List from the Select menu.

Remember, too, that you can *delete* a field from a particular layout. For example, if you're creating "Hello! My name is:" stickers, you certainly don't need each person's phone number to appear on his badge (unless it's *that* kind of party). So you can delete the phone number field from the layout; you do *not* lose any data you've typed in. The phone number field still *exists* — just not in this layout. Using the New Layout command in the Edit menu, you can create another layout . . . and another . . . and so on, until you've had your fill of data rearrangement.

When you're finished designing layouts, return to data entry mode by choosing Browse from the Select menu.

Finding

Once you've got some data typed in, you can manipulate it in all kinds of fun and exciting ways. Choose Find from the Select menu to get what appears to be a blank layout. Type what you're looking for into the appropriate blanks. For example, if you're trying to find everybody who lives in ZIP code 90210, you'd fill out the Find dialog box this way:

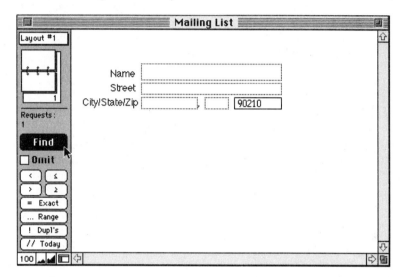

Then click the Find button. After about one second, you'll be returned to Browse (data entry) view, where you'll see the results of your search. This is important — FileMaker is *hiding* the records that *didn't* match your search requirements. You haven't lost them; they're just out of sight until you choose Find All from the Select menu. You can prove this to yourself by consulting the little book at the left side of the screen. It will say "Records: 194, Found: 22." That means FileMaker still knows there are 194 addresses in your mailing list, but only 22 have ZIP code 90210 (and they're all attractive teenage models on a major TV show).

Sorting

To sort your records, choose Sort from the Select menu. FileMaker needs to know how you want to sort your records: by first name, ZIP code, nose length, or what? On the left side, you see a list of all the fields in your database; just double-click the one by which you want to sort. (If you want to sort by last name and then sort by first name *within* each common last name, now double-click First Name.) Finally, click Sort.

Other steps

There's a million other cool things FileMaker can do. For example, it can look up a piece of info (like a phone number) from *another* FileMaker file and copy it into the appropriate place in *this* file. FileMaker also has a powerful Scripts command, which works a lot like a macro program (see "QuicKeys," following). In other words, you can make the program find all names added since last week, sort them by last name, switch to the Mailing Label layout, and print them — all with a single command from the Scripts menu. These rarefied pleasures are not, however, for the unenlightened. Grab whichever is closest — the manual or your resident computer guru person.

QuicKeys

QuicKeys is a *macro program.* (Bet you'd been hankering for some more lingo, hadn't you? It's been awhile since you had a good term to roll around on your tongue.)

A macro is an automated series of mouse or keyboard steps, which you'd otherwise have to perform manually. It's a shortcut, bub. Mouse and keyboard tasks aren't particularly strenuous, of course, except that sometimes you can get tired of performing them, especially if you have to repeat the same steps over and over again.

Typical examples: You have to type a password into some program every day. Or you're asked to open each of 1,000 documents, change the font to Times 96-point bold, print, and save. Or you always sign your letters "With fondest and most lingering feelings of warmth and mutual support, Ingrid." All of these tedious and repetitive tasks can be automated using a macro program like QuicKeys so that only a *single keystroke* (of your choosing) triggers the Mac to do the chore itself.

QuicKeys is the easiest System 7-compatible macro program, and it can perform some amazing stunts. For example, you can make it open up a certain program or document with the touch of a key. It can type out the time or the date when you press another key. And so on. Here be the basics.

Teaching by example

The easiest way to create a macro is the voyeur method: You do whatever-it-is *manually,* while QuicKeys watches.

For example, if you've just installed QuicKeys, you should see "QuicKeys 2" listed in your Apple menu. When your pointer reaches those words, a *submenu* pops out to the right; choose Record Sequence from that submenu.

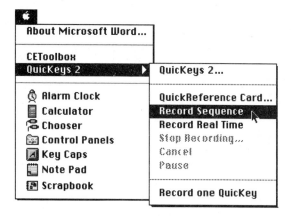

Suddenly a little blinking microphone appears where the ▇ normally is. This is QuicKeys's signal to you that it's paying attention. While you have such an attentive student, perform the task, or series of tasks, you'd like it to learn. Some examples: Type your return address; empty the Trash can; Print, then Save, then Quit; choose Bold, then Italic, then 12-point from the font menus; open the Calculator desk accessory; flap your arms; or whatever.

As you teach QuicKeys what you want it to do, there's just one caveat: If you want it to click something, make sure that whatever-it-is will always be in the *same place* on the screen. Suppose you drag an icon to the Trash can. When QuicKeys later tries to repeat what you did, it will click futilely in empty space, and drag *nothing* to the Trash can — because that icon is no longer there. Good bets for macros that involve clicking, therefore, are menus, desk accessories, and Tool palette icons — all of which are always in the same screen location.

Anyway, when you're done doing the task yourself, go back to the QuicKeys menu item in your Apple menu, and choose Stop Recording from the submenu. This box (or something like it) appears:

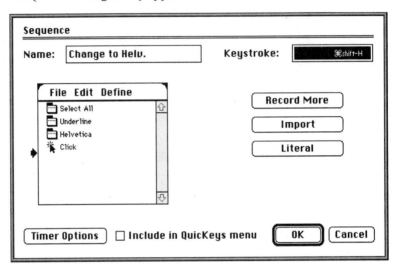

In the Name box, type a short description of what this macro is supposed to do. Press Tab to jump to the Keystroke box.

Now press the key or keys on your keyboard that you want to be the trigger. A great choice for a trigger key, by the way, is one of those otherwise useless function keys (F1, F2, and so on) that the IBM world is so bonkers about. If your keyboard has them, they're at the top of your keyboard. Another idea: Use the otherwise useless *Control* key, which you've probably never even noticed. For example, you might make Control-Q save your document and then quit. Or Control-R could type your return address.

In the lower-left quadrant of the screen, you can see QuicKeys's list of the individual steps that constituted this macro. Each type of action — a mouse click, text typed on the keyboard, a menu item selected — is represented by a different icon. You can cut, copy, paste, or delete these, but that's really a topic for your pal, the manual, to cover.

When you're done setting up the name and trigger key for this macro, click OK twice, and you're in business. Whenever you press the trigger key you specified, QuicKeys will perform that series of tasks by itself in very frantic succession. It's really something to see, too — you'll think your Mac has been inhabited by a ghost who's had way too much coffee.

Opening QuicKeys

For more specific, or more complex tasks, you may want to program macros manually (and not by example). For this, you can create a macro in the QuicKeys control panel.

There are several ways to bring up this panel. First, choose QuicKeys 2 from your Apple menu, and then choose QuicKeys 2 from the submenu. Alternatively, you can choose Control Panels from the Apple menu, double-click the QuicKeys icon and then click Open. Either way, you wind up facing a screen like this:

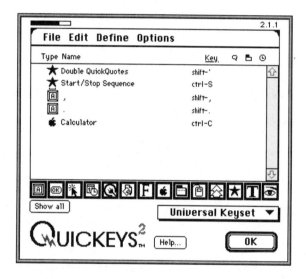

The key to creating a macro manually is the Define menu that appears within this panel. It lists 13 kinds of macros, as follows.

An *Alias* is a letter substitution. You type a W, but a P appears on the screen. That's a dumb example, of course, but that's the idea. A more useful use: Get QuicKeys to type a *period* instead of a > symbol every time you press Shift-period so that you don't keep typing "Born in the U>S>A>" by accident. (Don't confuse this kind of alias with what's called an alias by Apple in System 7. You'll find out about *that* kind of alias in Chapter 8. Sorry to interrupt.)

A *Button* is an on-screen button, like OK or Cancel. QuicKeys can click such a button automatically. What's especially nifty is that QuicKeys even knows — in the case of a checkbox-type button — whether the button is on or off. You can tell it to click a checkbox *only* if it's not already selected, for example.

A *Click* is a mouse click or a mouse drag. When you choose this from the Define menu, you'll be asked to *do* the click or drag, so the program gets the idea.

Date/Time types out the current date or time, in your choice of several formats.

Extensions are pretty neat. They're plug-in special-feature macros. One extension flips your color monitor to black and white (or back again), saving you a tedious trip to the Apple menu (and from there to the Monitors control panel). Another extension changes printers for you, in case you have more than one connected to your Mac. (Sorry, it's me again. Once again, QuicKeys has chosen a particularly unfortunate term since an *extension* is actually a special self-loading program in System 7 that you'll read about in Chapter 9. If you last that long.)

A *File* macro automatically launches a file, or a program, of your choice. It's peachy because you don't even have to know where the thing's icon is buried on your hard disk. I use Control-W to launch Word. I used Control-D to open the *Macs For Dummies* manuscript while I was writing it.

Don't worry about *FKEYs*. Hardly anyone uses them.

A *Menu/ DA* macro pulls down a menu item for you or opens a desk accessory. *Mousies* are various self-explanatory mouse actions, like scrolling down in a document, closing a window, or opening a window to full size.

A *Sequence* is several of the other types of macros, strung together. Using this kind of macro, you can construct long and complex macros.

Specials are miscellaneous handy macros. Shut Down, for example, safely turns off your Mac even if you're not in the Finder. And QuickQuotes automatically pops in a curly quote whenever you type in one of those boring straight ones (see "Top Ten Word Processing Tips" in Chapter 3).

Text is how you get QuicKeys to type out some text that's always the same: your end-of-a-letter closing; your return address; boilerplate text of any kind.

Finally, a *Real Time* macro is one that doesn't zip maniacally through the steps of the macro as fast as its little brain can manage. A Real Time macro performs the steps you teach it at exactly the same pace, with all the hesitations and mouse movements, at which you recorded it. You'd use a Real Time macro in a painting program to draw a cartoon smile, for example. If you used the Sequence kind of macro instead, QuicKeys would try to save time by drawing a line straight from the beginning point to the end point, which wouldn't look like a smile at all.

Any macro usually needs a little debugging. But once you've mastered the art of putting your Mac on autopilot, you'll save hours of cumulative time, which you can use to leave work early and play outside.

Apple File Exchange

Most people will never use this program, so I guess it really doesn't qualify for the top ten. Yet Apple File Exchange comes free with every Mac (it comes on those white System disks), and the few people who need a program like this *really* need it.

Apple File Exchange converts IBM PC files to Mac, and vice versa. You may have read, in the brochures, that your floppy disk drive is a SuperDrive capable of reading both Mac and PC disks — a technical achievement comparable to making a CD player play tapes.

What the brochure *doesn't* say is that it's not quite that easy. You don't slip a PC disk into the drive and watch its icon pop up on your screen. (Especially not the old 5 ¼-inch *really* floppy disks, which you have to first get transferred to Mac-style 3 ½-inch hard-shell disks before you can even think about any of this.)

No, what you do is launch Apple File Exchange first. *Now* you can insert a PC disk, and its contents will show up on the right side of the screen:

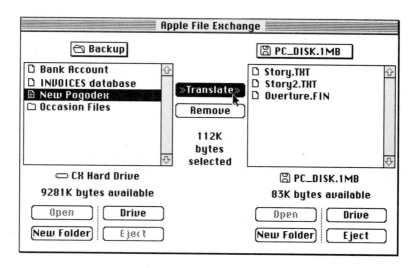

On the left, you see the contents of your hard drive. To convert a file, you just select it by clicking and then click the Translate button, as shown above.

You get exactly one converter included with Apple File Exchange — from MacWrite to DCA format, whatever that is. (Don't be disturbed if you don't own MacWrite; every word processor on the market can both create and open MacWrite documents.) You don't need any converter for text files; you can convert those easily in both directions, to and from a PC disk.

Apparently, you can get other kinds of converters to use with Apple File Exchange — ones that create (and translate) other kinds of IBM word processing formats — but dang if I've ever seen one.

Of course, if you're serious about exchanging files with PCs and PC clones, you might be better off with a program like MacLink. This incredible software gizmo, once installed in your Mac, *does* make PC disks' icons show up on the screen when they're inserted — no Apple File Exchange needed. What's more, MacLink comes with a zillion converters, to and from every kind of Mac and PC program. Furthermore, Apple recently came out with something called PC Exchange, which is supposed to do the same kind of thing.

The 5th Wave By Rich Tennant

"I'M GONNA HAVE A LITTLE TROUBLE WITH THIS 'FULL MOON' ICON ON OUR GRAPHICAL USERS INTERFACE."

Top Ten Programs That Aren't in the Top Ten

For your shopping pleasure and entertainment: a double-handful of neat programs that are worth looking into and often discussed at techno-savvy cocktail parties. ("Hi there, baby. Want to come up and see my FreeHand printouts?")

1. *FreeHand* or *Illustrator.* Primo, powerful, professional, pricey PostScript graphics programs. Be prepared to read the manual.

2. *Resolve, Lotus 1-2-3 for the Mac,* or *Wingz.* Full-featured spreadsheets that rival Excel, but aren't Excel, and therefore don't sell well.

3. *Now Up To Date.* A sensational calendar program: type your appointments onto the appropriate squares. Up To Date can then remind you of them, show your To Do list, and print out gorgeous daily, weekly, or monthly agendas.

4. *Quicken.* The world's greatest and least expensive checkbook/financial program. Perfect for home and very-small-business use. Prints your checks, balances your budget. When stretched, can even do accounts receivable and payable, profit and loss, and that sort of thing.

5. *Persuasion.* It's called *presentation* software. Lets you quickly and easily assemble slide shows — graphs, bullet charts, colorful diagrams — with a choice of many rich, unified color schemes. Print the slides onto slides or transparencies, or use the Mac itself to give a slide show.

6. *Kid Pix.* Mind-blowing, colorful, audio-equipped version of MacPaint. Designed for kids but equally addictive for adults. The drippy paintbrush runs, the eraser makes scritch-scratch sounds, and when you want to start over, the Dynamite Tool blows up your artwork. About $25.

7. *Microsoft Flight Simulator.* A great, almost too-realistic airplane simulator. It's three-dimensional, works in color, and has sounds. You can actually fly across the country — in real time.

8. *Microphone II.* You use this program if you have a modem (a phone hookup for your Mac). Lets you dial friends, bulletin boards, or on-line services like CompuServe. (More about these things in Chapter 8.)

9. *Super QuickDex.* A sizzlingly fast Rolodex program. Can pull up one person's card, out of 2,000, in less than half a second. Can even dial the phone if you have a modem. Easier to use than a hairbrush. If you'll want to do much printing, you may prefer the more feature-laden (but much slower) *DynoDex* or *Address Book Plus.* They print out your address books in a billion different formats.

10. *AppleTalk Remote Access.* Yo, PowerBook owners! Read Appendix E for the vital scoop.

• •

Summary

▶ Graphics programs work alike, but painting programs (that let you paint dots on the screen) and drawing programs (that only let you draw squares, lines, and circles) are very different.

▶ Excel is for calculations of numbers, which get updated instantly if you change any one number in the equation. FileMaker is a database so flexible it makes the Dewey decimal system look prehistoric.

▶ A macro program like QuicKeys is great for automating things you have to do the same way every day.

▶ Page layout programs like PageMaker and QuarkXPress let you arrange text and pictures on a page.

▶ Select, then apply . . . Select, then apply . . . Select, then apply . . .

• •

Chapter 7
More Stuff To Buy and Plug In

• •

In This Chapter

▶ Preserving your favorite belch sound forever

▶ Why a scanner is like an inside-out printer

▶ Hooking your Mac to the telephone line

▶ Making your Mac musical or cinematic

• •

*I*t's probably taken you at least a day to reach this part of the book, and I'll bet you're already chomping at the bit. "Filemaker — fiddlesticks! Printers — piffle!," you're no doubt exclaiming; "Give me something I, the Reader, can sink my teeth into!"

OK, O Reader. In this section you'll find out about several impressive and high-tech gadgets you can spend money on — yes, it's Credit Card Workout #4. These devices give the Mac eyes and ears, turn it into a national network, and turn it into an orchestra. You're not obligated to purchase any of them, of course. But knowing about some of the amazing things your computer can do will help you understand why a Mac is such a big deal.

Microphones

Almost every Mac model comes equipped with a little microphone. It's the circular thing that looks like a Munchkin smoke detector, about two inches in diameter, with a thin cord trailing out.

If you bought an older Mac, or for some other reason have a Mac model without a microphone jack in the back, a little money (as always) can remedy the situation. One microphone is called the

MacRecorder; another is the Voice Impact (both listed in the Resource Resource). Both plug into the jack marked by a telephone (in back of your Mac) and do everything the Apple mike can do, and more — they just cost more.

Anyway. You wouldn't be alone if you wondered what the point of a microphone was. Fact is, there isn't a whole heckuva lot you can do with it. Mainly what you do with it is record sounds — sentences, sound effects, belches, whatever you want. You can play back a sound by double-clicking its icon; or, using the Sound control panel, you can designate any sound to replace the beep the Mac makes when you make a mistake. (The offices of Mac freaks are filled with exclamations of *"Not!"* and "Bogus!" — the chosen error beeps of the Mac faithful. For more details on recording your own sounds see Chapter 8.)

Casper, the friendly technology

Still, you gotta wonder why Apple goes to the trouble of including a microphone — with a *tie clip* on the back, for heaven's sake — with every computer they make. Well, recent headlines have tipped their hand: It's a technology code-named Casper. It's *voice control.* No, your eyes aren't deceiving you; within a year or so, people will be controlling their Macs by talking to them. Maybe Apple's simply been readying us all for the big day, making sure that every Mac has ears. So watch your language.

Scanners

You've actually seen scanners before. They're usually known by their technical name: *copying machines.* Yup. When you put a piece of paper on the ol' Xerox machine, the scanner part (glass, bright light, funny hum) takes a picture of your document. Then the printer part prints the copy. Well, if you strip out the printer part, what's left is a scanner.

If the point of a printer is to take something on the *screen* and reproduce it on *paper,* then a scanner is the opposite — its function is to scan an image on *paper* and throw it up on the Mac *screen.* Once it's been scanned and converted into bits and bytes that the Mac understands (meaning that it's been *digitized),* you can manipulate it any way you want. Erase unwanted parts, make the background darker, give Uncle Ed a mustache, shorten your brother's neck, whatever. The more dignified use for a scanner is grabbing real-world images that you then paste into your own documents, particularly in the realm of page layout and graphic design. Got a potato-industry newsletter to crank out? Scan in a photo of some fine-lookin' spuds, and you've got yourself a graphic for page one.

O say can u OCR?

Unfortunately, when you scan a page of *text,* the Mac doesn't see English words. It sees lots of itty-bitty dots in funny patterns. When the image pops up on your screen after being scanned, you can't correct a typo — because it's not really text anymore, just a picture of text. (Analogy time: If you take a Polaroid of a handwritten grocery list, you can't then erase Charmin 8-Roll Pack from the *photo,* because it's no longer handwriting — just a picture of some.)

To convert that picture of text into a true text document, you need a piece of highly brainy software designed for *optical character recognition,* which is so unhelpful a term that people abbreviate it OCR out of sheer disgust. Using OCR, you can save yourself massive amounts of retyping; you can just roll the magazine article, book page, or other text document through your scanner, and wait while your OCR program examines each letter to decide its identity. The result is a text document that's about 98 percent correctly typed.

So how much is all this gonna cost you? A serious black-and-white scanner, one with a big plate of glass like a copier, is around $800. An OCR program costs between $200 and $800, depending on its sophistication.

One in the hand

If you doubt you'll be needing to grab images or text every day, you could consider a *hand* scanner. Instead of being a huge piece of machinery, a hand scanner is a little hand-held doodad, about five inches wide. You leave the document on the table, and roll this gizmo across it; the scanned image (usually four inches wide, max) appears in a strip on the screen. You can even get a hand scanner with built-in OCR, when you need to grab text. Hand scanners have their limitations — the four-inch maximum scan width, for one thing, and the fact that you have to drag the scanner across the page absolutely straight. But they cost less than half what the big guns do.

Modems

A modem is a phone hookup — a box that sits between the Mac and a phone jack.

Once your Mac is connected by phone to another computer, all kinds of neat things can happen. You can have a conversation with somebody at the other end, where everything each person types appears on both people's screens. You can transfer a file from your hard disk to somebody else's, even if they live in Tulsa or Zurich. You can drop electronic mail messages into people's electronic mailboxes, which they'll read the next time they check in. (Such messages are called *E-mail,* from the exclamation "*Eeee-hah! I don't have to send it through the mail!*") You can make plane reservations, order disks, check your stocks, send cartoon renderings of your face worldwide, and get all kinds of other info by using an *on-line service.*

E-mail: *Electronic mail. Requires some special software. You type a note on your Mac screen, click a Send button, and it pops up on the recipients' screens — provided they're connected to your Mac via a network.*

Depending on how much of a computerphile you intend to become, a modem can be as exciting an addition to your life as, say, taking up aerobics or getting cable TV. If your printer blows up, you could scream for help on an electronic bulletin board, and you'd get it. If you have Macs both at work and at home, you can send documents back and forth over the phone wires. Some people phone *all* their work in to the office; these people are called *telecommuters* (or *lucky slobs,* depending on whom you ask).

Another stupid etymology

Sorry to do this, but the weenies will claim I didn't do my job if I don't reveal the usual boring explanation for the word *modem.*

The word comes from the first syllables of the words *modulator* and *demodulator.* When a modem modulates, it's sending very rapid on/off pulses, kind of like a Morse code operator on a nicotine fit. That's how it talks to other computers. The computer on the other end translates (demodulates) those on/off signals back into intelligible text (or graphics or music or whatever you're sending).

In fact, if you have a PowerBook (a laptop Mac) with a modem, you can do something *really* neat. Suppose you're out in the Alaskan tundra, and you realize you left those critical third-quarter sales reports on your regular office Mac in Chagrin Falls, Ohio. If the Ohio Mac also has a modem, you can actually dial in to your office, turn on the Ohio Mac automatically, get the documents you need, turn off the Ohio Mac — all by long-distance remote control. As a matter of fact, you lucky so-and-so, instructions for performing this astounding high-tech stunt await you in Appendix E, "Long-Distance Computing: AppleTalk Remote Access."

Coping with bauds

Just like computers, modems come equipped with different amounts of speed and power; just like cars, the more speed you have, the more the thing costs. Instead of miles per hour, which would probably be a more user-friendly measurement, modem speed is measured by its *baud rate.* (Note the spelling. *Bawd* rate is something completely different, having to do with barroom womanizing in 17th-century England.) I wouldn't try to explain what a baud is even if I knew. I can tell you, though, that the available modem speeds are 300, 1200, 2400, 9600, and 14400 baud.

Almost nobody uses the first two anymore. The 2400 baud rate is by far the most common; 9600 and 14400 will certainly be the speeds-o'-the-future (but at this point are way-2-expensive).

In addition to the modem, you'll also need some software. If you want to communicate directly to another Mac, you'll need a program like MicroPhone, SmartCom, or White Knight (and so does the person on the other end of the phone). If, instead, you want to hook up to an *on-line information service* (see below), then you probably won't need to buy any software; the service you're subscribing to usually provides free software that works with their system.

And, of course, you'll need to rig some kind of phone-line connection for your modem, either by adding a Y-splitter jack to your existing phone line or by using a separate line.

Fax/modems

While we're talking about buying modems, you might also want to consider a *fax/modem.* For only about $50 more than the cost of a plain modem, you can get one that turns your Mac into a big gray fax machine. A fax/modem can receive any kind of fax; the incoming document appears on your Mac screen, where you can read it, print it on your printer, or throw it away.

To *send* a fax, you prepare the document you want to send on your Mac. For most people, that means typing it up in a word processor. This, of course, is the one major disadvantage to owning a fax/modem instead of a real (but much more expensive) fax machine: You can only send documents that are on the Mac. You can't fax someone, for example, an article from *MAD* magazine because it doesn't exist on your Mac screen. (Unless you go to the trouble of buying a scanner and scanning it in.)

On-line services

One of the neatest things you can do with a modem is dial into an on-line service. The most popular ones are called America Online and CompuServe. You get a local access phone number for each so that calling the service isn't a long distance call. But you pay by the hour while you're connected to the service: $4 per hour for America Online (nights and weekends, more other times) and about $13 per hour for CompuServe.

In reality, these services are gigantic rooms full of humming mainframe computers in Virginia (America Online) or Ohio (CompuServe), with gazillions of phone lines coming in so that thousands of computer users can dial in at the same time.

What you see on your screen, however, depends on the service you're using. America Online (and AppleLink, another popular one) looks just like the Mac screen you're used to: There are friendly icons and folders and buttons to click. If you want to send an E-mail message to somebody, you just click a button that says Send Mail. CompuServe, on the other hand, has no graphics at all; it's basically some small text that scrolls endlessly up your screen. Most people would agree that CompuServe (and GEnie, Delphi, and other text-based services) is much harder to navigate and learn, *even* if they buy a program called CompuServe Information Manager that adds an icon-based front end to that Mother of All Networks.

On both kinds of services, though, there are some wicked-cool things to do. You can find up-to-the-minute news, sports, and weather reports, for starters. There's an electronic ("on-line") encyclopedia, for those middle-of-the-night bursts of curiosity about dead German philosophers. You can actually hook into the same airline reservation systems that travel agents use, so you can literally book your own flights. You can send faxes to anybody in the world for about a dollar a page (even though you don't have a fax machine or even a fax/ modem). You can get help, overnight, for just about any computer problem.

What's especially fun about America Online is that you can have face-to-face meetings, live encounters, with up to 22 other people at once in an electronic "room." It's a real social encounter — wisecracks, social gaffes, falling in love, the whole bit — except you don't even have to comb your hair. Nobody knows your age, gender, weight, skin color, or whether or not there's spinach caught between your front teeth. There are also *private* rooms, where, legend has it, people from different parts of the world participate in the ultimate safe sex.

Bulletin boards

Much less exotic, but especially practical, are local electronic bulletin board services, known commonly (according to the Universal Rule that Computer Terms Must Be Cryptically Abbreviated) as *BBSs*. A BBS is local and run by some computer guru. Since they're local and usually free, they're somewhat less polished than the expensive commercial services, but they make up for the glitz by being hotbeds of local information. You wouldn't have much luck selling your used printer on a national service, for example, but you could put an ad on a BBS for nearby computer users to find.

Like the commercial services, BBSs usually stock a huge amount of trial software free of charge, which you can transfer to your own Mac (in a process called downloading). This kind of software is called *shareware* (a computer term I actually *like*) because the programmer who wrote it wants to share it with fellow Mac owners everywhere. Instead of paying $400 for a beautifully packaged, heavily advertised program, you could download a piece of shareware from a local BBS and pay only $15 for it. And your payment is on the honor system, at that: You only mail the guy his money if you really like the software. (Try *that* with a Microsoft program.) It's the ultimate try-before-you-buy, win-win, everybody's happy system.

So how do you find out the number of a local BBS since that's probably the best way to try out your new modem? Well, you can ask around, of course. But a surefire (albeit roundabout) method is to call Apple at 800-538-9696 and ask them what Macintosh User Group is nearest to you. Once you know, call up the user group and ask *them* what some phone numbers of local BBSs are. Then dial away and have fun! I can almost guarantee it — you won't remember having tied up the phone for so long since you were a teenager.

CD-ROM

Nothing spices up a good discussion like a baffling computer equipment acronym, y'know?

Fortunately, you already know half of this one: CD stands for Compact Disc, just like the ones that let you play Ella Fitzgerald on your compact disk player.

Instead of holding music, though, a CD-ROM disk holds computer information — *tons* of it. (Don't even worry about what ROM stands for. It'd leave you more confused than you may be already.)

If you have a CD-ROM player — a $400 gizmo that plugs into the back of your Mac — you can play CD-ROM discs. They contain pictures, sound, movies, graphics, and text . . . enough to keep you busy for days. Typical examples: One CD-ROM contains an encyclopedia, complete with color pictures, some of which are movies that show the motion of, say, the Venezuelan Sun Gekko. Another is a dictionary, where you actually hear a guy read the pronunciation of each word. Another CD-ROM is a video game — an *interactive* one, like a TV show where *you* control where the main character goes next.

Apple Computer vows that CD-ROM is going to be the next big thing. In fact, you can get a built-in CD-ROM player as an option on your Performa 600, IIvx, Quadra, or Centris Mac. We'll see. At the moment, there aren't all that many CD-ROM discs to choose from, and $400 is still too much for most people to pay for the privilege.

Music and MIDI

Oh, groan . . . it's another abbreviated computer term! All right, let's get it over with.

MIDI, pronounced like the short skirt, stands for Musical Instrument Digital Interface. What it *means* is "hookup to a synthesizer." What it *does* is let your Mac record and play back your musical performances, using a synthesizer attached to it. When you record, the Mac makes a metronome sound — a steady click track — and you play to the beat. Then, when you play back the music, your keyboard plays *exactly* what you recorded, complete with feeling, expression, and fudged notes; you'd think that Elvis's ghost was playing the instrument, except that the keys don't move up and down.

The advantage of recording music in this way (yup, there's a term for this, too — it's called *sequencing*) is that once you've captured your brilliant performance by recording it into the Mac, you can edit it. You can take *out* those fudged notes. You can transpose the piece into a different key. You can speed it up or slow it down, *without* affecting the pitch. Why? Because this isn't a tape recording; it's a *digital* recording. Your musical MIDI information is a stream of computer numbers that describe each note you play; the Mac might instruct the keyboard, for example, to "Play middle C, with this much volume, and hold down the note for one-tenth of a second."

A one-person orchestra

In the real world, the most useful application of MIDI information, though, is that a single musician (or even semi-musician) can make a recording that sounds like an entire band. How?, you ask, eyebrows raised.

Simple: You record one musical line at a time. You play the bass line, for example; the Mac records it, nuance for nuance. Now, while the bass line plays back, you record the piano part. Then while those *two* tracks play back, you record the violins, and so on. Hate to break it to you, but virtually *all* popular music (and advertising jingles) are now recorded this way: by one Mac musician alone in a studio with a big pile of realistic-sounding synthesizers. (And I still haven't recovered from finding out, at age eight, that the whole band isn't actually at the radio station every time a song comes on.)

What you need

What you *don't* need to make MIDI music on the Mac is much musical ability. Remember, you can record something as slowly as you want, at a tempo that would slow a turtle's pulse. Then you can just change the tempo when the music plays back, and instantly you sound like you've got 18 fingers and six hands.

You do, however, need a little box that connects your Mac to the synthesizer. It's called a MIDI *interface,* and it shouldn't cost more than about $50. You also need a program that can record and play back the music, called a *sequencing program.* Some easy-to-use and inexpensive ones are EZ Vision and Trax. And, of course, you need to get your hands on a synthesizer. Check out a music store and get jammin'.

Other things MIDI can do

Another popular use of the Mac is to make it write out your music for you in standard sheet music notation. Several *notation* programs (MusicProse, Encore, Finale) actually write down every note you play, let you edit it, add lyrics or chord symbols, and then print it out as gorgeous sheet music. These programs can even play back your music; you can listen to your masterpiece, correcting any wayward notes before committing them to paper. Presto, you're Mozart.

A Camcorder

"Say *what?*," you're saying. "This crazy author is suggesting I plug my camcorder into my computer? What's next, plugging my microwave into the vacuum?"

Hot: *(1) Expensive.* He bought a hot new computer. *(2) Trendy.* What do you use your new computer for? Well, nothing, but it's hot, isn't it?

It's true. The hottest new use of a Macintosh is as a movie-making machine. You can actually plug your VCR or camcorder into the computer and watch in awe as your home movies pop up on the Mac screen. Once you've captured your videos onto the Mac (or, more correctly, *digitized* them), with full color and sound, you can edit them, play them backward, edit out the embarrassing parts, or whatever. The technology and the movies are called QuickTime, and no other computer can do it.

The caveats of the proletariat

That's the end of the good news. QuickTime video editing is still very new. As a result, it takes some serious Mac horsepower: You need a fast color Mac, plus a video *digitizing card* (the thing you actually plug your VCR into), plus some movie-editing software. And you need a *lot* of hard disk space: Every minute of digitized movie on your Mac consumes about *15MB* of disk space (for those whose calculators don't work in megabytes, that's a hefty chunk of a typical hard disk). Even with all that, the movies play back pretty jerkily, in a tiny window about the size of a Triscuit.

At this writing, the most cost-effective way to get started making your own digital movies is to buy a Video Spigot. It's a digitizing card (a circuit board you install into your Mac IIsi, IIci, or whatever) that costs about $500. However, by the time you read this sentence (and probably before I'm even done writing it), the video product market will have changed considerably. New digitizing cards are supposed to cost about $2,000, but they'll be incredible; instead of watching jumpy, Max Headroom-ish movies in a window on your screen so small you need a magnifying glass, you'll be able to watch very smooth, full-screen movies with stereo sound!

They'll still take up tons of hard-disk space, though. Of course, people will just have to go buy additional hard disks to hold their movies. And when *they* fill up, then — hold on a second. Maybe it's time to talk about less expensive storage gadgets.

SyQuests, Bernoullis, and Tapes, Oh My!

In Chapter 2 you learned all about hard disks. You learned that the hard disk (usually built inside your computer) is a terrific place to store your data when the computer is turned off. You found out that it's sort of expensive, but it delivers data very quickly into the Mac's little head.

There's only one thing wrong with hard disks: Like closets, garages, and landfills, they fill up. No matter how much of a neatness nerd you are, even if you promptly throw away anything you're finished working on, you'll gradually watch your "MB available" count go down, down, down over the months, until your hard disk is completely full. (Thousands of experienced Mac users all over the world are sagely nodding their heads in sorrowful acknowledgment.)

So what are you supposed to do? Go back to writing on Post-It notes?

Well, you could buy another hard disk, of course. The one *inside* your computer is called an *internal* hard drive. If you buy another, you could plug it into the back of your Mac and have access to its contents as well. (This, as you may have guessed, would be called an *external* hard drive.) But that's an expensive proposition, and the darnedest thing of it is that *that* hard disk will fill up, too.

Remove it

For thousands of storage-starved people, the solution is to get a *removable cartridge* system. This device looks just like an external hard drive, except when the spinning platters get full, you can just pull them out of the machine (they're sealed into a plastic cartridge) and put in a new, blank, virgin cartridge. Since a cartridge only costs about $65, and a new hard disk costs $400, you can see why a removable cartridge is an attractive idea.

A removable-cartridge system solves another chronic problem, too: how to *back up* your data. To back up is to *make a spare copy of your important files,* so if something should happen to your main hard disk (or *you* do something to it) and all your files get erased, you haven't lost your life's work.

But placing a second copy of everything on the *same* hard disk doesn't make much sense; if the hard disk croaks, then you lose both copies. Many people copy their data onto floppy disks. That's certainly cheap but a bit inconvenient, especially if you work with large files that take forever to copy. With a removable-cartridge system, you can back up your entire hard drive in five minutes.

There are two primary makers of removable-cartridge systems: SyQuest and Bernoulli. A SyQuest drive costs about $600, and each 45MB cartridge is around $65. The newer SyQuest drives accept 90MB cartridges, which are slightly more expensive. The huge advantage of SyQuest drives: They're extremely common. Thousands and thousands of people own them, and cartridges can be swapped freely back and forth.

A Bernoulli removable-cartridge drive is, technologically speaking, a slightly superior solution. Each cartridge holds 90MB of data, and the cartridges are incredibly tough and long-lasting. (You hear occasional stories about a SyQuest cartridge going bad, but you never hear about a Bernoulli going bad.) The possible drawback: There aren't as many Bernoullis in the world, so finding a fellow cartridge-swapper isn't easy (if, indeed, you care).

Another possibility for making backup copies is a *tape drive.* Instead of storing your information on metal platters, a tape drive stores it on a plain old cassette-like tape. The advantage: The special tapes are dirt cheap. The disadvantage: They're slow as frozen ketchup. Also, you can't easily retrieve just one file from a tape-backup cartridge because the computer can't easily jump from one place on the tape to another. So don't bother with tape backup; I'm telling you about tape backup only so that you'll know to whom you're entitled to feel superior.

Networks

You already know what a network is. It's the television company that broadcasts stuff like "Love Connection" so you'll have something to watch when you're burned out from computer work.

In the computer world, though, a network is defined as *more than one Mac hooked together.* In some offices, hundreds of Macs are all interconnected. Some advantages of being networked: You can send an E-mail to other people, which

---

A network of one

You, too, can get in on the fun of networking, even if you don't have millions of Macs in your office. Read Chapter 5 to find out why *one* Mac and *one* printer, technically speaking, constitute a net-

work. And, actually, hooking up two Macs together isn't really that scary if you're using System 7. Use your System 7 manuals to guide you.

---

pops up on their screens; you can have access to each others' files and programs; and you can save money by buying just one printer (or scanner, or modem) for use with a whole bunch of Macs.

It's way, *way* beyond the scope of this book — or the knowledge of its author — to tell you anything about networking. This is the domain of SuperWeenies: consultants, gurus, computer whizzes, who are paid big bucks to come into a company and get it wired.

Plugging the Stuff In

Peripheral: *An expensive add-on gadget for your Mac, like a scanner, printer, or hard disk. From* peripheral vision, *which is how you'll see all this stuff cluttering up the edges of your desk.*

Suppose you win the lottery. You buy every Mac peripheral there is. Only two things left to do: give half your winnings to the IRS and figure out where to plug the stuff in. In Appendix A, you'll find a pretty good diagram of the jacks in the back of your Mac. Here's where everything goes:

> ✔ *Scanners, CD-ROM players, external hard drives, removable-cartridge drives, tape-backup devices:* the SCSI port. It's the wide one with screws on each side. So how are you supposed to plug in so many different things if there's only one port? Simple — by *daisy-chaining* them, one to another.

Daisy-chaining and SCSI

Daisy-chaining is the act of connecting more than one peripheral gizmo to a single jack on your computer, by plugging each into the back of another one. So called because, when you discover how frustrating it can be to connect multiple devices like hard drives, you'll be reduced to sitting in a field by yourself tying flowers together.

SCSI is the annoying acronym for Small Computer System Interface, pronounced even more annoyingly: "scuzzy." Actually refers to the wide jack with two rows of little holes, located on the back of the Mac.

Daisy-chaining is an act of utter bravery, however, and should not be undertaken until after you've read the "Scuzzy SCSI" section in Chapter 9. Until then, plug *one* machine only into the SCSI jack of your Mac.

✔ *Apple microphone:* There's a special jack, a miniplug, just for this.

✔ *Modems, MIDI interfaces (music), label printers, MacRecorder, or other nonApple microphones:* These all go into the modem port. It's the little round jobber marked by a telephone icon. So how are you supposed to plug more than one of these into your Mac? (No, there's no such thing as daisy-chaining modem-port devices.) You have two choices, both of which involve using only one device at a time. First, you can just unplug one device before using the next. Or second, you can get an A/B switch box that acts like a Y-splitter; you plug both modem port pluggables into this box and then turn a knob to select which one you want the Mac to pay attention to. (You can even buy an A/B/C/D box that accommodates *four* devices if you've really gone crazy with this kind of peripheral.)

Expansion slot: *A receptacle for a plug-in circuit board inside certain Mac models. Only the Classic, the Plus, the Classic II, and the PowerBooks lack expansion slots. The majority of people never use their expansion slots. You can fill your slots with things like accelerators (to make your Mac faster), digitizing cards (so you can make QuickTime movies), or internal fax/modems.*

✔ *Camcorder, VCR:* There's no built-in jack for this. But once you buy a digitizing card and install it into one of your Mac's *expansion slots,* there will be a new little jack protruding from the back of the Mac (extending from the card inside).

✔ *Printer, network:* You've probably figured out, all by yourself, that the printer gets connected to the printer port (another small, round jack, next to the modem port, and marked by a printer icon). But it's good to know that this is where you plug in the cabling for a network, too, if you have one. (So then where does the printer go if your printer port is used up by a network connection? Easy — it gets hooked into the network, so anyone can use it. See your resident guru for details.)

Top Ten Non-Costly Mac Add-Ons

Like people, Macs that go unaccessorized are likely to be shut out of the most important social functions. But not every add-on has to cost a million bucks, as the following list demonstrates.

1. *A mouse pad.* It's a foam rubber mat that protects the desk and the mouse from each other, gives your mouse better traction, and keeps cookie crumbs out of the mouse mechanism. Often carries the same kinds of promotional graphics as T-shirts and bumper stickers.

2. *A dust cover.* Basically a specially shaped bag you drape over your Mac at night to keep the dust storms out. You might get one for your keyboard, too.

3. *A glare filter.* I think they make the screen too dim, but lots of people use them and think they make the screen easier to look at.

4. *Disk boxes.* They hold your floppy disks. A nylon disk *wallet* holds about ten disks in a fold-up thing you can put in your breast pocket. Disk boxes hold between ten and 100 disks, and come in every possible material from plastic to polished teak.

5. *A carrying case.* For the Classic, Plus, SE, or PowerBook, these rugged, padded protective bags are extremely helpful in transporting your machine. Even if it's in one of these cases, don't ever check your computer on a plane (unless it's in the original cardboard box with its styrofoam protectors).

6. *A trackball.* People who don't like mice (computer mice, of course) often take great delight in replacing their Mac mouse with a trackball. A trackball looks like an eight ball set into a six-inch square base; you move the pointer on the screen by rolling the ball in place with your fingers. (The PowerBook has a built-in trackball, right in the center below the keyboard.)

7. *A surge suppressor.* This thing looks like an ordinary multiple-outlet extension cord from the hardware store, but it's supposed to have an additional benefit — circuitry that can absorb an electrical voltage surge, and thus protect your Mac from a wayward bolt of lightning. Not many people realize that the Mac already has a *built-in* surge suppressor, however; furthermore, a surge suppressor's value has long been debated. (They're not designed to protect you from acts of God, though. I've known people with surge suppressors whose Macs got fried by lightning, as well as people *without* surge suppressors whose houses were struck by lightning without affecting the Mac.) Let your paranoia be your guide.

8. *A one-switch multiple-outlet box.* In other words, an extension-cord thing that lets you plug in your Mac, hard drive, printer, and so on, so that they all turn on when you flip a single switch. Such devices usually have a surge suppressor built-in, by the way. My favorite is the PowerKey, which is designed especially for the Mac, has four surge-protected outlets, and lets you turn the Mac on by pressing the big triangle key on your keyboard (even if you have a Classic, Plus, SE, or LC, whose big triangle keys usually do nothing).

9. *A paper clip.* Man, talk about low cost. Nonetheless, the true Mac cognoscienti keep a straightened paper clip next to their machines — it's the only way to remove a floppy disk that's stuck in the disk drive. (See the sidebar in Chapter 3 entitled "Dweebs' Corner: Alternative disk tips" for instructions.)

10. *Spare printer cartridges.* Have an extra ribbon, cartridge, or drum for your printer (depending on what it is) at all times. Murphy's Law, or whatever law governs computers, states that the printer cartridge you're using now will not wear out until you're halfway through a large printing project that's due shortly and all the stores are closed.

● ●

Summary

▶ A microphone lets you record sounds and may one day let you talk some sense into your Mac.

▶ A scanner lets you scan your favorite Barry Manilow album covers so they show up on the Mac screen.

▶ Removable-cartridge and CD-ROM disks hold tons of information (but a CD-ROM is prerecorded).

▶ MIDI lets your Mac make music, and QuickTime lets your Mac make movies.

▶ The best stuff is expensive and becomes obsolete as soon as you buy it.

● ●

Chapter 8
Putting the Mouse to the Metal

· ·

In This Chapter

▶ Uncovering the forbidden secrets of the Option key

▶ Duplicating, finding, and splitting the personality of icons

▶ Vandalizing your own Mac, without spraypaint or a sledge hammer

▶ Utilities with no monthly bill

· ·

*I*f this book were a weekend in Tahoe, it would now be Sunday afternoon. If it were a movie, you'd be watching the car chase. If it were a box of cereal, the free decoder ring, in its little cellophane wrapper, would just have dropped into your bowl. Yes, kids, you're on the home stretch. It's payoff time.

This chapter is about honing the basic skills you already have. It's about becoming more efficient in the way you work — shortcuts, hidden secrets, and slick tricks to astonish your friends. And it's about turning the basic Mac that *millions* of people have into one that's unmistakably yours.

Maybe it'd be better if I avoided the term that's about to apply to you . . . *power user.* Maybe those words will strike fear once again into your soul. But even if you started *out* as a Mac virgin, either leery or outright petrified about the alien technology before you, by now you've almost completely mastered the Mac. The only tidbits left to explore are the ones normally classified as — yes — *power-user secrets!*

The Efficiency Nut's Guide to the Option Key

Yeah, yeah, everybody knows that you can close a window by clicking its close box. But you didn't fork over good money for this book to learn something that's on page 1 of the Mac manual.

No, these tips are much choicer. They show you how to unlock the power of that most overlooked of keys, the Option key. It's been placed closer to you than any letter key on the keyboard — and that's no accident.

Closing all windows at once

Suppose you've opened a gaggle of folders, and their windows are lying open all over the screen. And suppose that the niggling neatness ethic instilled in you by your mother compels you to clean up a bit. Here's the "before" picture:

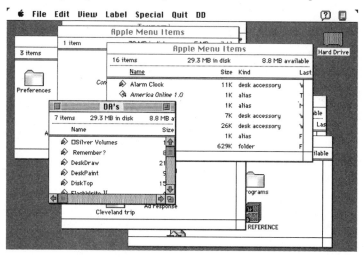

You could, of course, click the close box of each window, one at a time. But it's far faster to click only *one* window's close box while pressing the Option key. Bam, bam, bam — they all close automatically, one after another. Here's the "after" picture:

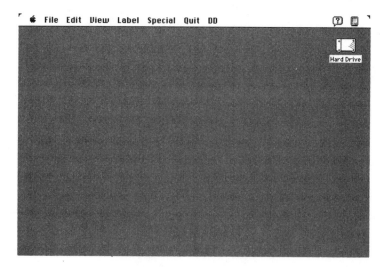

Windows and folders: developing tunnel vision

When you're trying to find a document icon that's inside a folder inside a folder inside a folder, it's hard to avoid having COWS (Cluttered, Overlapping Windows Syndrome). By the time you finally arrive at the darned icon, your screen is filled with windows.

If you press Option while double-clicking each nested folder, though, the Mac will neatly close the *previous* window before opening the next one. Criminy — this computer even *cleans up* after you!

In the figure below, you could press Option while double-clicking the Oregon folder (left); the USA folder that contains it would automatically close as the new window opened (right):

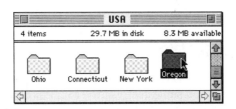

OK. So here we are in the Oregon folder. What if we want to backtrack and go back to the USA folder (or the World folder)? There's a little-known trick that lets you jump to the folder that *contains* it: Press the ⌘ key, and click the window's title!

In the figure above, you ⌘-click the word Oregon at the top of the window. Now you slide down the pop-up menu that lists the nested folders, from innermost to outermost. Let go when you reach the folder you want (below left); the Mac opens the folder you selected (below right).

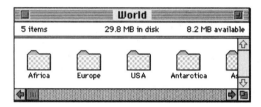

If you press Option as you choose the new folder name, you'll simultaneously close the original nested window.

Taking out the trash

Let's review: You drag an icon on top of the Trash can, and the icon disappears. The Trash can bulges. You smile gently at the zaniness of it all. Now you choose Empty Trash from the Special menu, and a little message appears on the screen, saying something like:

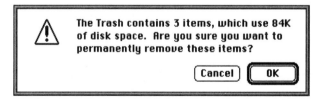

> ⚠ The Trash contains 3 items, which use 84K of disk space. Are you sure you want to permanently remove these items?
>
> [Cancel]   [**OK**]

The silence of the trash

You can tell the Mac you *never* want to see the "Are you sure . . . " message when you choose Empty Trash. Here's the secret: Click the Trash can icon. From the File menu, choose Get Info.

See the checkbox at the bottom? It says "Warn before emptying." Click this checkbox so that the X disappears.

That's all very well and good, but busy Americans concerned with increasing their productivity may not always have time for such trivial information. Therefore, if you want to dump the trash, but you *don't* want that message to appear, press our friend Mr. Option Key while you choose Empty Trash. (Option is also the key for emptying the trash when the Mac tells you there's something "locked" in the Trash can.)

Multitasking methods

As you discovered early on, the Mac lets you run more than one program simultaneously. (Remember when you tried some tricks with both the Note Pad and the Calculator open on the screen at once?) You can switch from one program to another by choosing its name from the Application menu at the top right of your screen, marked by the ▣ icon (or the icon of whatever program is currently in front).

We haven't yet examined the other commands in this menu, such as Hide Others and Show All. These are anti-COWS commands that help keep your screen neat and clean. For example, suppose you're trying to use the Calculator, but so many other programs are running that your eyes cross:

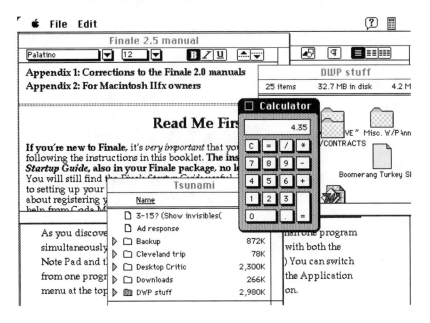

By choosing Hide Others from the Application menu, all windows that belong to other programs disappear, leaving the frontmost window all by itself:

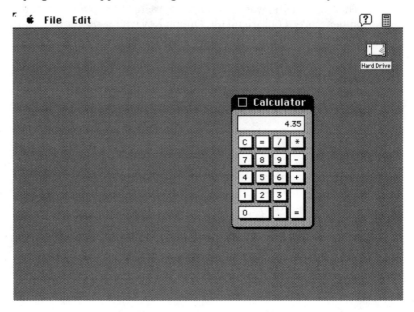

The other programs *are* still running, and they *do* still exist, but their windows, plain and simple, are now hidden. You can verify this by checking the Application menu, where you'll see that their icons appear dimmed.

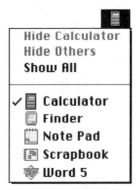

So how does the Option key play into all this? When you switch from one program to another, you can make the program you're *leaving* hide itself automatically if you press Option while choosing the new program's name (or clicking in its window). That way you always keep nonessential programs hidden.

Making an instant document copy

In most Mac graphics programs, the Option key has a profound effect on a selected graphic item: It peels off a copy of the selected graphic as you drag the mouse. For example, the left eye (below) is selected and then Option-dragged to the right:

You can accomplish essentially the same thing in the Finder, making duplicates of your files instead of eyeballs. Normally, when you drag an icon from one folder to another *on the same disk,* of course, you simply move that icon. But if you press Option while dragging an icon to a new folder (or to the Desktop — the gray background), the Mac places a *copy* of the file in the new folder and leaves the original where it was.

Alphabetize them icons!

For the neat freak, there's nothing worse than a mass of messy icons cluttering a window. If you choose Clean Up Window from the Special menu, the Mac will align each icon to an invisible grid so that at least they're neatly arranged. But (1) that won't alphabetize them, and (2) that won't maximize space in the window by eliminating gaps.

If you press (guess which key?) Option while choosing Clean Up Window, though, it changes to say Clean Up by Name. And the effect is totally different — the Mac (1) alphabetizes your icons, and (2) moves them so that they take up as little window space as possible.

Funny little hidden Option key stunts

Control panels: *Little programs that govern the way your Mac works: the color of the background, how fast your mouse pointer moves, stuff like that. To see your list of control panels — and to play around with them — choose Control Panels from the ★ menu.*

Those wily Apple guys! The sneaky programmers! The funsters in Apple Land have buried all kinds of amusing little surprises in the control panels and other places (of System 7). Try these:

✔ The weird little Map control panel lets you find any major city by latitude and longitude, and tells you what the time zone difference is. If you Option-double-click the Map control panel, the map will appear at double size.

✔ You use the Monitors control panel to switch from color to black and white (if you have a color monitor, of course). If you hold the mouse down on the little "7.0" in the upper-right corner, you'll see a list of the programmers. Press Option while you do so, and watch the smiley face — you'll find out what they really think of you.

✔ When you're in the Finder, the item under the Apple menu normally says About This Macintosh. Choose it to view some critical specifications about your machine — how much memory it has, for example. But if you press Option while choosing it, the command changes to say About the Finder and shows you a pleasant Silicon Valley scene. Wait long enough, and you'll eventually see some scrolling credits.

Buried Treasures

Did you enjoy those obscure, mostly useless Option key tricks? Then you'll really love these equally scintillating techniques, not one of which requires the Option key.

How to find a lost file

You haven't really poked around much with the Find command, but it's a doozie. Just choose Find from the File menu (or use the keyboard equivalent ⌘-F), and this box appears:

```
╔══════════════════ Find ══════════════════╗
║                                           ║
║  Find: ███████████████████████████████    ║
║                                           ║
║  ┌─────────────┐     ┌────────┐ ┌───────┐ ║
║  │ More Choices│     │ Cancel │ │ Find  │ ║
║  └─────────────┘     └────────┘ └───────┘ ║
╚═══════════════════════════════════════════╝
```

In the highlighted text box, type a few identifying letters of the name of the file you're looking for. For example, if (by some improbable cosmic accident) you can't find your System Folder, you could just type *SYS* and then click Find (or press the Return key). It doesn't matter whether you type capitals or lowercase letters because the Finder will look for the nearest file that *contains* (not necessarily *begins with*) the letters you've specified.

You can buy any of a zillion programs and desk accessories that are designed to find lost files. But the Finder's Find command is the only one that actually produces the lost file, opening its folder for you and highlighting the icon:

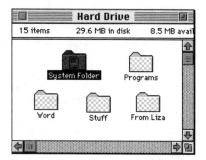

But what if there are several files on your disk that contain the same letters? Easy. Each time the Find command displays the wrong icon, choose Find Again from the File menu. Or just press ⌘-G, as in, "Guess again, diskbrain." The Mac will hunt through your files and highlight the next one it finds that contains those same letters.

If you click the More Choices button, the dialog box expands to show you some other search criteria, such as date, file size, and so on. You could, if you really wanted to, find a certain document whose name you couldn't remember, but that you're certain you created at 3 p.m. during a NoDoz-crazed fit on August 4th.

Make an alias of a file

In the File menu, there's a command called Make Alias. Although you might expect this command to generate names like One-Eyed Jake or Bubba Wilcox, the term *alias* in the Macintosh world represents something slightly different — a duplicate of a file's icon (but not a duplicate of the file itself). You can identify the alias icon easily because the filename is in italics, as shown in the following figure. (The original file is on the left.)

Word 5

Word 5 alias

What's neat about aliases is that, when you double-click an alias icon, the Mac opens the *original* file. If you're a true '90s kinda person, you might think of the alias as a beeper — when you call the *alias,* the *actual* file responds.

K: *Short for* kilobyte, *which means 1,000 bytes. One thousand bytes is either about a paragraph's worth of information or a lot of mosquito attacks, depending on how much you enjoy puns.*

So who on earth would need a feature like this? Well, there's a little bit more to the story. An alias, for one thing, only requires a tiny amount of disk space (a couple of K) — so it's not the same as making an *actual copy* of the original file. (And you can make as many aliases of a file as you want.) Therefore, making an alias of something you use frequently is an excellent time-saver — it keeps the alias icon (and thus the real file) readily accessible, even if the real file is buried four folders deep somewhere.

Another very common trick: Place an alias of a program, or a document, into your menu, where you don't have to open *any* folders to get at it.

Here's the drill:

1. Click the real icon.

2. Choose Make Alias from the File menu.

3. Open your System Folder.

4. Drag the alias into the folder called Apple Menu Items (within the System Folder).

5. Now look in your menu.

Sure enough — there's your file! Select it from the menu to open the original file.

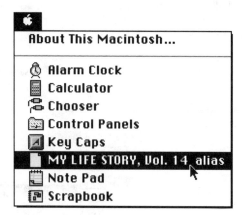

And yet, because you used an alias, the *real* file can be anywhere on your hard disk or on a different disk. You can move the real file from folder to folder or even rename it, and the alias still opens it properly.

Caution!

When you trash an alias, you're only deleting the alias. The original file is still on your disk. If you delete the *original* file, however, the alias icons will remain uselessly on your disk, rebels without a cause, babies without a mother, days without sunshine. When you double-click an alias whose original file is gone, you'll just get an error message.

Likewise, if you copy your inauguration-speech file's *alias* to a floppy disk, thinking that you'll just print it out when you get to Washington, think again: You've just copied the alias, but you *don't* actually have any text. That's all in the original file, still at home on your hard disk.

Creating the L.L. Mac catalog

Every now and then, you might find it useful to create a list of files or folders on your disk. But it's hardly worth your time to go to the Finder, look at the first file's name, switch to your word processor and type it and then repeat with the second file. Here's a much faster way:

1. Select the files whose names you want to copy. (You might want to use the Select All command in the Edit menu, at which point you can press the Shift key and click "off" the items you don't want.)

2. Choose Copy from the Edit menu.

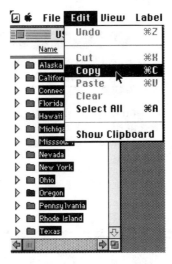

3. Launch your word processor (or even the Note Pad desk accessory, under the menu), and choose Paste from the Edit menu. Presto: a neatly typed list of file names!

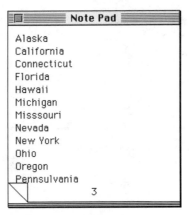

(P.S. — The list can't be a terrifically long one; the Mac copies only 256 characters of text at a time, but you can always repeat the process.)

Have it your way — at "Icon King"

You don't have to accept those boring old icons for files, programs, and folders. If you want anything done around the Mac, heaven knows, you've got to do it yourself.

1. Go into HyperCard or MacPaint or some other program that lets you draw stuff. Make a funny little picture. And I mean *little* — remember, you're drawing a replacement icon for some hapless file. Like this guy here, for example:

2. Copy it to the Clipboard.

3. Go to the Finder, and click the file whose icon you want to replace.

4. Choose Get Info from the File menu so that this box appears:

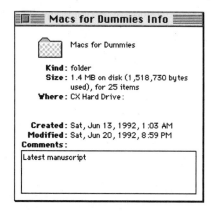

5. See the folder icon in the upper left? Click that sucker —

and then paste away!

From now on, that little picture will be the new icon for the file (or folder or disk). To restore the original icon, do the Get Info business, but click the icon and press the Clear key.

Taking a picture of the screen

In this book, you've probably noticed a number of pictures that illustrate objects on the Mac screen (like the picture of the Get Info window). Now I'll show you how to take your own snapshots of the screen.

It involves pressing three keys simultaneously: Command (⌘), Shift, and 3. You'll hear a satisfying *kachunk!* camera shutter sound. After a moment, a new file appears in your hard disk window, called Picture 1. (If you take another shot, it'll be called Picture 2, and so on.) If you open this Picture file (with the TeachText program that came with your Mac, for example, or any graphics program like MacPaint), you'll see that you've successfully captured the entire screen image.

Unfortunately, you don't have much control over this photo session business. You can't take any pictures while a menu is pulled down, and you can't take a picture of only *part* of the screen. (You can buy programs for those tasks: Screenshot and Capture, for example.)

So why did I wait until this chapter to clue you in on this? Easy — I didn't want you to write and illustrate your *own* Mac book before you'd finished reading this one!

Just saying no

There's a wonderful keyboard shortcut that means *no* in Mac language. It could mean *No, I changed my mind about printing* (or copying or launching a program); *stop right now.* It could mean *No, I didn't mean to bring up this dialog box; make it go away.* Or: *No, I don't want to broadcast my personal diary over worldwide E-mail!* Best of all, it can mean *Stop asking for that disk! I've already taken it out of your slot! Be gone!*

And that magic keystroke is ⌘-period (.).

When you begin to print your Transcripts of Congress, 1952-1992, and you discover — after only two pages have printed — that you accidently spelled it "Transcripts of Congrotesque" on every page, ⌘-period will prevent the remaining 14 million pages from printing. Because the Mac has probably already sent the next couple of pages to the printer, the response won't be immediate (but will be light-years quicker than waiting for Congress).

Or let's say you double-click an icon by mistake. If you press ⌘-period *right away,* you can halt the launching and return to the Finder. And if the Mac keeps saying, "Please insert the disk: Purple Puppychow" (or whatever your floppy disk was called), you can tell it to shut up by doing that ⌘-period thing over and over again until the Mac settles down with a whimper. Show it who's boss.

Colorizing, Editing the Menus, and Other Cool Acts of Vandalism

The great thing about the Mac is that it's not some stamped-out clone made in Korea. It's one of a kind — or it will be after we get through with it. These tips illustrate some of the ways you can make the Mac match your personality, sensibility, or décor.

Changing the background pattern

When you first turn on a new Mac (Performas not included), the desktop area (the background) presents a lovely shade of uninteresting gray. You can easily change this to any other pattern of black-and-white dots — or, if you have a color Mac, to any elaborate arrangement of colored dots. Here's how.

From the Apple menu, choose Control Panels. Double-click the General Controls icon, and you'll see this:

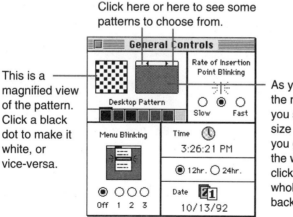

Click here or here to see some patterns to choose from.

This is a magnified view of the pattern. Click a black dot to make it white, or vice-versa.

As you edit the dots in the magnified view, you see an actual-size view here. When you get the pattern the way you want it, click here to fill in your whole desktop background.

As shown in the diagram, the upper-left quadrant of the General Controls panel contains the tools you need to change the backdrop pattern. At left, there's a magnified view, which lets you easily edit each dot that constitutes the overall pattern. At right, you see the overall pattern — in other words, you see what's in the "magnified view" repeated over and over again.

If you have a color (or grayscale) monitor, you can use the row of eight colored squares beneath the magnified view. Double-click one of these squares to change the color it displays. Once that's done, treat these color swatches as a palette — click a swatch and then start clicking dots in the magnified view to change their colors.

Anyway, the point is that when you're finished editing the magnified view at left (to show, for example, your initial), you have to click in the normal-size view (to its right) to make the pattern "take" and fill in your desktop backdrop.

Here are a few pattern ideas to get you started.

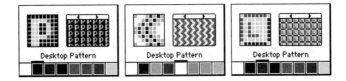

Color-coding your icons

There's another pretty neat colorization feature that hardly anyone uses, but it's still worth knowing about: color-coding. All you do is select an icon or a whole passel of them, and choose a color from the Label menu.

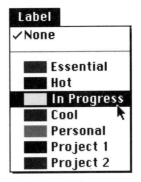

If you don't have a color monitor, you can still attach descriptive labels to your icons (Essential, Hot, In Progress, and so on), even though you won't see the colors.

Two questions, then: (1) How do you change the colors and labels into something more useful, and (2) what's the point?

Well, it seems like most people never bother with labeling their icons. You could argue, though, that it makes life more convenient since you can sort by label (you could see all your In Progress files grouped together in a window). You can also use the Find command to search for a file that has a certain label. You might give one label to everything related to, say, a certain book project — "Idi Amin: The Sensitive Side" — and then when it's time to back up your work, use the Find command to round up all files with the Idi Amin label, so you can copy them all at once. (Or, when the project is over, you could happily *delete* them all at once.)

Anyway, if you *do* want to use this feature, you'll probably want to change the labels Apple suggests (Essential, Hot, In Progress, and so on) to something more useful. To do that, choose Control Panels from the Apple menu. When the Control Panels window appears, double-click Labels.

To change the wording of a label (remember, you're actually changing the wording of the Label *menu*), just double-click a label and type in something new. To change the color — if your monitor is thus equipped — click the color swatch; a dialog box appears where you can select a new color by clicking.

Blue language

Here's one more treat for color monitor owners: You can make highlighted text turn some color other than drab black. In other words, when you select some text in your word processor, it usually looks like this:

Tenderly, gasping through her tears, she daubed his fevered forehead with a rag soaked in

To change the highlighting so that it looks more like, well, a highlighter, choose Control Panels from the Apple menu. When the Control Panels window appears, double-click Color. This Control Panel appears:

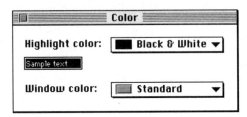

By choosing a new color from the upper pop-up menu, you can make your highlighted text any color you want, like this:

a vile mixture of Jack Daniels, sparkling water, and Pond's skin cream.

Let your innate fashion sense be your guide.

Views

Open the Views control panel. This baby is the control freak's best friend — it can change almost every aspect of the way the Finder displays icons.

Using the font and size controls at the top of the window, you get to choose what text style you want the Mac to use for all icons in the Finder. If your vision is going — or you're trying to demonstrate the Mac to a crowd — make the font huge. If you want to make your icons as high as possible per square inch, pick a tiny, compact type style. A couple of unorthodox possibilities are shown here:

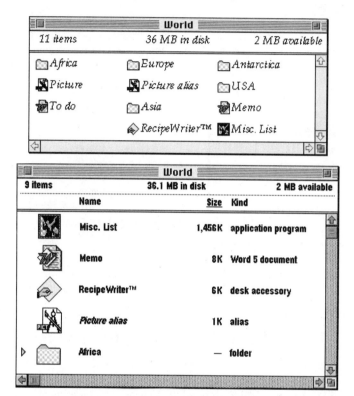

The Icon Views controls let you specify how icons should arrange themselves when you drag them around. If you select "Always snap to grid," icons will smartly jump into position whenever you drag them and let go, according to your Icon Views setting: "Straight grid" places them into neat rows, and "Staggered grid" offsets every other icon so that their names won't overlap when they're placed side by side.

The List Views control governs how icons appear when you're viewing them in a list format.

All those checkboxes on the right side ("Show size," "Show kind," and so on) control which pieces of information show up when you're in a list view. "Calculate folder sizes" is neat because it lets you see how much disk space each folder takes up. (If this checkbox isn't selected, then all you get is an unhelpful "—" in the Size column of a list view.) However, turning on this option tends to gum up the works, making window contents appear more slowly. Finally, "Show disk info in header" puts a separate information strip at the top of each window, which shows you how full your disk is.

List views

There are two ways to view your files in the Finder: as icons or in a vertical list. You choose how you want them arranged using the View menu.

You control which items appear ("by Size," and so on) in the View menu by your checkbox selections in the Views control panel. That is, if you've elected to show only the Size and Date of each file, then you won't see "by Kind" or "by Comments" in the View menu.

View

by Small Icon
✓by Icon
by Name
by Size
by Kind

These two commands let you arrange your icons freely.

The remaining commands create list views and determine how your files are sorted: alphabetically, by file size, by type, and so on.

ResEdit: Menu-editor of the gods

There's a free program called ResEdit (pronounced RESSS-edit, and short for "resource editor"). It doesn't come with your Mac, but you can get a copy from your Apple dealer, depending on how convincingly you grovel; or you can definitely get it from a Mac user group or dial up an on-line service like America Online.

Most Mac books steer such a wide berth around ResEdit that you'd think it had swine flu or something. They'll tell you it's scary, that you could wreck your software with it, that it's too powerful for beginners.

All of that is technically true, but that's like warning you to stay away from your printer because you might drop it on your big toe. In the hands of someone drunk, foolish, or in love, *any* activity is dangerous.

Anyway, what ResEdit lets you do, among other things, is change what the menus say. You can also alter the ⌘-key shortcuts in the menus. If this appeals to you, here's a quickie guide. If you have too much of a life to worry about menu commands, then fast forward ahead.

1. Double-click ResEdit to launch it.

2. When you see the jack-in-the-box, click the mouse to make it go away.

   A list box opens, letting you select the program whose menus you want to mangle.

3. Double-click the program's name. (In the example below, I'm hacking up a program called Extractor.)

   A weird-looking window opens up:

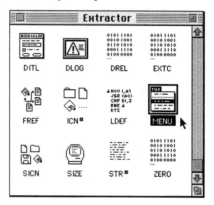

4. Look for the one that says MENU, and double-click it. Now you see the menus in that program, like this:

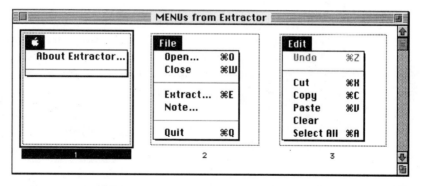

Double-click the menu you want to change. In the resulting dialog box, you'll see how easy it is simply to type in new names for things. (For each menu item, you'll also see the ⌘ key equivalent listed in the lower right. You could make ⌘-S be Quit instead of Save, if you were really that kooky.)

In no time at all, you can make the menus more helpful to you or more colorful or just *different:*

Using that microphone

With most new Macs, you get a free microphone. It's not exactly the same one Madonna licks in her videos, but it's good enough for what we're about to do. And that is to change the little beep/ding sound the Mac makes (when you make a mistake) into some other sound, like "Oops!" or a game show "wrong answer" buzzer or a burp or something (depends on your mental age, I guess).

Here's how it works:

1. From the Apple menu, choose Control Panels.

2. Double-click the Sound icon.

3. When you see the Sound control panel, click the Add button (if your Mac didn't come with a microphone, the Add button will be dimmed). Now you see this:

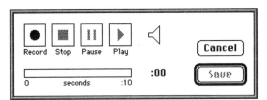

Play me

Here's a way to play a sound that doesn't even involve opening a Control Panel. If you're a double-clicking kinda person, open your System Folder and then double-click the System file. It opens into a window, where you'll see a list of all your fonts and all your sounds. Just double-click any sound's icon to hear it played.

4. To record, just click Record and speak into the microphone.

> Be ready to click Stop when you're done, or else you'll accidentally include a bunch of silence and fumbling at the end of your sound.

There's a plethora of ways to play back your new sound. You could, mnemonically enough, click the Play button. Then again, you could click Save and give the sound a title so that you'll be able to preserve it for your grandchildren. When you return to the list of sounds in the Sound control panel, click your new sound's name to play it. If you leave it selected in the list, though, you've just selected it to be your new error beep.

Utilities with No Monthly Bill

Even as you've been taking your first tremulous steps on this most wondrous of computers, thousands of hackers, in a grand effort to make this insanely great computer even greater, have been slaving away late at night, for weeks at a time, subsisting primarily on three-cheese pizza and Jolt cola ("All the sugar! And twice the caffeine!").

You'd be amazed at the things they come up with. Today you can buy programs that make your hard disk hold more, automatically type out your return address on cue, or — most important of all — put an animated sarcastic moose in a corner of your screen. These are called *utility* programs; here's an overview.

Compression programs

Run a large file through a *compression* program, and it emerges from the other end at about half its original size. (Too bad you can't run the government through one.) Multiply that size-reduction process by all your files, and all of a sudden your hard disk can hold twice as much. It's almost like getting a second hard drive free.

Geek's nook

If you own a modem (a phone hookup for your Mac), you'll discover another great benefit to owning a file-shrinker — if a file is smaller on your disk, it'll take less time to send over the phone lines. And when you're paying by the minute, that means cold, hard cash.

The best-known file-compression program is StuffIt. The *best,* however (if you ask me), is DiskDoubler. This ultra-clever program adds a new menu to your menu bar in the Finder, containing Compress and Expand commands. To shrink a file, just click it and then choose Compress.

Best of all, DiskDoubled files decompress themselves automatically — a double-click does the trick. Why is that a big deal? Because in other compression programs, you have to launch a special program each time you want to compress or decompress a file.

Screen savers

If you've ever seen the ghost of a cash machine's welcoming screen permanently etched in the display, you'll understand the reason for *screen savers.* By automatically blanking the screen after a few minutes of disuse, these programs ensure that your Mac monitor won't suffer the same burn-in syndrome if you accidentally leave the computer on for the whole week you're in Acapulco. To signal you that the computer is still on, however, a screen saver must bounce some moving image around the screen. That's where the fun comes in.

The programmers of these utilities figure: If you've got to display some "I'm still on!" signal on the monitor, it might as well be entertaining. That's why today's screen savers let you choose from dozens of different patterns or animations to fill your screen while you're ignoring the Mac: wild, psychedelic lava-lampish images, sharks swimming back and forth, fireworks, swirling lines, slithering worms, and so on. The most popular commercial screen saver is After Dark, which displays the now-famous Flying Toasters in Space or a Lawnmower Man whose riding mower gradually eats up whatever document you were working on. You get your regular screen back by touching the mouse or keyboard.

Do you really need one of these? Nah. You'd have to leave your Mac sitting idle for days to get screen burn-in. On the one-piece Macs, you can just turn down the screen brightness; on a Color Classic, you can use the built-in Screen Power Saver. But frankly, screen savers are really, really neat, and sort of *de rigeur* among the computing élite. And they help you justify having bought a color monitor.

The bright person's guide to dim screens

Here's how you dim your screen. On a Macintosh Classic or Performa 200, choose Control Panels from the Apple menu, double-click Brightness, and move the slider. On a Mac Plus, SE, or SE/30, there's a dial built into the underside of the front of the screen. (Two-piece Macs have a brightness dial on the side of the monitor, but it doesn't go all the way down to black.)

Anti-virus software

A computer virus, as you may have read, is a program written by some jerk from a dysfunctional family who seeks to bolster his own self-worth by gumming up other people's Macs. There have been a dozen or so Macintosh viruses — little self-duplicating programs that attach themselves to innocent software, whereupon they duplicate some more, until every disk that passes through your floppy-disk drive is infected. You can't get a computer virus unless you (1) swap disks with friends or (2) use a modem to connect to other Macs over the phone.

Once infected, your Mac usually just acts weird: beeps occasionally, slows down, that kind of thing. No widespread Mac virus has ever destroyed files. Nonetheless, that potential exists. Playing on the resulting paranoia, many companies have offered anti-virus programs for sale, cleverly charging you money for an update every time a new virus is discovered. Virex, S.A.M., and Gatekeeper are a few.

My advice is not to spend any money at all on this — instead, get Disinfectant, which is free. It watches over your Mac, tells you if you've contracted a virus, and wipes it out for you. (Disinfectant comes from the usual sources of non-commercial software: Your local user group has it, and you can get it from a dial-up on-line service or bulletin board.)

The Talking Moose and other just goofy stuff

There's no good reason for you to spend any time or money in acquiring these things. It's worth knowing, however, that this computer of yours actually has a decent sense of humor.

The Talking Moose is a hilarious, nearly indescribable little software doodad. It makes a cartoon moose pop up in the corner of the screen every few minutes, utter a sarcastic or silly morsel, and then disappear again. "Let's get a move on," he'll say after a few minutes of boredom. Or: "We never go out anymore."

If such silliness piques your interest, you may also want to consider Sound-Master. This one is *shareware* — not sold in any store — and it finally gives you a good use for that microphone of yours. It lets you designate a sound for the Mac to play when it ejects a disk, starts up, shuts down, or does any other conceivable computer action. This means you can jazz up your holiday season with fa-la-las or make the Mac shut down with a parting shot like "Now get some exercise, lardball." The most famous example is making the Mac say *Bleeccchh!* when spitting out a disk, although playing the Looney Tunes theme upon startup isn't too shabby either.

Top Ten Free or Almost-Free Utility Programs

A moose may be charming, as the producers of "Northern Exposure" will tell you, but it's expensive. Your other Mac utilities don't have to be. Here are ten good ones, all of them shareware. (In case you missed it, you get shareware from a user group, electronic bulletin board, or on-line service like America Online.)

1. *MaxAppleZoom.* Look at your monitor when the computer is on. See how there's a fat black band around the edges of the glass? What a waste! If you have an Apple 13-inch color monitor with a standard Mac II Video Card, MaxAppleZoom eliminates that ¾-inch band of darkness around the perimeter of your monitor, filling every single pixel behind the glass with usable image, right up to the plastic collar. Suddenly you've got 17 percent more screen area — as though you traded in your 13-inch monitor for a 14-incher.

2. *Disinfectant.* As described above.

3. *Compact Pro* or *StuffIt Classic.* File-compression programs. Not as convenient — and not nearly as fast — as DiskDoubler, but then again much cheaper.

4. *SoundMaster.* As described above — at last your Mac can make yawning sounds and grouchy mumbling when you wake it up in the morning.

5. *System 7 Pack.* When Apple upgraded its system software (i.e., all that junk in the System Folder) to System 7, many Mac owners rejoiced. But a few sighed because System 7 makes things in the Finder slower — things like opening windows and copying files. But System 7 Pack, written by a teenager in New Jersey, takes care of both problems. It makes windows open faster and makes your Mac copy files three times faster.

6. *SCSI Probe.* You power up the Mac, but your hard-drive icon doesn't appear. If you have SCSI Probe (or the nearly identical SCSI Info), you can find out the make, model, capacity, and SCSI address of every SCSI device attached to your Mac, and more. It has a Mount button that can often bring a SCSI device on-line if it's acting flaky. (SCSI is like that.) More about SCSI in Chapter 9.

7. *Save-O-Matic.* The software for the chronic Mac procrastinator: a safety net for people who forget to save their documents regularly. This thing'll do it *for* you, every five minutes or ten minutes or whatever you specify.

8. *Remember?.* It's a desk accessory calendar thingie. You type your appointments into its clean, colorful calendar, and it actually reminds you of each

upcoming event. If you want, it presents you with a list of the day's schedule when you turn the computer on in the morning. If anybody cares, I think it's better than most of the high-priced calendar/reminder programs.

9. *Moire.* It's a screen saver, as described above. No, it doesn't have flying toasters or lawnmower guys. But what the heck — it's free, and the patterns it bounces around on the screen are plenty pretty.

10. *Pixel-Flipper.* Do you know how to switch your color monitor to black-and-white (and back again)? It's a long, boring process: Choose Control Panels from the Apple menu, double-click Monitors, and click Color or Black-and-White. The whole thing is much easier if you get Pixel-Flipper, which pops a menu up anywhere you click, from which you choose any setting: black-and-white, color, whatever.

• •

Summary

▶ The Option key unleashes secrets, plays hidden movies, and tidies up your windows.

▶ The Finder has some built-in features that make life worth living: the sizzlingly fast Find command, for example, or the Make Alias command that lets a file be in two places at once.

▶ Using the Views, Color, Sound, Labels, and Monitors control panels, you can brainwash the Mac into looking and sounding like anything you want.

▶ Utility programs, both free and expensive, protect the Mac's screen, protect it from viruses, put talking animals in the corner, or make your files take up less disk space. We have the technology. We can make the Mac better, stronger, faster.

• •

Part III
Becoming Your
Own Guru

The 5th Wave — By Rich Tennant

TOM'S COMPANY OCCASIONALLY CONDUCTED SPOT CHECKS TO MAKE SURE THE EMPLOYEES WEREN'T SNEAKING THEIR MACINTOSHS INTO THE OFFICE.

Pencil box,...Rolodex,... large glowing chefs hat, nope, no Macintosh here.

In this part...

Now it's time to take the bull by the horns, the sword by the hilt, the fish by the gills, and really take off. First, I bestow unto you Chapter 9, the Mother of All Troubleshooting Sections. And then you'll find out where to go from there, with your trusty Mac ever by your side.

Chapter 9
When Bad Things Happen
to Good Machines

• •

In This Chapter

▶ The top ten problems encountered by beginners and how to solve them

▶ The next ten after that

▶ The next ten after that

▶ A bunch of others

• •

Introduction to Computer Hell

As a new computer owner, it probably doesn't cheer you up very much that this troubleshooting guide is the fattest part of the book.

But let's face it: Computers are appliances — and, as such, they have minds of their own. And, like other expensive appliances (cars, homes, pacemakers), they tend to get cranky at the worst possible times.

Fortunately, several million Mac users have been this way before, and they've uncovered the most common glitches already; you'll find them, and their solutions, explained here. Again fortunately, most computer problems cost you nothing but time.

Some computer glitches also cost you some data (that is, your work). Well, you've been told to floss if you want to keep your teeth; I'm telling you to back up your work if you want to keep your data, job, and sanity. Saving your work frequently and making backup copies minimizes the number of midnight sobbing sessions you'll have when your important projects vanish into what's left of the ozone.

The three most common causes of computer problems

A guy once called a software company in a panic. "Help!" he told the help-line woman. "Your program made my monitor go out!"

The woman tried to soothe him. "Don't worry," she said. "A cable probably came loose. Why don't you look in back of the computer to see if everything's connected?"

The guy replied, "How can I look back there? It's too dark — the power in my building is out!"

That story is a tactful, nonthreatening way of introducing one very common cause of computer glitches: operator error. Nothing's actually *broken,* but there's something simple that you, the operator, may have overlooked. Be sure to read the "Top Ten Beginner Troubles," below.

Another common cause of computer troubles arises when you attach other equipment (or peripherals, as the Mac intelligentsia call them) to the back of the Mac. Be sure to read "Scuzzy SCSI," below, for some chilling truths on this topic.

By far the most common and frustrating computer problem, though, is caused by software bugs. Writing a software program that works with every Mac model, under every circumstance, and is compatible with all *other* programs, is spectacularly difficult. It's like trying to work out the seating for a 100-guest dinner party, where no two people of different political, dietary, or hygiene habits can be seated together — and everyone, incidentally, happens to be schizophrenic. There are just too many variables; and in the computer world, everything changes all the time.

System crash: *The Mac suddenly stops working, usually displaying a picture of a short-fused bomb accompanied by the not-very-comforting words "Sorry, a system error has occurred."*

System freeze: *The cursor freezes in place on the screen and neither the mouse nor the keyboard works, but no error message appears.*

Therefore, even when Silicon Proboscis Software thinks it's ironed out every single bug in its nose-imaging plastic surgery program, *you* may have trouble with it because there's something on *your* hard disk that's incompatible with that program. The result may be a system crash, a freeze, or something equally horrifying.

Shooting your own troubles

extension: *In this context, a System extension is a little miniprogram that you drop into the System Folder. It adds some feature to the Mac — one that automatically dims your screen after a few minutes of idleness, adds a little clock to your menu bar, protects your disk against computer viruses, and so on.*

Therefore, what I'd *really* like to teach you is how to be your *own* Mac guru: how to ferret out the cause of a problem yourself.

There are only a certain number of ways a person can set up a Mac. The elements are what model it is; how much memory it has; what printer it's connected to; what *extensions* and control panels are in its System Folder; what order you take steps in; what program you're using; and how everything's wired together.

When something doesn't work, then, the object is to try changing *one* of those variables and repeating whatever-it-is-that-didn't-work.

Here are a couple of typical examples.

Walter, a New Jersey tollbooth operator, tries to print out a picture he made of a Maserati flying off the highway at high speed — but nothing comes out of the printer. Flicking his earlobe, he wonders whether it's the *printer* that's not working or the *program*. To find out, he goes to his word processor, types TESTING TESTING and prints *that*. It works. Now he knows that the printer works fine — the problem is related to the drawing program. Next he success-fully prints a different document from the same drawing program, and thus learns that the problem is with his Maserati document, not the drawing pro-gram in general.

Extensions folder: *A special folder inside the System Folder that houses System extensions. In fact, if you drop an extension's icon on top of the System Folder icon, the Mac will place it in the Extensions folder automatically.*

Or Nina, the political figurehead for an emerging third-world nation, is given an expensive fax/modem as a bribe by a company that wants to strip-mine for sulphur. She hooks it up, drops the necessary software (an extension) into her System Folder, and tries to send a fax — but the mouse freezes, unmovable, on the screen. Calmly, she wonders what's unusual about her particular Macintosh that would cause a popular gizmo to malfunction. She opens the Extensions folder and removes all the extensions that didn't originally come with her Mac: a screen saver, a spelling checker, and Adobe Type Manager. She restarts the Mac, and this time the fax/modem works beautifully. She correctly assumes that the fax/modem's extension has a *conflict* with one of her other extensions; with a little experimentation, she is able to figure out which one, and the desecration of her country's natural resources proceeds unhindered.

Do you see the connection between Walter and Nina? Each became a Mac sleuth, changing one variable at a time, until the problem was cornered. Neither one knew *what*, technologically speaking, the problem was. But both figured out *where* the problem was, and that's the first step to working around it and getting on with your life.

Here, then, is a chapter full of typical snafus encountered by typical Mac users. If you never need to refer to this section, the gods smile on you; read it anyway, to find out how lucky you really are.

The Top Ten Beginner Troubles (That Don't Actually Need Shooting)

If you've read this book to this point, a couple of these troubles will seem obvious. But believe me, I've seen these typical troubles zap the confidence of many a first-timer.

1. *The screen is all gray, there's no window open, you can't find any files or folders, but the Trash can is in the corner.*

   If you want a window to appear, you have to open a disk icon. In the upper-right corner of your screen, there's an icon representing a disk. Point to it and double-click the mouse button to make it open into a window.

2. *You try to work, but nothing happens except beeping. Every time you click the mouse button, there's another beep.*

   When the Mac requests some information from you, it displays a *dialog box* — a box with some questions for you to answer. This one, for example, appears when you try to print:

LaserWriter "Silentwriter 95"	7.1.1	**Print**
Copies: 1 Pages: ⦿ All ○ From: [ ] To: [ ]		Cancel
Cover Page: ⦿ No ○ First Page ○ Last Page		
Paper Source: ⦿ Paper Cassette ○ Manual Feed		
Print: ○ Black & White ⦿ Color/Grayscale		
Destination: ⦿ Printer ○ PostScript® File		

What's not very nice about dialog boxes, though, is that they commandeer your Mac. You're not allowed to do *anything* until you answer the questions and get rid of the box. If you try to keep working, the Mac will keep beeping at you, and the box will sit on your screen until doomsday.

Every dialog box, therefore, has a button you can click to make the box go away. Usually you can choose a button that says OK or one that says Cancel. (In the figure above, the buttons say Print and Cancel.) Anyway, you have to click *one* of those buttons before the Mac will return control to you.

3. *You double-click an icon, but you get an irritating message that says "Application not found" (or something equally unhelpful).*

   This is a confounding one for beginning users. As it happens, it's also a confounding one for *experienced* users. So I'll refer you, at this point, to the same item in the section below called "Error Messages."

4. *A menu command is gray, and you can't choose it.*

   The Mac is smarter than most computers (although that's not saying much). Among other things, it can tell when something's appropriate. If there's no floppy disk in the disk drive, for example, the Eject command in the menu is dimmed because there's nothing to eject! So the Mac saves you some trouble, selectively dimming menu commands according to the context.

```
┌──────────────┐
│ Special      │
├──────────────┴───┐
│ Clean Up Window  │
│ Empty Trash   ⌘T │
├──────────────────┤
│ Eject Disk    ⌘E │
│ Erase Disk...    │
├──────────────────┤
│ Restart       ⌘R │
│ Shut Down        │
└──────────────────┘
```

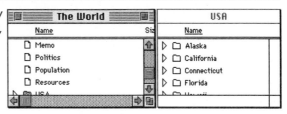

Active window: When more than one window is open on the screen, you can see all of them, but you can only work in one at a time. The frontmost window, in which you're working, is called the active window. You can tell it's active because (1) its title bar has pinstripes, and (2) its scroll bars appear. In the figure at right, The World is active, but USA is inactive (as usual).

Some other examples: According to the noun-verb scheme of the Mac (as discussed in Chapter 1), Cut and Copy aren't available if you haven't first selected some text or graphics that you want to cut or copy. Close Window is dimmed if there isn't a window open. The entire View menu is dimmed if no window is *active* — even if there is an *open* window.

5. *There's a pile of stuff next to the Trash can.*

All the Mac books and manuals tell you how you chuck a file you no longer want: Drag its icon "to the Trash," meaning the Trash can icon in the lower-right corner of your screen.

What's usually *not* made absolutely clear is that, as you drag the icon to the Trash can, you have to place the *tip* of the arrow cursor directly *on* the Trash can icon. You have to see the Trash can itself turn black.

That may seem awkward, especially if you're dragging a whole group of icons at once. For example, in the illustration below at left, one of the icons being dragged is already bumping up against the edge of the screen.

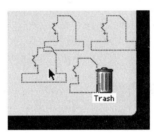 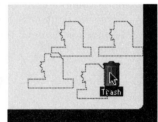

You have to ignore that, though, and keep on moving the mouse until the arrow is directly on the Trash can (above right).

6. *You're word processing, and suddenly all your text disappears.*

There are two possibilities, neither of which means you've really lost your text.

First of all, not everyone is aware that, when you fill up a screenful of text, a word processor automatically shoves that screenful upward off the top of your screen, in effect advancing you to the next clean sheet of paper.

This diagram shows how the first page of text has scrolled off the top of the window:

As she slipped out of the silky almost-nothing she'd been wearing, her shiny chestnut hair cascaded down across her creamy shoulders.

"What you *don't* know about me, Arthur," she cooed, "is that I'm not a woman at all."

An odor of electrical smoke touched his nostrils, and he looked in horror as her graceful, womanly fingers—the very fingers he'd kissed only moments before—grappled with a seam near her collarbone. His breath quickened. A clock ticked. Somewhere, in the distance, a wolf howled.

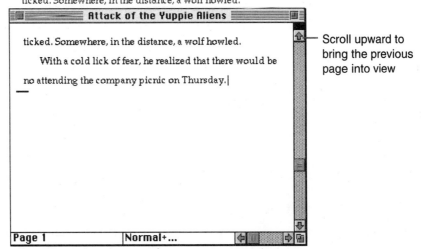

ticked. Somewhere, in the distance, a wolf howled.

With a cold lick of fear, he realized that there would be no attending the company picnic on Thursday.|

Scroll upward to bring the previous page into view

But suppose you *do* know all about scroll bars and scrolling. And you scroll, and you decide that your text really *has* disappeared.

You may well be the victim of another not-immediately-obvious Mac "feature": that any highlighted text, from a single letter to a 4,000-page encyclopedia, is *instantly replaced* by the next keystroke you type. Usually this is handy: If you want to replace the word "kickback" with the words "incentive payment," you don't have to *delete* the word "kickback" first. You just select it (below top) and then type (below bottom):

> to accept the occasional <mark>kickback</mark> of
> to accept the occasional incentive payment| of

The danger is that, if you've inadvertently (or advertently) selected a bunch of text, and you touch *any* key — the spacebar, Return key, or any letter — you'll replace everything you've selected with a space, a Return, or a letter.

If this happens, the solution is easy: Choose Undo from the Edit menu.

If it's too late for Undo — in other words, if you've done something else *since* deleting the text (because Undo only undoes the *most* recent thing you do) — you may be able to recover some of your text. Close your document *without* saving changes. Reopen it. At least you'll see as much text as was there the last time you saved your work.

7. *There's a thin horizontal line all the way across your color monitor.*

Believe it or not, *all* Apple 13-inch and 16-inch color monitors show this faint line (it's about a third of the way up the screen). It's a shadow cast by a wire inside. Just grit your teeth and remember: "It's a Sony." (Sony makes these monitors.)

A word to writers

If you're a writer, or anybody who plans to do a lot of typing, there's a way to protect yourself against *any* of the text-loss problems described above. Even if you (1) experience a system crash before you've had a chance to save your work, or (2) accidentally replace all your text, or (3) *deliberately* delete some text, but then later wish you hadn't, there's a little piece of software that can save you. It's called Last Resort, and it lurks in the background of your Mac, silently logging everything you type into a text file. You never see it, never notice it — *but,* if the unmentionable happens, you can open the Last Resort text file and recover everything you've typed (ever since you installed Last Resort, in fact). See the Resouce Resource for info.

8. *You drag a file into a window, and it disappears.*

   Once again, you have to watch your tip, if you'll excuse the expression. When you drag an icon, it's the cursor arrow's *tip* that actually marks where the icon is going, *not* the icon itself. What probably happened is that you accidentally released the icon when the arrow tip was on top of a *folder* within the window, as shown here:

   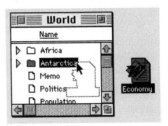

   As a result, the Mac dropped the file *into* the folder, making it disappear from the screen.

9. *You can't print.*

   There's a delightfully thorough discussion of printing problems later in this chapter.

10. *You become addicted to working with your Macintosh. The image of the Trash can gets burned into your corneas. Friends, family, and job seem to recede and eventually go away.*

   Congratulations! You've graduated from this book.

Error Messages

Let's start the Troubleshooting session in earnest with a few good old American Error messages. Yes, kids, these are the '90s equivalent of "DOES NOT COMPUTE." These are messages, appearing in an *alert box* like the fictional one shown below, that indicate something's wrong.

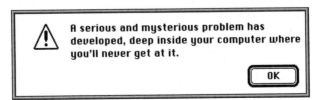

Note that these aren't the same as *System errors,* which are described later; a System error box shows a bomb with a short fuse and indicates a much graver problem.

"Application is busy or missing," or "Application not found."

I promised to return to this one: Here we go.

First resort: Not everything in the Mac world is meant to be a plaything for you. The Mac reserves a few files for its own use. If it came with your Mac — like the Scrapbook file, the Clipboard file, and so on — then you at least get *someplace* when you double-click an icon: The Clipboard file opens up into a window where you can see the most recent stuff you copied; the Note Pad file automatically launches the Note Pad desk accessory; and extensions or control panels at least identify themselves (with a message on the screen, like "System Extension: This file adds functionality to your Macintosh").

Preferences folder: *One of the special folders inside your System Folder. It contains private data files that are used exclusively by* other *programs* and are not meant for you to mess with.

But if you double-click a file belonging to non-Apple software — like any file in the Preferences folder, for example, or various other support files for non-Apple stuff — you'll just get a beep and an unhelpful error message.

That's what's going on *most* of the time.

Second resort: Every now and then, though, you'll double-click a file that you yourself created, and *still* you get the "Application not found" message. Refer back to Chapter 3, where you learned about programs and the documents they produce (like parents and children). In this case, you're trying to open a document (child), but the Mac can't find its parent (the program used to create it). So if you double-click a Word document, but the Word program itself isn't on your hard disk, then the Mac will shrug its shoulders and tell you, in effect, "Yo — how am I s'posed to open this?" To remedy the situation, copy the application program back onto the hard disk.

Third resort: Sometimes you may get the "Application not found" message *even* if (1) you're positive it's not a System file that you can't open, and (2) you're sure that the document's parent program is on the disk. (You double-click a Word document, and you're told that the application — Word — can't be found, even though it's *sitting right there* on the disk in plain sight!)

In a situation like this, the Mac's genealogical gnomes have become confused: The computer has lost track of which program is associated with which kinds of documents. Don't ask me how such confusions happen: Just rejoice that it's an easy problem to fix. In the words of Mac gurus everywhere, "You gotta rebuild the Desktop."

Now then. Before you grope for your woodworking tools, let's analyze this concept of rebuilding the Desktop. The Desktop referred to is a very important file on your disk. So how come you've never seen it? Because the Desktop file is *invisible*. (Yes, Mac icons can be invisible. Remember that if you ever get involved in antiterrorist espionage activity.) It's something the Mac maintains for its own use.

In the Desktop file, the Mac stores two kinds of information: First of all, it stores the actual pictures used as icons for all your files; second, it stores information about the parent-child (program-document) relationships you're having trouble with.

If the Desktop file becomes confused (which results in the "not found" message), you have to reset it. You have to brainwash it, forcing it to unlearn the misconceptions that are giving you trouble, and relearn the correct relationships between documents and the programs that gave birth to them. See the "Rebuilding the Desktop file" sidebar for instructions.

Last resort: There's one more circumstance when you'll get this message: If you try to open a generic text or graphics file that's not associated with *any* particular program.

(Sigh.) Yes, I know, this contradicts everything you've learned about programs and documents being like parents and children. But suppose somebody wants to give you a memo they've written, yet they're not sure which brand of word processor you own. The smart thing would be to give you the memo in *text-only* format: a generic, no-frills, raw-typing format. A text file. Or, as the weenies say, an *ASCII* (pronounced ASKie) text file. No matter what program was used to create this file, *any* word processor (even on non-Mac computers, for that matter) can open it.

Rebuilding the Desktop file

Restart the computer (choose Restart from the Special menu). As it starts gearing up to turn on again, press and *hold* the Option and ⌘ keys. Don't let go. Keep them down until the Mac explicitly asks you if you want to "rebuild the Desktop." (Obviously, you should click OK.)

Once that's done, your document double-clicking will work (if, in fact, the parent program is on the disk). And your Mac, having been cleansed of all obsolete icon pictures, will also run faster and more smoothly.

However, a text file generally isn't double-clickable. To read it, you launch your word processor *first.* Then use the Open command in the File menu. The usual list box appears, and you'll see the text file listed there. Double-click to open it.

The same applies to generic picture documents, too; the weenie-word here is *PICT* files. If you try to double-click a generic PICT file, you'll be told (yawn) "Application not found." Once again, the solution is to launch your graphics program (like MacDraw) *first* and then open the PICT file via the Open command.

"There is not enough memory to open Word."

This is a biggie. It gets a section all by itself; see "Out of Memory," below.

"The application LightningDraw has unexpectedly quit."

You're probably out of memory. Once more, see "Out of Memory," below.

However, even if your Mac has plenty of memory, the individual *program* that just "unexpectedly quit" may not have enough memory allotted to it. See the sidebar on page 239 to find out how to give your program a more generous helping of memory.

"The disk is full."

This means the disk is full. It happens to the best of us: Over time, your hard disk gets fuller and fuller. Then, with only a megabyte of storage space to go, you try to do something (like saving an important file), and you're told there's no more elbow room.

You'll have to make some more room. From the Application menu, choose Finder. Root through your files and find some things to throw away. Drag them to the Trash can, and don't forget to *empty* the trash (using the Empty Trash command in the Special menu).

Application menu: *The menu in the upper-right corner of all System 7-equipped Macs, which you use to move from one open program to another.*

Which brings up an interesting point for which I couldn't find any other logical place in the outline: what all that crud in your System Folder is and what you can safely toss. Otherwise it's just taking up valuable disk space.

Double-click the System Folder, and let's do some hunting. (Some of these items may be in the Extensions or Control Panels folders *within* the System Folder.) Don't worry about trashing this stuff: If you ever need it again, you can just reinstall it from your white Apple system disks.

- ✔ Anything with the word DAL in it. This is for huge monolithic corporations where you're trying to plug the Mac into some giant humming mainframe computer behemoth named Hal. Toss it.

- ✔ Anything with the words AppleShare, File Sharing, Sharing, Network, Users and Groups in the title. All these files are associated with networking Macs together. If you're a solo Mac user, throw them away. You not only gain disk space, you also get some memory back that those things use.

- ✔ Easy Access and CloseView. Designed for the motion- and vision-impaired, respectively. Easy Access lets you move the cursor by pressing keys instead of using the mouse. CloseView blows up the screen image.

- ✔ Unnecessary printer drivers. There are probably tons of these in your Extensions folder. Each has the name of (and has an icon that looks like) a common Apple printer: ImageWriter, LQ ImageWriter, AppleTalk Image-Writer, blah blah blah. Thing is, though, that you probably only use *one* printer. Throw all the *other* ones away.

- ✔ Monitors and Color. Toss these if you use a black-and-white Mac and only one monitor. (Yes, some people actually use more than one monitor attached to the same Mac.)

- ✔ Portable and Battery. Toss these unless you have a PowerBook or an old Macintosh Portable. Sack 'em.

- ✔ Brightness. You only need this if you have a Mac Classic. (Other Macs have a dial that controls the brightness of the screen.)

"The Print Monitor has reported an error." or "Can't open printer."

Look these up in the Printing troubleshooting section.

"Can't empty trash."

There's probably a locked file in the Trash can. Press Option while choosing Empty Trash from the Special menu.

"An error occurred while writing to the disk."

Something went wrong while you were trying to save a document — probably your disk was full, or it's a flaky floppy disk. (See "Floppy Disk Flukes" for more information on flaky floppies.)

"Microsoft Word prefers 2048K of memory. 2000K is available."

Once again, you're out of memory. The Mac will give you the chance to launch the program anyway — but it'll run slowly and may crash if you get too ambitious with your work. See the "Memory tactics" sidebar for a more lucid explanation.

Out of Memory

As a service to you, the Tremulous Novice, I haven't even whispered a word about Memory Management, which is a whole new ball of wax. I've hoped that you'd never need to think about it. Memory only really becomes an issue when you get the message "There is not enough memory to Open Word" (or whatever program you're trying to open) — and that's why you're reading about memory in this troubleshooting chapter.

Your Mac has a fixed amount of memory. Think of it as a station wagon. You can pack it with camping gear, or you can pack it with your kid's birthday party friends, but probably not both. Even if you manage to cram in the kids and the gear, if you *then* try to cram in the dog, somebody in the family is going to say, "There is not enough room to take Bowser."

That's what the Mac is trying to tell you.

Each program you open consumes a chunk of the Mac's limited memory. You're entitled to run as many programs as you wish simultaneously: the Note Pad, the Calculator, your word processor, and so on, *provided* they all fit into the amount of memory your Mac has. If you try to open one too many programs, you'll get that message about the dog. *(You* know what I mean.)

Memory tactics

Here's how you can get a clue.

✔ Go to the Finder. From the menu, choose About This Macintosh. This helpful dialog box appears, showing several important numbers about your use of memory:

This is how much memory your Mac has. (If you want to convert this number to megs, mentally replace the comma with a decimal point.)

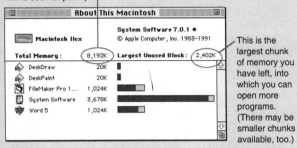

This is the largest chunk of memory you have left, into which you can open more programs. (There may be smaller chunks available, too.)

In the bottom part of the box, you can see what's already taking up memory and how *much* each program is taking up (see those bar graphs?).

You may find it useful, however, to *change* the amount of memory each of your programs uses. For example, if you're experiencing a lot of system crashes, the program may need a bigger memory allotment. And if memory is at a premium, you may be able to give a program *less* memory, freeing some up for other purposes.

Here's how:

✔ Quit the program whose memory appetite you want to change. Click its icon.

✔ From the File menu, choose Get Info. This box appears:

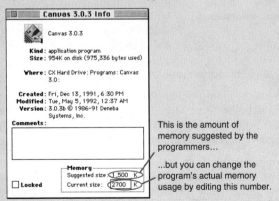

This is the amount of memory suggested by the programmers...

...but you can change the program's actual memory usage by editing this number.

✔ Change the number in the Current size (or, in System 7.1, the Preferred size) box. It's the amount of memory the program will actually consume when you run it. Unless the system crashes make life seem more interesting, don't set the Current size much below the Suggested size, though.

First resort: Quit programs

If you're told you're out of memory, then the easiest way out of the situation is to quit one of the programs you're already running. (You quit a program by choosing Quit from the File menu.) So if you're running Word, and you try to open the Calculator, and you're told there's not enough unused (free) memory, you'll just have to quit Word first.

Actually, unless you use System 7.1 (find out by chosing About This Macintosh from the Apple menu), there's a *pre*-first resort here: Make sure that there's an icon called System 7 Tune-Up in your Extensions folder, within the System Folder. And make sure it's version 1.1.1 or later. If you don't find it, and you've even checked your white Apple floppy disks looking for it, get System 7 Tune-Up right away from a user group or an Apple dealer (it's free). It makes the Mac much kinder and gentler when it comes to dealing with you and your Mac's memory, thus eliminating some of these out-of-memory messages.

Second resort: Make the Mac give back some memory

Quitting programs, of course, isn't a very convenient solution — especially if having multiple programs open is part of what you're *trying* to do, like copying numbers *from* the Calculator *to* Word.

megabyte (MB): *A unit of measurement for things like memory and disk space. A typical Mac comes with 2, 4, or 8 megabytes of memory installed.*

Therefore, your next attempt to solve the problem should be to make the Mac itself use up less memory. Oh yes indeed, the Mac's own behind-the-scenes operations use memory like a silicon hog — at a minimum, System 7 grabs 1.5MB of your memory. If your Mac only has 2MB to begin with (or even 4), you can see already why it's easy to run out of memory.

Here are some tricks to make the Mac use less memory.

✔ Use fewer *extensions,* the little auto-loading programs whose icons appear across the bottom of the screen when you start up the Mac. Each one that didn't originally come with your Mac (screen savers, menu clocks, virus-checkers, and so on) eats up another nibble of your memory.

✔ Turn off File Sharing. Those of you advanced enough to be using this complicated feature know who you are. March right up to that Control Panel in the Apple menu, young man/woman, choose Sharing Setup, and click the Stop button. You'll immediately get back one-fifth of a megabyte of memory.

And while you're shutting things off, open the Chooser (by selecting its name from the ⬥ menu), and select AppleTalk Inactive, if it's not already. If you have a laser printer, you've just killed your ability to print — but you've reclaimed another one-fifth of a meg of memory. Turn AppleTalk back on when you have to print.

✔ Turn off Adobe Type Manager (ATM) if you have it. And how do you know? Choose Find from the Finder's File menu and look for it. (Actually, if you have ATM, you'll probably remember buying it for $7.50.) This amazing piece of type enhancement software is nifty (see "Technology to the rescue" on page 97), but it gulps up memory like there's no tomorrow. Either turn it off or turn it down (use its Control Panel to decrease its memory allotment).

✔ Another potentially huge memory-stealer is the Disk Cache. This little gimmick is something you can blissfully ignore for most of your computing days . . . until you start running out of memory.

Suppose you're innocently word processing, and you make some text boldface. Because the word processing program resides on your hard disk, the Mac consults the disk to find out how it's supposed to create bold type. This disk-reading business takes, let's say, one second. If you use boldface a lot, those one-second disk searches are going to cumulatively slow down you and your Mac.

Therefore, the Mac reserves a piece of memory (called the Disk Cache) just for such frequent pieces of information. *Now* when you make text boldface, the Mac consults the disk (taking one second), but stores the "how-to-make-bold" information in the Disk Cache. The *second* time you need to create bold text, the Mac *already knows* how to do it; your text becomes bold in ¹⁄₁₀₀ of a second (because memory delivers information to the Mac's brain 100 times faster than the disk). Cumulatively, all those little tidbits of information the Mac stores in the Disk Cache give you quite a speed boost.

The larger this piece of memory, the faster your Mac will go. But there's the rub — if you make this Disk Cache memory *too* big, you'll use up memory that you could be using to run programs.

Even if I've totally lost you, here's what to do when you're strapped for memory: From the Apple menu, choose Control Panels and double-click Memory. Clicking the arrow as shown below, make the Disk Cache smaller (you can go all the way down to 32K).

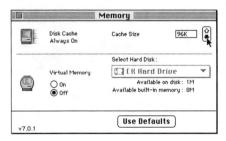

This has been a long explanation for a small reclamation of memory, I know, but it feels good to know what's going on behind the scenes, don't it?

Third resort: Defragment your RAM

Sometimes the Mac will appall you: Here it is, the equivalent of a whole *room* full of 1950s-style computers, yet it can't even add.

Here's the scenario. Your Mac has 5MB (megabytes) of memory, let's say. You know your System uses up 1.5MB. And you're running Excel, which let's suppose takes 2MB.

And now you try to launch MacPaint, which we'll suppose needs 1.5MB of memory. And you get the out-of-memory message! How can this be — after all, the System (1.5) and Excel (2) together only use up 3.5 of your 5MB. There ought to be 1.5MB left over, right? What's going on?

Memory fragmentation, if you must know. It works like this: At noon, you start the Mac. Your memory usage looks like this:

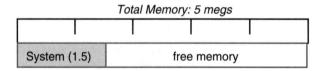

Then at 12:05, you open the Calculator. For this example, let's say its memory requirement is half of a megabyte. When you then launch Excel, your Mac's memory map looks like this:

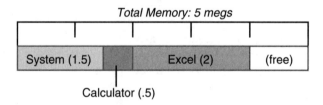

At 12:15, you close the Calculator. Your memory map looks like this:

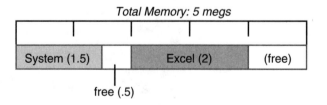

If you look at this last drawing, you'll see you can't now launch MacPaint (which needs 1.5MB) because there aren't 1.5MB of *contiguous* memory left! Because of the sequence, you've inadvertently chopped your remaining memory into two smaller chunks, neither of which alone can fit MacPaint.

The solution to the I-*know*-I-have-enough-memory-to-launch-this syndrome is to *quit* all your programs so that only the Finder is running. *Then* launch all the ones that are supposed to fit in your Mac's memory; and this time, it will work.

Fourth resort: Starve your software

So far we've assumed that each program has a certain memory requirement — 1MB, 2MB, 3-potato, 4. What you may not realize is that *you* can determine how much memory a program eats up. See the "Memory tactics" sidebar on page 239 for instructions.

Why is this useful? Because sometimes when you first install a program, the Current size (the amount of memory it consumes) is set to a much higher number than it needs to be, which can only make your memory-shortage problems worse. Word, for example, comes set to 2048K (which equals 2MB), when it *really* only needs 1MB, or less, to run. Its programmers assumed that you'd be using all its fancy features: the grammar checker, the thesaurus, the automatic hyphenator, and so on. And besides, those programmers tend to do *their* work on Macs the size of a Buick.

If you *don't* plan to use these features, drag them out of the Word Commands folder, and by all means reset Word's memory allotment to something more reasonable.

Fifth resort: Virtual memory

There's another rather technical but interesting possibility for avoiding out-of-memory problems. Fortunately, it lets you run programs whose combined memory requirements add up to much more than your Mac's memory should be able to handle. Unfortunately, it requires you to learn a new term. Ponder this tradeoff for a moment; then read on if you dare.

The term is *virtual memory*. Under this scheme (unique to System 7, and not available on Mac Classic, SE, LC, or Plus models), the Mac attempts to use the *hard disk* as emergency memory.

Virtual: *A '90s computer word meaning fake.* Virtual memory *isn't really memory, and* virtual reality *isn't really real. I don't know why they don't just say "fake," or* faux *if they're after prestige. Maybe it's because* virtual *has more syllables. I guess it gives computer-weenies virtual status.*

Suppose your Mac has 4MB of memory, but you want to run both Limerick-Writer (which requires 2MB) and BrailleMeister (which also requires 2MB). Since your System requires 1.5MB by itself, you can already see that 2 + 2 + 1.5 is going to equal more than your 4MB.

But if you were using virtual memory, the Mac would allow you to run both programs simultaneously. And where would it get the extra 1.5MB of memory it needs to fit everything? It would use an empty hunk of hard-disk space.

Read this slowly: When you're in LimerickWriter, the Mac stashes the excess 1.5MB worth of BrailleMeister information on the hard disk. Then when you bring the BrailleMeister window to the front, the Mac quickly feeds that 1.5MB worth of information back into actual memory, displacing that amount of LimerickWriter instructions (which, needless to say, it writes back onto the hard disk). Each time you switch programs, the Mac juggles the overflow.

This doesn't take place instantaneously. That's a lot of information for the Mac to shuttle back and forth between memory and the hard disk. (Maybe it's time to reread Chapter 2, where memory and hard disks are described in pulse-quickening detail.) In fact, there may be quite a lag when you switch from one program to another. But a little waiting sure beats not being *able* to run those two important programs at once.

For some mysterious technical reasons, the amount of hard-disk space the Mac needs to perform this stunt isn't just the amount of pretend memory you want to *add* to your real memory. That is, if your Mac has 5MB of memory, and you'd like your Mac to think it has 8MB, you can't just set aside the difference (3MB) in hard-disk space; golly, no. You have to allow a chunk of disk space that's the size of *all* the memory — real and imagined; in this case, 8MB.

OK. All that having been said and read, let's get to the actual process of using virtual memory.

1. From the ⚹ menu, choose Control Panels. Double-click Memory.

   The control panel appears, like this:

```
┌────────────────────────────────────────────────────┐
│ ▭▭▭▭▭▭▭▭▭▭▭▭▭  Memory  ▭▭▭▭▭▭▭▭▭▭▭▭▭ │
│                                                      │
│   ▢▢     Disk Cache        Cache Size    ┌─────┐ ⇧  │
│   ▢▢     Always On                       │128K │ ⇩  │
│                                          └─────┘     │
│  ················································      │
│                          Select Hard Disk :         │
│                          ┌──────────────────────┐   │
│          Virtual Memory  │ 🖴 DOCU            ▼ │   │
│   ◉       ● On           └──────────────────────┘   │
│           ○ Off            Available on disk : 10M   │
│                     Available built-in memory : 8M   │
│                          After restart   ┌─────┐ ⇧  │
│                                          │10M  │ ⇩  │
│                                          └─────┘     │
│  ──────────────────────────────────────────────     │
│                      ┌──────────────────┐            │
│   v7.0.1             │  Use Defaults    │            │
│                      └──────────────────┘            │
└────────────────────────────────────────────────────┘
```

See the Virtual Memory area? If not, then your Mac isn't equipped for this feature. (Some of the older ones aren't, and neither is the original Classic or the original LC.)

2. From the pop-up menu, specify the hard disk you want the Mac to use as its temporary fake-memory dumping ground.

If you only have one drive — the one inside your Mac — skip this step.

3. Using the little up and down arrow keys, specify how big you want that virtual memory file (on your hard disk) to be.

Remember, there has to be a chunk of empty hard-disk space that's big enough to hold the *total* of your real memory and the extra, phony memory you'd like to have.

Don't create total memory more than double your *real* memory. If you have 4MB of RAM, your total memory (including virtual) shouldn't exceed 8MB; things will get so slow as to be unworkable.

The Mac may tell you that there's not enough room on your disk. Maybe it's time to go on a cleaning binge.

When you're done setting up your virtual memory setup, restart the Mac.

Last resort: Buy more

After a certain point, knocking yourself out to solve out-of-memory problems (like those listed above) reaches a point of diminishing returns. You get so worn out from workarounds that it's not worth doing.

At that point (or much sooner), just spring the $35 per megabyte and *buy more memory.* You can get it from any mail-order company (like MacConnection). You can install it yourself, very easily, into any Mac that has a separate monitor. Installing it into a one-piece Mac like a Classic is trickier and requires some funky tools. Anyway, when you call a mail-order company to buy memory, tell them what Mac you have and find out what you'll need. Sometimes they send you a how-to video, which is very handy, and when you're done with it, you can use it to record "The Simpsons."

Fair warning: Installing memory yourself is not that difficult, but you should know that if you cause any other part of the computer to malfunction as a result of your installation, you risk voiding the one-year Apple warranty.

Having lots of memory to kick around in is a joy. Your Mac runs faster, has fewer crashes and glitches, and acts like a new machine. It's a situation I heartily recommend.

Starting Up

Problems you encounter when you turn on the Mac are especially dishearten-ing when you're a new Mac user. Does wonders for your self-esteem to think that you can't even turn the thing *on* without problems.

No ding, no picture

First resort: Chances are very, very, very good that your Mac simply isn't getting electricity. It's probably not plugged in. Or it's plugged into a power strip that has an On/Off switch that's currently in Off. Or, if it's a PowerBook, the battery is completely dead. (Plug in the adapter for fifteen minutes.)

Second resort: If you have a two-piece Mac, you turn the machine on by pressing the triangle key on the keyboard — maybe the keyboard isn't plugged in. Check that.

Last resort: If that's not the problem, then your Mac is as dead as Elvis. Get it in for repair. But that's virtually never the actual problem.

Ding, no picture

If you hear the startup chime (or ding) but the monitor doesn't light up, then something's wrong with the monitor.

First resort: Is the screen brightness turned up? On most Macs, there's a bright-ness dial on the edge of the monitor. On a Classic, you have to use the Bright-ness control panel.

Second resort: I don't mean to insult your intelligence — but is it possible you have a screen saver program installed? To find out if that's the cause of the current blackness, click the mouse button. If the screen picture doesn't appear, read on.

Screen saver: *A little program that runs behind the scenes; after it notices that you haven't touched the Mac for several minutes, it blanks out the monitor to prevent an image from getting permanently etched into the screen.*

Third resort: If you have a two-piece Mac, the monitor has to be (1) plugged into the Mac, (2) plugged into a power source, *and* (3) turned on. (Not everybody realizes that your monitor has an On/Off switch.) Often the monitor is plugged into the AC outlet on the Mac itself; that's OK.

Last resort: Does your monitor require a graphics card? Some do. Of course, if your Mac needs a graphics card, you would have discovered this problem the very first day you got your system.

Picture, no ding

Every Mac makes a sound when it's turned on. In fact, even if you've set the volume level of your Mac's speaker to zero (using the Sound control panel), you still get a sound when you start up the Mac.

First resort: Look at the little speaker jack in the back of the Mac. If there's some kind of plug in it — usually some kid's Walkman headphones, a cord connected to a stereo, or occasionally a pretzel stick — then no sound can come out of the Mac speaker.

Last resort: There's a remote possibility that somebody, mucking around inside your two-piece Mac, unplugged the speaker-wire cable. Find that person, yell firmly into his or her nearest ear, and insist that the cable (inside the Mac) be reconnected.

Four separate musical notes

If you hear an arpeggio, then something's seriously wrong inside the Mac. (Why is the music prettier the worse the problem? I guess life's just like that.)

Fortunately, 80 percent of the time you hear this just after installing new memory. It means that one of the memory chips is loose or defective — something you (or whoever installed the memory for you) can fix relatively easily.

First resort: If you've just installed or otherwise messed around with the memory chips in your computer, that's certainly the problem. Reopen the Mac. Carefully remove each memory chip and reinstall it, checking the little centipede legs to make sure none are bent. Come to think of it, get someone who knows what he or she's doing to do this.

Second resort: The other common source of funny startup notes is a SCSI problem of some kind. Yes, I know we haven't defined this in awhile; see "Scuzzy SCSI" on page 254 for instructions — or, for a quick fix, just unplug any external hard drives or scanners from the SCSI jack (the very wide one) in the back of the Mac, and try starting up again.

Last resort: If it's truly not a memory chip or a SCSI problem, call your Apple dealer. This baby's sick.

A question mark blinks on the screen

System Folder: *The all-important folder on your disk that tells the Mac how it's supposed to work, what the screen looks like, and all that stuff we take for granted.*

The blinking question mark is the Mac's international symbol for "I've looked everywhere inside me, and I can't find a System Folder anywhere."

Usually the System Folder is on your hard disk. If it's an *external* hard disk (one that's plugged into the back), check to make sure it's plugged in and turned on and securely connected to the Mac. If you have other pieces of equipment attached to your external hard drive, like a scanner, you might have a SCSI problem. See "Scuzzy SCSI" on page 254.

If your hard disk, like most people's, is inside the Mac, the blinking question mark means that it's not working right — or that it's working fine, but somehow your System Folder got screwed up. In either case, here's what to do.

First resort: Panic. (Who are we kidding? I know you're going to do this anyway.)

Second resort: After ten seconds of that, turn the Mac off and try starting again. Or just press the Restart switch (see the sidebar below).

Third resort: Find a floppy disk with a System Folder on it. The best bet is the white System disks that came with your Mac; the one called Disk Tools usually does the trick. Put it into the disk drive.

If it pops out again, then it doesn't have a System Folder. If you arrive at some kind of Installer screen, then you must have used a System Software Installer disk, and (alas) it's not going to help you get going.

The Restart switch

Almost every Mac has this switch. There are always two buttons side by side, somewhere on the Mac's casing — and the one with a left-pointing triangle is the Restart switch.

Pressing this plastic button is the same as turning your Mac off then on again — except that it doesn't send a wall of sudden electricity thudding into the machine's delicate electronics, and

thus is better for your Mac. It's good to keep the Restart switch in mind when you have a System freeze or crash, too.

Old Macs, like the Plus and SE, come with the Restart switch loose in the box; you have to install it yourself. And the LC series and Performa 400 have no Restart switch; instead, you press Control-⌘-Escape to make the Mac restart.

But if the Mac happily accepts the disk, gives you the smiling Mac picture, and goes on to the familiar desktop, look for your hard disk's icon to appear. If it's there, in its customary upper-right-corner-of-the-screen position, reinstall the System software (using those same white floppies, starting with the Install disk) and start over — after first making sure you have a copy of everything useful on the disk, of course.

Fourth resort: If the hard drive icon still doesn't appear, read "Scuzzy SCSI," below.

Fifth resort: This one is really, *really* technical. I've never even seen it work. But repair people say it could theoretically work. It's called (do *not* learn this term) *zapping the PRAM.* (They pronounce it PEA-ram.)

First, turn off (or restart) your Mac. Then turn it on again, but hold down four keys at once: Control, Option, P, and R; don't let go until the "Welcome" screen flashes a second time. Supposedly this can help.

Last resort: If nothing has worked, and you still can't make your hard-drive icon appear on the screen, then your hard drive is sick. Call up your local dealer or Mac guru, and do *not* freak out — chances are very good that all of your files are still intact. (Just because the platters aren't spinning doesn't mean they've been wiped out, just as your Walkman tapes don't get erased when the Walkman runs out of batteries.)

In fact, you can probably rescue the data from your disk yourself if you buy a disk recovery program like Norton Utilities for the Mac. That won't fix the drive, but it'll let you grab anything useful off the disk in case the drive's ailment is terminal.

"Sorry, a System error has occurred."

This grammatically ungraceful message pops up under various circumstances; see "System Crashes and Freezes," below. When it appears while the Mac is starting up, though, it's almost certainly what the nerds call an *extension conflict,* or an *INIT* conflict.

Trouble is, each extension was written by a programmer who had no clue what *other* extensions you'd be using. The result: Two extensions may fight over the same piece of memory, resulting in that polite disclaimer, "Sorry, a System error."

These things are super easy to fix, once you know the secret. Shut off your Mac and then turn it on again (or just press the Restart switch). But this time, as it's starting up, hold down the Shift key. Keep it down until (1) you see the message "Extensions off," or (2) you arrive at the desktop, whichever you notice first.

Now you're running without *any* of your cute little extension programs. No screen saver, no macro program, and so on. Burrow into your System Folder to find the Extensions folder, where these little guys live. Drag a few of their icons out of that folder (and out of the System Folder) onto the gray desktop — that's how you prevent *selected* extensions from loading. You don't have to throw them away; just take them out of the System Folder and restart the computer. (Use the Restart command in the Special menu.)

If the Mac doesn't crash this time, then you can pretty much bet that one of the extensions you removed was the guilty party. If it *does* crash again, repeat the whole process, but take some more extension icons out of the System Folder.

Through trial and error, eventually you should be able to figure out which pair of extensions doesn't get along. Sometimes just renaming one so that it alphabetically precedes its enemy is enough to solve the problem.

Some crazy program launches itself every time you start up

In the words of Mac programmers everywhere: "It's a feature, not a bug."

Inside the System Folder, there's a folder called Startup Items. Look inside it. Somebody put a program or document in there.

Anything in the Startup Items folder automatically opens up when you turn on the Mac. It's supposed to be a time-saver for people who work on the same documents every day.

System Crashes and Freezes

There are two scary conditions that are enough to make even semi-pro Mac jockeys swallow hard and feel a little helpless. A system *crash* is when this message appears on the screen:

Your current work session is over, amigo. You have to restart the computer. Anything you've typed or drawn since the last time you saved your work is gone. (Safest way: Press the Restart switch, as described in "The Restart switch" sidebar on page 248.)

A system *freeze* is different — and, as horrific computer nightmares go, it's preferable. You get no message on the screen. Instead, the mouse cursor freezes into place. You can't move the cursor, and nothing you type on the keyboard changes anything. The Mac, as far as you can tell, has silicon lockjaw.

Escaping a System crash

You can't. Restart the computer (don't even bother trying to click the Restart button on the *screen*, which usually doesn't do anything).

What you *can* do is understand why system crashes occur. Ninety percent of the time, they're related to memory: either you're out of it, your program is out of it, or two programs are fighting over the same piece of it.

First resort: Increase the amount of memory allotted to the program you were using, as described in the "Memory tactics" sidebar on page 239. Give it 150K more, for example.

Second resort: There may be a bug in the program that's crashing; call up the company that makes it and ask. More likely (and this is what the company will probably tell you), the program's incompatible with something in your System Folder. Go through the taking-extensions-out-of-the-System-Folder routine described on page 250.

Third resort: If that step didn't stop the crashes, there may be some other weird memory-related thing going on under the hood. Some programs are allergic to virtual memory, for example; so your second step should be to turn off Virtual Memory, described on page 243. And if you're advanced enough to know what "32-bit addressing" is, go to the Memory control panel and turn it off. A lot of programs break out in puffy hives when *that* is on, too.

Fourth resort: You may have a SCSI conflict on your hands, especially if more than one external gizmo is plugged into your Mac. See "Scuzzy SCSI," below.

Fifth resort: It's possible that something in your System Folder got gummed up. Reinstall the System software. (1) Turn off the Mac. (2) Insert the white Install 1 disk into your disk drive. (3) Turn on the Mac. (4) Double-click the icon called Installer; follow the directions on the screen.

Sixth resort: You don't, by any chance, have *two* System Folders on your hard disk, do you? That's like throwing two baseballs at once to a Little League shortstop — chances are he'll panic and won't catch either one. Usually people have added another System Folder accidentally, in the process of copying new software onto the hard disk from a floppy. If you don't want your Mac to (forgive me) drop the ball, use the Finder's Find command and search for "system" to make sure you have only one.

Last resort: If you're *still* having system crashes, particularly if they don't seem to be related to any one program, then the fault may lie in the way your hard disk was prepared. Once again we're wading in waters too technologically deep for my comfort. But particularly if you're using a Mac purchased in 1991 or before (in other words, before System 7), frequent system crashes are a telltale sign that you need to *reformat* the hard disk.

That tiresome task involves copying *everything* off the disk (onto a million floppies, for example, or just onto another hard disk), and using a hard disk formatting program to erase it completely. One such reformatting program is on your white Disk Tools disk that came with your Mac; it's called Apple HD SC Setup. Other popular programs are SilverLining and FWB Hard Disk Utility. Or if you bought an external hard drive, you may have a drive formatting program on a floppy disk that came with it.

In any case, the main thing is to ensure that your formatting program is *System 7-compatible*. (The programs I specifically named above all are compatible.)

When you've completely erased and reformatted your hard drive, copy all your intellectual belongings back onto it. You'll probably be amazed at how many fewer crashes you experience.

System freezes

If your system freezes, and your cursor locks in place, you can't save the work in the program you were working on. You don't, however, have to sell your Mac or even restart it. Instead, try this amazing keystroke: ⌘-Option–Esc. (It's about the only time you'll ever use the Esc key.)

If it works, you'll get a dialog box that says "Force [this program] to quit?" Click Force Quit, and you exit the program you were working in.

So what's the big whoop? Well, if you had several programs running, this technique only dumps the one you were working in — the one that crashed. You now have a chance to enter each of the *other* programs that are still running and save your work (if you haven't done so). Then, to be on the safe side, restart the Mac.

And what causes a system freeze? Pretty much the same kinds of things that cause system crashes (see above).

A note about the ID numbers or error messages in the bomb box

In the "Sorry, a system error has occurred" box, there's usually an ID number or a cryptic little error message (like "bad F-line instruction" or "Unimplemented trap").

They're of absolutely no value in figuring out what went wrong. Yes, there are some published tables that list them and what they mean. But in the "what they mean" column, it always says something like "software error." Big help, huh?

Scuzzy SCSI

I've tried to shield you as much as possible from the term SCSI and all it entails. But since it's (alas) one of the most common sources of trouble, it's time to put on the overalls and get dirty.

If there's nothing attached to your SCSI jack in the back of the Mac (like a scanner or a removable cartridge drive), then you *have* no SCSI problems, and you should skip this entire section. You don't know how lucky you are.

What's SCSI?

They pronounce it "scuzzy" for some reason. Here on the East Coast, we used to pronounce it "sexy," which I prefer, but the Valley girls and boys held sway.

Anyway, it stands for Small Computer System Interface (or *Serial* Interface, or *Standard* Interface, depending on where you look it up — it's such a messed-up technology they can't even get the *name* right). It describes the widest connector on the back of your Mac: the *SCSI port*. It also describes the fattest cable of any Mac appliance: the *SCSI cable.* And it describes the kind of hard drives, scanners, SyQuest drives, computer CD players, and other gadgets that you attach to this jack: *SCSI devices.* It also describes the type of information that flows from those devices through those cables to that jack along the *SCSI chain.* But the term you hear most often is: *SCSI problems.*

What's especially frustrating to people who write computer books is that you can't pin SCSI down. Even if you obey the "rules," which I'll give you anyway, things still go wrong.

The only good thing to say about SCSI problems is that once you've figured out the problem with your setup, that problem is gone for good.

System crashes, slow-as-molasses performance, no external drive icon, scanner won't work

These are only a few of the delicious symptoms you have to look forward to in the world of SCSI problems. Now here are some of the equally delicious solutions.

First resort: Unhook the SCSI devices from your Mac. That's right, put the Mac back the way it was when you bought it: bald and buck naked, with nothing attached. This way, at least, you can figure out if SCSI *is* the problem. If the problem went away, then you have a SCSI problem indeed.

Second resort: Somewhere in this book I've mentioned that you can string more than one SCSI device together, or *daisy-chain* them, which is how you can use both an external drive and a scanner (for example) even though the Mac only has one SCSI jack. When the Mac attempts to talk to various devices along this SCSI train, it must be careful not to say "start scanning!" to the hard drive or "start spinning!" to the scanner. In other words, it has to address its messages carefully.

For that reason, every SCSI device in the world has a *SCSI address* between 0 and 7. Usually there's a little number wheel that looks like a one-digit odometer, on the back or the bottom of your SCSI device. Each SCSI device connected to your Mac must have a *different* SCSI number (address) so that the Mac can speak to each one individually.

The Mac, since it's part of the chain, has a SCSI number: 7. If you have an internal hard drive, it has a SCSI number too: and it's always 0. So for your external drives, scanners, and so on, you can choose numbers from 1 to 6; just make sure that no two have the *same* number, or you're cruisin' for a bruisin'.

Third resort: I wish I didn't have to mention SCSI Rule #2: The last device on the chain has to be *terminated.*

When I say terminated, I mean taken out and shot.

But if you've paid good money for these things, I suppose you'd prefer to keep them. The second meaning for terminated is a little bit more complicated.

As the Mac sends its little instructions to the various SCSI devices attached to it, it shoves them out the door with such force that they sometimes go all the way to the end of the cable and *bounce back* toward the Mac. Sometimes they make it all the way back, in which case you get nutty problems like a hard drive icon showing up *twice* on the screen.

To soak up any messages that were pushed with too much oomph, you're supposed to put a sort of electronic shock absorber at the beginning and the end of the line of devices. This absorber, Arnold Schwarzenegger notwithstanding, is called a *terminator.*

If your Mac has an internal hard drive, like most Macs, then you don't have to worry about the beginning terminator: Your SCSI chain is already terminated inside. And if you only have one SCSI device outside your Mac in addition, you also don't need a terminator on the outside end. (I'm perfectly aware that this contradicts Rule #2. But it doesn't contradict Rule #3, which is that these rules don't always apply. Including Rule #3.)

Once you have two or more SCSI things attached to the back of your Mac, though, it's time to start thinking about termination. You add termination by attaching a three-inch stopper plug (called, obviously, a terminator) to the empty SCSI jack of the last device on the chain. Some devices, however, have a terminator *switch* on the back or bottom, which you can just flip between terminated or unterminated positions.

Worst of all, some devices may or may not be *internally* terminated, meaning you can't *tell* whether or not they're already terminated. And Rule #4 is that you don't want a device in the *middle* of the chain to be terminated! And the only way to find out whether or not a device is internally terminated (if it's not in the manual) is to call up the cheap, lazy company that made it. And if it *is* internally terminated, that device *must* go at the end of the SCSI chain.

Gosh, isn't this awful?

So if you have *two* devices that are both internally terminated — well, you're basically up the creek. You can't use them both at once. You may be able to call up the company and have them explain to you, over the phone, how you open up the case and, with a pair of pliers, rip out the little circuits that terminate the device . . . but it's an ugly, unenviable operation.

I guess the point is that, when you shop for hard drives, scanners, or other SCSI devices, don't buy one that's terminated internally. It only means trouble.

Fourth resort: Try rearranging the physical order of the devices in your SCSI chain. It makes no sense, and there's no Rule of SCSI about it, but sometimes that makes things work when nothing else does. And at this point, you're entitled to be a little irrational.

For Mac IIfx owners only

You people have an additional SCSI Rule to worry about. When it comes time for you to add a SCSI terminator plug at the outer end of your SCSI chain, you're supposed to use a special, black, IIfx terminator plug.

Truth to tell, though, my best friend has a IIfx, and she uses a regular, gray, non-IIfx plug, and it works fine. Yet another SCSI Rule that doesn't seem to work.

Fifth resort: If everything else seems hunky-dory, then it's conceivable that the trouble is the *combined lengths* of your SCSI cables. They're not supposed to add up to more than 20 feet or so, and, like speeches and Willie Nelson songs, the shorter the better.

Last resort: OK. You've made sure every device has its own address. If you have more than one external SCSI device, you've terminated the last one. But things *still* aren't working right.

In this case, try taking *off* the terminator. I'm perfectly serious: Rule #5 of SCSI is: If a rule isn't working, try breaking it. Here at home, for example, I have a hard drive and a SyQuest removable-cartridge drive both plugged into the back of my Mac. And *no* external terminators. What sense does that make? I don't know — but I do know that if I follow Rule #2 and add a terminator, then nothing works, and my hard-drive icon doesn't appear on the screen.

Someday we'll laugh and tell our grandchildren, "Why, when I was your age, we used to have to *add terminator plugs to our external devices!*" Until that golden day, though, we have to put up with this cranky and unpredictable technology. Good luck to you.

Printing Problems

After the brutal experience of solving SCSI snafus, these'll seem like child's play.

"Printer could not be opened." or "Printer could not be found."

First resort: These messages appear when you try to print something without turning on the printer first (or letting it warm up fully). Turn it on, wait a whole minute and then try again.

Second resort: Of course, it may be that you haven't performed the critical step of selecting the printer's icon in the Chooser desk accessory. (Or even if you did, the Mac sometimes gets a little feebleminded and forgets what you selected in the Chooser. Just repeat the procedure.) See Chapter 5 for step-by-step instructions.

Last resort: Maybe a cable came loose. Track the cable from your Mac's printer port (make sure it's really the printer port, especially since the modem port looks exactly like it) all the way to the printer. If it all seems to be firmly connected, try replacing (1) the cable or (2) the little connectors.

A million copies keep pouring out

This big-time hazard for novices has to do with Background Printing (see page 108). When you print something, *nothing happens* for a minute or two. (The Mac is storing the printout behind the scenes so that it can return control of the Mac to you.) Trouble is, you don't *know* what the delay is. All you know is that the printer isn't printing. So you choose the Print command again. And again. But the Mac is duly storing all your printing requests; at some moment when you least expect it, all of those copies will start to print!

To stop them, choose Print Monitor from the Application menu (page 56); select each document and click Cancel Printing.

You get jagged text in your laser printouts

First, punish yourself by rereading Chapter 5 so that you'll understand the terms *screen fonts, PostScript fonts,* and *TrueType fonts.*

If you're getting jagged printouts, then you prepared your document using either (1) city-named fonts that aren't TrueType fonts, or (2) downloadable PostScript fonts that have no printer font files in the System Folder. (Again, all of these terms are explained in Chapter 5.)

First resort: If you prepared your document using a non–city-named font like Franklin Gothic, for example, then it's probably not one of the ten basic fonts that are built into your laser printer. (They're listed on page 101.) If this is a font you bought, find the floppy disk and locate the *printer font file* — the one with an abbreviated name, like FrankGoth. Drag it on top of the System Folder icon and try again.

Second resort: If you are trying to print a non–city-named font, but you can't find the corresponding printer font file, you'll have to choose a different font for your document.

Last resort: And if you used a city-named font that's printing out jagged, you're equally out of luck; that font simply wasn't designed for use with a laser printer. Again, you'll have the best luck with one of the fonts shown in the sidebar, "The ten great city fonts" in Chapter 5 on page 92.

Likewise, you may be printing a graphic that's *bitmapped,* from a program that has *Paint* in the title (SuperPaint, MacPaint, and so on). The trouble here is that the Mac no longer thinks of your text as *text;* it knows only about a bunch of dots in a certain pattern, and they'll never print out smoothly.

While printing, you get a message that a font is "not found, using Courier"

Same deal. Your Mac can't find the printer font file for the font you're using. Read the solutions under "You get jagged text in your laser printouts," above.

Nothing comes out of the printer

Sometimes the Mac fakes you out: It goes through the motions of printing, but nothing ever comes out of the printer.

First resort: Is there paper in the paper tray, and is the tray pushed all the way in?

Or if it's an ImageWriter: Is the little Select light on? If not, push the Select button.

Second resort: Alas, your document is probably overwhelming the printer's feeble memory, and the printer is giving up. You can try using fewer different fonts in the document. Try printing only a page at a time. Or try using fewer *downloadable* fonts in the document — that is, fonts that aren't built into the printer (see #3 of "Top Ten Free Fun Font Factoids" in Chapter 5).

Third resort: If you're printing something complicated, there may be a messed-up graphic. Programs like SuperPaint, FreeHand, and Illustrator are known for generating very complex, sometimes unprintable graphics. For example, here's a graphic from SuperPaint that won't print out:

If you're printing something that includes both text and graphics, try removing your graphics and printing the same document — if it prints without the graphics, you know where the problem is. Call up the graphics program company and loudly complain.

Last resort: If your printer truly has run out of memory, you can usually pay to have it upgraded with more memory. In the computer world, as always, a little cash can surmount almost any problem.

Print Monitor won't go away

If you're using the generally wonderful Background Printing option, as described in Chapter 5, sometimes you may encounter the bizarro Print Monitor program.

What's so baffling is that you never remember launching this program by double-clicking. But there it is, listed in your Application menu. And sometimes it beeps at you, demanding some intervention on your part (such as when the printer runs out of paper).

Anyway, you can't make Print Monitor quit on cue. To make it really go away, you have to cancel any printing jobs it's still working on (by clicking the Cancel button). Then go to another program. Eventually, Print Monitor should disappear from your Application menu.

Streaks on Laser printouts

If they're *dark* streaks, then there's some crud on some element of the paper path inside the laser printer. Open the lid. Examine the rollers (but be careful if the printer has just been on — those rollers get incredibly hot): You're looking for a single blob of grit or toner dust. Clean it off with a Q-tip, preferably damp with alcohol (the Q-tip, not you).

Also look at the series of thin one-inch diagonal wires. Make sure those are sparkling clean.

If there are *light* streaks on the printouts, open the printer lid. Remove the toner drum (usually a big black plastic thing) and gently rock it from side to side. Basically, you're running out of toner dust; this procedure may give you a couple days' worth of extra time, but you'll be needing a new cartridge soon.

Every time you turn on the laser printer, it cranks out a stupid start-up page

This is an annoying one, but easily fixed. See #8 in "Top Ten Free Fun Font Factoids" in Chapter 5.

Finder Foulups

The Finder, you'll recall, is your home base. It's the Desktop. It's the Trash can and icons and all that stuff. It's where you manage your files, rename them, copy them — and sometimes have problems with them.

The Find command doesn't find a file that you know is there somewhere

The Find command is pretty literal. Suppose you're looking for a letter called "Mr. Ted Smith." You use the Find command, and where it says "Find what," you type "Mr. Smith," or "Mr.Ted Smith" (see the missing space?), or "Mr Ted Smith" (no period), or "Mr. WilliamSmith." In any of these circumstances, the Find command will draw a blank. Try searching for "smi," or "Mr.", or any portion of the letters you're certain of.

Capitalization, however, *doesn't* matter.

Of course, the problem may not be what you type into the "Find what" box. You may have misspelled the name of the file itself — say, "1993 Salries" — and no matter how many times you search for the word "salaries," the Finder will always come up empty-handed.

You try to rename an icon, but the Mac highlights some other icon

To rename an icon, click once on it and then press Return (or click its name and wait a second) so that the little rectangle appears around its name.

Now you can edit the name.

If you start to type *before* the little rectangle appears, though, the Mac will think you're trying to select an icon by typing its name, and it will highlight the icon whose name most closely matches what you're typing. It's a feature, not a bug.

You can't rename a file

The file is probably locked. Click on it, choose Get Info from the File menu, deselect the Locked checkbox.

```
┌──────────────────────────────────────────┐
│ ▓▓▓▓▓▓▓▓▓   Review Info   ▓▓▓▓▓▓▓▓▓        │
├──────────────────────────────────────────┤
│   ▨                                        │
│  ▨▨▨  Review                               │
│                                            │
│     Kind : Word 5 document                 │
│     Size : 18K on disk (16,896 bytes used) │
│                                            │
│   Where : Tsunami :                        │
│                                            │
│                                            │
│  Created : Wed, Jun 17, 1992, 4:41 PM      │
│ Modified : Wed, Jun 17, 1992, 6:51 PM      │
│  Version : n/a                             │
│                                            │
│ Comments :                                 │
│  ┌─────────────────────────────────────┐  │
│  │                                     │  │
│  │                                     │  │
│  │                                     │  │
│  └─────────────────────────────────────┘  │
│ ⊠ Locked  ▶        ☐ Stationery pad        │
└──────────────────────────────────────────┘
```

Floppy Disk Flukes

Floppy disks are cheap and handy and make excellent coasters. But when they start giving you attitude, read on.

When copying a file to or from a floppy disk, you get a message that a file "could not be copied and will be skipped"

This one's a pain, isn't it?

First resort: If you were copying a whole group of files, try dragging the troublesome file by itself.

Second resort: Make a duplicate of the file (click it and choose Duplicate from the File menu). Now try copying the duplicate.

Third resort: If the unruly file is a document, launch the program that created it. For example, if it's a Word file, launch Word.

Now go to the Open command in the File menu and try to open the file. If it opens, use the Save As command to save it onto a different disk.

Fourth resort: Eject the disk. Open and close the sliding shutter a couple times. Manually rotate the round hub. Try again.

Fifth resort: Try inserting the obnoxious floppy into somebody else's Mac.

Last resort: With a little expenditure, you can almost certainly retrieve the file. The rescue programs are called things like 911 Utilities (the best for floppies) or Norton Utilities (best for hard disks). They're listed in Appendix C, the Resource Resource.

The Mac keeps asking for a disk that you've ejected

First resort: You probably ejected the disk by using the Eject Disk command in the Special menu. In general, that's a no-no, precisely because the Mac will continually ask for it.

You can get out of this scrape by pressing ⌘-period several times. And next time, eject a disk using the Put Away command in the File menu (or by dragging the disk icon to the Trash can).

Last resort: Sometimes, even if you use Put Away, a ghost of the disk's icon remains on the screen, and the Mac keeps asking for it, and ⌘-period doesn't solve anything. In this case, you probably opened a file on that disk — and it's still open. As long as something on that disk is open, the Mac won't forget about the disk; it would be like canceling the space program while some astronauts were in the middle of a mission.

Choose the program in question from the Application menu, and make sure you close all documents. Now you should be able to drag the disk icon to the Trash can.

You can't rename a disk

In System 7, you can't rename those really old, "single-sided," 400K disks. Period. You also can't rename any disk you're sharing on a network (you power users know who you are).

You can't get a floppy disk out

First resort: Press ⌘-Shift-1. That should pop out the disk, even if you can't see its icon.

Last resort: Use the paper clip trick described in the sidebar "Dweebs' Corner: Alternative disk tips" on page 45.

You insert a floppy, and the Mac says "This disk is unreadable. Do you want to initialize it?"

If it's a brand new disk fresh out of the box, there is *no* problem. *All* brand new floppies are initially unreadable, unless they have already been initialized. Go ahead and click Erase, and go through the disk-naming process that the Mac takes you through. But if it's a disk you've used before, you certainly don't want to destroy it.

First resort: Click Eject. *No*, you do not want to initialize (that is, erase) the disk.

Second resort: Remember that there are three different kinds of floppy disks: single-sided (400K), double-sided (800K), and high-density (1,400K). If you have an older Mac (say, one made before 1990), it may not have a high-density disk drive, and you may be trying to insert a high-density disk that it can't read. Again, the main thing is that you do *not* give the Mac permission to erase the disk; just take it to a more modern Mac, rescue the files, and bring them home on a kind of disk that *your* Mac can read.

Third resort: If it's a disk that you know has data on it, and you have a disk drive of the right type, then there may be something actually wrong with the disk. Eject it, shake it around a little. Try it a couple more times.

Fourth resort: There may be something wrong with your disk *drive* — and not the disk itself. That's easy enough to find out: Insert the disk in another Mac's drive.

If it does turn out to be a problem with your drive, the culprit is often dust and crud. Some of my technoid friends say it's dangerous (static-wise) to use a vacuum or blower in the disk drive slot, but I've actually rescued a disk drive or two this way (and have never damaged one).

Fifth resort: Buy a recovery program like 911 Utilities. If anything can get your files off that disk, 911 can.

Sixth resort: You're not trying to insert an IBM PC disk into your Mac, are you? If you are (having read in the ads that any Mac can read a PC disk), give it up — it's not that simple. You're going to need some special software, described on page 175, if you want your Mac to read PC disks.

Last resort: If the problem is not your disk drive, and even 911 can't get your data off the disk, then the disk is really broken. Don't even erase it and reuse it: Throw it away!

One of the most common sources of zapped floppies, by the way, is magnetic damage. Just like audio tapes, a disk stores information by magnetizing tiny particles of metal stuff. So if the disk gets magnetized by accident, the metal particles get rearranged into some random pattern that the Mac correctly deems "unreadable."

Below are the most popular ways to destroy floppies magnetically:

> ✔ telephones (big-time magnetic impulses when they ring)
>
> ✔ the ImageWriter (heavy electromagnets near the control panel)
>
> ✔ the left side of your one-piece Mac, or the right back corner of your two-piece Mac (electromagnetic power supply)
>
> ✔ other magnets and appliances

And by the way: I know this sounds crazy, but *somebody* has to put this into print because I've met a couple of hysterical new Mac owners who could've been saved. Don't put refrigerator magnets on or near your Mac. That hard disk inside the machine is, after all, a disk, and magnets do to disks what gravity does to a watermelon dropped at 39,000 feet.

Your floppy disks don't hold the amount they're supposed to

It's true. You can't fit 800K of information on an 800K disk, nor 1.4MB on a 1.4MB disk.

The missing storage capacity is filled by an invisible file, on every disk, called the *Desktop file.* This file is the Mac's accounting department and is described in more detail under "Error Messages," on page 233. The point is that it takes up 7K or more on every disk. If it's taking up a lot more than that, you may have a *bloated* Desktop file; see the "Rebuilding the Desktop file" sidebar on page 235 for instructions on slimming it down.

Software Snafus

This part describes things that can go wrong while you're working: problems in programs, for example. See also "System Crashes and Freezes " and "Error Messages."

Disappearing text

This one's covered under "The Top Ten Beginner Troubles (That Don't Actually Need Shooting)."

In FileMaker: Missing information

FileMaker, the world's most popular Mac database, sometimes misleads novices into thinking that their information has been lost. That impression is a result of FileMaker's clever ability to *hide* data. For example, you can ask your Rolodex file to show you only the names of people who weigh more than 250 pounds, or something; the name and address information for everybody skinnier will be *hidden*.

To restore all names to the screen, choose Find All from the Select menu. They should reappear.

In Excel: ##### in a cell

In Excel and other spreadsheets, it's a simple matter to make a cell wider or narrower. But if you make a cell so narrow that it chops off the number inside it, the program displays #####. (Other spreadsheet programs display something similar.)

You can see why it does this; otherwise, only *part* of the number would show up, possibly misleading you into thinking (for example) that your quarterly earnings are only $56, instead of $56,456,890.

In HyperCard: No menu bar

Actually, in certain HyperCard documents, the menu bar has been deliberately hidden by the programmer. The combination of keys ⌘-Q still quits the program, though.

If you'd like the menu bar to reappear, press ⌘-spacebar.

A whole document window just disappears

Every now and then — and this happens even to the greats — you'll be trying to do something with the mouse, when suddenly your entire spreadsheet (or manuscript or artwork) vanishes, and you find yourself in the Finder. No message appears — no "Save changes?," no "System error," nada.

What's probably happened is that, in the process of clicking the mouse, you accidentally clicked *outside* your document window. Of course, clicking a window (or outside a window) is the universal Mac signal that you want to bring some *other* open program to the front.

If your arrow's aim misses the document window (usually when you're trying to use a scroll bar, as shown below), you're most likely to click the gray background — the Finder.

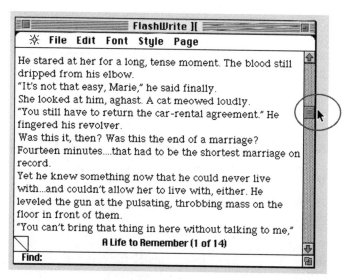

The Finder promptly jumps to the front, showing your folders and files, and the document you were working on gets shoved into the background. (All together now: "It's a feature, not a bug.")

Now you know why, in the Performa Macs, Apple decided to make the Finder get hidden automatically whenever you launch a program.

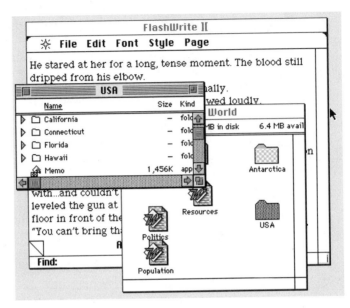

To bring it back, choose the name of the program you were in from the Application menu.

Miscellaneous crashes, freezes, beeps, and goofy or sluggish behavior

For details on freezes and crashes, see "System Crashes and Freezes" on page 250.

First resort: Something may have gotten messed up in the program itself. Find the original master disks, and install the program onto your hard disk again. (Throw away the copy you've been using.)

Second resort: Call the company that makes the program. It's their job.

Third resort: If everything on your Mac has seemed to be getting slower and slower lately, see the sidebar "Defragmenting your disk," below.

Last resort: It's extremely unlikely, but possible that your Mac has been invaded by a computer virus. Basically, though, the problem is almost never related to a virus. You can find out for sure by running a virus-checker program, like Disinfectant or Symantec Anti-Virus (both listed in Appendix C, the Resource Resource).

Hard-Disk Horrors

If you're like many Mac users, you wind up storing your whole life on that disk: appointments, finances, explosive secret diary, the works. That's a lot of trust to place in an inanimate mechanical device that's all moving parts. Back up your work all the time — and rely on this section when things go wrong.

The hard-drive icon doesn't show up

If it's an external drive, either it isn't on, it isn't plugged in right, or its SCSI setup isn't right (see "Scuzzy SCSI" on page 254). If we're talking about the drive inside your Mac, it's probably a SCSI problem.

It's theoretically possible that your drive is broken, too. Bummer.

Sluggish behavior

If copying, launching, and quitting programs (and opening and closing windows) seem to be taking longer than when you first bought your Mac, it's probably time to give your hard disk a physical. See the sidebar "Defragmenting your disk."

Defragmenting your disk

Over time, you create and throw away a lot of files.

Your hard drive, if you'll indulge me, is like a closet maintained by this guy I know who's always in a hurry. When guests are coming over, he cleans up the living room and throws everything into the closet, although not particularly neatly. Every now and then, when he gets time, he unpacks the closet and repacks it neatly, putting everything in a tidy, organized place.

The hard drive, too, is in a hurry. When you ask it to save a file, it doesn't wait around: It shoves that file wherever it can find space. Sometimes that even means sticking the file in *two* places, splitting it up as necessary. Over time, more and more files are stored on your hard disk in pieces. It's no big deal: When you need that file again, the hard drive remembers where all the pieces are and is perfectly able to bring it back to the screen.

But all this hunting for pieces slows the drive down. And like our busy closet keeper, it's very satisfying, every six months or so, to reorganize the files on your disk so that they're each in one piece, neatly placed end-to-end on the hard drive surface.

There are two ways to *defragment* your drive (which is the term for it). First, you can copy everything onto other disks, erase the hard drive, and copy the files back onto it. Second, you can buy a program just for defragmenting your drive. These programs are called things like Norton Utilities and DiskExpress.

You threw something away by mistake

First resort: If you haven't chosen Empty Trash from the Special menu, you're in good shape. Just double-click the Trash icon. Its window opens, so you can rescue any files therein by dragging them back to your hard-disk icon.

Last resort: If you've already emptied the Trash, you're not out of luck. Chances are very good that you can still recover the last several dozen files that you threw away, using a *data recovery program* like Norton Utilities or Mac Tools Deluxe. The more you've used your Mac since you threw something away, the less chance you have of getting it back. See Appendix C, the Resource Resource, for information on getting these programs, and see their manuals for instructions.

Cursor, Keyboard, and Mouse Nightmares

These aren't the most common glitches you're likely to encounter, but they're just as frustrating.

The mouse is sluggish, jerky, or sticky

This is a very common problem. Like children, mops, and mimes, a mouse does its work by rolling around on the ground, and it's bound to get dirty.

To clean it, turn it upside down in your hand. Very firmly rotate the round collar counterclockwise so that you can remove it. Dump the rubber ball into your hand; wash it off under the faucet, and let it air-dry completely.

In the meantime, go to work inside the socket where the ball usually is. With tweezers or something, pull out any obvious dust bunnies and hairballs. The main thing, though, is those three little rollers inside the cavity: You'll probably see a stripe of accumulated gunk around their circumferences. With patience, a scissors blade, and a good light, scrape off that stuff, preferably making an effort not to let it fall inside the mouse. Keep turning the mouse right side up and tapping it on the table to dislodge stuff.

When you put it all back together, you and your mouse will both be much happier.

Double-clicking doesn't work

You're probably double-clicking too slowly, or else you're moving the mouse a little bit during the double-click process.

The cursor freezes on the screen and won't move

This is a system freeze, or system hang. Read all about it under "System Crashes and Freezes" on page 250.

Then again, your mouse (or keyboard) cable may have come loose. Plug everything in firmly.

Something really weird starts suddenly: Beeps and menus get stuck down

If it's not your Mac, or if it *is* your Mac and you just aren't very tuned in, the culprit may be a little add-on program that makes menus jump down when the cursor touches them, even when you're *not* pressing the mouse button. I've always thought this kind of program is somewhat cruel, but some people claim that it saves them some effort.

If you're using a trackball, you may be the victim of a similarly stupid feature: a button on the trackball that, when clicked, makes the Mac think you're pressing the mouse button *all the time.* For the rest of your computing day, the Mac will think that the button is down, even if you frantically click the *regular* mouse button or try to quit the program or anything. Only when you again touch the click lock button does the Mac free the pointer from its bondage.

Nothing appears when you type

First resort: Well, obviously, you can't just type at any time and expect to see text appear. You have to be either in a word processor or in a text-editing area (like a dialog box or in the little text-editing rectangle when you're renaming an icon).

Second resort: Check the cable between the keyboard and the Mac. Make sure it's *very* firmly plugged in at both ends.

Incidentally, the keyboard and mouse cables are especially sensitive to being plugged and unplugged while the computer is on. Be religious about shutting off the Mac before plugging and unplugging them. (That's especially true of SCSI cables. The same is *not* particularly true of modem and printer cables, though.)

Keyboard shortcuts aren't working

Suppose you try to press ⌘-P to print or ⌘-Q to quit, and nothing happens. Chances are pretty good that your Caps Lock key is engaged, and so you're not sending the Mac the signal you think you're sending. (Of course, well-written programs should be aware of that and not care whether the Caps Lock is down or not.)

• •

Summary

▶ The Mac is a murky marvel of mixed-up software and hardware. To solve a problem yourself, change one variable at a time.

▶ The most common software problems, like system crashes and freezes, are caused by conflicting or unruly *extensions,* which are little add-on programs that load every time you turn on the Mac.

▶ The most common *hardware* problems, like system crashes and freezes, are caused by multiple appliances attached to your Mac's SCSI port. Figuring out how to solve the problem is a black art, but there are five SCSI rules, which, when either obeyed or ignored, will almost certainly either fix the problem or not.

▶ Your Mac has a finite amount of memory; when you open more than one program, you may run out of it. But the savvy Mac operator has a bag of tricks for getting around "out-of-memory" messages.

▶ If something bad happens to a disk, you can attempt to resurrect it yourself. If those attempts fail, it's time to buy a disk rescue program.

• •

Chapter 10
Beyond Point-and-Click: Where to Go from Here

In This Chapter

▶ Facing the future, credit card in hand

▶ Where to turn when things go wrong

▶ Now get outside for some fresh air

Credit Card Workout #5: Upgrades and Accelerators

As I warned you in Chapter 1, your Mac's lifespan is limited — not in terms of usefulness but in terms of cutting-edgeness. You'll find that your Mac model, though once top-of-the-line, becomes bottom-of-the-heap insultingly quickly as new models roll out of Silicon Valley.

The advice I'm about to give you may be difficult to follow, but it's something I firmly believe: If the Mac does what you need it to do, *you don't have to keep up with technology*. The impulse to keep your Mac current for its own sake will be strong, but I promise you that your personal worth does *not* ride on the processor speed of your Mac.

A woman in my building uses a 1984 Mac with one-eighth of a meg of memory. She owns one program — the very first version of MacWrite. She's in heaven.

Now then. If some *software* comes out that requires a more powerful Mac, and you require that program, that's a different story. At that point you have a couple of options:

✔ You can upgrade or accelerate your Mac by having a dealer install a more powerful circuit board inside. These upgrades are provided both by Apple and by other companies. Needless to say, Apple's upgrades are twice as expensive as non-Apple ones; what you're basically buying is the logo —

and, if your Mac is still under warranty (or Apple's extended warranty program, called AppleCare), an Apple upgrade won't nuke your safety net. A non-Apple upgrade probably *will* cancel your warranty — but if your Mac's warranty has already expired, there's no reason not to consider it.

✔ You can sell your old Mac and buy a more recent model. Believe it or not, this is often the more economical route. It's more effort, of course. But there are plenty of places to sell your Mac: the classifieds, user groups, bulletin boards at the library or the gym, and any of a number of national computer brokerages. These last advertise in *Macworld* and *MacUser* magazines.

Where to Turn in Times of Trouble

You *do* own the world's most forgiving, self-explanatory computer. But sometimes things will go wrong.

In the official Macintosh doctrine, the dealer from whom you bought your computer is supposed to be your Answer Person.

Yeah, right.

If you have a Performa model, you were lucky enough to get two toll-free phone numbers, good for one year: one for advice and the other to summon somebody *to your house* (or wherever the Mac is) to fix the Mac free if something's broken. Otherwise, as I've no doubt etched permanently into your brain by now, your next resort should be a local user group, if you're lucky enough to live in a pseudo-metropolitan area. A user group, of course, doesn't exist to anwer *your* personal questions; you still have to do some phoning and hobnobbing and research. But a user group *is* a source of sources. You can call up and find out who will know the answer to your question.

Of course, you could always turn to Apple. Their $2-per-minute help line is 900-535-2775. Or you can listen to some canned questions-and-answers at 408-257-7700, for which you're charged nothing but the long-distance call.

The other great source of help, as I've said, is an electronic meeting place like America Online, where you may get your question answered instantly — and if not, you can post your question on a bulletin board for somebody to answer overnight. As a matter of fact, *I'm* there, ready to receive your praise or, if it must be, your wrath, for stuff I've gotten you into. My E-mail address there is Pogue.

As for your continuing education: After spending a month's salary on a computer, I'll bet you can afford $20 more for a subscription to *Macworld* or *MacUser* magazine. I'll warn you that huge chunks of these rags will go right over your head. Heck, chunks of them go over *my* head. But in every single issue, you'll find at least one really useful item. You can learn all kinds of things just by reading the ads. And if you're not in touch with the computer nerd world at least by that tenuous thread — via magazine — then you might miss stuff like free offers, recall notices, warnings, and other consumer-oriented jazz.

Save Changes Before Closing?

If you do decide to pursue this Macintosh thing, I've listed the phone numbers of major user groups, dial-up services, and magazines in Appendix C, the Resource Resource, along with contact information for the products I've mentioned.

But wait a minute — the point of this book wasn't to convert you into a full-time Mac rabbit. It was to get you off the ground. To give you just enough background so you'll know why the computer's beeping at you. To show you the basics and help you figure out what the beanie heads are talking about.

Don't let them intimidate you. So *what* if you don't know the lingo or have the circuitry memorized? If you can turn the thing on, get something written up and printed, and get out in time to enjoy the sunshine, you qualify as a real Mac user.

Any dummy knows that.

Top Ten Topics Not Covered in This Book

Here's a who's who of topics I don't think any new Mac user needs to bother with. If you have the slightest interest in any of them, the shelves are full of geekier books than this one.

1. Networking.

2. Programming.

3. Any add-on that costs over $2,000.

4. Color separations.

5. Multimedia. Nobody even knows what it is.

6. Hard-disk partitioning. Too many syllables.

7. Publish and Subscribe. If you really want to get into it, it's in your Mac manuals.

8. How data is stored on a disk. If you never need to know something, why bring it up?

9. Security. There are all kinds of fancy ways to lock up your Mac. If you're really interested, call up Mac Connection and ask about what they can sell you.

10. The terms *ROM, interleave, SIMM, initiate, user-definable, SIMM, DRAM, implement, CDEV, nanosecond, kerning, VRAM, magneto-optical, token-ring, Ethernet, directory,* or *DOS.*

Appendix A

How to Buy (and Set Up) a Macintosh

● ●

*G*etting started with a Mac really involves three steps (or four, if you count reading this book): deciding which model to get, figuring out where to buy it, and setting it up. This delightful appendix will guide you through all three with as few tension headaches as possible.

The Product Line

At this writing: *Spring 1993. Of course, I fully expect this little table to be up-to-date for about as long as a newspaper. Apple introduces (and kills off) Mac models every few months.*

Since the Macintosh first appeared on the scene, there have been 40 different models. There are 18 still being made by Apple — at *this* writing. Each one is available in several different configurations of features.

Table A-1:	The Macintosh Product Line
*(current models in **boldface**)*	
Macintosh (128K)	Macintosh LC
Macintosh 512K	Macintosh LCII
Macintosh 512KE	**Macintosh LCIII**
Macintosh Plus	Macintosh IIsi
Macintosh SE	Macintosh Portable
Macintosh SE fdhd	Macintosh Classic
Macintosh SE/30	**Macintosh Classic II**
Macintosh II	**Macintosh Color Classic**
Macintosh IIx	PowerBook 100
Macintosh IIcx	PowerBook 140
Macintosh IIfx	**PowerBook 145**
Macintosh IIci	PowerBook 170

continued

Table A-1:	The Macintosh Product Line *(continued)*
PowerBook Duo 210	Macintosh Quadra 950
PowerBook Duo 230	Performa 200
PowerBook 160	Performa 400
PowerBook 165c	Performa 600
PowerBook 180	Performa 600CD
Macintosh Quadra 700	Macintosh IIvx
Macintosh Quadra 800	Macintosh Centris 610
Macintosh Quadra 900	Macintosh Centris 650

Yeah, right — and you're supposed to be able to walk into a computer store, browse the brochure for a minute, make instant sense of all those numbers and specs, and know which Mac model you want? Not a chance. But by the time you finish this chapter, you're going to know precisely what to say to the sales person. (But say it nicely because computer hardware dealers are usually susceptible to being haggled down to a lower price.)

First, let's decide how *big* a Mac you want to get. Physical size has absolutely nothing to do with price or power — mainly it has to do with chic quotient and your interior decorator. The Macintosh comes in four basic sizes:

✔ **One-Piece**. These one-piece models, called *compact Macs* by Apple, are about two feet tall. All you do is plug in the keyboard and the power cord, and you're off and running. The screen is built-in. Apple calls it a nine-inch screen, but that's cheating — they're measuring diagonally. It's actually about seven inches wide and five inches tall, so you can see a five-inch-tall slice of a page all the way across.

The advantages of one-piece Macs are that they're inexpensive, and they're relatively transportable (there's a handle built into the top). They weigh about 15 pounds, and you can get a carrying case for them. They fit into the overhead rack of an airplane, just barely. Especially if you take out the little foam pillows first. (Of the rack, I mean. Not the computer.)

The disadvantage is that expanding one-piece Macs (juicing them up to make them faster) is a pain since you have to dismantle the case. Also there's the screen size. For word processing, most people think it's perfectly adequate. But art and graphic design people go nuts if they can't see an entire page on the screen at once, and some people don't like the fact that compact Macs only come with black-and-white screens. (Read on for information about color screens.)

The most basic one-piece Macs are the Plus, the SE (both discontinued, but used ones are usually fine) and the Classic. As Macs go, these models are dirt cheap — well under a thousand bucks — and for word processing, doing mail merges (form letters), balancing your checkbook, non-color games, and spreadsheet work, they're dandy. For more demanding software — graphics, music processing, page layout (graphic design), tapping into the school computers to change your grades, and so on — spend a little extra for added speed in the SE/30 (discontinued but good) or the Classic II (which is sold as the Performa 200).

Actually, there's another one-piecer that doesn't quite match my description: the Color Classic. It's bigger and heavier than the standard Classic, but it's fast, and it's got a ten-inch *color* screen.

🖙 **Two-Piece.** Two-piece Macs, called *modular* by Apple, involve two pieces of equipment: the computer itself and a separate screen (called the *monitor)*. When computer nerds want to show off, they call the part that's *not* the monitor a *CPU*. Got that? You have two pieces to buy — a monitor and a CPU.

CPU: Stands for Central Processing Unit. Well, that made everything clear, now, didn't it?

No, you're not going to be able to transport *this* baby without the original shipping cartons (and a luggage cart). But buying a separate monitor grants you the power of choice: large or small, black-and-white or color, tall or wide. (Also Apple and non-Apple, for that matter — the golden rule is that anything with the Apple logo on it costs 15 percent more than the same gadget from somebody else.)

The modular Macs are also easily expandable. The lid pops right off, just like the lid of a shoebox. Of course, the inside of the computer looks nothing like the inside of a shoebox. There are a lot of wires and chips and stuff, but they're very neatly arranged, and whatever you want to install slips into a very obvious place. Modular Macs include anything with the Roman numeral II in it (except the Classic II, of course), as well as the Macintosh LC, Performa 400 or 600, and Centris.

✔ **Laptops.** These Macs are called PowerBooks. They're dark gray, two inches thick, weigh under seven pounds, and are every bit as powerful as the models we've been discussing. They open like a book when you're using them; one side has the keyboard, and the other has the screen. You can plug a PowerBook in or use the battery, which lasts about two hours per charge. (Airport waiting lounges, public restrooms, bus terminals . . . You'd be amazed at how good you'll become at finding power outlets on the road once you own a PowerBook. See Appendix B for a detailed discussion of these amazing gadgets.)

Typing on a PowerBook is slightly less comfortable than on a desktop Mac, you pay more, and you can only expand one with considerable hassle and expense (unless you have a Duo Dock; see Appendix B). But a PowerBook is indispensable for anyone who travels. And a PowerBook is definitely the Mac to have if you're trying to catch the eye of an attractive stranger across the aisle. (Especially if you've got one with a color screen.)

✔ **Floortops.** OK, nobody calls these floortops except me. They're the Quadra series — the top of the line.

Actually, they're two-piece modular Macs, but they're so big and suped-up and powerful and fast and expensive that they deserve their own category. You should buy a Quadra if you do color graphics, work with video or movies, work in complex architectural programs, or have some other requirement for all the speed money can buy.

The Only Three Numbers That Matter (Besides the Price)

You'll hear all kinds of numbers and specifications tossed around when you go Mac shopping. But the only three that matter are (1) hard disk space, (2) memory, and (3) the processor chip number.

✔ **Hard disk space.** The first number that matters is the *size of the hard disk inside the Mac.* The size is measured in *megabytes,* or, if you're at a cocktail party, you can say *megs* for short. Larger disks are more expensive.

How much do you need? Well, the stuff you'll be creating (letters, manuscripts, whatever) is pretty small; a 500-page book might take up *one* megabyte of your hard disk. But today's *software programs,* like a word processing program, are huge; count on each one taking up a megabyte by itself. Whether you understand any of this or not, believe it: A hard disk fills up quickly. Get at least a 40MB hard disk.

The first question you might ask in the computer store, then, is — "Yo. Does this Mac have a 20-, 40-, or 80-megabyte hard disk?" No salesperson will take *you* for a ride.

✔ **Memory.** When you press Play on a VCR, it reads the video cassette's contents and throws the video information up onto the TV screen. When the TV is off, you can't watch your movie, but you sleep well knowing it's still safely stored on the tape.

Similarly, your Macintosh reads what's on the *hard disk,* and throws an electronic copy of it up on your computer screen, where you can look at it, make changes, whatever. While it's on the screen, it's *in memory.*

What the hey?!

I'm perfectly aware that these are strange, alien terms unless you've already looked over Chapter 2, where hard disks and memory are discussed in nauseating detail. Essentially, the bigger the hard disk, the more stuff (text, pictures, music, numbers, whatever) you can store. And memory is related to the computer's capacity to run programs — the more the memory, the more you can do with your software programs.

What's confusing about memory is that it's measured in the *same units* as hard-drive space — megabytes. But memory is much more expensive than disk space, so you get a lot less of it. Where hard drives are typically 40MB or 80MB, a Mac usually comes with 2MB or 4MB of memory. The more you have, the more you can do with your computer simultaneously (type into one window, draw in another, and so on). In general, you need at least 4MB of memory to do anything useful.

Intelligent Computer Comment Number Two, then, is: "How much RAM do I get in this Mac? Two megs? Forget it! I can't even *breathe* in two megs."

By the way, newspaper ads often give you both of these first critical numbers (memory and disk space) at once. You might read, for example, "Mac Classic 2/40." In your newfound savvy, you know that this computer has 2MB of *memory* and a 40MB *hard drive* for permanent storage. A Mac Classic 4/80 is better.

✔ **Processor chip**. The third important number is the name of the primary processor chip. (As endless *Newsweek* articles and specials on "Nova" have no doubt informed you, a *chip* is a rat's nest of tiny circuits, etched into a piece of silicon the size of a couple of postage stamps.) The heart of a Macintosh is a chip, about an inch square, that's actually manufactured in the millions by a completely different company. (It's Motorola; that's why *Apple* stock goes down when there are negative headlines about Motorola).

The higher the model number of this chip, the faster the Mac. There are three models of processor chip used in current Macs: 68000, 68030, and 68040. You don't have a choice for a specific model of Mac. The Classic, for example, has a 6800 chip, and that's all there is to it. All other current models use the 68030 or 68040 chip.

This information is of absolutely no value, except to explain something that you might hear bandied about in the computer store. "Um, I think you should get a Centris because it's got the oh-4-oh-chip, y'know."

You'll smile knowingly. "Yeah? Well so do the Quadra 700, 800, and 950," you'll retort.

Their eyebrows will go up with newfound respect.

Nerd's nook

OK, OK, there's actually a *fourth* variable that accounts for the performance differences among Mac models — the *clock speed*. That's something like the blood pressure. It's how fast the data moves through the machine's circuits. That explains why the Classic II, the IIsi, and so on, have different prices and run at different speeds, even though they all use the same Motorola 68030 chip.

OK, So Which One?

It's my professional opinion that, no matter what you'll be using a Mac for you need at least 4MB of memory and a 40MB hard drive (a 4/40 configuration, the insider would say). Beyond those stats, buy a Mac according to your plans for it.

Here's a list of some typical things you might use a Mac for and the Mac models that are suited to each task. Remember that the two-piece Macs (and the Color Classic, and the PowerBook 165c) are the only ones that do color. Remember, too, that you can upgrade almost any Mac at any time to make it faster or more powerful — but performing that kind of surgery to the one-piece Macs isn't exactly do-it-yourself, and you *can't* do such enhancements to the laptops yourself.

Table A-2:   **Choosing the Right Mac for the Job**

Task	Classic	Classic II / Performa 200	Color Classic, LC II, Performa 400	LC III	PowerBook 145, 160	PowerBook 165c	PowerBook 180	Duo 210/230	Centris 610/650	IIvx, Performa 600	Quadra 700	Quadra 800/950
Word processing, mail-merge	•	•	•	•	•	•	•	•	•	•	•	•
Typing-instruction programs	•	•	•	•	•	•	•	•	•	•	•	•
Black-and-white painting programs	•	•	•	•	•	•	•	•	•	•	•	•
Hooking up to the phone (by modem)	•	•	•	•	•	•	•	•	•	•	•	•
Rolodex and calendar programs	•	•	•	•	•	•	•	•	•	•	•	•
Networking (sending E-mail)	•	•	•	•	•	•	•	•	•	•	•	•
Simple database files	•	•	•	•	•	•	•	•	•	•	•	•
Kids' programs (black-and-white)	•	•	•	•	•	•	•	•	•	•	•	•
Spreadsheets, checkbook programs	•	•	•	•	•	•	•	•	•	•	•	•
Music recording (from a synthesizer)		•	•	•	•	•	•	•	•	•	•	•
Color games, color kids' programs			•		**	•	**	**	•	•	•	•
Page layout, graphic design			•		•	•	•	•	•	•	•	•
Color graphics (painting and drawing)			•		**	•	**	**	•	•	•	•
Music notation (sheet music printing)					•	•	•	•	•	•	•	•
Photo retouching					**	**	**	**	•	•	•	•
Medium and complex databases					•	•	•	•	•	•	•	•
QuickTime (digital movie-making)*					**	•	**		•	•	•	•
3-D graphics "rendering"/modeling										•	•	•
Approximate street price, in thousands	1	1.2	1.2	1.2	2	3.4	3	2.2/2.5	2.5	2/2.5	4	4.5
Modular, compact, laptop?	C	C	C/M/M	M	L	L	L	L	M	M	M	M
Processor chip (68000, 68030, 68040)	0	30	30	30	30	30	30	30	30	40	40	40
Clock speed	16	16	16	25	25	33	33	25/33	32	20/25	25	33
Expansion slots	0	0	1	1	0	0	0	3†	3	3	2	3/5

*   requires a very large hard disk and at least 5 megs of memory

** If connected to a separate color monitor (PowerBook 160, 165c, 180, 210, and 230 models only). For the Duo models, this requires a Dock; see the next footnote.

†   Requires a Duo Dock (about $1000) or a Duo MiniDock (about $500); see Appendix B.

As you can see, you get a Classic II if you're strapped for cash. The LCIII, while more expensive, is an incredible deal: so much horsepower for so little money. For page layout and design work, you'll want a two-piece Mac so you can buy a screen large enough to show you a whole page (or more). And for serious professional number-crunching — work with video, 3D graphics, hardcore scientific projects — you can get a Quadra or Centris, although some software isn't yet compatible with it.

Macintosh as a Second Language

Let's see how much of that tech-talk you were able to absorb.

In the grocery: "Nice to see you! Say, you ought to come over to my house. My husband just got a Macintosh PowerBook 145 4/40. It's neato."

Translation: Well, you know from the table that there are four current laptop Power-Books: models 145, 160, 165c, and 180. So her husband got the bottom-of-the-laptop line computer, with 4MB of RAM (just enough) and a 40MB hard drive — the 4/40 configuration. (He'll probably fill up that baby's hard drive with stuff in about three months.)

In Entertainment Weekly: "The film's special effects were created using a Macintosh IIfx with an installed 040 accelerator card."

Translation: OK, well, you see from the table that the IIfx is a powerful machine, but it comes with a 68030 processor. The special-effects people needed more horsepower, so they expanded it — they opened the lid and slipped in a circuit board (which they purchased from a non-Apple company that makes such things). This circuit board has a 68040 chip on it — the same one that makes the Quadra such a racehorse — so these special-effects wizards essentially turned their not-quite-top-of-the-line IIfx into a real workstation.

On a bulletin board: "FOR SALE: Macintosh Plus. Color monitor, 2 expansion slots. $3,000. Call Sid."

Translation: This guy has no idea what he's talking about. The Plus is black-and-white, it has no expansion slots, and that's about six times too much to pay for a used machine!

If you understand that much, the worst is over. You're ready to begin your assault on the computer marketplace — informed, armed, and ready for anything.

Buying a Monitor

If you've decided to become the proud owner of a two-piece Mac (a Mac II-something, a Quadra, Centris, LC or equivalent), you have to decide what kind of screen (monitor) to get.

You can classify monitors either by shape or by display color. For instance, you can get a *portrait* or *full-page* display, which is big enough to show you a full 8½-inch × 11-inch page at a time (below left).

There are also *two-page* displays, which (needless to say) show two side-by-side pages at a time (above middle). The most popular Apple color monitors, on the other hand, have a screen just shy of nine inches wide and seven inches tall. They're called *landscape* monitors because they're wider than they are tall, and they don't quite show you a full page at a time (above right). These Apple color monitors are referred to as the 12-inch, 13-inch and 14-inch displays. The 12-inch monitor is cheap, but avoid it; everyone I know who has one complains about it. The 13-inch is fantastic but pricier. For about half as much you can get a slightly lower quality 14-inch monitor which, despite its name, shows exactly the same amount of screen area as the 13-inch.

For writing, virtually any size screen will do. Even if you can only see half a page at a time, you can always *scroll* the display up or down, to see what you wrote on the previous (or next) page. If you plan to do any graphic design — that is, page layout of brochures or newsletters — you'll probably want at least a full-page display. And if you're going to do professional page design work, such as laying out a book, then get a two-page display.

Black-and-white, gray scale, color

The least expensive screens show you black writing against a white background, just like a typewriter. For writing, finances, spreadsheets, music, databases, calendars, Rolodexes, and 90 percent of the other day-to-day Mac tasks, black-and-white is all you'll ever need. Black-and-white screens are also the fastest; you almost never have to wait for the computer to "paint" the screen from top to bottom, as you do when you're working in color.

I've never understood why anybody would want a *gray-scale* monitor, the next step up. These monitors don't just have black and white; they can also display any shade of gray. Unless you make your living by (1) doing photo retouching or (2) painting London fog scenes, a gray-scale monitor seems to be a slightly useless creation: If you don't need color, get a black-and-white monitor and save the money. And if you need gray scale, you may as well get a color monitor, which can *become* a gray-scale monitor with the click of a button.

Color monitors are the most expensive, and they make everything appear on the screen slightly slower. There are some things that absolutely demand a color monitor: games, color graphics, presentations and some business charts, digital movies (called QuickTime movies), and so on. Otherwise, color is purely a luxury. Everything on the screen appears more 3D. Certain programs make clever use of color — for example, a drafting program might display light blue graph paper lines behind the black lines you draw.

In the olden days (in other words, last year), that would have been the end of the color story. You got to see great, rich, stunning color on the screen, but everything you printed came out in black and white. Color printers cost way too much for any individual to buy.

Recently, though, the prices of color printers have plummeted. Now you can buy a high-quality color printer for $4,000, or one with a more limited palette of colors for $1,000. I wouldn't advise getting a color printer for everyday correspondence and such, but if you're ever hired to design rough sketches for a movie poster or something, keep those cheapie color printers in mind.

Monochrome monitors

The computer nerds refer to black-and-white screens as *monochrome* monitors. Joke's on them, though. *Monochrome* doesn't actually mean black and white. Technically speaking, it means a color monitor with only one color — black. In other words, a gray-scale monitor, which is something totally different.

A little bit about 8-bit and 24-bit color

If you decide to get a color monitor, your decision-making isn't over yet. The techno-bullies of the world have foisted several different *kinds* of color upon us: *8-bit, 16-bit,* or *24-bit* color. All you need to know is that 24-bit color is more expensive, slower to appear on the screen, and much more realistic. *Realistic* is a term that only matters if you plan to work with photos or movies on the screen. If not, 24-bit is for the pros, and it's overkill for everyone else. (An additional note: Most current Macs give you 8-bit color; all you have to do is plug your monitor into a built-in jack. If you one day decide that you can't live without photo-realistic colors on your screen, you can buy and install a *video card* [a circuit board] to get 24-bit color — you don't need a whole new monitor.)

When you're choosing a monitor, remember that a color monitor is *also* a gray-scale monitor *and* a black-and-white monitor. (An on-screen control panel lets you switch from one mode to another.) As you read this book, look over the possibilities of color and see if any of them appeal to you. Otherwise, black and white is the faster, less expensive way to go.

By the way: Apple Computer's specialty is computers. Anything else you have to buy — monitor, keyboard, printer — is often made better, and priced lower, by other companies. This fact makes getting your computer system more complicated because you may be getting different pieces of it from different sources. If you don't mind spending, say, 12 percent more for the convenience of one-stop shopping (at a computer store, for instance), by all means get an all-Apple system.

One less thing to buy — maybe

In the olden days, color Macs didn't have built-in color-monitor circuitry. You'd have to pay $400 for a video card *and* buy a monitor.

Nowadays, Apple is more generous: they've built the required circuitry for basic (8-bit) color into all current Macs (and even some discontinued ones like the IIsi and the IIci). Today, the primary reason to buy a video card is to gain 16-bit or 24-bit (more realistic) color.

Be ye warned, though. By using the Mac's own brain to process the visual information (instead of shoving it over to a video card to do), you slow down your Mac. If you're shopping for a new Mac and plan to use its built-in video feature instead of buying a card, try one at a computer store to make certain you won't be impatient waiting for the screen picture to update itself.

For weenies only

You really, really want to know where terms like *8-bit* and *24-bit* come from? Don't say you weren't warned.

Remember color theory from high school physics? Mixing the three primary colors red, yellow, and blue is supposed to be able to produce any color in the rainbow.

Well, to display a color picture, the Mac has to remember the precise amount of those colors to mix for *each individual dot on the screen*. Think about it: Dot number 15 is 21 percent red, 79 percent blue, and so on, for each dot. That's an awful lot of information to store for each of 307,200 dots.

To save expense, trouble, and memory, the most popular Mac monitors only reserve 8 bits of the Mac's brain to describe the color of each dot. (You can think of a *bit* as one word of computer description, a unit of electronic information.) So even though a particular dot can be any color under the rainbow, the *total number of colors* that can appear on an 8-bit color monitor is 256. That may sound like a lot of colors, but there are thousands more shades needed to produce a convincing rainbow.

The pros, then, get much more expensive monitors that use far more information to describe the color of each dot — 24 bits, in fact. With that much description power, the Mac can display *millions* of different colors at once. In fact, every dot on the screen could be a different color, and you'd still have millions of colors to choose from that couldn't fit on the screen.

All this thinking and describing the Mac has to do for 24-bit color (sometimes stupidly called 32-bit color, by the way — it's the same thing) means the screen gets painted pretty slowly. Of course, the Basic Rule of Computing states that whenever there's a computing inconvenience, some company will invent an expensive gizmo that solves it. The slow speed of 24-bit monitors is no exception: For a couple grand more, you can get an *accelerated* graphics card, which makes it possible to see 24-bit images almost as quickly as 8-bit ones on an *un*accelerated screen.

Where to Buy Your Mac

I'm going to assume that you're not in Donald Trump's tax bracket and that you're looking for ways to get the most Mac for the least lira.

The Apple university discount

First of all, you should know that Apple practically gives Macs away to students and teachers. (I think the discount is between 25 and 40 percent.) If you're affiliated with a college, find out if the school's bookstore is a member of this delightful program. There's no possible way to find lower prices on Mac equipment.

Mail order

If you're not fortunate enough to be a student or faculty member, the next least-expensive way to get a new Mac is probably through a mail-order catalog. These outfits take out big ads in the Macintosh magazines like *Macworld* (which, I say with no small conflict of interest, is my favorite) and *MacUser*. Of course, you can't exactly browse the merchandise, and so it's assumed that you already know what you want when you call up one of these places.

If everything goes smoothly, mail order can be a nifty deal: You save hundreds by avoiding sales tax, you get a pretty good price, and you don't have to haul anything home in the car. The trouble with mail order, though, is that things can get pretty ugly if things *don't* go right. What if the thing is broken when it arrives? Suddenly you've got the burden of packing it up, shipping it back to the company, and persuading them to replace the equipment (*if* they'll even consider it). Mail order is for gamblers: You can score big, but you can also get shafted, and you won't have anywhere to turn for help.

Computer stores

A computer store, on the other hand, is likely to have higher prices. You'll have to pay sales tax. But you also get a human being to blame when things get fouled up.

In theory, a computer dealer is also supposed to answer your questions and help you with installation. In practice, unfortunately, buying a computer at a store is still a crapshoot: Good dealers are relatively rare, and lousy dealers are everywhere. There's a notorious New York City dealership, for example, that makes a regular practice of advertising rock-bottom prices. Then, when you show up, they mention that you'll "probably also want to buy" several items normally included in the package — the mouse, for example, or a cartridge if you're buying a printer.

The other advantage to buying a Mac at a dealer is service. It's very important for you to know that under Apple law, *any* Apple dealer must repair a Mac or Apple printer *for free* if it's still covered by its one-year warranty, regardless of which dealer sold it to you. Don't let any dealer tell you otherwise.

Unfortunately, dealers who offer great repair service are also rare. The *quality* of the repair isn't really an issue — almost always, they'll fix what ails the machine and give it back to you in good shape. Instead, the issue is turnaround time; it's not going to help you or your business much if you have to spend six weeks without your Mac.

So how are you supposed to know good dealers (and their repair guys) from bad? There's only one way: Ask around. Of course, depending on where you live, getting the word-of-mouth report may be easier said than done. If you're at a loss as to whom you should ask, start by finding the nearest Macintosh user group (by calling Apple's user group listing hotline, 800-538-9696).

Consumer stores

There they are, right next to the blenders and microwaves: the Macintosh Performa series. These Macs are *only* sold through non-computer stores like Sears, Silo, Price Club, and office-supply stores. Because the usual clerks can't be expected to know anything about computers, Apple covers you with toll-free phone numbers — one to call with questions and one to call if something breaks. For one year, Apple will actually send somebody to your house to fix the Mac.

The Performa 200, 400, and 600 are essentially the same machines as the Classic II, LCII, and IIvx, which are sold through usual computer stores. And they're priced about the same, but they come with free software. Their special version of System 7 makes using them even easier — but at the expense of some minor features, like the ability to customize the background screen pattern. If you don't mind that, then the Performas are a good deal.

Used Macs

Finally, you can buy a used Mac. Once again, the luck of the draw determines how satisfied you'll be. To a certain extent, you can tell how much abuse a Mac has had by looking at it. But a visual exam won't tell you about the funny noise the hard drive makes only after it's been on for 20 minutes or the monitor that's been in for repair three times already or the ball of cat hair wedged inside the disk drive.

In other words, there are three rules for buying used equipment. First, determine that you're willing to forgo the comfy Apple warranty for the sake of saving money. Second, be sure the asking price really is low enough that the savings is meaningful, particularly with discontinued Mac models like the SE/30 or the LC. (Some naïve sellers, who don't understand the Inviolable Rule of Instant Obsolescence, think they can recoup their full purchase price when they sell their used Mac. Don't fall for it — be sure you've compared the asking price with a computer store's new Mac price.)

And finally, test the Mac as much as possible before you buy it. Above all, test the disk drive (by inserting a floppy disk and copying a file onto it), the printer port (by printing something), and the mouse (by rolling it around on the desk).

Credit cards

It doesn't thrill me to break the news to you, but you're going to be spending a lot of money even *after* buying your Mac. We haven't even discussed buying a keyboard yet. (Here's the discussion: Wherever you're buying your Mac, you can also buy a keyboard. But it'll cost about $50 more than a superior keyboard from a mail-order company.) And you're going to need software. As hobby costs go, computing isn't exactly crocheting.

As long as you're committed to this plunge, a word of solemn advice: Put everything on a credit card, especially when you're buying by mail order. Thousands of Mac users have avoided getting ripped off by the occasional fly-by-night operation because they charged it. (As you probably know, the credit card company doesn't pay your bill if you're disputing the charge — an incredible layer of protection between you and companies that send you the wrong item, a broken one, and so on.)

I Took Off the Shrink-Wrap! Now What?

Setting up the Mac should take less than 20 minutes. All you have to do is plug in three cables. (If you have a two-piece Mac, you also have to set up the monitor. And if you have a printer, you have to hook that up, too — see Chapter 5.)

Ergo . . . ergonomics

First of all, figure out where you're going to put the most expensive appliance you've ever bought. You probably already know, but make sure you're ergonomically correct. In my opinion, the principal principle is: When you're seated at your desk, and you're in typing position, *your elbows can't be lower than your wrists*. Otherwise, if you plan to do a lot of work at the computer, you may wind up with a nasty and painful disease, called Carpal Tunnel Syndrome, which never goes away until you stop using the computer.

The next ergonomic lesson is one learned from painful experience by thousands of home-office users: Don't put the monitor in front of a sunny window. It turns out that your pupils shrink to accommodate the bright window light. But since you're trying to focus on the relatively dim Mac screen, your optic system gets confused and strained, and it's hello, headache.

Finally, I suppose I should mention ELF. No, this elf isn't the little man inside the Mac who runs around obeying your every command. It stands for Extremely Low-Frequency radiation. There are a few scientists who've been saying (without much hard proof one way or another) that electrical appliances emit a very subtle, low dose of radiation. If you sit very close to an appliance for a very long period of time, the theory says that your cancer risk increases. (Computers are supposedly the biggest risk — not many people sit all day hunched in front of their blenders.)

Macworld magazine tests discovered that you have to sit *really* close to your Mac to get any of this radiation. In fact, by the time you move 28 inches away, the level of ELF radiation is zero. That's arm's length. If ELF radiation concerns you, then just stay arm's length from the nearest monitor and you'll be OK. (Furthermore, all of this applies primarily to two-piece Macs; the compact Macs don't emit anything but good vibes.)

Getting plugged

Of course, your manuals are the best instructions for setting up the Mac. But here are the basics.

Everything plugs into the back of the Mac. Take a look: There are a whole assortment of plugs back there. They're labeled with little symbolic pictures, called *icons*. (Get used to icons. They're the cornerstone of the Mac's graphic nature.) The sidebar shows the back of a typical Mac and what you can plug in.

If your new Mac is a laptop (the PowerBook), there's nothing to set up. Plug it in, open the back panel, hit the round On/Off button, and flip back to Chapter 1.

If your Mac *isn't* a PowerBook, study the diagram in the "The back of the Mac, Jack" sidebar. Using it as your guide, plug the power cord into the power jack and the keyboard into the ADB port. Most people then plug the mouse into the other side of the keyboard. But some Macs have a second ADB port for the mouse; do whatever feels good.

If you have a Mac Plus, SE, Classic, or Performa 200, your installation is complete. Flip back to Chapter 1.

If you have a two-piece Mac, and your monitor *didn't* come with a separate circuit board (video card), plug the monitor's two cables into the monitor power and video out jacks, as shown in the sidebar diagram. You're all set.

If you did get a video card, you have to open the cover and install it. It's entirely possible that your dealer already did this for you. Call up and ask. Otherwise, follow the instructions that came with your monitor.

Finally, plug the monitor's video cable into the jack on the back of the video card which now protrudes through the back of your Mac. Then plug the monitor's power cord into the monitor power jack.

You're ready for business. For instructions on hooking up your printer, see Chapter 5.

Switching the Mac on

Quick! Flip to Chapter 1!

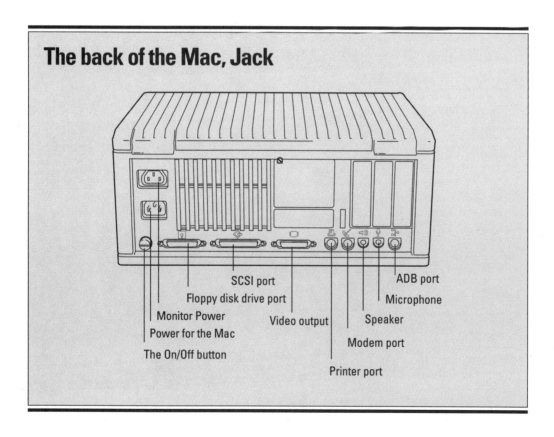

The back of the Mac, Jack

SCSI port

Floppy disk drive port

Monitor Power

Video output

Power for the Mac

The On/Off button

Printer port

Modem port

Speaker

ADB port

Microphone

Top Ten Things You Get Free with Your Mac

Enjoy this list. This is probably the last time you'll get anything free in your entire computing career.

1. A mouse.

2. A floppy disk drive built into the front.

3. HyperCard Player. (See Page 122.)

4. A one-year warranty that covers parts and labor at *any* Apple dealership.

5. A set of white System software disks (except Performa models).

6. A power cord.

7. A coupon for a free mouse pad or subscription to *Macworld* magazine.

8. Instruction manuals.

9. A guided tour disk ("Macintosh Basics" or "Mouse Practice").

10. A registration card. Fill it out, send it in.

Appendix B
The PowerBook Survival Guide

● ●

*I*t's a little bit mind-blowing when you find out that a tiny PowerBook Duo 230 has more computer horsepower than a Mac IIci. Apple made almost no compromises: The speed, storage capacity, memory, and back-panel jacks on a PowerBook are almost exactly the same as regular Macs — but they're crammed into a book-sized case that weighs five or six pounds and conceals dirt. Recent models' screens (160, 180, Duo) show different shades of gray, and the non-Duos have a jack that lets you plug in a separate color monitor. Heck, the 165c even has a built-in color screen and much more stunning color screens are slated for upcoming models.

In fact, working on a PowerBook is so much like working on a regular Mac that you may forget to make certain allowances. Use these tips to help you get extra mileage out of your machine and its battery.

Get a Case

The PowerBook comes with neither handles nor a carrying case. There are a million cases for sale, designed to carry and protect the PowerBook and accessories; call up one of the mail-order companies like Mac Connection. Almost all of them are tough, attractive, and beautifully designed (the cases, I mean, not the mail-order companies). A company called Magenta Seven even sells a lightly padded slipcover with handles, for people who don't need a full-fledged case because they carry the laptop in a briefcase.

Power Options

There are all kinds of ways to milk more juice out of your PowerBook battery; they're outlined in the Top Ten list below.

In the meantime, consider buying a power accessory or two. Car (or boat) cigarette lighter adapters for the PowerBook are available from Lind or Empire Engineering; Lind also makes a five-pound, bricklike superbattery that keeps your PowerBook kicking for eight hours (compared with the regular battery's two or three). Keep that in mind the next time you have to fly to Europe. There's even a battery pack from Interex that takes regular flashlight batteries (a set of eight provides eight hours of juice).

My favorite alternative-power product, though, is a second Apple PowerBook battery. Not very innovative, I know, but you really get your $99 worth from the thing.

The contact information for these companies is in Appendix C, the Resource Resource; unfortunately, I can't guarantee that these companies or products will still be around by the time you read this. That's the computer biz, I guess.

When Trouble Strikes

One of the best things you bought with your PowerBook was Apple's emergency-repair program. For the first year, you can call Apple at 800-SOS-APPL, wherever you are. They'll send a messenger to pick up your sick PowerBook, repair it in one day, and overnight it back to you — all at *no charge.* Ladies and gentlemen, an American bureacratic program that really works.

Before you dial, though, you may as well know ahead of time that burned-out *pixels* (the tiny square dots of your screen) may not qualify as broken. Apple says that up to five burned-out pixels (on a PowerBook 170 or 180) are within its definition of "not really broken." Yeah, well, I bet *their* PowerBooks don't have burned-out pixels.

Keeping an Eye on Juice

Mac insiders have known for years about SuperClock!, an ingenious System extension that puts a digital time readout in the upper-right corner of your screen, like this:

When you install it on a PowerBook, though, a funny thing happens: You also get a battery "fuel gauge" so that you can keep an eye on your battery life:

A solid black battery indicates a full charge; as the battery juice runs out, the blackness empties out of te little battery icon. (You get SuperClock! wherever fine shareware is sold: on electronic bulletin boards or from a local user group.)

Alternatively, of course, you can just leave the Battery desk accessory open on the screen in a convenient place.

Those Darned X-Ray Machines

Some people claim that airport security X-ray machines are bad for your Power-Book. Others claim that X-rays can't hurt electronics. The first group replies that "It's not the X-rays, it's the magnetic fields in the conveyer-belt mechanism." So the second group, getting annoyed, replies that they *always* put their PowerBooks through the machine and have never had a problem. The first group, claiming it's better to be safe than sorry, rebuts that it's no big deal to turn the machine on for inspection (which is the alternative to running it through the machine) and throws a spitball at the second group.

Finally, both groups agree to disagree and start swapping tips on maximizing battery life.

Walking During Sleep

Then a few minutes later, they start arguing again. Some people will tell you that you should never transport the PowerBook when it's in Sleep mode. They point to the Apple manual, which does indeed tell you to fully Shut Down your Power-Book before moving it. The other group scoffs and tells you that they carry their machines around all the time while asleep (the machines, not the owners) with no problems.

Sleep mode: *A low-power condition for a Macintosh laptop. Very similar to Off, actually, except that the contents of memory are preserved. When you wake up the computer (by touching a key), you're right where you left off, complete with programs and documents open.*

The first group insists that you'd better let sleeping laptops lie, elaborating on Apple's concern — that you might really bump the heck out of the PowerBook, enough that a key gets pressed, which will wake up the computer, which will start the hard disk spinning, which puts your data at risk of another bump. The living-dangerously group kicks sand in the faces of the conservative group, jeering that such a sequence of events is incredibly unlikely and insisting that it's OK to carry the thing around, as long as you don't dribble it like a basketball.

Insta-Printer

You can get a fax/modem as an optional accessory for any PowerBook. (Global Village and PSI make superior fax/modems for the PowerBook.)

That's not the tip, though. The tip is that if you have a built-in fax/modem, you really don't need to lug along a printer (even if you did have the money to spend on a portable Diconix printer). Instead, just fax the document you want to print *to yourself,* using a fax machine at the airport or hotel to receive the fax you're sending from the laptop. Ingenious, eh?

Preventing Your Battery from Bursting into Flame

 If you carry an extra PowerBook battery with you, keep it in a baggie. (Or, if a plastic battery case didn't come with your PowerBook, call Apple and get your free one.) Otherwise, it's theoretically possible for a paper clip or a coin to create a short circuit between the battery terminals, starting a fire.

And, as we all know, it's impolite to smoke in public.

Sittin' on the Dock

If you bought a PowerBook Duo 210 or 230, you must've turned this 4-pound beauty over and over in your hands, mystified as to where you're supposed to plug stuff in. There's no place to hook up a monitor; no SCSI connector for plugging in another hard drive; there isn't even a floppy-disk drive!

Then again, you don't *need* any of those items when you're sitting on the airplane typing, and that's exactly what Apple discovered. That's why there's the Duo Dock — a housing that sits on your desk at home, which has expansion slots, a floppy drive, and every connector you can think of. (The MiniDock is a more portable, less full-fledged piece of gear that only adds the jacks and a monitor connector.)

You can plug in a big-screen monitor, a regular keyboard, and a mouse. So when you come home from your trip with the PowerBook Duo, you slide the laptop into its dock. It gets slurped inside like a videocassette, and presto: you've just handed all your data — and the Duo's brain — to the machine on your desk, so you can now work merrily away as though it wasn't a laptop at all. Pretty cool.

When You Get Desperate

Now look, I don't want to get angry letters from spouses and significant others, blaming me for converting their beloveds into hermitic power nerds. What I'm about to tell you should be socked away in the back of your mind, only for emergencies.

 It's about airplanes and airports. We all know that PowerBooks and airplanes were made for each other. But what you may not know is what to do when the dreaded "Your screen has been dimmed" message pops up, warning you that you only have a few minutes of battery power remaining, and you're in the middle of a brilliant brainstorm.

 First of all, I happen to know that there are publicly available power outlets at every gate of every airport (and bus and train station, too). They're there, actually, for the benefit of the cleaning staff's vacuums, and as such they're sometimes concealed on the side of a pillar. And I happen to know that they're *never* convenient to a seat, so if your Mac habit is stronger than your pride, you're going to have to sit on the floor.

I also know what to do when you run out of juice *on the plane.* Yes, that's right: I'm going to call to your attention the electric razor outlet in the bathroom of almost every plane in America. You feel like an absolute idiot, of course, wedged in there on that toilet with your adapter cord snaking up to the plug above the doll-sized sink, while your laptop recharges.

That's what I've been *told,* anyway. Naturally, *I* would never do anything that pathetic.

Top Ten Tips for Maximizing Battery Power

Many new PowerBook owners are devastated to find that, instead of getting "two to three" hours of life out of each freshly charged battery, they only get 90 minutes or so. These excellent tricks will solve that problem in a hurry.

1. The backlighting for the screen uses up *half* of the power. The more you turn it down, the longer your battery will last.

2. I've actually overheard PowerBook owners asking the airline gate agent for a seat not merely next to a window but on a particular *side* of the plane, and now I know why. They want to be where the sun will be shining. Bright sunlight is enough to illuminate a PowerBook screen, so you can turn the backlighting all the way off.

3. As you go through life with your PowerBook (model 140 through 180), repeated partial chargings of your nickel-cadmium battery gradually decrease its potential life. The problem is called the *memory effect* (camcorder batteries do this too), and it results from not allowing the battery to fully discharge before recharging begins.

   To restore the battery to its good-as-new, virginal, strong-as-ever condition, deliberately let it run down to the ground. That's right: Just keep your PowerBook on, not letting it sleep, and click OK every time a message appears telling you that the battery is running down. At the very end, the Mac will literally tell you "Good night," and it will put itself to sleep. You've now drained the battery — and undone the memory effect — and it's now OK to plug the adapter in to charge it.

   When the battery is finally restored, it should last much longer. Do this routine once a month.

4. If you want to get serious about tip #3, you can actually buy a device that performs that whole sequence automatically. It's called a Battery Reconditioner/Charger, and it's made by Lind. It plugs into the wall; you put your battery into it, and it deep-empties the battery, then safely refills it to full. The whole cycle takes over seven hours, but the company claims that it rejuvenates the battery even more than the process described in tip #3 does. (Lind also makes a charger for the PowerBook 100 battery, which is a lead-acid battery, and thus doesn't suffer from the memory effect.)

5. When you want to make sure your battery is as full as it can be, allow all day for it to recharge — and don't trust the Battery desk accessory fuel gauge. You see, the PowerBook battery gets charged 80 percent full in only two hours or so. At that point, the Battery gauge will tell you that it's full. But to charge the battery fully — to charge that extra 20 percent — it takes another *five or six hours* of what they call "trickle charging." (This isn't true of Duo, whose battery charges fully in two hours.)

6. Turn off AppleTalk! This incredible power drain will sap a half hour of life from your battery. To do so, choose Chooser from your Apple menu. In the lower-right corner, make sure that AppleTalk Inactive is selected.

7. If you're not going to use the machine, even for a couple of minutes, put it to sleep by choosing Sleep from the Special menu.

8. If you have a PowerBook 160, 170, or 180, choose Battery from the Apple menu, and select PowerSaver. This option slows down the Mac's brain and dims the screen slightly — and makes your battery last longer.

9. If your PowerBook has a built-in modem, quit your modem software promptly when you're finished telecommunicating. Otherwise, as long as that modem program is open, the Mac is sending precious juice to that modem.

10. The other major drain to your battery is hard disk usage. Whenever you hear that darned disk spinning, it's like voltage down the drain.

The only way to completely avoid using the hard disk is to transfer *everything* you'll be working on into memory. If everything's in memory, the Mac never needs to wake up the hard disk, and your PowerBook can run happily for hours and hours. (I've heard people say they get five hours from a charge this way.)

If you have 6MB of RAM or more in your little gray marvel, read on.

In order to fit everything into memory, you need to create a *RAM disk* — a portion of memory that the Mac believes to be a big floppy disk. A RAM disk even shows up on the screen as a floppy disk icon. But anything you drag onto its icon is copied into memory, and stays there.

To create a RAM disk on your PowerBook, choose Control Panels from the Apple menu, and double-click Memory. This window opens:

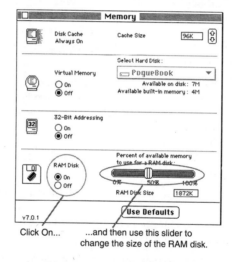

Click On...   ...and then use this slider to change the size of the RAM disk.

Click On, as shown, and then drag the slider until the "RAM Disk Size" number is large enough to contain (1) your System Folder, (2) your program, and (3) your document. This can become a game of mental Twister if you're not careful — even though you're going to be putting these items into *memory,* the size you're worried about is *not* how much memory they need to run. You're worried about how much *disk space* they take up at the moment.

You're not going to be able to pull this off at all, unless you strip down your System Folder. If I were you, I'd start with the absolutely minuscule System Folder on the Disk Tools disk that came with your PowerBook — with only a single font and no desk accessories, it only takes up 1.2MB of disk space. (I doubt you'll survive for very long with only Geneva 9-point type, though, so feel free to add another small font or two.)

Once you've prepared this mini System Folder, carry it on a floppy disk with your PowerBook. Now here's how it all works.

Set up the RAM disk, as described above. Restart the computer by choosing Restart from the Special menu. When the Mac comes alive again, you'll see the RAM disk on the screen:

Onto this imaginary disk, copy your stripped-down System Folder, the program you'll be using, and the document you'll be using. Once that's done, choose Control Panels from the Apple menu, and double-click Startup Disk; in the window that appears, select RAM Disk. Restart the PowerBook.

If all has gone well, the Mac will now use the RAM Disk as the startup disk and heed the instructions in *its* System Folder instead of the one on the hard disk. If you now double-click the program on the RAM Disk and use its Open command to open your *document* on the RAM Disk, you've successfully created a completely memory-based workstation. The Mac will *never* need the hard disk, and will thus never waste any battery power making it spin.

When you save your work, you'll be saving changes to the document on the RAM Disk — which isn't, of course, a disk at all. In other words, you'll be making changes in memory and *saving* them into another part of memory!

If this were happening on any normal Mac, you'd be scolded for attempting anything so foolish. After all, what if your system crashes? Then everything in memory — including the document you've been working on — vanishes forever, right? Aren't you out of your mind to save a document into RAM?

On a PowerBook, no, because the contents of its memory are preserved, even if you put the machine to sleep, and even if you restart the machine. (*Restart*, friends, *not* Shut Down. If you Shut Down, you *will* lose the contents of the RAM disk.) So if you do have a system crash, don't do anything rash, and *don't shut off the computer by pushing the On/Off button.* Instead, take a pencil or a straightened paper clip, and carefully push it into the tiny hole on the back of the machine — the Restart switch, which is marked by a little left-pointing triangle. The machine will restart, once again using the System Folder on the RAM Disk, and there you'll find your document, safe and sound.

Appendix C
The Resource Resource

Magazines

Macworld
800-234-1038

MacUser
800-627-2247

MacWeek
609-461-2100

User Groups

New York Macintosh
  Users' Group
212-645-2265

Boston Computer Society
BCS/Mac
617-625-7080

BMUG
415-849-9114

Apple User-Group
  Info Line
800-538-9696

Products Mentioned in This Book

1-2-3 for Macintosh
Lotus Corp.
617-577-8500

911 Utilities
Microcom Systems Inc.
919-490-1277 ext. 310
919-490-6672 (FAX)
919-419-1602 (8,1,N) BBS

**Adobe Type Manager
(ATM)**
Adobe Systems
415-961-4400
800-833-6687
800-521-1976 ext. 4400
(to order ATM for $7.50)

After Dark
Berkeley System Design, Inc.
415-540-5536

Amazing Paint
CE Software
515-224-1995

America Online
America Online Inc.
800-827-6364

Animation Works
Gold Disk
213-320-5080

Baseline Publishing
901-682-9676 ext. 108 or 107
  (customer support)
901-682-9691 (FAX)
800-926-9677
  (automated ordering)

Bernoulli
IOMEGA
801-778-1000
800-456-5522

Capture
Mainstay
818-991-6540

ClarisWorks
Claris Corp.
408-727-8227

CompuServe
617-661-9440
800-873-1032

Connectix
415-324-0727

DeskPaint
Zedcor
602-881-8101
800-482-4567

DeskWriter
Hewlett-Packard
800-752-0900

Disinfectant
Freeware: John Norstad, author. Available from any on-line modem service, or send a self-addressed stamped sturdy envelope and an 800K disk to the following address. People outside the US may send an international postal reply coupon instead of US stamps (available from any post office).
John Norstad
Academic Computing and Network Services
Northwestern University
2129 Sheridan Road
Evanston, IL 60208

DiskDoubler
Fifth Generation Systems
800-873-4384

Encore
Passport Designs
415-726-0280

Excel
Microsoft Corp.
206-882-8080
800-426-9400

EZ Vision
Opcode Systems, Inc.
415-369-8131

Finale
Coda Music Software
612-854-1288

Flight Simulator
Microsoft Corp.
206-882-8080
800-426-9400

FreeHand
Aldus Corp.
206-628-2320

Gatekeeper
Available from on-line services

GreatWorks
Symantec Corp.
408-253-9600
800-441-7234

Hard Disk ToolKit
FWB
415-474-8055

HyperCard
Claris Corp.
408-727-8227

Illustrator
Adobe Systems
415-961-4400
800-833-6687

KidPix
Broderbund Software, Inc.
415-492-3200
800-521-6263

Last Resort
Working Software
408-423-5696

MacConnection
800-800-4444

MacLink Plus
DataViz
800-733-0030

MacRecorder
Macromedia
415-442-0200

Mac Tools Deluxe
Central Point Software
800-947-9443

Mac Warehouse
800-255-6227

Mac Zone
800-248-0800

MacPaint
Claris Corp.
408-727-8227

MasterJuggler
ALSoft
713-353-4090

MenuFonts
Dubl-Click Software
818-888-2068

MicroPhone
Software Ventures
415-644-3232

ModuNet
Data Spec
818-772-9977

MusicProse
Coda Music Software
612-854-1288

MyAdvancedLabelMaker
MySoftware Company
415-325-9372

Nisus
Paragon Concepts
619-481-1477

Norton Utilities for the Macintosh (NUM)
Symantec Corp.
408-253-9600
800-441-7234

Now Up-to-Date
Now Software
503-274-2800

Now Utilities
Now Software
503-274-2800

PageMaker
Aldus Corp.
206-628-2320

Persuasion
Aldus Corp.
206-628-2320

PhoneNet
Farallon
(415) 596-9100

PowerBook Battery Recharger
Lind Electronics Design
612-927-6303

PowerBook Car/Boat Adapter
Empire Engineering
805-543-2816

Power Partner (battery pack)
Interex
316-524-4747

QuarkXPress
Quark
303-934-2211
800-356-9363

Quicken
Intuit
415-322-0573
800-624-8742

QuicKeys
CE Software
515-224-1995

Resolve
Claris Corp.
408-727-8227

Screenshot
Baseline Publishing
901-682-9676 ext. 108 or 107 (customer support)
800-926-9677 (automated ordering)

SilverLining
La Cie
800-999-0143

Studio/1
Electronic Arts
415-571-7171
800-245-4525

StuffIt
Aladdin Systems, Inc.
408-761-6200

Suitcase II
Fifth Generation Systems
800-766-7283

Super QuickDex
Casady & Greene, Inc.
408-624-8716
800-359-4920

SuperPaint
Aldus Corp.
206-628-2320

Symantec Utilities for the Macintosh (SAM)
Symantec Corp.
408-253-9600
800-441-7234

SyQuest
415-438-5500
800-245-2278

Talking Moose
Baseline Publishing
901-682-9676 ext. 108 or 107 (customer support)
800-926-9677 (automated ordering)

Trax
Passport
415-726-0280

UltraPaint/ArtWorks
Deneba Software
305-594-6965
800-622-6827

VideoSpigot
SuperMac
408-245-0646
408-245-2202

Virex
Microcom Systems Inc.
919-490-1277 ext. 310
919-490-6672 (FAX)
919-419-1602 (8,1,N) BBS

Voice Impact
Articulate Systems
800-443-7077
617-935-5656

White Knight
The FreeSoft Company
412-846-2700

Wingz
Informix
913-599-7100
800-438-7627

Word
Microsoft Corp.
206-882-8080
800-426-9400

WordPerfect for the Macintosh
WordPerfect Corp.
801-225-5000
800-321-4566

WriteNow
T/Maker Company
415-962-0195
415-962-0201 (fax)

Appendix D
The Techno-Babble Translation Guide

• •

accelerator
The pedal you press while driving to pick up your very first Mac. Also, an expensive circuit board you can install to make your Mac faster and slightly less obsolete and less compatible.

active window
The window in front. Usually, only one window can be active; you can recognize it by the stripes across the title bar, like this:

ADB
An acronym for Apple Desktop Bus, which describes the cables and jacks used by the keyboard and mouse: *Could you believe that dimwit!? He plugged his printer into the ADB port!*

alert box
A message that appears on the screen; the Mac's attempt to maintain an open and communicative relationship with you. Unfortunately, as happens so often in relationships, the Mac tends to communicate only when something is wrong. An alert box is marked either with the International

Exclamation Point or a warning hand, like this:

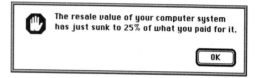

Apple menu
The menu at the far left of your menu bar, marked by a piece of black or multi-colored fruit. In the Apple menu, you'll find a listing of your desk accessories (miniprograms like the Calculator), as well as any files, folders, documents, control panels, and even disks (or their aliases) you care to see there. (To add something to the Apple menu, drop its icon into the Apple Menu Items folder within your System Folder.)

AppleShare
Some kind of trademarked name for the way interconnected Macs communicate with each other. You'll never need to know this.

AppleTalk
Another trademarked name, also having to do with Macs talking to each other. You *may* need to know this term if you have a laser printer because AppleTalk is the language it speaks to your Mac. AppleTalk must be "active" to print; choose the Chooser from the

 menu, and you'll see where you turn AppleTalk on or off. (PowerBook user alert: Turn AppleTalk off for the plane rides — you'll gain a whole half-hour of battery life.)

application
Nerd word for *program*.

Application menu
The rightmost menu on the menu bar (if you have System 7), marked by an icon. This menu lists whatever programs you have open and shows a check mark next to the frontmost program. You can switch from one program to another by choosing their names from the Application menu.

ASCII
The most interesting thing about this term (which means "text file") is its weird pronunciation: *ASKie*. Good name for a Labrador, don't you think?

ATM
Short for Adobe Type Manager, a piece of software that makes certain fonts look really great on the screen (and in nonlaser printouts). It's free, for only $7.50.

background printing
A feature that returns control of the Mac to you immediately after you use the Print command; the Mac will print your document taking its own sweet time, always giving priority to what you're doing on the screen. The alternative, known as *background printing is off*, takes less time to print — but takes over the Mac, preventing you from working, displaying a "now printing" message until the printing is over.

baud rate
The speed of a modem (see *modem*). Directly related to the price.

BBS
An electronic bulletin-board system. That's where a Mac in somebody's house is connected to a phone line or two, so you can dial in with your modem (see *modem*) and post messages for other people to see. You can also read their messages. Good place to advertise that you're selling your used Mac stuff and to get dates.

beta test
Means "test," but adding a Greek word makes it more important-sounding. Used exclusively when applied to software: When a program is still so buggy and new that a company doesn't dare sell it, they give it away (to people who are then called "beta testers") in hopes of being told what the bugs are.

binary
Capable of counting only up to 2: how a computer thinks. Or anything that can only be in one of two conditions, like a Morse code signal, a light switch, or a public restroom.

bit
You'd think it was the past tense of *byte* (see below). Actually, it's a tiny piece of computer information not even big enough to bother with.

bitmap
A particular arrangement of black dots on your white screen. To your eye, a particular bitmap might look like the letter A (bit-mapped text) or a coffee mug (a bitmapped graphic); to the computer, it's just a bunch of dots whose exact positions it has to memorize.

boot
(1) Western footwear. (2) To start up the computer. (3) To fire somebody for having

accidentally erased the hard drive: *He was booted out of here so fast, you could have heard a résumé drop.*

bug

A programming error in a piece of software, caused by a programmer too wired on Jolt and pizza, that makes the program do odd or tragic things when you're working to beat a deadline.

bus

A form of public transportation. What's the big deal?

button

There are two you'll have to deal with: the big square one on the mouse, or the many oval or round ones you'll see on the screen that offer you options.

byte

A piece of computer information made up of bits. Now *that* made everything clear, didn't it?

CAD

Computer-aided design (i.e., architectural programs).

Caps Lock

A key on your keyboard responsible for messing up pages and pages of manuscript if you're one of those people who doesn't look up much from the keyboard. It makes every letter you type come out as a capital. Doesn't affect numbers. Press it once to get the capitals; press it again to return to normal.

CD-ROM

A computer compact-disc, requiring a special $400 CD-ROM player. CD-ROMs can show pictures, play music or voices, display short animations or movies, or display reams and reams of text. (A typical CD holds 600 megs of information; compare with the measly 80-meg hard disks that come in the more expensive Macs.)

cdev

Short for Control Panel.

Chooser

A desk accessory, therefore listed in the menu, that lets you specify what kind of printer you have. Failure to use this thing when you first set up your Mac is the Number One reason beginners can't print.

click

(v.) The cornerstone of the Macintosh religion: to point the cursor at an on-screen object and then press and release the mouse button.

clip art

Instead of possessing actual artistic ability, graphic designers can buy (or otherwise acquire) collections of ready-made graphics — little cutesy snowmen, city skylines, Santa Clauses, whatever — that they can use to dress up their newsletters, party invitations, or threatening legal notices.

Clipboard

The invisible holding area where the Mac stashes any text or graphics that you copy using the Copy command. The contents of the Clipboard get vaporized when you turn off the Mac (or copy something new).

close box

The little square in the upper-left corner of a window (as opposed to the little square who sold you the Macintosh) which, when clicked, closes the window.

color separation

The technique used in offset printing, where four separate metal plates (each one sopped in ink of a different color) are used to print a full-color image.

Command key

The one on your keyboard that has a ⌘ symbol on it. When it's pressed, the letter keys on your keyboard perform commands instead of typing letters: ⌘-P = Print, ⌘-S = Save, ⌘-Q = Quit, and ⌘-Z = undo (well, they can't *all* be mnemonic).

command

Something you'd like the Mac to do, like Print or Play or Make Me Rich.

Control key

A useless key that does absolutely nothing.

Control Panel

A little window full of settings that pertain to some aspect of the Mac's operation. There's a control panel for the mouse, another for the keyboard, another for the monitor, and so on. To view the selection of control panels, choose (what else?) Control Panels from the ⬤ menu.

Copy

Do you really need a definition of *copy?*

CPU

What it *stands for* is central processing unit. What it *means* is the actual computer — in the case of two-piece Macs, the box that contains the real brains, as distinguished from things like the monitor, the printer, and the keyboard.

CRT

Man, those geeks really get into cryptic acronyms for simple things, don't they? CRT is the screen. If you must know, it stands for cathode ray tube.

cursor

The pointer on the screen, whose position you control by moving the mouse across the desk.

daisy chaining

The act of stringing together a bunch of different add-on appliances, like a CD player, a hard disk, or a scanner, by plugging one into the back of the next, very much like an elephant conga line.

data

Isn't he that white-makeup guy on *Star Trek: The Next Generation?*

database

An electronic list of information — like a mailing list — that can be sorted very quickly or searched for a specific name.

DA

Short for desk accessory.

defragment

To restore something that's all broken up and scrambled into one continuous chunk. Usually refers to the information in memory or on a hard disk but can also be applied to hamburger meat.

Delete key

In the typewriter days, this key was named Backspace. In my opinion, it still *should* be called that. I make it a habit to magic-marker the word *Backspace* on every keyboard I encounter.

desktop file

A file the Mac maintains for its own use, in which it stores information like what your icons should look like and which kinds of documents can be opened by which programs. This file is invisible — but when it becomes damaged or bloated and starts causing problems, it's not quite invisible enough for most people.

desktop publishing

The act of cranking out nice-looking print-outs from your Mac, instead of paying to have it typeset. Despite the fact that the PowerBook is equally adept at creating beautiful printouts, the term *laptop publishing* still hasn't quite caught on yet.

desktop

(1) The top of your desk, where the Mac sits, as in *I don't want a laptop; I want a desktop computer.* (2) (Capitalized) The home-base environment, where you see the Trash can and icons and all that stuff. Also known as the Finder. (3) The actual, usually gray, background of that home-base view. You can drag an icon out of its window and onto this gray tablecloth and announce to your coworkers that you've just placed an icon on the desktop.

dialog box

The message box the Mac puts on the screen when it needs more information from you (like the one that appears when you print, asking how many copies you want). Because the Mac doesn't, thank God, actually talk back to you, and instead just listens to what *you* say, a better name might be *therapist box.*

digitize

Computerese for *digest.* It's what happens to sound, pictures, video, or any other kind of real-world sensory experience once the Mac converts it into its own internal numerical digestive tract.

digitizing board

A circuit board that converts video or TV pictures into files on your Mac.

disk cache

A secret feature for making your Mac faster at the expense of memory; the Mac memorizes a few things you do a lot and keeps them in a wad of memory called the disk cache, where they'll be immediately accessible. You set the size of the disk cache (the amount of memory reserved) using the Memory control panel.

disk

Oh, come on, you know *this* word.

disk drive

The machinery that actually reads what's on a disk. If we're talking hard disk, the disk and the drive are built into a single unit. If we're talking floppy, the disk drive is the slot in the face of the Mac into which you insert a floppy disk.

document

A file that you create with a program, like a memo (using a word processor), a logo (using a graphics program), or a spreadsheet (using a spreadsheet program).

dot-matrix

A kind of low-quality printer and the printouts it makes. The ImageWriter printer is a dot-matrix printer.

dots per inch

A gauge of visual clarity, both on printouts and on the screen. The Mac's crystal-clear screen became famous for having a very high resolution — 72 dots per inch, or 72 *dpi.* A laser printer is much sharper, though, capable of printing at 300 dpi.

double-click

One of the most basic Mac skills, without which you can't do anything but stare at the blank screen. Involves placing the on-screen pointer on an icon and, without moving it, pressing the mouse button twice quickly. If you double-click an icon, it always opens into a window; double-click a word to select it.

download

To transfer a file from one computer to another over the phone wires. If you're on the receiving end, you *download* the file. If you're on the sending end, you *upload* the file. If you're the phone company, you *love* the file.

downloadable font

Every laser printer comes with a basic set of typefaces built into it. You're welcome to use fonts that aren't in that built-in set, but the Mac has to send them to the printer (it has to *download* them) before the printer can start spitting out pages.

drag

(1) To position the cursor on something, press the mouse button and move the mouse while the button is still down. (2) What it is when your disk drive breaks the day after the warranty expires.

drawing program

A graphics program that creates circles, squares, and lines. The Mac stores each object you draw as an object unto itself, rather than storing the status of each screen dot; see *painting program* and *bitmap*.

driver

A smallish file on your disk that tells the Mac how it's supposed to relate to a specific piece of equipment, like a printer or a scanner, that it's never heard of before. A translator.

E-mail

Electronic mail. Messages that you read and write on the Mac screen, without ever printing them. May also be short for Earthmail since no paper (and no rain forest acreage) is involved.

Enter key

A key, obviously, with the word "Enter" on it. It almost always does the same thing as the Return key.

expansion slot

The new notch you have to use on your belt when you've been putting on weight. Also, the socket for an add-on circuit board inside certain Mac models.

extended keyboard

A slightly more expensive keyboard than the "standard" one; the extended one has a row of function keys (F1, F2) across the top, which don't do anything, and a little bank of keys that say PgUp, PgDown, and stuff.

extension

Miniprogram that you install by dropping it into your System Folder (whereupon the Mac puts it into the Extensions folder). From that moment on, the extension will run itself when you turn on the Mac and be on all the time. Examples: virus protectors and type enhancements.

fax/modem

Like a modem (see *modem*) but costs more and also lets you send or receive faxes from your Mac screen.

field

Computerese for *blank*, like a blank on a form.

File Sharing

A built-in feature of System 7, wherein you can make any file, folder, or disk available for other people to go rooting through (as long as they're connected to your Mac by network wiring).

file compression

Making a file take up less disk space by encoding it into a more compact format, using (what else?) a *file-compression program* like StuffIt or DiskDoubler. The trade-off: stuffing something down (and later expanding it when you need it again) takes a few seconds.

file

The generic word for one of the little icons in your Macintosh. There are two kinds of files: *programs,* that you purchase to get work done, and *documents,* which are created by programs. See also *program* and *document.*

Finder

The "home-base" view when you're working on your Mac. It's the environment where you see the Trash, your icons, and how little space you've got left on your disk. Also known as the Desktop or "that place with all the little pictures."

FKEY

One of those cool techno-sounding words that nobody's ever pinned down to one meaning. Can refer to (1) the row of keys across the top of some keyboards, the *function* keys, labeled F1, F2, and so on. Or (2) a special built-in keyboard shortcut involving the ⌘ and Shift keys plus a number; the ⌘-Shift-3 function key, for example, takes a snapshot of the screen, and ⌘-Shift-1 ejects a floppy disk.

flat-file database

A shopping list, Rolodex, or phone book; a simple collection of information. On a Mac, you can do things to your database like

search or sort; *flat-file* means it doesn't have fancy interconnections to other lists, like a "relational" database does.

floppy disk

The hard 3 ½-inch square thing you put into your disk drive slot. Comes in three capacities: 400K (single-sided), 800K (double-sided), and 1400K (quadruple-sided, or high-density). When magnetized by being placed too near an appliance, often used as a windshield scraper.

folder

In the Mac world, a little filing-folder icon into which you can drop other icons, like your work, for organizational purposes. When you double-click a folder, it opens into a window. Also, the name of the high-speed machine that creases and envelope-stuffs the junk mail you're going to start getting from computer companies.

font

(1) Apple's usage: a single typeface. (2) Everyone else's usage: a typeface family or package.

Font/DA Mover

An obsolete, obtuse, and obstinate utility program that came with every Mac for years. Used for adding or removing fonts to/from your Mac (and adding or removing desk accessories). With System 7, thank God, the Font/DA Mover is history.

fragmentation

When something gets broken up into little pieces. Usually refers to the files on your hard disk (which, over time, get stored in little pieces all over the disk, making it slower) or the memory in your computer (see *defragment*). Also can apply to your window after you throw the computer through it in frustration.

freeze
When your cursor becomes immovable on your screen, and you can't type anything, and your Mac locks up, and you get furious because you lose everything you've typed in the last ten minutes.

Function key
See *FKEY*.

gray scale
A form of color image or color monitor, where all the colors are different shades of gray, like all the images in this book.

grow box
Slang for Resize Box. (See *resize box.*)

hang
(1) Freeze (see *freeze*). (2) Knack: *Hey, I'm actually getting the hang of this. I'm no dummy!*

hard copy
A synonym for *printout,* used primarily by the kind of people who have carphones and say "let's interface on this".

hard disk
A hard drive.

hard drive
A hard disk. That is, the spinning platters, usually inside your Mac but also purchasable in an external form, that serve as a giant-sized floppy disk where your computer files get stored.

hardware
The parts of your computer experience you can feel, and touch, and pay for. Contrast with *software.*

header
Something that appears at the top of every page of a document, like "Chapter 4: The Milkman's Plight" or "Final Disconnection Notice."

highlight
To select, usually by clicking or dragging with the mouse. In the Mac world, text and icons usually indicate that they're selected, or highlighted, by turning black. In the barbecue world, things indicate that they're, um, *ready* by turning black.

HyperCard
A program that once came with every Mac. Sort of a Rolodex gone mad. Can be an appointment book, a diary, a kid's game . . . whatever you make of it.

icon
A teensy picture, an inch tall, used as a symbol for a file, a folder, or a disk.

ImageWriter
A low-cost, high-noise, low-speed, low-quality Apple dot-matrix printer.

INIT
The dweeb's word for *extension* (see that).

insertion point
In word processing, the blinking, short vertical line that's always somewhere in your text. It indicates where your next typing (or backspacing) will begin.

K
Short for *kilobyte,* a unit of size measurement for computer information. A floppy disk usually holds 800K or 1,400K of data. All the typing in this book fills about 1,500K. A full-screen color picture is around 1,000K of information. When your hard disk gets

accidentally erased, it's got 0K (but that's not OK).

kerning
In type-intensive Mac work like creating a newspaper headline, the act of squishing two letters slightly closer together to make better use of space so that you can fit the phrase AN ALIEN FATHERED MY 2-HEADED BABY on one line.

landscape
The natural environment you gradually forget about as you become addicted to the Mac. Also used to describe the sideways orientation of a piece of paper.

laptop
Where a PowerBook computer is when you're working on the plane.

laser printer
An expensive printer that creates awesome-looking printouts.

launch
To open a program: *He just sits at that computer all day long, moving icons around, because he hasn't figured out how to launch a program yet.*

LCD
The technology that creates the flat screen on the PowerBook laptop computer, marked by the tendency for the pointer to fade out if moved too quickly. Stands for either "Liquid Crystal Display" or "Lost the Cursor, Dammit."

leading
(*LEDding*): The vertical distance between lines of text in a document. Single-spaced and double-spaced are measurements of leading. *His term paper was 33 pages short,*

so he increased the leading and hoped the professor wouldn't notice.

LocalTalk
The hardware portion of a Macintosh network: the connectors and cables that plug one Mac into another.

macro
A predefined series of actions the Mac does automatically when you press a single key — like launching the word processor, typing "Help! I've been inhabited by a Mac poltergeist," and printing it — all by itself. Requires a special macro program.

MacroMaker
A macro program that used to come free with your Mac. Doesn't work with System 7.

math coprocessor
The kid whose algebra homework you used to copy.

MB
Short for *megabyte*.

megabyte
Another unit of disk-storage space or memory measurement (see *K*). Used to measure hard disks and other large storage devices. There are about 1,000K in a megabyte.

memory
The electronic holding area, which only exists when the Mac is turned on, where your document lives while you're working on it. Expensive and limited in each Mac.

menu
A list of commands, neatly organized by topic, that drops down from the top of the Mac screen (when you click its title).

menu bar
The white strip that's always at the top of the Mac screen, containing menu titles. Not to be confused with *bar menu,* or wine list.

modem
A phone attachment for your Mac, so you can send files and messages to other computer users all over the world, and prevent anyone else in the house from using the phone.

modifier keys
Keys that mess up what the letter keys do. Famous example: the Shift key. Other examples: ⌘ (Command), Option, Control, and Caps Lock.

monitor
What you should do to your blood pressure when you find out how much computer screens (monitors) cost and weigh.

mouse
The little handheld gray thing that rolls around on your desk and controls the movement of the cursor and is such an obvious target for a rodent joke that I won't even attempt it.

mouse button
The square plastic button in the middle of the mouse.

mouse pad
A piece of plastic-topped foam rubber that protects the mouse and desk from each other and gives the mouse good traction. Often bears a logo or slogan like "Sony Disks: We're always floppy."

MultiFinder
Before Apple invented System 7, you could only run one program at a time. To paste a graphic into a letter, you'd have to quit your graphics program, launch the word processor, and paste the picture. Using Multi-Finder, a special optional software add-on, you could have the graphics and word processing programs both open at once. (In System 7, you can *always* have more than one program open provided you have enough memory.)

multimedia
Something involving more than one medium, I guess. Mainly an advertising gimmick.

network
What you create when you connect Macs to each other so that you can send messages or transfer files from one to another without having to get up and run down the hall with a floppy disk in your hand (a networking system fondly called *SneakerNet*).

NuBus
The special kind of expansion slot (see *expansion slot*) found in any Mac II-style computer. Contrast with *PDS,* the slot found in a Macintosh LC. And no, there was never an OldBus.

OCR
Short for optical character recognition, where you run an article you tore out of *Entertainment Weekly* through a scanner, and the Mac translates it into a word processing document on your screen, so you can edit it and remove all references to Cher.

on-line
Hooked up: *Let's get this relationship on-line.*

painting program
(1) A program with the word Paint in the title (like MacPaint or UltraPaint) that

creates artwork by turning individual white dots black on the screen (by creating a *bitmap*; see that). (2) An adult-education course for would-be watercolorers.

partition

To use special formatting software that tricks the Mac into thinking that your hard disk is actually *two* (or more) disks, each with its own icon on the screen. Like subdividing a movie theatre into a duplex, but less expensive.

PDS

Stands for processor direct slot, and is the kind of *expansion slot* (see that) in a Mac LC. Incompatible with *NuBus* (see that, too).

peripheral

(1) Add-on: a printer, scanner, CD drive, dust cover. (2) The kind of vision by which you'll see your spouse leave you forever because you're too consumed by the Mac.

PICT

A confusing-sounding acronym for the most common kind of picture file: *Just paste that image of Sculley's head into your word processor, Frank; it's only a PICT file, for heaven's sake.*

pixel

One single dot out of the thousands that make up the screen image. Supposedly derived from *pic*ture *el*ement, which doesn't explain how the X got there.

pop-up menu

Any menu that doesn't appear at the top of the screen. Usually marked by a down-pointing black triangle. Doesn't actually pop *up*; usually drops down.

port

(1) A jack or connection socket in the back of your Mac. (2) Where boaters dock so they can recharge their PowerBook batteries.

portrait

A right side-up piece of paper; the opposite of *landscape* (see that). Also a right side-up monitor that can show a full page at once (as in "a portrait display monitor").

PostScript

A technology, a printer, a trademark, a kind of font, a computer code language for displaying or printing text or graphics, a way of life. All of it means high-quality type and graphics, and all of it means heaping revenues for Adobe, the company that invented it.

PRAM

Parameter RAM . . . the little piece of memory maintained by your Mac's battery that helps explain why the Mac always knows the date and time even when it's been turned off for a week.

Print Monitor

A program that launches itself, unbidden, whenever you try to print something when Background Printing is turned on (see *background printing*). Print Monitor is also the program that tries to notify you when something goes wrong with the printer, like when a piece of paper gets horribly mangled inside.

printer font

The printer half of a PostScript font (the other half is the *screen font*). Must be in your System Folder, and you must have one printer font for each style (bold, italic, and so on). An eternal nuisance.

program

A piece of software, created by a programmer, that you buy in order to make your Mac do something specific: graphics, music, word processing, number-crunching, or whatever.

Publish and Subscribe

A fancy new version of copy-and-paste that's part of System 7. Lets you paste information (like a graphic) from one document into another (like a memo), such that when you make a change to the original (the graphic), the copy (the memo) is changed automatically.

radio button

What you see in groups of two or more when the Mac is forcing you to make a choice between mutually exclusive options:

```
A System error has occurred. What result
would you like?
○ Loud, static buzzing
◉ Quietly blink to black
○ A two-minuite fireworks display
```

RAM

Term for *memory* (see *memory*) designed to intimidate non-computer users.

RAM disk

A way to trick the Mac into thinking that it has an extra floppy disk inserted, but the disk is actually a chunk of memory set aside to *resemble* a disk (complete with an icon on the screen). A built-in option on the PowerBooks and Quadras.

reboot

Restart.

rebuilding the Desktop

One of several desperate methods that can be used in the event of something screwy

going wrong with the Mac. Involves holding down the ⌘ and Option keys while the Mac is starting up.

record

(n.) Other than its obvious definitions, the computer-word *record* refers to one "card" in a database, such as one person's address information. Contrast with *field,* which is one *blank* (like a ZIP code) within a record.

relational database

A complex information list that you hire somebody to come in and set up for you, where each list of information (like a mailing list) is interconnected to another list (like People Who Never Pay on Time).

removable cartridge

Like a hard drive with free refills: a storage device (usually made by SyQuest or Bernoulli) that accepts huge-capacity disks, so you never run out of disk space (until you run out of the ability to buy more cartridges).

ResEdit

A free program that lets anybody do some hacking to any program — changing what the menus say, altering the keyboard shortcuts, or really screwing up the works.

resize box

The small square at the lower-right corner of a window that, when dragged, changes the size and shape of your window.

resolution

(1) A number, measured in dots per inch, that indicates how crisply a printer or a monitor can display an image. (2) A New Year's vow, like "I will spend five minutes away from the computer each day for family, exercise, and social activity."

restart switch

A little plastic switch, marked by a left-pointing triangle, on the side molding of most Macs that, when pressed, safely turns the Mac off and on again.

ROM

A mediation mantra you can use when contemplating the ROM chips, where the Mac's instructions to itself are permanently etched.

sans serif

A font, like Helvetica or Geneva, with no little "hats" and "feet" at the tip of each letter.

scanner

A machine that takes a picture of a piece of paper (like a Xerox machine), and then displays the image on your Mac screen for editing.

Scrapbook

A desk accessory, found in your ❡ menu, used for permanent storage of graphics, text, and sounds. (Not the same as the Clipboard, which isn't permanent, and only holds one thing at a time.) To get something into the Scrapbook, copy it from a document, open the Scrapbook, and paste it. To get something out of the Scrapbook, use the scroll bar until you see what you want, and copy it (or cut it).

screen saver

A program that darkens your screen after you haven't worked for several minutes. Designed to protect an unchanging image from burning into the screen, but used more often as a status symbol.

scroll

To bring a different part of a document into view, necessitated by the fact that most computer monitors aren't large enough to display all 60 pages of your annual report at once.

SCSI

Stands for Small Computer something Interface. The second S may stand for *standard,* or *system,* or *serial,* or something else, depending on whom you ask. Only used in the following five terms.

SCSI address

Refers to a number you have to give each SCSI device (see *SCSI device*) plugged into your Mac, using a little switch or thumb-wheel on the back. Can be between 0 and 7, except that the Mac is always 7 and the internal hard disk is always 0. If two SCSI devices have the same SCSI address, you're in big trouble.

SCSI cable

A fat cable with a 25- or 50-pin connector at the end. Used to join SCSI devices to each other. Total length of all your SCSI cables can't be more than about 20 feet, or you're in big trouble.

SCSI device

A scanner, CD player, external hard drive, printer (sometimes), removable-cartridge drive, external floppy-disk drive (sometimes), or other piece of equipment that you attach to the wide SCSI port in the back of your Mac. When you attach more than one of them (by plugging each into the back of the previous one), you have to obey certain rules (outlined in Chapter 9), or you're in big trouble.

SCSI port

The wide connector in the back of your Mac.

SCSI terminator

A plug that is supposed to go on the last SCSI device attached to your Mac. If you don't use one, you're in big trouble; although sometimes you're in big trouble if you *do* use one. See Chapter 9.

serif

(n., adj): a term used to describe a font that has little ledges, like little "hats" and "feet," at the tip of each letter, like Times or this font.

shareware

Programs that are distributed for free, via electronic bulletin board or on a floppy disk from user groups. The programmer requests that you send $10 or $20 to him or her, but only if you really like the program.

Shut Down

The command in the Special menu that turns off your Mac.

SIMM

It stands for Single In-line Memory Module, which I suggest you immediately forget, and it refers to memory chips.

sleep

A command, and a condition, that applies only to PowerBooks or the Mac Portable. Sort of like Off, except that the Mac remembers everything you had running on the screen. So when you want to use the computer again, you just touch a key, and the whole computer wakes up, the screen lights up, and you're in business again. Used to conserve battery power.

slot

An *expansion slot*. See that.

software

The real reason you got a computer. Software is computer code, the stuff on disks: programs (that let you create documents)

and documents themselves. Software tells the hardware what to do.

spooler

A program that allows *background printing* (see that).

spreadsheet

A program like an electronic ledger book, so you can type in columns of numbers and have them added up automatically.

stack

A document created by the HyperCard program.

startup disk

A startup disk is a floppy or hard disk that contains a System Folder (including a particular set of fonts, desk accessories, and settings for running your Mac). *The* startup disk is the one you've designated to be in control (in the event that there's more than one to choose from). The Startup Disk *control panel* is what you use to specify *the* startup disk.

stationery pad

A System 7 feature. Click a document icon, choose Get Info from the File menu, select Stationery Pad. From now on, when you double-click that icon, it won't open; instead, an exact *copy* of it opens. Saves you the hassle of pasting the same logo into every memo you write because you can paste it into your Stationery Pad document just once.

StyleWriter

A low-cost, quiet, high-quality, slow-speed Apple inkjet printer.

submenu

In some menus, you're forced to choose from an additional set of options, which are marked in the menu by a right-pointing triangle. When your pointer is on the main menu command, the submenu pops out:

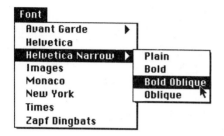

SuperDrive

The kind of floppy-disk drive found on every Macintosh except the Plus and early Mac II's and SE's. Called Super because it can read high-density (1.4 MB) floppy disks instead of the un-super 800K disks and because it can theoretically read IBM-format disks.

System 6

One version of the Mac's controlling software. Faster, but harder to use, than System 7. Requires 1MB of memory, or less.

System 7

The more recent version of the Mac's controlling software. More attractive, easier to use, more powerful, and slower than System 6. Requires at least 2MB of memory and, because it's a lot of software, requires a hard disk (because it doesn't fit on a floppy).

System 7.1

The first version of the Mac system software that's not free; you have to pay $35 for it. Adds two features to System 7: a Fonts folder that contains all manner of font files (TrueType, screen fonts, printer fonts); and WorldScript, the ability to convert all Mac screen elements into a different language, like Japanese (requires special drop-in language modules). System 7.1 is also

modular; you can add new features to it just by dropping in plug-in software tidbits as they become available.

System disk

A *startup disk* (see that entry).

System file

The most important individual file inside a System Folder. Contains the Mac's instructions to itself, and stores your fonts, sounds, and other important customization information. A Mac without a System file is like a broke politician: It can't run.

System Folder

The all-important folder that the Mac requires in order to run. Contains all kinds of other stuff also defined in this glossary: the System file, the Finder, fonts, desk accessories, printer fonts, and so on. Always identified by a special folder icon:

System Folder

system crash

Where something goes so wrong inside your Mac that a bomb appears on the screen with a message "Sorry, a System error has occurred!" — or not. Sometimes the whole screen just freaks and makes buzzing noises and gets filled with static, like a TV station going off the air.

telecommunication

Communicating with other computers over the phone lines. Requires a modem.

telecommute

To work in T-shirt and slippers in a messy apartment, spending not one penny on transportation, and sending work in to the office over the phone wires. Requires a modem and an ability to be alone for days on end without going insane.

terminator
See *SCSI terminator.* Or see an Arnold Schwarzenegger movie.

third party
(1) A company other than Apple: *You didn't get a mouse pad with your Mac? Well, of course not; you buy that from a third party.* You, by the way, are the second party. (2) The New Year's Eve get-together at which you get the drunkest.

TIFF
Stands for tagged image file format, and is the kind of graphics-file format created by a scanner.

title bar
The strip at the top of a window, where the window's name appears. Shows thin horizontal stripes if the window is *active* (in front of all the others).

toner
The powder that serves as the "ink" for a laser printer. Runs out at critical moments.

trackball
An alternative to the mouse. Looks like an 8-ball set into a pedestal, which you roll to move the pointer.

TrueType
A special font format from Apple that ensures high-quality type at any size, both on the screen and on any printer. Rival to PostScript but costs much less (nothing, in fact: comes with System 7).

user group
A local computer club that usually meets once a month and acts as a local source of information, and a place to unload your obsolete equipment to unsuspecting newcomers.

video card
A circuit board required by any two-piece Mac (except the IIsi, IIci, and Quadra) in order to see anything at all on the monitor; something else you have to buy.

virtual memory
A chunk of hard-disk space the Mac sets aside, if you wish, to act as emergency memory. (More on this in Chapter 9.)

virus
Irritating, self-duplicating computer program designed (by the maladjusted jerk who programmed it) to gum up the works of your Mac. Easily prevented by using Disinfectant or another virus barrier.

window
A square view of Mac information; in the Finder, a window is a table of contents for a folder or a disk. In a program, a window displays your document.

word wrap
A word processor's ability to place a word on the next line as soon as the first line becomes full.

WYSIWYG
Short for What You See Is What You Get, one supposed reason for the Mac's superiority over other computers. Means that your printout will precisely match what you see on the screen. Isn't always true.

zoom box
The tiny square in the upper-right corner of a window (in the title bar) that, when clicked, makes the window jump to full size.

Appendix E
Long-Distance Computing:
AppleTalk Remote Access

● ●

*I*f you have a PowerBook, or if you travel much, you may be interested in this decidedly non-dummyish topic. In fact, most people would call me nuts for including these instructions in a book for beginning Mac mavens. But I feel confident that once you see the astonishing potential of the technology known as *remote-access computing,* you'll think it was worth slogging through.

Until recently, every PowerBook came with a little program called AppleTalk Remote Access (which, to be consistent with the industry wags, I'll hereafter call ARA). Now they charge $200 for it. Anyway, using ARA and a modem, you can use one Mac to dial into another, thousands of miles away, and get files from it. Or read E-mail, print out a note for a coworker, or even use programs on the remote Mac.

That means you no longer need to nervously pack up the PowerBook for each trip you make, racking your brains to make sure you've copied everything you'll be needing from your remote Mac. If you forget a file, you can always phone home. The remote Mac shows up on your PowerBook screen as a plain old icon, as though it's simply another hard disk attached to your PowerBook.

Setting Up ARA

To make all this work, you need a pair of modems (one at home, and one for your PowerBook). The cheapie 2400-baud modems work but so unbelievably slowly that you might not think it's worth the trouble. You're better off using 9600-baud modems, which cost around $300 each. You also need both Macs (the caller and the callee) to be running System 7.

The only other thing you need to worry about is the phone line itself. In order to dial into your Mac at home, its modem has to be connected to a phone line. I'll leave it up to you to decide whether to (a) actually set up a dedicated phone line just for your modem, or (b) buy a $70 switcher box for your *regular* phone line, which, when a call comes in, automatically knows whether it's for the Mac or for your answering machine. I'd suggest, though, that you also buy a Power-Key Remote, a little gizmo from Sophisticated Circuits that turns your Mac on automatically when you call in (and turns it off when you're done).

That's a lot of physical setup, but I swear it's going to be one of the neatest things you've done with your Mac.

Now comes the complicated part that you'd never be able to figure out on your own. Stay with me, and follow these steps — you don't even have to know *what* you're doing, as long as you just *do* it — and you'll be remote-accessing in a trice.

Setting up your home Mac

1. Make sure System 7 is installed on the home Mac, including its File Sharing feature. If you don't have File Sharing or aren't sure, insert the first Install disk of the System 7 floppy-disk set. In successive dialog boxes, click OK; Customize; File Sharing; Install. Feed System 7 disks to the Mac as requested.

   When everything has been installed properly, you'll find about ten new files in your System Folder or in folders therein.

2. Insert the AppleTalk Remote Access disk, and double-click Installer. Click OK, and then click Install. When the installation process is over, your home-base Mac's System Folder will now contain two dozen more files, control panels, and specific modem modules (scripts).

3. Restart the Mac.

4. From the menu, choose Control Panels. Double-click Sharing Setup. In the Sharing Setup dialog box, enter your name and a password (optional). *Remember your Owner Name and Password!* If, when you try to dial in later and don't precisely type this information, you won't be granted access to your own Mac.

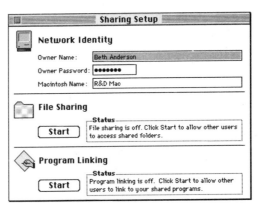

5. Click the upper Start button. Eventually, the button will change to say Stop. Close Sharing Setup.

6. Open the Users & Groups control panel. Double-click the icon representing your own name. In the dialog box that appears, determine how much access you want to give yourself.

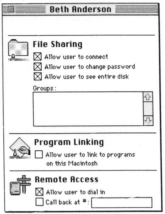

Be sure you select "Allow user to dial in" in the Remote Access section.

7. Click your hard-drive icon and choose File Sharing from the File menu. A dialog box appears; click "Share this item and its contents." Close the window, and save changes.

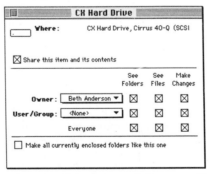

Repeat this step with any other disks or folders you'll want to access from the road.

8. Open the Remote Access Setup control panel. From the pop-up menu, specify the model and brand of modem attached to the home-base Mac. (If your modem brand isn't listed, you're not necessarily out of business; call the modem company to find out if they can send you an ARA script for your modem. If the modem company sends you a script, put it in your System Folder and then do this step over.)

Make sure "Answer calls" is selected.

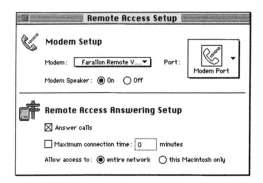

If you have an automatic-shutdown program (such as the PowerKey Remote control panel), set it up now to turn off your Mac a few minutes after you're done working with it.

The home-base Mac should now be ready for action.

Setting up the PowerBook

1. Install AppleTalk Remote Access, as described in step 2 above.

2. Open the Remote Access Setup control panel. From the pop-up menu, specify the model and brand of modem attached to the PowerBook.

3. Double-click the Remote Access program icon.

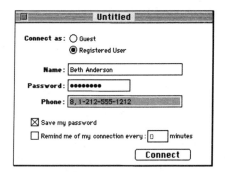

Enter your name and password exactly as you entered them in Step 4 of "Setting up your home Mac." In the Phone blank, enter the phone number of your home-base Mac's modem. (In this illustration, the number is preceded by 8 — to dial out from a hotel room — and a comma, which makes the dialing process pause for two seconds.) Unless you're worried about somebody stealing your PowerBook and using it to call up your home Mac, select "Save my password," so you won't have to retype it each time you call in. Choose Save from the File menu so that you create a connection document you can use again.

Click Connect. Your modem should start dialing like mad.

4. Watch the Remote Access Status dialog box:

When you've successfully connected, the Status line will display the name of your home-base Mac. (Don't forget to allow plenty of time for the host Mac to start up, load its extensions, and so on. ARA may even give up, claiming that nobody's answering the phone. Just try clicking the Connect button again; by this time, your home Mac has almost certainly finished starting up.)

5. From the menu, choose Chooser. In the Chooser, click AppleShare. On the right, you'll see the name of your Mac. Double-click its name; a dialog box appears.

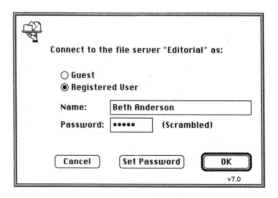

6. Once again, enter your name and password (if you've set one up). Click OK. Now you see a list of any disks or folders for which you turned on File Sharing in step 7 above. Double-click the one you first want to access. The disk or folder's icon should now appear at the right side of your Power-Book screen, where you can open it and use its contents as usual.

To save time, select it now and choose Make Alias from the File menu. Next time you want to dial in, just double-click the alias; you'll be able to skip steps 2–5.

Once you're hooked up to your home Mac, don't forget that you're actually placing a phone call — and if it's long distance, you're paying for every connected moment. So do some planning before you call, so you don't waste time, and be sure to click Disconnect when you're finished working with your home Mac.

Didn't I tell you this was the coolest thing ever?

Index

8-bit, 16-bit, 24-bit color monitors, 287–288
300 dpi editing, 139
800 numbers, for user groups, 110, 185, 303
911 Utilities, 263, 264, 265, 303
68000, 68030, 68040 processor chips, 282
/ (division operator), 162, 166
– (minus sign), 162, 166
* (multiplication operator), 162, 166
. (period), Command key and, 208–209, 263
+ (plus sign), 162, 166
(pound signs), in Excel cells, 266

—A—

About This Macintosh dialog box, 202, 239
accelerators, 273–274
  for color screens, 288
  defined, 307
accent marks, 126
accessories, sources for, 303–306
active windows, 229
ADB port, 292, 293, 307
add-ons, 179–194
  camcorders, 188–189
  CD-ROMs, 185–186
  computer problems and, 226
  connecting, 191–192
  microphones, 179–180
  MIDI, 186–188
  modems, 182–185
  networks, 190–191
  scanners, 180–181
  sources for, 303–306
  tape drives, 190
  ten non-costly, 192–194
  See also removable-cartridge drives; SCSI
Address Book Plus, 177
address book programs, 51, 122, 177
addresses, SCSI, 255, 319
Adobe Systems, 303
  Apple Computer and, 93, 97–99
  Illustrator, 99, 135, 177, 259, 304
  type style utility, 115
  See also PostScript entries
Adobe Type Manager (ATM), 303
  defined, 308
  memory and, 241
  PostScript fonts and, 103
  screen display and, 97
  TrueType fonts and, 98–99
After Dark, 218, 303
airplane simulator, 177

airplanes
  power outlets in, 299
  using PowerBook on, 299
airports, power outlets in, 299
alert boxes, 233, 307
  See also error messages
alias icons
  versus Alias macro, 173
  trashing, 205
  use of, 203–205
Alias macro, 173
alphabetical listing. *See* list-view
Always snap to grid command, 213
Amazing Paint, 303
  See also painting programs
America Online, 111, 184, 303
  getting help from, 275
  shareware from, 214, 220
"An error occurred while writing to the disk," 238
animation, HyperCard and, 134
Animation Works, 177, 303
anti-virus programs, 219, 268
apostrophes, straight versus curly, 86
Apple Computer
  Adobe Systems and, 93, 97–99
  AppleTalk, 108, 240–241, 300, 307
  fax/modems, 297
  LocalTalk connectors, 105
  monitors, keyboards, printers and, 287
  Motorola Corporation and, 282
  and obsolescence, 7
  StyleWriter printer, 91, 100, 102, 104, 320
  university discount, 288
  See also ImageWriter II printer; LaserWriter printers; TrueType fonts
Apple Desktop Bus (ADB), 292, 293, 307
Apple File Exchange, 175–176
Apple HD SC Setup, 253
Apple menu
  About This Macintosh dialog box, 202, 239
  active programs and, 78
  alias icons and, 204–205
  Chooser, 87, 105–108, 109, 257–258, 309
  defined, 307
  desk accessories, 52, 53
  File Find command, 20
  Option key and, 202
  PowerSaver command, 300
  See also Control Panels
Apple Menu Items folder, 53
Apple User-Group Info Line, 110, 185, 303
AppleLink, 184
AppleShare, 307

AppleTalk, 108, 307
  batteries and, 300
  memory and, 240–241
AppleTalk Remote Access, 183, 323–328
appliances, floppy disks and, 265
"Application is busy or missing," 234–236
Application menu, 56–60
  defined, 236, 308
  disk eject problems and, 263
  function of, 57
  Hide Others command, 199–200
  multitasking and, 199–200
  Note Pad icon and, 57
  Print Monitor program, 260
  saving and, 76
  Show All command, 199–200
"Application not found," 229, 234–236
"The application [program name] has unexpectedly quit," 236
applications, 308
  See also programs
Arc Tool, 135, 138, 142
architectural programs, 309
arrow keys
  in Excel, 159
  highlighting with, 23, 46
  moving insertion point with, 63–64
  troubleshooting problems with, 270–272
Arrow Tool, 135
ASCII text files, 235–236, 308
asterisk (*), 162, 166
At Ease, 47
ATM. *See* Adobe Type Manager (ATM)

—B—

Background command, 128, 129
background pattern, changing, 209–210
background printing, 108–109, 308, 320
  printing problems and, 260
backing up, 84, 190, 225
backlighting, battery life and, 299
Backspace. *See* Delete key
Balloon Help, 47
Baseline Publishing, 303
batteries, 295–296, 298, 299–302
  AppleTalk and, 300
  clocks for, 296
  maximizing power of, 299–302
  memory effect in, 300
  for PowerBook, 295–296
  PowerSaver command and, 300
  RAM disks and, 301–302
  recharging, 299–300
  reconditioner/charger, 299, 305
  safety and, 298
  Sleep mode and, 300
  startup problems and, 246
Battery desk accessory, 296, 300
Battery file, System Folder, 237

Battery Reconditioner/Charger, 299, 305
baud rate, 183, 308
BBSs. *See* bulletin boards (BBSs)
beeps
    changing error, 216–217
    troubleshooting, 228–229
Berkeley Macintosh Users' Group
        (BMUG), 303
Bernoulli drives, 190, 191, 303
beta test, 308
binary, 308
bit, 308
bitmap, 308
bitmapped fonts
    defined, 92
    identifying on Font Size menu, 93
    laser printers and, 100
    versus PostScript fonts, 93, 94, 113
    printing problems and, 258
    type styles and, 96
bitmapped graphics, versus object-
        oriented graphics, 134
black-and-white display, switching to
        color, 174, 221
black-and-white monitors, 285–286, 287
black-and-white painting programs, 138
blink rate, of insertion point, 61
blinking question mark icon, 13, 20, 40,
        248–249
BMUG (Berkeley Macintosh Users'
        Group), 303
bold text, 69–70
    in Excel, 160
    fonts and, 95–96, 115
    Ribbon controls and, 145
    troubleshooting problems with,
        114–115
bomb box, 226, 250–251, 253
bookkeeping programs, 177
booting, 11–14
    defined, 19, 308–309
    troubleshooting problems with,
        246–250
Boston Computer Society, 303
brightness, screen, 218, 246
Brightness file, memory and, 237
Browse Tool, 127, 131, 133
Brush tool, 127, 138
bugs
    computer problems and, 226, 252
    defined, 309
bulletin boards (BBSs)
    defined, 308
    getting help from, 275
    modems and, 185
    shareware from, 219, 220, 296
    software for, 177, 183
bus, 309
Button macro, 174
Button Tool, 127, 132
buttons
    creating, 130–132
    defined, 309
    macros for, 173
    programming, 132–133
    radio, 318
byte, 309

— C —

cables
    connecting printers with, 104–105
    keyboard, 271, 272
    mouse, 271, 272
    printing problems and, 257
    SCSI, 254, 257, 272, 319
    speaker-wire, 247
CAD (computer-aided design), 309
Calculate folder sizes control, 213
calculated fields, 166
calculation, automatic in Excel, 160–161
Calculator
    Copy and Paste and, 55–60
    multitasking and, 199–200
    opening, 57
    use of, 53–55
calendar/reminder programs, 51, 122,
        220–221, 283
camcorders, 188–189, 191
"Can't empty trash," 237
"Can't open printer," 237
Canvas. *See* drawing programs
capitalization
    Find command and, 203, 261
    of text, 65–66
Caps Lock key, 272, 309
Capture, 208, 303
cards. *See* HyperCard
Carpal Tunnel Syndrome, 291
carriage returns. *See* Return key
cartridge drives. *See* removable-
        cartridge drives
case. *See* capitalization
cases, carrying, 193, 295
Casper, 180
cathode ray tube (CRT), 310
    See also monitors
cdev, 309
CD-ROMs, 185–186, 191, 309
cells, Excel, 157, 160–162, 266
centering text, 71
Central Processing Unit (CPU), 279, 310
Centris. *See under* Macintosh computers
characters
    formatting, 69–70
    Ribbon controls and, 145
    showing hidden, 69
    spacing of, 71
    substitution macros, 173
charts, in Excel, 162–163
checkbook programs, 177
    Macintosh models and, 279
chips, memory, 282
Chooser
    background printing and, 109
    defined, 309
    printing problems and, 257–258
    selecting printers with, 87, 105–108
cities, Map control and, 202
citizen keys, 37
city-named fonts, 92, 95, 99–103
    printing problems and, 258
Claris Corporation
    ClarisWorks, 51, 122–134, 177, 303
    HyperCard and, 123, 304
Classic Macintosh. *See under* Macintosh
        computers
Clean Up by Name command, 201

Clean Up Window command, 201
Clear key, Calculator, 57
Click macro, 174
clicking
    defined, 17, 309
    double-clicking, 23, 38, 312
    guided tour and, 19
    icons, 20–21
    macros and, 171, 174
    Option key and, 197
    outside document window, 267–268
    Shift-clicking, 39, 136, 146
clip art, 309
Clipboard
    Copy command and, 56, 58
    Cut command and, 86
    defined, 309
clock speed, 282
clocks
    batteries and, 296
    setting time and type of, 61
close box, 22, 77, 309
closed spacing, 147
CloseView, 237
closing
    all windows, 196
    files, 22, 77
cloverleaf symbol, 37–38
Cluttered, Overlapping Windows
        Syndrome (COWS), 197, 199
Color Classic. *See under* Macintosh
        computers
Color control, 212
color display, macro for, 174
Color file, System Folder, 237
color menus, 142
color monitors, 285–288
    8-bit, 16-bit, 24-bit, 287–288
    advantages/disadvantages of, 286
    black-and-white, gray-scale monitors
        and, 287
    color printers and, 286
    customizing display on, 209–212
    horizontal line on, 232
    switching to black-and-white display,
        174, 221
    video cards and, 247, 287, 288, 292,
        322
    See also monitors
color painting programs, 138
color printers, color monitors and, 286
color separation, 310
color swatches, Control Panels, 210,
        211
ColorStudio. *See* painting programs
Command key
    +Option+Esc combination, 253
    +period (.), 208–209, 263
    canceling printing with, 110
    defined, 310
    ejecting floppy disks and, 45, 264
    highlighting, 146
    as modifier key, 37–38
    rebuilding Desktop and, 235
    windows and, 197
    See also keyboard shortcuts
commands, 310
    See also menu commands
communications. *See* modems
compact Macs, 278, 283
Compact Pro, 220

compression programs, 217–218, 220, 296, 313
CompuServe, 184, 303
computer problems. *See* troubleshooting
computer stores, purchasing from, 289–290
computer viruses, 219, 268
computer-aided design (CAD), 309
conferencing, on-line, 184–185
Connectix, 303
consumer stores, 290
Content Tool, QuarkXPress, 155
contiguous memory, 243
Control key
    defined, 310
    macros and, 172
    as modifier key, 37–38
    zapping the PRAM and, 249
Control Panels, 60–61
    Calculate folder sizes control, 213
    cdev and, 309
    Color control, 212
    color swatches on, 210, 211
    defined, 202, 310
    Desktop Pattern control, 61, 209–210
    dimming screens with, 218
    File Sharing control, 240
    General Controls, 60–61, 209–210
    Icon Views controls, 213
    Label menu control, 210–211
    List Views controls, 213
    Map control, 202
    Memory controls, 241, 244–245, 252, 300–301
    Monitors control, 202, 287
    Option key and, 202
    QuicKeys and, 173–174
    RAM disks and, 300–301
    Show disk info control, 213
    Sound control, 180, 216–217
    switching color/black-and-white display, 174, 221
    Views control, 212–213
    Virtual Memory control, 244–245
Copy command
    versus Cut command, 86
    keyboard shortcut for, 59–60
    use of, 55–56, 58
copy shops, 116
copying
    alias icons and, 203–205
    files, 43–44
    Option key and, 46, 201
copying machines, scanners and, 180
cost, of Macintosh computers, 283
COWS (Cluttered, Overlapping Windows Syndrome), 197, 199
CPU (Central Processing Unit), 279, 310
crash, system. *See* system crash
credit cards, purchasing with, 291
CRT (cathode ray tube), 310
    See also monitors
curly quotes, 86, 174
cursor
    defined, 15, 310
    I-beam, 64–65
    system freeze and, 226
    in word processing, 63–64
    See also insertion point
cursor keys. *See* arrow keys

Cut command
    Cut-and-Paste
        versus drag-and-drop, 147
        moving text with, 86
        keyboard shortcut for, 59

— D —

daisy-chaining
    defined, 191–192, 310
    SCSI problems and, 255
DAs. *See* desk accessories
data, 310
Data Entry view, FileMaker Pro, 163
data recovery programs, 263, 264, 265, 270
data types, 165
database programs, 51
    Macintosh models and, 283
    See also FileMaker Pro
databases
    data types and, 165
    defined, 163, 310
    fields and, 164–166, 312
    records and, 165, 169, 318
    relational versus flat-file, 164, 313, 318
date, setting, 61
Date macro, 174
date-stamping documents, 148
dealers, purchasing from, 289–290
debugging macros, 174
defragmenting
    defined, 310
    hard drives, 269
    memory, 242–243
Delete key
    defined, 310
    in FileMaker Pro, 166
    in Note Pad, 54
    selection tools and, 139
    in word processing, 63, 65
Delphi, 184
deselecting text, 66
design, computer-aided (CAD), 309
desk accessories
    Battery, 296
    Calculator, 51, 53–60
    calendar/reminder utility, 220–221
    Chooser, 87, 105–108
    Font/DA Mover, 97
    Key Caps, 126
    macro for, 174
    Note Pad, 51, 53–60
    Scrapbook, 319
DeskPaint, 303
    See also painting programs
Desktop
    changing pattern of, 61, 209–210
    defined, 13, 311
    locating files on, 21
    rebuilding the, 235, 318
    See also Finder
Desktop file
    defined, 310–311
    floppy disks and, 265
    rebuilding, 235, 318
desktop publishing
    defined, 311
    laser printers and, 92
    See also PageMaker; QuarkXPress

DeskWriter printer, 91, 303
    connecting to Macintosh, 104
    resolution of, 102
diacritical marks, 126
dialog boxes
    About This Macintosh dialog box, 202, 239
    defined, 72–73, 311
    highlighting in, 73
    Open command dialog box, 74, 81–82
    Page Setup dialog box, 108, 114, 139
    Print dialog box, 109–110
    Save dialog box, 74–77, 83
    Tab key in, 110
    troubleshooting problems with, 228–229
Diconix portable printer, 298
digital recording, 186–187
digitizing, 181, 188–189, 192, 311
digitizing board, 311
dimmed menu commands, 17, 75, 229–230
dimming screens, 218, 299, 300
ding, startup, 246–247
Disinfectant, 219, 220, 268, 304
disk boxes, 192
Disk Cache, 241, 311
disk drives
    defined, 42, 311
    port for, 293
    SuperDrive, 175, 321
    troubleshooting problems with, 264
    used computers and, 290
    See also floppy disks; hard drives; RAM disks; removable-cartridge drives
"The disk is full," 236–237
"This disk is unreadable: Do you want to initialize it?," 42, 264–265
disk with question mark icon, 13, 20, 40, 248–249
disk recovery programs, 249
Disk Tools disk
    reformatting program on, 253
    starting Macintosh and, 13
    startup problems and, 248
DiskDoubler, 218, 296, 304
DiskExpress, 269
disks. *See* floppy disks; hard drives; RAM disks
displays. *See* monitors
division operator (/), 162, 166
Document Layout palette, QuarkXPress, 156–157
documents, 311
    See also files
dot matrix printers, 90, 311
dots per inch (dpi), 93, 311
    See also resolution
double quotes
    macro for, 174
    straight versus curly, 86
double-clicking, 23, 38, 312
double-sided floppy disks, 42, 264
double-spacing text, 71
download, 312
downloadable fonts, 113–114, 312
    printing problems and, 258, 259
dpi (dots per inch), 93, 311
    See also resolution

dragging
  defined, 17, 312
  and dropping text, 147–148
  folders, 38
  guided tour and, 19
  icons, 20–21
  macros for, 174
  to select text, 65–66
drawing programs, 134–137, 312
  creating icons with, 207
  generic graphics files and, 235, 236
  grouping/ungrouping objects,
    136–137
  Macintosh models and, 283
  monitors and, 285
  Option key and, 201
  versus painting programs, 134
  Shift key and, 136
  Tool palette, 135–136
  See also graphics programs; painting
    programs
drivers
  defined, 312
  printer, 106–108, 237
Duo (and Duo Dock). *See under*
    PowerBook
Duplicate command, 46, 262
dust covers, 193
DynoDex, 177

—E—

8-bit color monitors, 287–288
Easy Access, 237
Edit menu
  Background command, 128, 129
  Copy command, 55–56, 59–60, 86
  Paste command, 57–60, 86
  Undo command, 59–60, 130, 232
editing
  painting program graphics, 139
  text in drawing programs, 137
Eject Disk command, 17, 44, 263
electronic bulletin boards. *See* bulletin
    boards (BBSs)
electronic mail, 182, 184, 312
ELF (Extremely Low-Frequency
    radiation), 291-292
Ellipse Tool, 135, 138, 142
E-mail, 182, 184, 312
Empire Engineering, 295, 305
Empty Trash command
  deleting folders with, 40
  full disks and, 236
  locked files and, 199, 237
  Option key and, 198–199, 237
  recovering files after, 41, 270
  in System 6, 40
  in System 7, 46
Encore, 188, 304
Enter key, 312
  See also Return key
envelopes, printing, 91
Eraser tool, 127, 138, 141
error beep, changing, 216–217
error messages
  "An error occurred while writing to
    the disk," 238
  "Application is busy or missing,"
    234–236
  "Application not found," 229,
    234–236

"Can't empty trash," 237
"Can't open printer," 237
copying files and, 262–263
Empty Trash and, 198
"Extensions off," 249
floppy disks and, 262–263, 264–265
fonts and, 259
"Force [program name] to quit?," 253
in HyperCard, 122
"Printer could not be found," 257
"Printer could not be opened," 257
"[Program name] prefers 2048K of
    memory. 2000K is available,"
    238
"Sorry, a system error occurred,"
    226, 250–251
  ID numbers in box, 253
  startup problems and, 249–250
"System Extension: This file adds
    functionally to your
    Macintosh," 234
system freeze and, 226
"The application [program name]
    has unexpectedly quit," 236
"The disk is full," 236–237
"The Printer Monitor has reported
    an error," 237
"There is not enough memory to
    open [program name]," 236
"This disk is unreadable: Do you
    want to initialize it?," 42,
    264–265
"You have changed your current
    printer....," 108
"Your screen has been dimmed," 298
  See also troubleshooting
Escape key
  function of, 37
  restarting with, 253
Excel. *See* Microsoft Excel
expansion slots, 192, 312, 316
extended keyboards, 312
extension cords, 193
extensions
  conflict of, 249
  defined, 312
  versus Extensions macro, 174
  memory and, 240
  System, 227
  System errors and, 249
Extensions folder, 227, 237
  System 7 Tune-Up in, 240
Extensions macro, 174
"Extensions off," 249
external hard drives
  connecting, 191
  versus internal, 33, 189
  reformatting programs and, 253
  SCSI problems and, 254–257, 269
  startup problems and, 247, 248
  troubleshooting problems with, 269
  See also hard drives
Extremely Low-Frequency radiation
    (ELF), 291-292
EZ Vision, 187, 304

—F—

F keys, 37, 172, 314
fax/modems, 183–184, 297–298, 312
Field Tool, 127, 131
fields, 164–165, 312
  calculated, 166

file compression programs, 217–218, 220,
    313
  PowerBook and, 296
File Find command, 20
File macro, 174
File menu
  Duplicate command, 46, 262
  Find Again command, 203
  Locked checkbox in, 262
  Make Alias command, 203–205
  New Card command, 130
  New Folder command, 35–36
  Open command, 22, 74, 81–82
  Page Setup command, 108, 114, 139
  Print command, 109
  Print Preview command, 144
  Put Away command, 44, 263
  Quit command, 83
  Save command, 32–33, 72–77, 81, 83
  Stationery Pad, 320
  See also Find command
File Sharing, 240, 312–313
FileMaker Pro, 51, 163–170
  data entry, 166
  data types and, 165–166
  database types and, 164
  fields, 164–166
  Find command, 169
  hidden data, 266
  layouts, 167–169
  navigating in, 166
  records, 165, 166
  saving in, 165
  Scripts, 170
  Sort command, 169
  starting a file, 164–166
  troubleshooting problems with, 266
  views in, 163
files
  alias icons and, 203–205
  ASCII text, 235–236, 308
  backing up, 84, 190, 225
  closing, 22, 77, 309
  compressing, 217–218, 220, 313
  converting IBM and Macintosh,
    175–176
  copying, 43–44, 46, 201, 262–263
  creating lists of, 206
  defined, 313
  ejected disks and open, 263
  finding, 20, 202–203
  graphics, 235, 236, 322
  locked, 199, 237, 262
  macros for launching, 174
  opening generic text or graphics, 235
  opening new versus existing, 79–80
  PICT, 236
  recovering from Trash can, 77, 79,
    80–82, 270
  recovery utilities for, 263, 264, 265,
    270
  renaming, 262
  saving, 72–77, 82–83
  in System Folder, 237
  text-only, 235–236, 308
  troubleshooting problems with, 233,
    234–236, 262–263
  See also folders
Fill Down command, Excel, 162
Fill Right command, Excel, 161–162
Finale, 188, 303
financial programs, 177
Find Again command, 203

Find command
    capitalization and, 203, 261
    FileMaker Pro and, 169
    versus Find File command, 20
    More Choices option and, 203
    troubleshooting problems with, 261
    use of, 202–203
Finder
    Application menu and, 78
    defined, 313
    locating files with, 21, 76, 202–203
    Option key and, 201, 202
    Trash can and, 21
    troubleshooting problems with,
        261–262
    See also Desktop
FKEY, 313
FKEYs macro, 174
flat-file databases, 164, 313
Flight Simulator, 177, 304
floortop Macintosh computers, 280
floppy disks, 41–45
    backing up, 84, 190, 225
    boxes and cases for, 193
    converting IBM and Macintosh,
        175–176
    copying, 46
    copying from, 43–44, 262
    defined, 27–28, 313
    Desktop file and, 265
    displaying available space on, 213
    double-sided, 42, 264
    ejecting, 44–45, 47, 194, 263–264
    error messages and, 262–263,
        264–265
    high density, 42, 264
    IBM versus Macintosh, 42, 175–176,
        265
    icon, 43
    initializing, 42–43, 264–265
    locking and unlocking, 41
    magnetic damage and, 265
    naming, 42–43
    paper clips and, 45, 194, 264
    renaming, 46, 263
    single-sided, 42, 264
    sizes of, 42, 264
    tips for using, 45–47
    troubleshooting problems with, 238,
        262–265
    viewing contents of, 43
    write protecting, 41
    See also disk drives; hard drives;
        RAM disks; removable-
        cartridge drives
folders, 35–41
    closing, 40
    copying, 43–44, 46
    creating, 35–36
    creating lists of, 206
    defined, 313
    deleting, 40
    displaying size of, 213
    Extensions, 227
    locating, 23
    locking, 46
    moving, 38–40
    naming, 36
    renaming, 46
    saving files into, 74–77
    selecting multiple, 38–40

    in System Folder, 237
    viewing subfolders in, 25
    views of, 24–25, 45–46, 212–214
Font Size menu, 93
Font Substitution option, 113
Font/DA Mover, 97, 112, 313
fonts, 92–104
    aesthetics of, 85
    built into Postscript laser printers,
        113
    choosing, 70
    city-named and non-city-named, 92,
        95, 99–103, 258
    defined, 92, 313
    downloadable, 113–114, 258, 259, 312
    error messages and, 259
    facts about, 112–117
    identifying, 99–103
    installing, 97, 111
    menu display of, 115–116
    in painting programs, 141
    point-size of, 94
    PostScript versus bitmapped, 93, 94,
        113
    printer, 95–97, 98, 100–101, 317
    printing problems and, 258, 259
    removing, 111–112
    Ribbon controls and, 145
    screen, 95–97, 98, 112
    serif versus sans serif, 116–117, 319,
        320
    sources for, 110–111
    standard on Macintosh, 112
    Styles and, 149
    substitution of, 113
    table of printers and fonts, 103–104
    See also Adobe Type Manager
        (ATM); bitmapped fonts;
        PostScript fonts; TrueType
        fonts; type styles
Fonts folder, 100, 111, 112
Fonts disk, 92, 111
footers, 86, 148
"Force [program name] to quit?," 253
formatting, 67–71
    characters, 69–70
    in Excel, 157–158
    paragraphs, 70–71
    Return key and, 68–69
    Styles and, 148–149
    typefaces, 70
formatting disks. See initializing disks
formatting programs, 252–253
forms, printing, 90
forward slash (/), 162, 166
fragmentation
    defined, 313
    hard drives and, 269
    memory and, 242–243
free/almost free utility programs,
    220–221
FreeHand, 99, 135, 177, 259, 304
freeze, system. See system freeze
full-page monitors, 285
function keys
    defined, 314
    function of, 37
    macros and, 172
FWB Hard Disk Utility, 253

— G —

Gatekeeper, 219, 304
General Controls window
    Desktop Pattern and, 209–210
    use of, 60–61
generic text/graphics files, 235–236
GEnie, 184
glare filters, 192
Global Village fax/modems, 297
glossary, 307–322
Grabber tool, 135, 138, 142
Grammar command, 149
graphics, bitmapped versus object-
        oriented, 134
graphics cards, 247, 287, 288, 292
graphics files, 235, 236, 322
graphics programs, 134–142
    creating icons with, 207
    drawing versus painting, 134
    generic graphics files and, 235, 236
    handles in, 136
    Macintosh models and, 279, 280, 283
    monitors and, 285
    Option key and, 201
    PostScript, 99, 135, 177
    printing problems and, 258, 259
    Shift key in, 136, 141, 142
    See also drawing programs; painting
        programs
Graphics Smoothing option, 139
grayed out menu commands, 17, 75
gray-scale monitors, 286, 287, 314
GreatWorks, 177, 304
grid, snapping icons to, 213
Group command, drawing programs,
    136–137
grow box, 314
guided tour, of Macintosh computers,
    18–20

— H —

Hand grabber tool, 135, 138, 142
hand scanners, 181
handles, in graphics programs, 136
hang, 314
    See also system freeze
hard copy, 314
Hard Disk Toolkit, 304
hard drives
    backing up, 84, 190, 225
    and copying floppy disks, 46
    copying from floppy disk to, 43–44
    cost of, 33
    defined, 21, 314
    defragmenting, 269, 310
    displaying available space on, 213
    explained, 28
    fragmentation and, 269, 313
    icon, 21, 249, 269
    internal, 33, 189
    versus memory, 30–31, 33
    partitions, 317
    PowerBook and, 296
    and purchasing a Macintosh, 281, 283
    reformatting, 252–253
    versus removable-cartridge drives,
        189

size of, 281
system crash and, 252
troubleshooting problems with, 236–237, 238, 248, 269–270
video editing and, 188
viewing contents of, 21–23, 82
virtual memory and, 33, 243–245
See also external hard drives
hardware, 314
headaches, monitors and, 291
headers, 314
use of, 86, 148
help, sources for, 275, 303
Hewlett-Packard, DeskWriter printer, 91, 102, 104
hidden characters, showing, 69
Hide Balloons command, 47
Hide Others command, 199–200
high density disks, 42, 264
highlighting
with arrow keys, 23, 46
changing color of, 211–212
Command key and, 146
defined, 314
in dialog boxes, 73
icons, 23
lost text and, 231
menu commands, 17
one line of text, 146
paragraphs, 70, 145–147
and replacing text, 231–232
sentences, 146
Shift key and, 146
shortcuts for, 146
text, 36, 55, 65–66
un-highlighting, 66
See also selecting
home movies, 188–189
Home stack, HyperCard, 122
horizontal scroll bar. *See* scroll bars
hot, defined, 188
humans, similarities of Macintoshes and, 25–26
humorous programs, 219
HyperCard, 122
Player, 122, 294
Hyphenation command, 149

— I —

I-beam cursor, 64–65
IBM disks, versus Macintosh disks, 42, 265
IBM files, conversion of, 175–176
Icon Views controls, 213
icon-based on-line services, 184
icons
"AAAAAAAGH," 14
alias, 203–205
versus alphabetical listing, 24–25
alphabetizing, 201
Apple on menu bar, 20
bomb, 226, 250–251, 253
Clean Up Window command and, 201
clicking and dragging, 19, 20–21
color-coding, 210–211
creating custom, 207–208
customizing display of, 212–214
defined, 314

disk with blinking question mark, 13, 20, 40, 248–249
double-clicking, 23
floppy disk, 43
fonts and, 100
"FWOOOD13," 13
hard drive, 21, 249, 269
highlighting, 23
Icon Views controls and, 213
labeling, 210–211
Laser Prep, 107
listing by, 24, 45–46, 100
locking, 46
moving, 19, 20–21
Note Pad, 56–57
open/closed spacing, 147
opening, 21–22, 23
Option key and, 201
printer driver, 87, 107, 258
printer installation and, 106–108
renaming, 46, 261
selecting, 21, 23, 38–40, 45
smiling Macintosh, 12–13
snapping to grid, 213
sound, 216
System 7, 20
text style of, 212–213
troubleshooting problems with, 269
TrueType fonts, 100
and turning Macintosh on, 12–14
used in book, 5
views of, 24–25, 45–46, 212–214
See also Trash can
ID numbers, in System error box, 253
Illustrator, 99, 135, 177, 259, 304
ImageWriter II printer, 90, 99, 314
Adobe Type Manager and, 102, 103
background printing and, 109
connecting to Macintosh, 104
floppy disks and, 265
printing problems and, 259
See also printers
indentation, setting, 147
initializing disks, 42–43, 264–265
INITs
conflict of, 249
defined, 314
System errors and, 249
TrueType, 100
inkjet printers, 91
insertion point
defined, 314
setting blink rate of, 61
in word processing, 63–64
See also cursor
Install 1 disk, 252
Installer program, fonts and, 110
Installer screens, 248
integrated programs, 51, 177
integrated video, 287
Interex, 295
internal hard drives, 33, 189
See also hard drives
internal SCSI terminators, 256
Invert command, 139
italics, 69–70
fonts and, 95–96
Ribbon controls and, 145
versus underlining, 85
Item Tool, QuarkXPress, 155

— J —

justification, of text, 71, 147

— K —

K (kilobyte), 204, 314–315
kerning, 315
Key Caps, typing symbols with, 126
keyboard shortcuts, 36–41
Caps Lock key and, 272
changing with ResEdit, 214–216
cloverleaf symbol and, 37–38
Copy command, 59–60
curly quotes, 86
defined, 6
ejecting floppy disks, 45, 264
Fill Right command, 162
Find Again command, 203
Find command, 202
formatting text, 70
halt, 208–209
Hand grabber tool, 142
highlighting icons, 23
HyperCard, 123
locating folders, 23
menu commands and, 36
modifier keys for, 37–38
New Folder command, 38
for no, 208–209
opening icons, 23
Paste command, 59–60
Save command, 72, 83
selecting all text, 85
selecting text, 146
troubleshooting problems with, 272
See also Command key; Control key; macros; Option key
keyboards
cables and, 272
extended, 312
purchasing, 287, 291
screen savers and, 218
system freeze and, 226
troubleshooting problems with, 270–272
keypad, Calculator and, 53
KidPix, 177, 304
kilobyte (K), 204, 314–315
Kind, sorting windows by, 25

— L —

Label menu, changing, 210–211
label printers, 192
labels
FileMaker Pro and, 163, 167
printing, 91
landscape, defined, 315
landscape monitors, 285
languages, page description, 93
laptop
defined, 315
See also PowerBook
Larger Print Area option, 114
Laser Prep icon, 107
laser printers
bitmapped fonts and, 100
Chooser and, 105–108

connecting to Macintosh, 104–105
in copy shops, 116
defined, 315
font size and, 93–94
fonts built into PostScript, 113
LaserWriter and, 258
memory and, 241
PostScript, 91–92
PostScript versus non–PostScript, 94
startup page, 116, 260
streaks on printouts of, 260
types of, 91–92
See also LaserWriter printers;
    PostScript laser printers;
    printers
LaserWriter Font Utility, 116
LaserWriter printers
connecting to Macintosh, 104–105
described, 91, 93–94
icon for, 107, 258
non-PostScript, 102
PostScript laser printers and, 91,
    93–94, 258
Select 300 model, 92, 102
See also laser printers; PostScript
    laser printers; printers
Lasso tool, 127, 128–129, 138
versus Marquee tool, 139–140
Last Resort, 232, 304
latitude, Map control panel and, 202
launch, defined, 315
layout programs. *See* page layout
    programs; PageMaker;
    QuarkXPress
LCI, LCII, LCIII. *See under* Macintosh
    computers
LCD (Liquid Crystal Display), 315
leading, 315
letter substitution macros, 173
Lind Engineering, 295, 299, 305
line spacing, 71, 147
Line Thickness menu, 136, 141, 142
Line Tool, 127, 135, 138, 141
Linking Tool, QuarkXPress, 156
LinkTo command, HyperCard, 133
Liquid Crystal Display (LCD), 315
List Views controls, 213
list-view
explained, 24–25, 45–46, 214
fonts and, 100
LocalTalk connectors, 105, 315
Locked checkbox, 46, 262
locked files, 46, 262
in Trash can, 199, 237
longitude, Map control panel and, 202
Lotus 1-2-3 for the Mac, 177, 303
lowercase, Find command and, 203

— **M** —

Mac Tools Deluxe, 270, 304
Mac Warehouse, 304
Mac Zone, 304
MacConnection, 41, 51, 304
MacDraw Pro. *See* drawing programs
Macintosh Basics disk, 18
Macintosh computers
IIcx, IIsi, IIci, IIvx, IIfx, 279
    choosing, 283
    differences between, 282

monitors and, 285, 287
movie-making and, 284
setting up, 292
IIvx, 186
accelerating, 273–274
addiction to, 233
advantages of, 6
back side of, 293
Centris, 12, 186, 278–280, 282, 285
Classic or Classic II, 11, 279, 282, 283–
    284, 290, 292
Color Classic, 12, 218, 279
clock speed and, 282
compact, 278, 283
connecting printers to, 104–108
cost of, 283
credit cards and, 291
customizing, 209–214
ELF radiation and, 291-292
floortop, 280
free software included with, 51, 175
guided tour of, 18–20
integrated video and, 287
laptop. *See* PowerBook
LC (I, II, or III), 11, 248, 279, 283–285,
    290
modular, 279, 280, 283
monitors, keyboards, printers and,
    287
as "Nerf" appliances, 23
obsolescence and, 7
one-piece
    advantages/disadvantages of,
      278–279
    magnetic damage and, 265
    power switch on, 11–12
    screen savers and, 218
    setting up, 292
    Shut Down command and, 18
    turning off, 15, 18
    uses for, 283
operation of explained, 31–33
Performa. *See* Performa
plugging in, 292–293
Plus, 11, 279, 283, 284, 292
Portable, 320
PowerBook. *See* PowerBook
processor chip and, 282–283
product line, 277–284
Quadra, 279, 280
    choosing, 283–284
    monitors and, 285
    processor chips and, 282
    setting up, 292
remote control of, 183
repair service and, 289
resources for, 303–306
SE, 11, 279, 283, 290, 292
selling, 274
setting up, 291–292
similarities of with humans, 25–26
turning off, 15
turning on, 11–14
two-piece, 279, 280, 285
    dimming monitor of, 218
    magnetic damage and, 265
    power-on switch on, 12
    setting up, 292
    troubleshooting problems with,
      246, 247
    turning off, 15
    uses for, 283

university discount and, 288
upgrading, 273–274
used, 290
warranties, 274, 289
what to get free with, 294
where to buy, 288–290, 303–306
See also PowerBook; purchasing
    guide; System 6 versus System
    7; System 7
Macintosh user groups, 275, 290
defined, 322
software from, 214, 219, 220
telephone numbers for, 110, 185, 303
MacLink, 176, 304
MacPaint, 304
KidPix version, 177, 304
See also painting programs
MacRecorder, 180, 191, 304
MacroMaker, 315
macros, 170–174, 315
clicking and, 171
creating by example, 171–172
creating manually, 173–174
debugging, 174
defined, 170, 315
macros for, 174
programs for creating, 170–174
types of, 173–174
See also QuicKeys
MacUser magazine
computer brokerages and, 274
getting help from, 275
mail order houses and, 52, 289
reviews in, 50, 51
toll-free number, 303
MacWeek magazine, 303
Macworld magazine
computer brokerages and, 274
ELF tests, 292
getting help from, 275
mail order houses and, 52, 289
reviews in, 50, 51
toll-free number, 303
MacWrite
Apple File Exchange and, 176
font menu display, 116
Magenta Seven carrying cases, 295
magnetic damage, floppy disks and, 265
magnetic fields, PowerBook and, 297
Magnifying glass tool, 135, 138, 142
mail order, purchasing via, 51–52, 289
Mailing Label layout, FileMaker Pro, 163
mailing labels
FileMaker Pro and, 163, 167
printing, 91
Make Alias command, 203–205
Map control panel, 202
margins
in Microsoft Word, 144, 147
setting, 67
Marquee tool, 127, 128–129, 138
versus Lasso tool, 139–140
Master Pages
in PageMaker, 150–151
in QuarkXPress, 156–157
MasterJuggler, 97, 304
math coprocessors, 315
math symbols, 162, 166
MaxAppleZoom, 220
Measurement palette, QuarkXPress, 157

megabytes (MB), 30–31, 240, 281, 282, 315
memory
    About This Macintosh dialog box and, 239
    Adobe Type Manager (ATM) and, 241
    adjusting a program's usage, 239, 243, 252
    AppleTalk and, 240–241
    contiguous, 243
    cost of, 33
    defragmenting, 242–243, 313
    Disk Cache and, 241
    downloadable fonts and, 113–114
    error messages, 236, 238
    explained, 27, 29–30, 32, 315
    extensions and, 240
    File Sharing and, 240, 312–313
    versus hard drives, 30–31, 33
    installing, 245, 247
    megabytes and, 30–31
    printer, 114
    printing problems and, 259, 260
    programs and allotment of, 239, 243, 252
    and purchasing a Macintosh, 281–282, 283
    RAM disks and, 33, 301–302
    Save command and, 72
    Single In-line Memory Modules (SIMMs) and, 320
    sound problems and, 247
    System 7 Tune-Up and, 240
    system crash and, 252
    troubleshooting problems with, 238–245
    virtual, 33, 243–245, 252, 322
Memory controls
    Disk Cache and, 241
    RAM disks and, 300–301
    virtual memory and, 244–245, 252
memory effect, in batteries, 300
menu bar
    Apple icon and, 20
    defined, 316
    programs and, 78
menu commands
    activating, 18
    Always snap to grid command, 213
    Background command, 128, 129
    blink rate of, 61
    choosing, 56
    Clean Up by Name command, 201
    Clean Up Window command, 201
    Copy command, 55–56, 58, 59–60, 86
    Cut command, 59, 86
    dimmed or "grayed out," 17, 75, 229–230
    Duplicate command, 47, 262
    Eject Disk command, 17, 44, 263
    File Find command, 20
    Fill Down command, 162
    Fill Right command, 161–162
    Find Again command, 203
    Grammar command, 149
    Group command, 136–137
    Hide Balloons command, 47
    Hide Others command, 199–200
    highlighting, 17
    Hyphenation command, 149

Invert command, 139
    keyboard shortcuts for, 36
    LinkTo command, 133
    Make Alias command, 203–205
    New Card command, 130
    New Folder command, 35–36, 38
    Open command, 22, 74, 81–82
    Page Layout command, 143–144
    Page Setup command, 108, 114, 139
    Paste command, 57–60, 86
    Paste Function command, 162
    PowerSaver command, 300
    Print command, 109
    Print Preview command, 144
    Publish and Subscribe commands, 318
    Put Away command, 44, 263
    Quit command, 83
    Restart command, 250
    Save command, 32–33, 72, 81, 83
    Select All command, 85
    Show All command, 199–200
    Show Balloons command, 47
    Show Clipboard command, 56
    Shut Down command, 15, 17–18, 47, 302, 320
    Sort command, 169
    Spelling command, 149
    Staggered grid command, 213
    Straight grid command, 213
    syntax of, 21–22
    Thesaurus command, 149
    Trace Edges command, 139
    transformation commands, 141
    Undo command, 59–60, 130, 232
    Ungroup command, 136–137
    See also Empty Trash command; Find command; menus
Menu/DA macro, 174
MenuFonts, 116, 304
menus
    choosing commands from, 56
    defined, 4, 315
    display of fonts in, 116
    editing with ResEdit, 214–216
    keyboard shortcuts and, 36
    macro for, 174
    pop-up, 75, 317
    pulling down, 15–17
    in Save File dialog box, 74–77
    submenus and, 320–321
    symbols in, 37
    tear-off, 127
    troubleshooting problems with, 271
    See also menu commands
messages. See error messages
mice. See mouse
MicroPhone II, 177, 183, 304
microphones, 179–180, 192
    jack for, 293
    using, 216–217, 219
Microsoft Excel, 51, 157–163, 266, 304
    bolding text in, 160
    cells, 157
        #### in, 266
        automatically-calculating, 160–161
        copying, 161–162
        formula, 162
    charts, 162–163
    Fill Down command, 162

Fill Right command, 161–162
    formatting numbers and text in, 157–158
    navigating in, 159
    Paste Function command, 162
    Sum button, 160
    troubleshooting problems with, 266
    See also spreadsheet programs
Microsoft Flight Simulator, 177, 306
Microsoft Word, 51, 143–149, 305
    date-stamping documents, 148
    dragging-and-dropping text, 147–148
    headers and footers, 148
    margins in, 144, 147
    page numbering, 148
    page views in, 143–144
    Ribbon controls, 145
    Ruler, 145–147
    spelling checker, 149
    Styles, 147, 148–149
    toolbar, 146
    See also word processing
MIDI interfaces, 186–188, 191
military time, setting, 61
minus sign (–), 162, 166
modem port, 191, 257, 293
modems, 182–186
    baud rate and, 183, 308
    bulletin boards and, 185
    cables and, 272
    connecting, 191
    defined, 316
    E-mail and, 182, 184
    fax/modems, 183–184
    file compression programs and, 217
    Macintosh models and, 283
    on-line services and, 182, 183, 184–185
    software for, 177, 183
modifier keys, 37–38, 316
modular Macs, 279, 280, 283
ModuNet, 304
Moire, 221
monitors
    Apple 12", 13", 14", 285
    black-and-white, 285–286, 287
    defined, 316
    gray-scale, 286, 287
    headaches and, 291
    horizontal line on color, 232
    increasing screen space on, 220
    landscape, 285
    Macintosh IIsi, IIci, and Quadra and, 287
    macros for, 174
    monochrome, 286
    power plug for, 293
    program needs and, 285
    purchasing, 285–288
    setting up, 291, 292
    switching color/black-and-white on, 174, 221
    troubleshooting problems with, 246–247
    two-page, 285
    two-piece Macintosh computers and, 279, 285
    types of, 285–286
    video cards and, 247, 287, 288, 292, 293, 322
    See also color monitors; screens

Monitors control, 202, 287
Monitors file, System Folder, 237
monochrome monitors, 286
More Choices option, Find command, 203
Motorola Corporation, 282
mouse
    cables and, 271, 272
    cleaning, 270
    clicking, 16–17
    defined, 316
    dragging, 17–18
    macro for, 174
    moving, 15–17
    moving insertion point with, 63–64
    pulling menus down with, 15–17
    screen savers and, 218
    system freeze and, 226
    troubleshooting problems with, 270–272
    used computers and, 290
    See also trackballs
mouse button, 316
mouse pad, 192, 316
Mouse Practice, 18, 293
Mousies macro, 174
movie making, 188–189, 280, 283
mufflers, for printers, 90
MultiFinder, 316
multimedia, 316
multiple-outlet boxes, 193
multiplication operator (*), 162, 166
multitasking, Option key and, 199–200
music notation programs, 188, 283
music processing programs, 186–188
    Macintosh models and, 279, 283
MusicProse, 188, 304
MyAdvancedLabelMaker, 304

— N —

911 Utilities, 263, 264, 265, 303
Name, sorting windows by, 25
Name-Tag view, FileMaker Pro, 163
naming
    floppy disks, 42–43
    folders, 36
    fonts, 92, 95, 99–103
    programs, 50
networks, 190–191, 316
    connecting, 192
    Macintosh models and, 283
    printers and, 104–105
    System Folder and, 237
New Card command, 130
New Folder command
    creating folders with, 35–36
    keyboard shortcut for, 38
New York Macintosh User's Group, 303
Newsweek magazine, 282
Nisus, 304
non-city-named fonts, 92, 95, 99–103
    printing problems and, 258
Normal view, 143
    Ribbon and Ruler in, 145
Norton Utilities for the Mac (NUM)
    address and telephone, 304
    data recovery and, 249, 263, 270
    disk defragmentation and, 269
notation programs, music, 188, 283

Note Pad
    Copy and Paste and, 55–56
    multitasking and, 199–200
    use of, 54–55
Note Pad icon, 56–57
noun-verb syntax, of menu commands, 21–22
Nova, 282
Now Up-to-Date, 51, 177, 305
Now Utilities, 116, 305
NuBus slots, 316
numbering pages, 148
numeric keypad, Calculator and, 53
numeric operators, 162, 166

— O —

object-oriented graphics, versus bitmapped graphics, 134
obsolescence
    Macintosh computers and, 7
    programs and, 49–50
OCR (optical character recognition), 181, 316
On/Off switch, 11–12, 293
on-line, defined, 316
on-line conferencing, 184–185
on-line services
    getting help from, 275
    modems and, 182, 183, 184–185
    shareware from, 219, 220
    software for, 177
    text-based versus icon-based, 184
Open command
    dialog box for, 74, 81–82
    and Save command, 81
    viewing hard disk contents with, 22, 82
Open spacing, 147
operator error, computer problems and, 226
optical character recognition (OCR), 181, 316
Option key, 195–202
    alphabetizing icons with, 201
    Control Panels and, 202
    copying with, 46, 201
    Finder and, 201, 202
    as modifier key, 37–38
    multitasking and, 199–200
    rebuilding Desktop and, 235
    Trash can/Empty Trash and, 198–199, 237
    typing symbols with, 126
    windows and, 196–198
    zapping the PRAM and, 249
outline type style, 96
Outline view, 144
output bureaus, 116

— P —

page description languages, 93
page layout programs
    Macintosh models and, 279, 283
    monitors and, 285
    See also PageMaker; QuarkXPress
Page Layout view, 143–144
    Ribbon and Ruler in, 145
page numbers, 148

Page Setup dialog box
    explained, 114
    Graphics Smoothing option, 139
    printer installation and, 108
page views, 143–144
PageMaker, 150–154, 305
    creating Master Pages, 150–151
    importing and editing text, 151–153
    Page menu, 153
    Pointer Tool, 153
    starting a document, 150
    Story Editor, 153
    Styles, 154
    Text Tool, 153
    Type menu, 153
    See also page layout programs
Paint brush tool, 127, 138
Paint bucket tool, 127, 138
painting programs, 138–142, 316–317
    color versus black-and-white, 138
    creating icons with, 207
    versus drawing programs, 134
    editing graphics in, 139
    generic graphics files and, 235, 236
    Graphics Smoothing option, 139
    Invert command, 139
    Macintosh models and, 283
    monitors and, 285
    Option key and, 201
    printing problems and, 258, 259
    text in, 131, 140–141
    Tool palette, 127–129, 138–142
    Trace Edges command, 139
    transformation commands, 141
    See also drawing programs; graphics programs
palettes. *See* thickness palette; Tool palette
Panorama II, 164
paper clips, 45, 194, 264, 302
paragraphs
    formatting, 70–71, 145–147
    highlighting, 70, 145–147
    indenting, 147
    justifying, 147
    margins of, 144, 147
    Return key and, 68–69
    Ruler and, 145–147
    selecting, 70
partitions, hard drive, 317
Paste command
    and Cut command, 86
    keyboard shortcut for, 59–60
    use of, 57–60
Paste Function command, Excel, 162
pattern, changing background, 209–210
Patterns menu, 130
PC disks, versus Macintosh disks, 42, 265
PC Exchange, 176
PDS (processor direct slots), 317
Pencil tool, 127, 138, 140
Performa 11, 12, 18, 88, 290, 218, 277, 279, 283
    buying, 290
    control panels and, 61, 88, 209
    CD-ROM player in, 186
    Documents folder, 81
    help and service, 275
    monitors, 285, 287
    self-hiding windows, 54, 57, 199, 200, 267

included sotware, 50-51
Restart switch, 248
turning on, 11–12
period (.), Command key and, 208–209, 263
peripherals
  computer problems and, 226
  defined, 191, 317
  See also add-ons; SCSI
Persuasion, 177, 305
PhoneNet, 305
Photoshop. *See* painting programs
PICT files, 236, 317
pixel, 317
Pixel-Flipper, 221
PixelPaint. *See* painting programs
planes, power outlets in, 299
plugs
  in back of Macintoshes, 293
  SCSI terminator, 255–257
plus sign (+), 162, 166
point size, of fonts, 70, 94, 95
Pointer Tool, PageMaker, 153
pointing
  defined, 16
  guided tour and, 19
  See also selecting
Polygon Tool, 135, 138, 142
pop-up menus, 75, 317
Portable file, System Folder, 237
portable printers, 298
portrait, defined, 317
portrait monitors, 285
ports
  defined, 317
  illustration of, 293
  See also SCSI port
PostScript, defined, 91, 93, 317
PostScript fonts
  versus bitmapped fonts, 93, 94, 113
  downloadable, 113–114
  history of, 93, 97–98
  printing problems and, 258
  screen versus printer, 95–97, 98
  versus TrueType fonts, 98–99, 101
  type styles and, 96, 100–101
  See also bitmapped fonts; fonts; TrueType fonts
PostScript graphics programs, 99, 135, 177
  See also graphics programs
PostScript laser printers, 91–92
  fonts built into, 113
  LaserWriter printers and, 91, 93–94, 258
  versus non-PostScript, 94
  See also laser printers; LaserWriter printers; printers
pound signs (#####), in Excel cells, 266
power accessories, PowerBook, 295–296
power outlets, in airports and airplanes, 299
Power Partner, 305
power plugs, on Macintoshes, 293
power switch, Macintosh, 11–12, 293
power up. *See* booting
power users, 59, 195
PowerBook, 280, 284, 295–302
  cases for, 295

color PowerBooks, 280, 283, 295
disk drive, 24
Duo and DuoDock, 24, 295, 298, 300
file compression programs and, 296
hard drives and, 296
magnetic fields and, 297
microphones and, 179
modems and, 183
power accessories for, 295–296, 305
RAM disks and, 300–302
Restart switch, 302
restarting, 302
setting up, 292
Shut Down command and, 302
Sleep mode, 297, 300, 302, 320
system crash and, 302
System Folder and, 237
trackball, 17
traveling with, 280, 298–302
troubleshooting problems with, 246
turning on, 12
uses for, 283
X-ray machines and, 297
  See also batteries
PowerBook Battery Reconditioner/Charger, 299, 305
PowerBook Car/Boat Adapter, 305
PowerKey, 193
power-on button, 12, 246
PowerSaver command, 300
PRAM
  defined, 317
  zapping, 249
Preferences folder, 234
presentation programs, 177
price, of Macintosh computers, 283
Print dialog box, 109–110
Print Monitor
  defined, 317
  printing problems and, 237, 260
Print Preview command, 144
printer cartridges, 194
"Printer could not be found," 257
printer drivers, 106–108, 237
printer fonts, 95–97, 98, 100–101, 317
  printing problems and, 258
"The Printer Monitor has reported an error," 237
printer port, 192, 257, 293
  used computers and, 290
printer spoolers, 109, 320
printers, 89–92
  Adobe Type Manager and, 102, 103
  bitmapped fonts and, 92–93
  cables and, 272
  choosing, 87, 89–92
  color, 286
  connecting to Macintosh, 104–105, 192
  DeskWriter, 91, 102, 104
  dot matrix, 90, 311
  error messages and, 237, 257
  fax/modems and, 298
  and fonts comparison table, 103–104
  inkjet, 91
  macros for, 174
  mufflers for, 90
  networks and, 104–105
  non-PostScript, 94, 102, 103
  portable, 298

print samples, 90
printer drivers and, 106–107
purchasing, 287
selecting with Chooser, 87, 105–108
spoolers for, 109, 320
troubleshooting problems with, 257–260
  See also ImageWriter II printer; laser printers; LaserWriter printers; PostScript laser printers; StyleWriter printer
printing
  background, 108–109
  canceling, 110
  in copy shops, 116
  envelopes, 91
  error messages and, 237, 257
  fax/modems and, 298
  forms, 90
  how to do it, 109–110
  labels, 91
  Larger Print Area option and, 114
  memory and, 241
  painting program graphics, 139
  streaks on laser printouts, 260
  tagboard, 91
  text in drawing programs, 137
  troubleshooting problems with, 257–260
  unwanted duplicate copies, 258
  used computers and, 290
Printing disk
  printer driver icons and, 87, 107, 258
printouts. *See* printers; printing
problems. *See* troubleshooting
processor chips, 282
processor direct slots (PDS), 317
product line, Macintosh, 277–280
professor discount, on Macintosh computers, 288
"[Program name] prefers 2048K of memory. 2000K is available," 238
programs, 121–178
  active, 57, 78
  address book, 51, 122, 177
  alias icons and, 204–205
  Apple File Exchange, 175–176
  architectural, 309
  backup, 84, 190
  beginner's top ten, 121–176
  bookkeeping, 177
  bugs, 226, 252, 309
  calendar/reminder, 51, 122, 220–221, 283
  checkbook, 177, 279
  defined, 49, 318
  determining active, 78
  FileMaker Pro, 163–170
  formatting, 252–253
  free with Macintoshes, 51, 175
  hard disk size and, 281
  humorous, 219
  HyperCard, 122–137, 266, 304, 314
  IBM/Macintosh conversion, 175–176
  integrated, 51, 177
  macro, 170–174
  macros for launching, 174
  memory allotment and, 239, 243, 252
  Microsoft Excel, 51, 157–163, 266, 304

Microsoft Word, 143–150
multitasking and, 199–200
music notation, 188, 283
music processing, 186–188, 279, 283
naming conventions of, 50
obsolescence and, 49–50
opening, 79–80, 83
PageMaker, 150–154, 305
presentation, 177
QuarkXPress, 154–157, 305
QuicKeys, 170–175, 305
quitting, 83
Rolodex, 51, 177, 283
spreadsheet, 51, 177, 266, 279, 283, 320
Startup Items folder and, 250
top ten not in beginner's top ten, 177
troubleshooting problems with,
    234–236, 250, 252, 266–268
video recording, 188–189, 191, 280,
    283
what to buy, 50–51
where to buy, 51–52, 303–306
See also drawing programs;
    extensions; graphics
    programs; page layout
    programs; painting programs;
    PostScript graphics programs;
    shareware; utility programs;
    word processing
PSI fax/modems, 297
Publish and Subscribe commands, 318
publishing. See desktop publishing
pull down menus, 15–17
purchasing guide, 277–290
    choosing the right Macintosh,
        283–284
    hard disk space, 281
    memory, 281–282
    monitors, 285–288
    processor chips, 282–283
    product line, 277–280
    what to get free, 293
    where to buy, 288–290, 303–306
Put Away command, 44, 263

— Q —

Quadra Macintosh. See under
    Macintosh computers
QuarkXPress, 154–157, 305
    Document Layout palette, 156–157
    importing text, 155, 156
    Linking Tool, 156
    Master Pages, 156–157
    Measurement palette, 157
    Text Block Tool, 156
    Tool palette, 154–155
    See also page layout programs
question mark icon, 13, 20, 40
    problems and, 248–249
question mark menu, 47
Quicken, 177, 305
QuicKeys, 170–174, 305
    clicking in, 171
    control panel, 173–174
    creating macros with, 171–172
    See also macros
QuickQuotes macro, 174
QuickTime, 188, 283
Quit command, 83

quotes
    macro for, 174
    straight versus curly, 86

— R —

radiation
    Extremely Low-Frequency (ELF), 291
    PowerBook and, 297
radio buttons, 318
RAM
    cost of, 33
    defined, 31, 33, 318
    defragmenting, 242–243
    PowerBook and, 301–302
    See also memory
RAM disks
    defined, 33, 318
    PowerBook and, 300–302
Real Time macro, 174
rebooting, 19, 318
recharging batteries, 299–301
recipe books, HyperCard and, 122
recording
    music, 186–188, 283
    sounds, 134, 216–217
    video, 188–189, 191
records
    defined, 165, 318
    finding, 169
recovery programs, 249, 263, 264, 265,
    270
Rectangle Tool
    drawing programs and, 135
    HyperCard, 128–129, 130
    painting programs and, 138, 142
    Rounded, 135, 138, 142
reformatting programs, 252–253
relational databases, 164, 318
Remember?, 220–221
remote control, 183
removable-cartridge drives, 189–190
    defined, 318
    installing, 191
    sources for, 303, 305
repair service, warranty and, 289
replacing text, 65–66
ResEdit, 214–216, 318
Resize box, 314, 318
resolution
    defined, 318
    in painting programs, 139
    print, 102
    screen, 93
Resolve, 177, 305
resources
    help, 275, 303
    purchasing, 303–306
Restart button, 251
Restart command, 250
Restart switch, 248, 251, 319
    PowerBook, 302
restarting, 19, 248, 250, 251
    Command+Option+Esc combination,
        253
    PowerBook, 302
résumés, creating in HyperCard,
    125–127
Return key
    in Excel, 159
    in word processing, 62, 68–69

Ribbon controls, character formatting
    and, 145
Rolodex programs, 51, 177, 283
ROM, 319
Rounded Rectangle Tool, 135, 138, 142
    See also Rectangle Tool
Ruler, paragraph formatting and,
    145–147
running headers and footers, 86

— S —

16-bit color monitors, 287–288
68000, 68030, 68040 processor chips,
    282
SAM (Symantec Utilities for the
    Macintosh), 219, 305
sans serif fonts, 116–117, 319
Save command
    explained, 32–33
    keyboard shortcut for, 72, 83
    and Open command, 81
Save dialog box, 73–77, 83
Save-O-Matic, 220
saving
    in FileMaker Pro, 165
    PowerBook RAM disks and, 301–302
    recovering lost text and, 232
    utility for automatic, 220
    See also backing up
scanners, 180–181, 191, 319
    file formats and, 322
    SCSI problems and, 254–257
    startup problems and, 247
Scrapbook desk accessory, 319
screen fonts, 95–97, 98
    TrueType fonts and, 112
Screen Power Saver, 218
screen savers, 218, 221, 246, 319
screens
    accelerators for color, 288
    battery life and, 299
    dimming, 218, 299, 300
    glare filters for, 193
    HyperCard Welcome, 122–123
    increasing usable space on, 220
    PowerBook and, 299
    resolution of, 93, 318
    taking pictures of, 208
    troubleshooting problems with,
        246–247
    See also monitors
Screenshot, 208, 305
Scripts, in FileMaker Pro, 170
scroll bars
    explained, 22, 85–86
    Hand grabber tool and, 142
    and lost text, 231
SCSI, 191–192, 254–257, 319
    startup problems and, 247, 248
    system crash and, 252, 254–257
    troubleshooting problems with,
        254–257, 269
SCSI addresses, 255, 319
SCSI cables, 254, 257, 272, 319
SCSI chain, 254, 255–256
SCSI devices, 254, 255–256, 319
SCSI Info, 220
SCSI numbers, 255
SCSI port
    connecting peripherals to, 191–192

defined, 254, 319
illustration of, 293
SCSI Probe, 220
SCSI terminators, 255–257, 319–320
SCSI utilities, 220
searching. *See* Find command
Select All command, 85
selecting
  all text, 85
  deselecting text, 66
  icons, 21, 23, 38–40, 45
  keyboard shortcuts for, 146
  menu commands and, 21
  multiple icons, 38–40
  paragraphs, 70, 145–147
  text, 55, 65–66
  See also highlighting
selection strip, highlighting and, 146
selection tools. *See* Lasso tool; Marquee
    tool
self-publishing. *See* desktop publishing
selling your Macintosh, 274
Sequence macro, 174
sequencing, MIDI, 186, 187
serif fonts, 116–117, 320
service, warranty and, 289
shadow type style, 96
shape tools, 127–129, 142
shareware
  bulletin boards and, 185
  defined, 320
  SoundMaster, 219
  SuperClock!, 296
  utility programs, 220–221
Shift key
  clicking while pressing, 39, 136, 146
  ejecting floppy disks and, 45, 264
  in Excel, 159
  in FileMaker Pro, 166
  graphics functions and, 136, 141, 142
  highlighting multiple icons with, 39
  as modifier key, 37
  selecting paragraphs and, 146
  startup problems and, 249–250
shortcut keys. *See* keyboard shortcuts
Show All command, 199–200
Show Balloons command, 47
Show Clipboard command, 56
Show disk info control, 213
showing hidden characters, 69
Shut Down command
  defined, 320
  ejecting disks and, 47
  PowerBook and, 302
  turning power off and, 15, 17–18
Shut Down macro, 174
silicon chips. *See* memory
Silicon Valley scene, 202
SilverLining, 253, 305
SIMMs (Single In-line Memory
    Modules), 320
single quotes
  macro for, 174
  straight versus curly, 86
single-sided floppy disks, 42, 264
Size, sorting windows by, 25
Size box, 22
slash (/), 162, 166
Sleep mode, 297, 302

batteries and, 300
defined, 320
slide show programs, 177
slots
  expansion, 192, 312, 316
  NuBus, 316
  processor direct (PDS), 317
Small Computer Serial Interface. *See*
    SCSI
SmartCom, 183
software
  defined, 320
  See also programs
software bugs, 226, 252, 309
"Sorry, a system error occurred," 226,
    250–251
  ID numbers in box, 253
  startup problems and, 249–250
Sort command, 169
sorting contents of windows, 25
Sound control, 180, 216–217
SoundMaster, 219, 220
sounds
  HyperCard and, 134
  recording, 216–217, 219, 220
  startup, 246–247
  in System file, 216
spaces
  aligning text with, 85
  between lines, 71, 147
  between paragraphs, 147
  between words, 63
spacing
  closed, 147
  line, 71, 147
  Open, 147
speaker jack, 247, 293
speaker-wire cables, 247
Special menu, 15–16
  Clean Up Window command, 201
  Eject Disk command, 17, 44, 263
  Restart command, 250
  Shut Down command, 17–18
  See also Empty Trash command
Specials macro, 174
speed, increasing System 7, 220
Spelling command, 149
spoolers, printer, 109, 320
Spray Can tool, 127, 138, 141
spreadsheet programs, 51, 177, 266, 320
  Macintosh models and, 279, 283
  See also Microsoft Excel
stacks. *See* HyperCard
Staggered grid command, 213
Start Page options, 116
startup disk, 320
Startup Items folder, 250
startup page, printer, 116, 260
startup problems, 246–250
Stationery Pad, 320
storage. *See* floppy disks; hard drives;
    memory; RAM disks;
    removable-cartridge drives
Story Editor, PageMaker, 153
Straight grid command, 213
straight quotes, 86
  macro for, 174
streaks, on laser printouts, 260
student discount, on Macintosh
    computers, 288
Studio 32. *See* painting programs

Studio/1, 305
  See also painting programs
StuffIt, 218, 220, 305
Style Name box, 148
Styles
  Microsoft Word, 147, 148–149
  PageMaker, 154
StyleWriter printer (I and II), 91, 320
  bitmapped fonts and, 100
  connecting to Macintosh, 104
  PostScript fonts and, 102
  See also printers
subfolders, 25
  See also folders
submenus, 320–321
Suitcase, 97, 116, 305
Sum button, in Excel, 160
Super QuickDex, 51, 177, 305
SuperClock!, 296
SuperDrive, 175, 321
SuperPaint, 305
  See also drawing programs; painting
    programs
surge suppressors, 193, 321
switch boxes, 191
switches
  Macintosh power, 11–12, 293
  Restart, 248, 251, 302, 319
  SCSI terminator, 256
Symantec Corporation
  Symantec Anti-Virus, 268
  Symantec Utilities for the Macintosh
    (SAM), 219, 305
symbols
  in menus, 37
  typing, 126
syntax, command, 21–22
synthesizers, MIDI and, 186–188
SyQuest drives, 190, 191, 305
System 6 versus System 7, 321
  Apple menu, 53
  Find File and Find commands, 20
  fonts and printers, 103–104
  identifying, 20, 40
  installing fonts, 112
  moving folders, 39
  renaming icons, 46
  selecting icons, 23
  Trash can, 40
  TrueType fonts, 100
System 7
  alias icons in, 173, 203–205
  Application menu and, 56
  bitmapped fonts and, 92
  creating Apple menu in, 53
  defined, 103, 321
  Empty Trash command, 46
  extensions in, 174
  formatting programs and, 253
  increasing speed of, 220
  installing fonts, 111–112
  LaserWriter Font Utility, 116
  networks and, 191
  printer drivers and, 106–107
  printer icons for, 87
  question mark icon, 20, 40
  question mark menu, 47
  Stationery Pad, 320
  TrueType fonts and, 98, 100
  virtual memory and, 243
System 7 Pack, 220

System 7 Tune-Up, 240
System 7.1, 103, 111, 239, 240, 321. *See*
      Fonts folder
system crash, 250–253
   defined, 321
   PowerBook and, 302
   programs and, 268
   Restart switch and, 248
   SCSI problems and, 254–257
   See also system freeze
System disks
   defined, 321
   Disk Tools disk, 13
   printer icons and, 87
System error boxes
   versus alert boxes, 233
   ID numbers in box, 253
System error message, 226
   startup problems and, 249–250
   system crash and, 226, 250–251
System errors. *See* system crash;
      system freeze
"System Extension: This file adds
      functionally to your
      Macintosh," 234
System extensions, 227
System file
   defined, 321
   removing fonts from, 111-112
   sound icons in, 216
   TrueType fonts and, 98, 100
System Folder
   Apple menu and, 53
   CloseView and, 237
   Control Panels folder and, 60–61
   defined, 248, 321
   Easy Access and, 237
   files and folders in, 237
   installing/removing fonts and, 111-112
   locating, 23
   networks and, 237
   Preferences folder, 234
   printer drivers in, 237
   RAM disks and, 301
   reinstalling, 249, 252
   starting Macintosh with, 13
   Startup Items folder, 250
   System extensions, 227
   troubleshooting problems with,
      248–249, 252
   TrueType fonts and, 100
system freeze
   defined, 226, 251, 314
   programs and, 268
   Restart switch and, 248
   troubleshooting, 253
   See also system crash
System Software Installer, 248

—T—

24-bit color monitors, 287–288
Tab key
   in dialog boxes, 110
   in Excel, 159
   in FileMaker Pro, 166
tab stops
   aligning text with, 85
   setting, 67, 147
tab wells, 147

tables
   choosing the right Macintosh, 283
   formatting margins in, 147
   Macintosh product line, 277
   Macintoshes, printers, and fonts,
      103–104
tagboard, printing on, 91
tagged image file format (TIFF), 322
Talking Moose, 219, 305
tape drives, 190
teacher discount, on Macintosh
      computers, 288
tear-off menus, 127
telecommunications, 321
   See also modems
telecommuters, 182
telephone numbers, for user groups,
      110, 185, 303
telephones
   floppy disks and, 265
   modems and, 182
terminator switches, 256
terminators, SCSI
   defined, 319–320
   internal, 256
   SCSI problems and, 255–257
text
   aligning, 85
   cutting and pasting, 86
   deleting, 64–65
   deselecting, 66
   dragging-and-dropping, 147–148
   in drawing programs, 137
   formatting, 67–71
   in graphics programs, 131, 140–141,
      259
   inserting, 63–64
   justifying, 71
   macro for typing, 174
   replacing, 65–66
   Ribbon controls and, 145
   scanners and, 181
   selecting, 36, 55, 65–66, 70, 146
   troubleshooting problems with,
      230–232, 259
   See also word processing
Text Block Tool, QuarkXPress, 156
Text Box Tool, QuarkXPress, 155
text fields, HyperCard, 131–132
text files, ASCII, 235–236, 308
Text macro, 174
Text tool, 127, 130, 138, 140–141
   PageMaker, 153
text-based on-line services, 184
text-only files, opening, 235–236
"The application [program name] has
      unexpectedly quit," 236
"The disk is full," 236–237
"The Printer Monitor has reported an
      error," 237
"There is not enough memory to open
      [program name]," 236
Thesaurus command, 149
thickness palette, 136, 141, 142
third party, 322
"This disk is unreadable: Do you want to
      initialize it?," 42, 264–265
Tidbits disk
   LaserWriter Font Utility on, 116
TIFF (tagged image file format), 322

time, setting, 61
Time macro, 174
title bar
   defined, 22, 322
   multiple windows and, 24
toll-free numbers, for user groups, 110,
      185, 303
toner
   defined, 322
   streaked printouts and, 260
toner cartridges, 194
Tool palette
   drawing program, 135–136
   HyperCard, 125–127
   painting program, 138–142
   QuarkXPress, 154
   selection tools in, 139
Trace Edges command, 139
trackballs, 193, 322
   PowerBook and, 17
   troubleshooting problems with, 271
   See also mouse
transformation commands, 141
transparencies, programs for, 177
Trash can
   alias icons and, 205
   clicking and dragging, 19
   deleting with, 40, 230
   ejecting disks with, 45
   Finder and, 21
   full disks and, 236
   locked files in, 199, 237
   Option key and, 198–199, 237
   recovering files from, 40–41, 270
   in System 6, 40
   troubleshooting problems with, 230
traveling, PowerBook and, 280, 298–302
Trax, 187, 305
troubleshooting, 225–272
   basic approach to, 227–228
   beeps, 228–229
   cursor problems, 270–272
   dialog box problems, 228–229
   dimmed menu commands, 229–230
   disappearing files, 233
   Finder problems, 261–262
   floppy disk problems, 262–265
   full disk, 236–237
   hard disk problems, 269–270
   horizontal line on color monitors,
      232
   keyboard problems, 270–272
   loss of text, 230–232
   Macintosh addiction, 233
   Macintosh setup and, 227–228
   memory problems, 238–245
   most common causes of problems,
      226
   mouse problems, 270–272
   operator error and, 226
   peripherals and, 226
   printing problems, 257–260
   program bugs and, 226, 252
   program problems, 266–268
   SCSI problems, 254–257
   startup problems, 246–250
   top ten beginner troubles, 228–233
   Trash can problems, 230
   window problems, 228
   See also error messages; system
      crash; system freeze

TrueType fonts
  and bitmapped fonts, 100
  defined, 322
  icon for, 100
  INIT for, 100, 104
  versus PostScript fonts, 98–99, 101
  printing problems and, 258
  removing, 111
  screen fonts and, 112
  System 6 and, 100
  and System 7, 98, 100
  See also bitmapped fonts; fonts;
      PostScript fonts
turning off, 15
turning on. *See* booting
two-page monitors, 285
type styles
  font menu list of, 115–116
  PostScript fonts and, 96, 100–101,
    115
  printing, 114–115
  Ribbon controls and, 145
  setting, 67
  See also fonts
typefaces. *See* fonts
typewriters, versus word processors,
  67–68

—U—

UltraPaint, 305
  See also painting programs
underlining, 69–70
  fonts and, 95–96
  versus italics, 85
  Ribbon controls and, 145
Undo command, 130
  lost text and, 232
  use of, 59–60
Ungroup command, drawing programs,
  136–137
un-highlighting text, 66
university discount, on Macintosh
  computers, 288
unlocking
  files, 199, 237, 262
  floppy disks, 41
  free version of HyperCard, 123–125
upgrades
  Macintosh, 273–274
  software, 50
uppercase. *See* capitalization
used Macintoshes, purchasing, 289
user groups, 275, 290
  defined, 322
  software from, 214, 219, 220, 296
  telephone numbers for, 110, 185, 303
utility programs, 217–221
  anti-virus, 219, 268
  automatic save, 220
  backup, 84, 190
  calendar/reminder, 220–221
  defragmentation, 269
  file compression, 217–218, 220, 296,
    313
  free/almost free, 220–221
  increasing screen display, 220

increasing System 7 speed, 220
  recovery, 249, 263, 264, 265, 270
  screen savers, 218, 221, 246
  SCSI, 220
  sound recording, 219, 220
  switching color/black-and-white
    display, 221
  See also programs

—V—

VCRs, 188–189, 191
vertical scroll bar. *See* scroll bars
video cards, 247, 287, 288, 292, 293, 322
video output port, 293
video recording, 188–189, 191, 280, 283
VideoSpigot, 188, 305
View menu
  choosing Ribbon and Ruler from, 145
  dimmed, 230
  explained, 24, 45–46, 214
  fonts and, 100
  Page Layout command, 143–144
  Views control and, 212–214
views
  in FileMaker Pro, 163
  in Word, 143–144
Views control, 212–214
Virex, 219, 305
virtual memory, 33, 243–245, 322
  system crash and, 252
viruses, 219, 268, 322
voice control, 180
Voice Impact, 180, 305

—W—

warranties
  repair service and, 289
  upgrades and, 274
Welcome screen, HyperCard, 122–123
"What you see is what you get"
    (WYSIWYG), 93, 95, 322
What-if scenarios, in Excel, 161
White Knight, 183, 305
windows
  active, 229
  Clean Up Window command and, 201
  Cluttered, Overlapping Window
    Syndrome (COWS), 197, 199
  defined, 322
  listing contents alphabetically, 24–25
  opening icons into, 21–23
  Option key and, 196–198
  shutting down and, 47
  sorting contents of, 25
  tips for using, 45–47
  troubleshooting problems with, 228,
    267–268
  using multiple, 24
Wingz, 177, 305
Word. *See* Microsoft Word
word processing, 54–56, 61–71
  aligning text, 85

ASCII files and, 235–236
  backup and, 84
  character formatting, 69–70
  defined, 32
  deleting text, 64–65
  Field Tool and, 131
  hard disk size and, 281
  headers and footers, 86
  I-beam cursor, 63–64
  inserting text, 63–64
  insertion point, 63–64
  justification, 71
  line spacing, 71
  Macintosh models and, 279, 283
  monitors and, 285
  moving text, 86
  paragraph formatting, 70–71
  quitting, 83
  replacing text, 65–66
  retrieving files, 80–82
  Return key and, 62, 68–69
  saving files, 72–77, 82–83
  software, 51
  spacing in, 62–63
  text-only files and, 235–236
  tips for, 85–87
  troubleshooting lost text, 230–232
  type styles and fonts, 69–70
  versus typing, 67–68
  See also Microsoft Word; Note Pad
word wrap, 63, 322
WordPerfect for the Macintosh, 306
wrists, Macintosh setup and, 291
WriteNow, 51, 306
WYSIWYG Menus, 116
WYSIWYG ("What you see is what you
    get"), 93, 95, 322

—X—

X-ray machines, PowerBook and, 297

—Y—

"You have changed your current
    printer....," 108
"Your screen has been dimmed," 299
Y-splitters, 183, 191

—Z—

zapping the PRAM, 249
Zoom box, 22, 322
zooming
  Magnifying glass tool and, 142
  in PageMaker, 153

IDG Books Worldwide Registration Card

Macs For Dummies

Fill this out — and hear about updates to this book and other IDG Books Worldwide products!

Name _____

Company/Title _____

Address _____

City/State/Zip _____

What is the single most important reason you bought this book? _____

_____

Where did you buy this book?
- ❑ Bookstore (Name _____)
- ❑ Electronics/Software store (Name_____)
- ❑ Advertisement (If magazine, which? _____)
- ❑ Mail order (Name of catalog/mail order house _____)
- ❑ Other: _____

How did you hear about this book?
- ❑ Book review in: _____
- ❑ Advertisement in: _____
- ❑ Catalog
- ❑ Found in store
- ❑ Other: _____

How would you rate the overall content of this book?
- ❑ Very good   ❑ Satisfactory
- ❑ Good   ❑ Poor
- Why? _____

What chapters did you find most valuable? _____

What chapters did you find least valuable? _____

What kind of chapter or topic would you add to future editions of this book? _____

_____

Please give us any additional comments. _____

_____

How many computer books do you purchase a year?
❑ 1   ❑ 6-10
❑ 2-5   ❑ More than 10

What are your primary software applications?
_____
_____
_____

Thank you for your help!

❑ I liked this book! By checking this box, I give you permission to use my name and quote me in future IDG Books Worldwide promotional materials. Daytime phone number_____ .

❑ FREE! Send me a copy of your computer book and book/disk catalog.

- -

Fold Here

Place
stamp
here

IDG Books Worldwide, Inc.
155 Bovet Road
Suite 310
San Mateo, CA 94402

Attn: Reader Response / Macs For Dummies

Order Form

Order Center: (800) 762-2974 (7 a.m.–5 p.m., PST, weekdays)
or **(415) 312-0650**
Order Center FAX: (415) 358-1260

Quantity	Title & ISBN	Price	Total

Shipping & Handling Charges

Subtotal	U.S.	Canada & International	International Air Mail
Up to $20.00	Add $3.00	Add $4.00	Add $10.00
$20.01–40.00	$4.00	$5.00	$20.00
$40.01–60.00	$5.00	$6.00	$25.00
$60.01–80.00	$6.00	$8.00	$35.00
Over $80.00	$7.00	$10.00	$50.00

In U.S. and Canada, shipping is UPS ground or equivalent. For Rush shipping call (800) 762-2974.

Subtotal _____

CA residents add
applicable sales tax _____

IN residents add
5% sales tax _____

Canadian residents
add 7% GST tax _____

Shipping _____

TOTAL _____

Ship to:

Name _____

Company _____

Address _____

City/State/Zip _____

Daytime phone _____

Payment: ☐ Check to IDG Books   ☐ Visa   ☐ MasterCard   ☐ American Express

Card # _____   Expires _____

Please send this order form to: IDG Books, 155 Bovet Road, Suite 310, San Mateo, CA 94402.
Allow up to 3 weeks for delivery. Thank you!

BK=BOBMDM

- -

Fold Here

Place
stamp
here

IDG Books Worldwide, Inc.
155 Bovet Road
Suite 310
San Mateo, CA 94402

Attn: Order Center / Macs For Dummies